ATTENTION, SHOPPERS!

Princeton Studies in American Politics
Historical, International, and Comparative Perspectives
Paul Frymer, Suzanne Mettler, and Eric Schickler,
Series Editors
Ira Katznelson, Martin Shefter, and Theda Skocpol,
Founding Series Editors

A list of titles in this series appears in the back of the book.

Attention, Shoppers!

American Retail Capitalism and the Origins of the Amazon Economy

Kathleen Thelen

PRINCETON UNIVERSITY PRESS

PRINCETON AND OXFORD

Published by Princeton University Press
41 William Street, Princeton, New Jersey 08540
99 Banbury Road, Oxford OX2 6JX

press.princeton.edu

All Rights Reserved

Library of Congress Cataloging-in-Publication Data

Names: Thelen, Kathleen Ann, author.
Title: Attention, shoppers! : American retail capitalism and the origins of the Amazon economy / Kathleen Thelen.
Description: Princeton : Princeton University Press, [2025] | Series: Princeton studies in American politics: historical, international, and comparative perspectives | Includes bibliographical references and index.
Identifiers: LCCN 2024034172 (print) | LCCN 2024034173 (ebook) | ISBN 9780691266510 (hardback) | ISBN 9780691266527 (paperback) | ISBN 9780691266558 (ebook)
Subjects: LCSH: Retail trade—United States—History. | Trade regulation—United States—History. | Consumers—United States—History. | BISAC: POLITICAL SCIENCE / History & Theory | BUSINESS & ECONOMICS / Industries / Retailing
Classification: LCC HF5429.3 .T44 2025 (print) | LCC HF5429.3 (ebook) | DDC 381.0973—dc23/eng/20241004
LC record available at https://lccn.loc.gov/2024034172
LC ebook record available at https://lccn.loc.gov/2024034173

British Library Cataloging-in-Publication Data is available

Editorial: Bridget Flannery-McCoy and Alena Chekanov
Production Editorial: Natalie Baan
Cover Design: Felix Summ
Production: Lauren Reese
Copyeditor: Leah Caldwell

This book has been composed in Adobe Text and Gotham

10 9 8 7 6 5 4 3 2 1

To Ben

CONTENTS

The United States stands out among the rich democracies as a shopper's paradise and the quintessential consumer society. Alongside Walmart, Amazon stands astride a retailing landscape dominated by huge lean retailers whose business model is premised on squeezing suppliers and workers to deliver goods to American consumers at lightning speed and for "everyday low prices."

What accounts for the spectacular success of these companies? Economists view the rise of these mega-retailers in much the same way as they did mass producers, as the natural culmination of technological and organizational innovations that could grow to maturity in the country's large domestic market. Legal scholars attribute the rise of companies like Amazon to a resurgence in monopoly power made possible by changes in American antitrust jurisprudence since the 1970s and 1980s that privilege "consumer welfare," defined in terms of efficiency and price. Political scientists, focused mostly on the politics of production, have not had much at all to say about retailing—though a large literature on the emergence of America's consumption-driven growth regime places heavy emphasis on the expansion of consumption and consumer credit set in motion by government policies in the 1930s in response to the Great Depression.

By contrast, I trace the origins of the Amazon economy to the late nineteenth century, as large, low-cost retailers capitalized on the uniquely permissive regulatory landscape of the American political economy to outgrow the capacity of the government to regulate them. While their counterparts in Europe faced strong countervailing forces and a far less congenial regulatory landscape, large-scale retailers in the United States enjoyed judicial forbearance and often active government support as they grew in scale and scope. Their initial successes allowed them to assemble an ever-growing political support coalition that could then be weaponized to head off subsequent regulatory efforts.

This book tracks these processes through three broad phases that build toward the ascendance of the Amazon economy we know today: (1) the construction of a mass market and the rise of retail capitalism in the late nineteenth and early twentieth centuries, (2) the politicization of consumption and the backlash against chain stores in the 1920s and 1930s, and (3) retail's resurgence and the triumph of low-cost, low-wage discount retailers in the post–World War II period. Analyzing the American case in comparative perspective and over a long time-frame, this book uncovers the roots of a bitter equilibrium in the United States, one in which large low-cost retailers have come to dominate the retail landscape and in which vast numbers of low-income families have come to depend on them to make ends meet.

———

Writing this book took me on a journey that was at once deeply familiar and entirely new. Almost all of my previous work explored industries in which I have never worked, and countries in which I have lived only as a foreigner. What made this project so familiar is that, as it turns out, tracing the evolution of American retail capitalism involved recovering a part of my own history. At the same time, and because it was so different from everything I had written before, this project also took me far outside my comfort zone. It required deep dives into literatures that I had not previously engaged with much: the rich literature on American political development, the vast legal scholarship on antitrust, and areas of European economic history and politics that were wholly new to me.

All this newness meant that I would surely have lost my way had it not been for the guidance, support, and encouragement that I received throughout the journey. I owe an enormous debt of gratitude to the many colleagues who have generously shared their time and expertise at various stages in the evolution of this book: Nick Allen, Melike Arslan, Lucio Baccaro, Jens Beckert, German Bender, Gerry Berk, Giovanni Capoccia, Dan Carpenter, Bruce Carruthers, Colleen Dunlavy, Willy Forbath, Chase Foster, David Grewal, Rod Hick, Martin Höpner, Anna Ilsøe, Torben Iversen, Bill Kovacic, Jim Mahoney, Cathie Martin, Lisa Miller, Ive Marx, Renate Mayntz, Darius Ornsten, Mary O'Sullivan, Sanjukta Paul, Erik Peinert, Paul Pierson, Amy Pond, Jonas Pontusson, Monica Prasad, Ben Preis, Andreas Reisenbichler, Brishen Rogers, Fritz Scharpf, Daniel Schlozman, Fredrik Söderqvist, Chloe Thurston, Carolyn Touhy, Gunnar Trumbull, and Andreas Wiedemann. A number of economic historians—including Hartmut Berghoff, Lendol Calder, Louis Hyman, Jan Logemann, Laura Phillips Sawyer, and Sebastian

Teupe—offered comments and input that was incredibly important as I made my way through decades of retail history in Europe and the United States. I am particularly grateful to Louis Hyman, whose support and input in the early stages of this study were especially formative, and to Jan Loge-mann, whose input and enthusiasm for the project gave me confidence in its overall direction. I am indebted as well to a group of legal scholars, including Kate Andrias, Willy Forbath, Brian Highsmith, Amy Kapczynski, Sanjukta Paul, Katharina Pistor, Brishen Rogers, and especially Sabeel Rahman, who have taught me so much about how to think about the interaction of law and politics in the American context.

Several colleagues contributed in ways that merit special mention. My former student and now colleague and collaborator Chase Foster has taught me almost everything I know about contemporary European competition law. Peter Hall has read and provided his legendarily copious and insightful comments on everything I have ever written, and I thank him for his intellec-tual leadership and personal generosity. I am grateful to my MIT colleague Devin Caughey for cheering me on as I transgressed into his subfield of American politics, and from whom I have learned a great deal about Ameri-can political development (including as a student in his graduate seminar). Over the past five years, I have worked especially closely with an exceptional group of scholars—Jacob Hacker, Alex Hertel-Fernandez, and Paul Pierson (along with our fabulous postdocs Sam Trachtman, Sam Zacher, and Sophie Jacobson)—to launch the Consortium on the American Political Economy (CAPE). The collaboration with my fellow CAPErs has profoundly shaped my thinking about the American political economy. It is a gift to work closely with dear friends whose own work so inspires me. Their influence will be obvious to anyone who reads this book.

Two book workshops—one with scholars of European political economy at the Max Planck Institute for the Study of Societies in Cologne and one with experts on American political development—were critical to whipping the manuscript into shape. My colleagues in Cologne vet pretty much every-thing I write, and this book benefited from input at the MPIfG workshop by Melike Arslan, Lucio Baccaro, Jens Beckert, Benjamin Braun, Timur Ergen, Chase Foster, Sinisa Hadziabdic, Anke Hassel, Martin Höpner, Alexander Hoppe, Sebastian Kohl, Fritz Scharpf, Saila Stausholm, and Lisa Suckert. I am particularly grateful to the institute's directors, Lucio Baccaro and Jens Beckert, for their support over many years now. The all-star cast of participants in the APD workshop on this book brought both insight and enthusiasm. Heartfelt thanks to Amel Ahmed, Andrea Campbell, Sara

Chatfield, Jonathan Obert, Emily Zackin, and especially Devin Caughey for organizing the event.

I was fortunate to have been able to call on the help of a group of extremely talented graduate students whose work on the project was critical to its completion: Cory Adkins, Ayelet Carmeli, Matias Giannoni, Morgan Gillespie, Serene Ho, Angie Jo, Katharin Tai, and Lukas Wolters all provided superb research assistance at various points. Morgan deserves a special shout-out for the spectacular work she did on the manuscript in the final stages. I'm grateful as well to Kate Searle and Jen Greenleaf for tracking down hard-to-find sources. Jen in particular went above and beyond by tracking down one key source in her own public library.

This book is better for the input I received at presentations at a number of research institutes and universities in North America and Europe, including, among others, the American Academy in Berlin, the Center for European Studies at Harvard, the Free University of Berlin, Georgetown Law School, the Max Planck Institute for the Study of Societies, Northwestern University, Oxford University, the University of Bayreuth, the University of California at Berkeley, University Carlos III of Madrid, the University of Geneva, the University of Innsbruck, the University of Konstanz, the University of Mainz, the University of Toronto, and Yale University. I thank MIT (and especially my chair, David Singer) for institutional support for all that I do, and the Institute for Advanced Study at the Technical University of Munich, where I spent a very productive nine months in 2022–23.

I am also grateful to my wonderful editors, Bridget Flannery-McCoy and Alena Chekanov, for their enthusiasm for this project, and I am indebted to the entire Princeton University Press team for all they have done to improve and promote this work. It has been a pleasure working with them over the last several months.

Now the personal part. First, a quirk and a confession. As any author knows, there is always some quirky contingent event that sets a book in motion. For this one it was when our friend Takuto Sato discovered an old 1908 Sears catalog tucked away in the bookshelves of our New Hampshire lake house. From then on, the little paper on Amazon that I was writing at the time was destined to become a book and one that would have to cover the full 150 years that linked the great "wish book" of the late nineteenth and early twentieth centuries to the "everything store" of the twenty-first. The confession: this book would not have been possible without Amazon, or, more precisely, the third-party booksellers on that platform. With libraries closed during the pandemic, I relied on obscure Midwestern booksellers who provided me with materials, often discards from small rural public libraries, that provided many key insights that found their way into this book. What I wish for these third-party sellers is a way bigger cut of the profits that Amazon made off of me.

Friends and family sustained me in the process of writing this book, maybe even more than usual, since so much of it was written in a pandemic. Among the dear friends who helped me maintain my bearings, I thank Frank Dobbin and Michèle Lamont, Gisela Kühne-Groffebert and Hans Groffebert, Rajesh Gandhi and Bonnie Southworth, Kerry Scott, Cathie Martin, Jenny Mansbridge, David Soskice and Niki Lacey, Torben Iversen and Charla Rudisill. Zoom sessions with my sister Pat, brothers Mike and Erik, and sisters-in-law Nikki and Belle provided regular doses of much-needed levity, and I am especially grateful to have Pat and her family in my life. My Sherman Avenue friends—Jess and Jim Ticus, Sandy Waxman and Steve Bussolari, and Mike Pelletier and Arlene Levy—deserve a special shout-out for years and years of companionship and love. My own little family has been more involved in this project than any other in my career. My children Andy and Amelia (aka Emmy) buoyed me up with their interest, baiting me at dinner parties with leading questions on Amazon and antitrust. It has been a profound joy to watch them develop into such thoughtful, funny, empathic, and interesting adults; they amaze and inspire me. In the course of writing this book, Andy brought Liz Marsh first into our lives and then into our family, and we are all so much richer for the brightness and warmth she brings to everything she touches. Finally, and as always, my greatest debt is to my extraordinary husband Ben. How to thank him? I don't even know where to start.

PART I

Introduction

1

American Retail Capitalism and the Origins of the Amazon Economy

An upstart retail platform, led by a ferociously ambitious entrepreneur, is on the march. The company has been engaged in an aggressive strategy of relentless expansion, offering convenient at-home shopping for an ever-widening selection of goods while also maintaining low prices by generating huge sales volumes. Unsurprisingly, the company's success has provoked enormous antipathy among the small independent merchants who cannot possibly match its superior inventory and low cost. Critics complain that the company's profits are being underwritten by tax payers because of the central role the US Postal Service plays in delivering goods to customers. The firm's nonunionized employees bear the brunt of the monotonous but frantically paced work, in state-of-the-art warehouses deploying the latest technologies, on which the business model rests. The companies that supply many of the goods offered on the platform feel squeezed and trapped in a relationship of unequal dependence. Consumers, however, are smitten. They now have the luxury of shopping from home, choosing from a wide selection of every imaginable product, all available at unbeatable prices, with a money-back guarantee and special perks for preferred customers—and with everything delivered right to their door. What's not to love?

It is the turn of the previous century, and the company is Sears & Roebuck. Its hard-driving founder, Richard Warren Sears, had presided over the firm's spectacular growth with manic energy and flamboyant salesmanship. Mail order retail was an American innovation, and though the company was not the first in this space, within a decade of its launch it had come to dominate it. Originally offering only watches advertised on a one-page flyer, the company grew to become the original "everything store"—with catalogs of thousands of pages crammed with a breathtakingly wide array of products—everything from stump pullers to silk stockings. A marketing genius, Sears pioneered or, more often, perfected a host of consumer-facing innovations, including "send no money" purchasing to allow customers to inspect products before paying, generous money-back guarantees, and customer loyalty rewards programs. Like Amazon today, Sears made shopping cheap and easy—in the process satisfying but also generating seemingly insatiable demand on the part of American consumers.

Consumers occupy a central place in the political economies of all the advanced capitalist economies, but among its rich peers, the United States stands out as a shopper's paradise and the quintessential consumer society (Grewal and Purdy 2014). Consumption, and with it, shopping and retailing, are deeply baked into the American political economy and widely recognized as occupying center stage in the country's demand-driven growth model (Prasad 2012; Logemann 2012b; Baccaro and Pontusson 2016; Hassel and Palier 2021).[1] American consumers were watching TV and enjoying household conveniences such as washing machines and vacuum cleaners decades before their European counterparts (Berghoff and Spiekermann 2012; Logemann 2011). Today, no peer democracy depends as heavily as the United States does on domestic consumption to fuel economic growth (see figure 1.1).

Europe, of course, now has its own vibrant retail culture, one that also reflects the deep influence of American retailing actors and practices (De Grazia 2005). Nonetheless, striking differences remain (Logemann 2008, 2011, 2012b; 2021: 329–30). Credit plays a far less prominent role in supporting consumption in most European countries (Logemann 2008; Trumbull 2006b, 2012a; Wiedemann 2021). Excluding housing and other loans, consumer credit in the United States is over three times the EU average as a percentage of GDP, and more than twice that in Europe as a share of disposable income.[2] The average number of credit cards per person (aged

---

1. Carden notes that by the 2010s retail had "surpassed manufacturing as the leading sector in American economic growth" (2013: 402).

2. Figures are from the ECRI Statistical Package 2022, Centre for European Policy Studies (2023), figures 2.8 and 3.5.

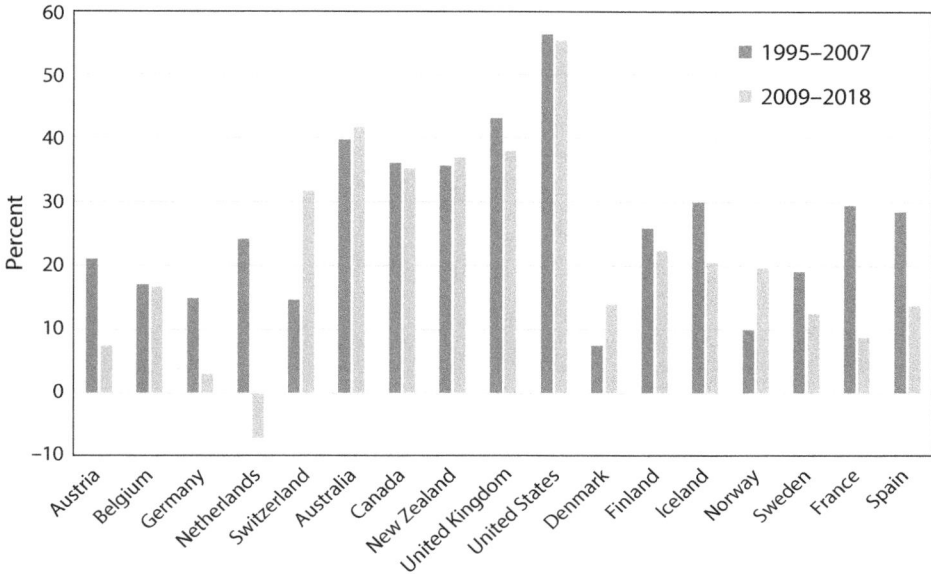

FIGURE 1.1. Contribution of domestic consumption to GDP growth, before and after financial crisis.
Source: Figures from Baccaro and Hadziabdic 2023. These figures are based on OECD input-output data, and they measure the share of total final demand growth that was satisfied by domestic private consumption (as distinct from investment, government consumption, and exports).

twenty-three and over) in the United States (four) is over twice the average in Europe (1.9 per person).[3]

There are also notable differences in the retail landscape. For starters, and as figure 1.2 shows, the United States features far more retail space per capita than peer democracies. This difference is partly a function of the large enclosed malls that one finds in most American suburbs. But it also reflects

3. For the United States, see Becky Pokora, "Credit Card Statistics and Trends 2024," *Forbes*, https://www.forbes.com/advisor/credit-cards/credit-card-statistics/. The average for Europe is actually the same as the average number of credit cards held by the youngest (Gen Z) Americans (ages eighteen to twenty-three, who will actually need them because, unlike in Europe, a credit card is often required for other functions—to secure a lease, buy a car, or even land a job, since many employers check credit scores before hiring). The figure for the number of Europeans with credit cards is also likely inflated by the inclusion of debit cards, which are more widely used in Europe. For Europe, see European Central Bank, "Payments Statistics 2021," https://www.ecb.europa.eu/press/pr/stats/paysec/html/ecb.pis2021~956efe1ee6.en.html#:~:text=The%20number%20of%20cards%20in,cards%20per%20euro%20area%20inhabitant; and https://www.spendesk.com/en-eu/blog/credit-card-statistics/.

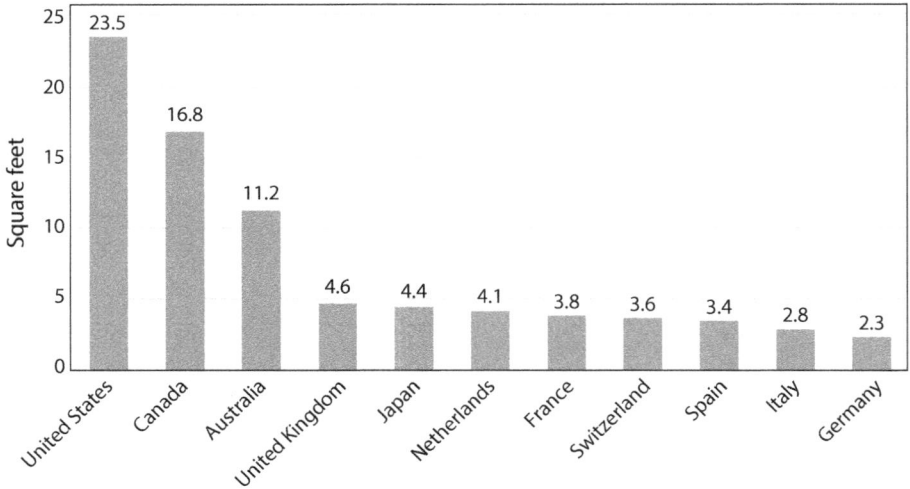

FIGURE 1.2. Retail space per capita in 2018, selected countries.
Source: Statista (accessed May 20, 2023).

the ubiquity of big-box discount centers across the United States. Walmart, for example, has over 5,300 stores in operation across all fifty states (Statista 2023); *Forbes* reports that 90 percent of Americans live within ten miles of a Walmart outlet.[4] In Europe, by contrast, such shopping meccas—while not absent—are far less prevalent, and downtown shopping areas in most countries have remained more vibrant.

Moreover, despite some convergence on American practices, there are still significant differences in retail operations. One of the most noticeable is that shopping hours are more restricted across most of Europe. Americans living or traveling abroad are often aggravated to find that in many European countries stores are closed on holidays and Sundays. Beyond shopping hours, European countries often impose further (less visible) restrictions on retailing operations, and sometimes on large retailers specifically, in an effort to protect small merchants or preserve central city shopping districts. Figure 1.3 presents comparative data on various restrictions on retail operations. It provides a cumulative measure of three types of regulation—restrictions on shopping hours, restrictions on promotions and discounts, and regulations pertaining specifically to large retailers. It shows

4. Stephen McBride, "Walmart Has Made a Genius Move to Beat Amazon," *Forbes*, January 8, 2020, https://www.forbes.com/sites/stephenmcbride1/2020/01/08/walmart-has-made-a-genius-move-to-beat-amazon/.

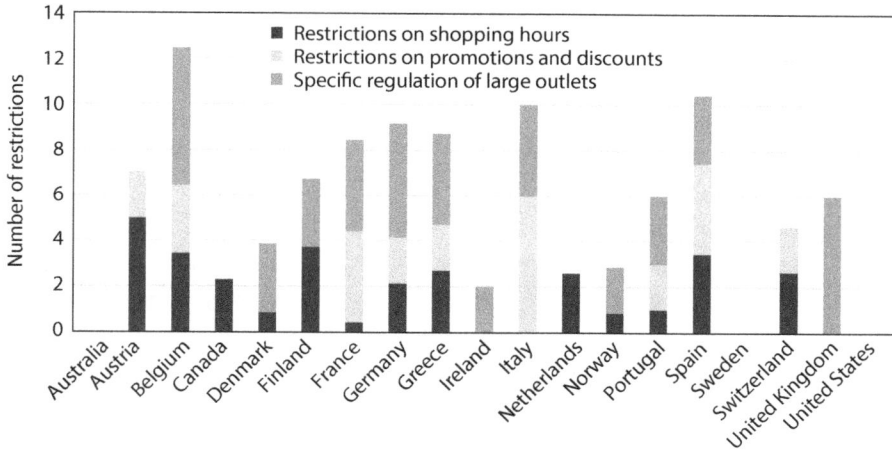

FIGURE 1.3. Restrictions on retail trade.
Source: OECD Data Explorer, "Regulation in Retail Trade 2013," https://stats.oecd
.org/Index.aspx?DataSetCode=RETAIL.

that different countries impose a mix of different regulations, but the United States stands out (alongside Sweden and recently liberalized Australia) for the unusually light regulations governing retail operations.[5]

And finally, shopping features far less prominently as a leisure activity than it does in the United States (Schor 1992: chap. 5). Indeed, the gargantuan Mall of America in suburban Minneapolis—with its twenty thousand parking spots and five-hundred-plus retail stores—beats out the Statue of Liberty among the top tourist attractions in the United States.[6]

Europe pioneered some significant advances in retailing (e.g., the department store), but it was American retailers who were responsible for many of the innovations that made shopping more accessible, and cheaper, especially for the masses. The list is impressive, and it includes not just mail order retail, but also installment purchasing, sales finance corporations, consumer credit

5. And the Swedish figure is somewhat misleading because issues such as shopping hours are regulated through collective bargaining rather than statute.

6. According to Wikipedia, accessed January 28, 2024, it is in fifth place. (Topping the list is Times Square, which is itself famous for its dense and flashing advertising billboards.) See https://en.wikipedia.org/wiki/Tourist_attractions_in_the_United_States. Another study, published in *Newsweek* in 2021, puts it at twenty-fourth (just edging out the Statue of Liberty). See Paulie Doyle, "The 25 Most Visited Tourist Spots in America," *Newsweek*, August 10, 2021, https://www.newsweek.com/most-visited-tourist-spots-america-disney-new-york-california-1616737.

ratings, the shopping mall, customer loyalty programs, the credit card, UPC (bar) codes, "Black Friday" and "Cyber Monday" promotions, and, of course, e-commerce. Innovations pioneered by American retailers are now ubiquitous across the globe, but the American model of mass distribution and the cultivation of consumers has a far longer history in the United States than in most of its peers.

This book provides an account of the origins of what I call "the Amazon economy." The Amazon economy is one in which consumption—and with that, retailing—plays a central role in driving economic growth. But it is also one that features a particular model of retailing—namely, ultra-lean retailing based on extremely narrow margins, dominated by players (such as Walmart and now Amazon) that enjoy enormous power over both workers and suppliers. It is an economy in which the low cost of distribution is partly underwritten by a precariously employed workforce whose low pay and unstable work hours are what allow for goods to be delivered to consumers at low cost and at almost any time of day. It is, in other words, a model that valorizes low prices and consumer convenience, and one that appears willing to accept, or ignore, the social costs that this model of retailing entails.

American lean retailing practices have diffused to other countries, and, indeed, a few foreign-based retailers have outdone their American counterparts in certain regards.[7] Yet the model originated in the United States and is still far more dominant there. Five of the ten largest private employers are all big discounters,[8] and the labor market as a whole features higher levels of labor market precarity than in peer democracies. As I have elaborated elsewhere (Thelen 2019), the United States stands out among the rich democracies both for its large low-pay sector (defined as employees earning less than two-thirds of the median wage) and for high levels of in-work

7. Germany's hard-discount grocery chains—Lidl and Aldi—have dramatically reduced costs by offering a restricted range of mostly private-label goods and by dispensing with much of the labor associated with presentation—often displaying goods on the pallets on which they were delivered. And Aldi in particular has made deep inroads into the American grocery sector with the purchase of Trader Joe's in 1979.

8. The most recent (2024) figures on the largest US employers show Walmart and Amazon with enormous leads (three to four times more employees compared to all others). The top ten also includes Home Depot, Kroger, and Target, as well as two major shipping couriers (UPS and FedEx), both of which are themselves key players in retail distribution. See https://stockanalysis .com/list/most-employees/, accessed 3/16/2024. In Germany and Denmark, by contrast, manufacturing firms still employ the largest number of workers (Davis and Sinha 2021: 4). For figures on employment in the retail and wholesale trades, see US Bureau of Labor Statistics, "Employees on Nonfarm Payrolls by Industry Sector and Selected Industry Detail," https://www.bls.gov/news .release/empsit.t17.htm.

poverty. The most recent figures for the size of the low-pay sector (2022) show a significant gap between the US (at 22.6 percent) and the OECD average (13.9 percent) (OECD 2023). Levels of in-work poverty are similarly striking, with the United States coming in at nearly 15 percent in 2019 against an OECD average of 9.3 percent (unpublished 2019 estimate by Hick and Marx; for 2017 figures see Hick and Marx 2023: 496, figure 34.1).

Retail workers in the United States themselves make up a large share of this American precariat: over three-quarters of them fall into the low-wage category (Ross and Bateman 2019:11). As a group they account for 8.4 percent of all low-wage workers in the United States (Ross and Bateman 2019: 11). According to a US Census Bureau report, over 15 percent of retail workers qualified for Medicaid in 2018, and over 10 percent fell below the poverty line.[9] The United States is thus characterized by a particularly bitter equilibrium, one in which large low-cost retailers have come to dominate the retail landscape and in which vast numbers of low-income workers now rely on them to make ends meet.

If we want to understand how we arrived at this place, we need to understand the way in which American retail capitalism has evolved. Analyzing the American case in comparative perspective and over a long time-frame—that evolution is what this book seeks to explain.

Prevailing Theories of Retail Capitalism

Given how prominently retailing and consumption figure in the economies of the rich democracies, it is surprising how little attention they have received in the comparative political economy literature (important exceptions include Chang et al. 2011; Rogowski and Kayser 2002; Trumbull 2006a; 2012a, 2014; Watson 2011). The vast majority of studies, my own work included, center on the politics of production. Hall and Soskice's influential "varieties of capitalism" framework (2001), for example, focuses entirely on the institutional configurations that shape what firms produce (based on a country's "comparative institutional advantage") and how they produce it (based on differences in the infrastructure supporting different production strategies in liberal versus coordinated market economies).[10]

9. D. Augustus Anderson, "A Profile of the Retail Workforce," US Census Bureau, September 8, 2020, https://www.census.gov/library/stories/2020/09/profile-of-the-retail-workforce.html.

10. Similarly, and relatedly, the "beneficial constraints" in operation in Streeck's classic work (1991) on diversified quality production are exclusively about the incentives and constraints faced by the producers of goods in these economies.

More historically oriented work on the origins of different political econ-omies is similarly fixated on producer groups, especially labor unions and manufacturing interests (Fulcher 1991; Swenson 2002; Thelen 2004). For the United States, specifically, we have superb accounts of the industrial titans who spearheaded a revolution in production (Josephson 1934; Chandler 1962). And the role played by American manufacturers in the development of mass production technologies—from Eli Whitney's interchangeable parts to Henry Ford's moving assembly line—figures centrally in the literature on the political economy of industrialization.

But mass production presupposes mass consumption and mass distri-bution, and to my knowledge there exists no sustained political-economic analysis of how the politics of *distribution* has shaped the American political economy over the past 150 years.[11] American retailers were no less transfor-mative than their more famous manufacturing counterparts. Aaron Mont-gomery Ward, Richard Warren Sears, John Wanamaker, Rowland Macy, Frank Woolworth, Sam Walton, and now Jeff Bezos have had as deep an impact on the shape of the American political economy as John Rockefeller, Andrew Carnegie, and Henry Ford.

There is a rich literature in history and sociology that documents the emergence of consumer culture in the United States. Lizabeth Cohen's magisterial *A Consumers' Republic* (2003) tracks the ways in which mass consumption in the post–World War II period transformed American poli-tics by giving rise to new social movements demanding inclusion in the American dream. Louis Hyman (2011, 2012) and Lendol Calder (1999) have brilliantly probed how consumer credit and mass consumption grew sym-biotically and in mutually reinforcing ways. There exist as well important comparative analyses that contrast aspects of the American and European consumer cultures and political economies (Beckert 2011, 2016; Berghoff 1999; Berghoff et al. 2016; Berghoff and Spiekermann 2012; De Grazia 2005; Logemann 2008, 2011, 2012b; Kocka 1997; Teupe 2016). These and other sociologists and economic historians have made signal contributions to our understanding of consumer culture.

But what have political economists had to say about the rise of large, low-cost retailing? The short answer is: not much. Economists mostly offer apolitical explanations of the triumph of mass retailing in the United States

---

11. Dunlavy and Welskopp (2007: 58) identify this as a significant gap in the literature. Bar-tholomew Watson's excellent 2011 thesis, discussed below, focuses primarily on the post–World War II period. There are of course some wonderful accounts of individual entrepreneurs and companies by historians, and I draw on them here.

(for a similar critique, see O'Sullivan 2019; Dunlavy 2024). It is a story of technological and organizational innovations animated by entrepreneurs responding rationally to the opportunities afforded by America's large domestic market to enhance productivity and efficiency through scale and scope. Chandler's analysis of Sears is the classic on this point (Chandler 1962: chap. 5). More recent variations on the same argument can be found in Baily and Solow (2001), Basker (2007), and Bronnenberg and Ellickson (2015). A more surprising example of this line of argument is Philippon (2019), who—while otherwise sharply critical of the concentration of corporate power in the American political economy—nonetheless holds Walmart up as an example of "efficient concentration" (2019: 31–35).[12]

Yet as Chandler's own research suggested, the large private retailers that rose to dominance in the United States were not the only alternative; indeed, a very different model of mass distribution took shape in Europe, where consumer cooperatives dominated the retail landscape in the nineteenth century and into the twentieth (Chandler 1990: 255–61). More generally, and as Bensel emphasizes, the largely unregulated national market that these large American retailers conquered was not "an historical 'given'" (2000: 16) but was itself politically constructed.[13] In fact, as we will see, the size of the domestic market was not a help but a hurdle for America's first mass retailers, one that they only overcame with a very significant assist from the government. American retailers did not simply respond to market opportunities; they created them by exploiting regulatory gaps to grow in scale and scope—and with a great deal of help from the courts.

Legal scholars working in the rich "law and political economy" tradition often attribute the rise of dominant players like Amazon to a resurgence in monopoly power in the post–World War II period. Most famously, perhaps, Lina Khan's seminal analysis (2016) places much of the blame on an important shift in antitrust jurisprudence beginning in the 1970s and 1980s, with the ascendance of the so-called Chicago school, which puts "consumer welfare," routinely defined in terms of price, at the heart of antitrust theory and practice. She traces the growing influence, in both legal and political

12. Philippon (2019) contrasts such examples of "good concentration" from "bad concentration" (as in the American airline industry) according to whether the efficiency gains from concentration have resulted in lower prices to consumers ("good concentration") or excess profits ("bad concentration").

13. See also McCurdy 1978 on the legal construction of the national market; and Dunlavy 2024 on the central role played by the US Department of Commerce in promoting product standardization in the 1920s.

circles, of Robert Bork's work in prompting the "shift in antitrust away from economic structuralism in favor of price theory" (2016: 717).

The rise of the Chicago school is clearly important, and antitrust policy and jurisprudence play central roles in the argument developed in the pages below. So while I agree with Khan about the importance of antitrust in the rise of the Amazon economy, I show that in retailing specifically, the changes since the 1970s are just the latest chapter in a far longer story, one in which large, low-cost retailers have almost always enjoyed a privileged position in the American antitrust regime. American antitrust doctrine played a key role in the late nineteenth century, not just in defeating the worker (and/or small-retailer) cooperative associations that thrived in many parts of Europe as alternatives to large private retailers, but also in hobbling other organized interests—labor unions, trade associations (especially of small manufacturers), and other organized business groups—that elsewhere placed various constraints on the growth of big retail.

Even in periods of heightened antitrust scrutiny, low-cost retailers were often spared or even given a boost. For example, in 1911, the very same year that it ordered the dissolution of the Standard Oil empire, the Supreme Court sided with a large discount drugstore against a small manufacturer of patent medicine in the landmark *Dr. Miles* case that banned resale price maintenance contracts—coding both as involving illegal acts in restraint of trade (see chapter 5 for a full discussion). Similarly, and as discussed in chapter 7, even in the "golden era" of antitrust enforcement in the years following World War II, the courts handed discounters crucial victories in their battles with producers over pricing. In short, American antitrust jurisprudence had tilted the playing field toward low-cost large retailers long before Robert Bork came on the scene, and their growth to dominance has allowed them to solidify an impregnable alliance with consumers that has so far proved durable in the face of numerous subsequent political and legal challenges.

Political scientists, as noted above, have generally not had much at all to say about the rise of mass retailing, focusing much more on the politics of production than distribution. Bartholomew Watson's (2011) dissertation comes closest to the present study by identifying different varieties of retailing. In his analysis, the American model of lean retailing is distinct from alternative arrangements in Europe that involve more collaborative relations with workers and suppliers. Watson argues that the European and American models of retailing, previously similar, diverged beginning in the 1960s. My own analysis, however, suggests something like the opposite: I show that the pre–World War II differences between Europe and the United States were far greater, and I argue that the postwar trend is, if anything, toward convergence (De Grazia 2005).

An adjacent literature in comparative political economy has explored important aspects of consumption and consumer politics, topics that are clearly related to the politics of retailing that lie at the center of the present study. Ronald Rogowski and colleagues, for example, have argued that majoritarian electoral systems provide incentives for policymakers to cater to consumers, while proportional representation systems empower producer groups (Rogowski and Kayser 2002; Chang et al. 2011). While suggestive of important differences, Rogowski et al. do not problematize the very different ways in which "consumer interest" is defined—and defended politically—cross-nationally. Gunnar Trumbull addresses this very issue, exploring how different forms of consumer mobilization and organization drove cross-nationally divergent approaches to consumer protection in the 1960s and 1970s (Trumbull 2006a, 2012b; 2014). The present study draws on Trumbull's work on the postwar period while also taking a broader historical sweep to emphasize the central role played by antitrust policy and regulatory fragmentation in shaping the balance of power between small and large retailers, between manufacturers and mass retailers, and between large retailers and their employees, as conflicts among these groups played out in the legislatures and courts at both the federal and state levels over the twentieth century as a whole.

A further body of work in political economy emphasizes the importance of *credit-based* consumption in defining and sustaining different growth regimes (Wiedemann 2021, Baccaro and Pontusson 2016; Ansell 2014; Thurston 2018; Carruthers 2022; SoRelle 2020, 2023). Most of these scholars trace the origins of America's demand-driven growth regime to the actions of the government in the 1930s in response to the Great Depression and to the extraordinary expansion of consumer credit after World War II (Trumbull 2014; Cohen 2003; Schragger 2005). The embrace of a consumption-driven growth model in the postwar period clearly plays a role in the flourishing of mass retailing. However, as Calder (1999) and Hyman (2011) emphasize, mass retailers were not just beneficiaries, they were themselves central players in promoting consumer credit long before the New Deal and indeed even long before the banks got into the game.[14]

---

14. To give just one example, credit cards were not invented by bankers but by America's large retailers (Calder 1999: 16–17, 72; Hyman 2011: chap. 4, 117–18). Today, most American teenagers still secure their first credit card not from a bank but through one of the large retailers in the United States (Gap, Old Navy, Target).

Moreover, the heavy focus on credit in the existing literature obscures the role of large discount retailers that eschewed credit as they grew. These big discount retailers are crucial to the story for the way they accelerated the decline of American manufacturing and the emergence of the low-wage, low-cost equilibrium that distinguishes the current period from the golden era of postwar economic growth.

Comparisons to Europe can help clarify the distinctive trajectory of American retailing. In this book, I compare the United States to the United Kingdom, Germany, and two Scandinavian countries (Sweden and Denmark). While a full analysis of a century of retailing across each of these other cases falls beyond the scope of the current project, I have sought to include sufficient detail to highlight the distinctive features of American retailing. Moreover, the comparisons that I chose are designed to address key theoretical issues at the heart of the argument. Thus, for example, the UK provides a comparison to a fellow common-law country that nonetheless featured a very different competition regime. Germany allows for comparison to another federal country, but one whose regulatory landscape is not as fractured as the United States'. And Sweden and Denmark provide the opportunity to underscore differences to other countries with widely dispersed rural populations in which—unlike the United States—agrarian and working-class cooperatives thrived as major retailers.

The Argument in Brief

The evolution of American retailing followed a distinctive trajectory. Whereas in Europe large-scale private retailers faced a host of legal and political obstacles throughout the late nineteenth century and much of the twentieth century, in the United States they grew in a far more permissive regulatory landscape. The constraints imposed on mass retailers in Europe (some, though not all, still in effect today) with which American firms have largely *not* had to contend are many. They include effective national-level restrictions on price competition, special taxes and rules pertaining to retail businesses over a certain size,[15] licensing arrangements that restrict entry into the sector, urban planning rules that limit where large retailers can locate, and regulations

---

15. In some cases such taxes were partly a reaction to American-style firms entering (or threatening to enter) these markets, examples of the kind of transatlantic exchanges of which Logemann (2019) and Rodgers (2000) have both written, and a reminder that my analysis of European and American retail practices involves comparison across countries that are not wholly independent cases.

governing store opening hours, not to mention the indirect impact of stronger unions and sectoral bargaining on the wages and benefits European retailers are often required to pay (Tagiuri 2021; Carré and Tilly 2017). Viewed in a broad comparative perspective, it is clear that large American retailers have historically enjoyed unusually clear sailing compared to their counterparts abroad. Large-scale American retailers grew in scale and scope not simply through their own ingenuity but by taking advantage both of a uniquely permissive legal landscape and of opportunities for regulatory arbitrage that were not available to their counterparts in Europe.

An important article by the legal scholar James Q. Whitman (2007) can provide an initial orientation for the argument developed in the chapters to follow. Setting aside the usual "well-worn" distinction between common-law and civil law traditions within his own discipline, Whitman draws out a contrast between what he calls America's "consumerist" and Europe's more "producerist" legal orders. His definition of a producerist legal order is one in which the law looks out first and foremost for the rights of producer groups (farmers, workers, small firms)—that is, actors "on the supply side of the market." Such a legal order conceives of workers as a producer class with rights to engage in collective self-help, while also recognizing the rights of other producer groups—for example, "the rights of competitors in a given industry to be protected against 'unfair competition' [and] the rights of small retailers to be protected against big discount stores" (2007: 345). Whitman contrasts this with an alternative consumerist legal order—most fully realized in the United States—that tends instead "to emphasize the right of consumers to buy goods and services at competitive prices" (2007: 346).[16] The distinction, he emphasizes, is not hard and fast; it is a difference in degree and emphasis rather than in kind. However, it is central to his account of what appear to be relatively durable differences in the "values embraced by different legal cultures" (2007: 347). Focusing especially on the postwar period, Whitman is primarily concerned with the question of whether continental Europe's traditional producerism is giving way to American-style consumerism. His answer is no: despite some pressures for convergence, "continental law continues to resist economic consumerism" (Whitman 2007: 372).

---

16. Whitman also includes in the consumerist orientation a concern for the interest of consumers in quality and safety, but he notes that while this *consumer protection* interest is wholly compatible with producer protection, "only *economic* consumerism represents a true menace to the producerist outlook" (2007: 347).

But how did these distinct legal cultures take root, and what impact did they have on the interest group landscape and on retailing and distribution in particular? The distinction Whitman draws, between producerist and consumerist legal orders, shares some striking similarities to the distinction between coordinated and liberal market economies that lies at the heart of the "varieties of capitalism" (VofC) framework as elaborated by Peter A. Hall and David Soskice (2001). Indeed, many of the arrangements that define Europe's coordinated market economies are the same as those that also support a producerist politics as defined by Whitman. In particular, what distinguishes Europe's more coordinated variety of capitalism from the alternative Anglo-Saxon liberal variety is a rich associational landscape of producer groups that allows employers to coordinate among themselves (and with unions) to achieve joint gains through cooperation (Hall and Soskice 2001: chap. 1).

Yet the connection between Whitman's producerist/consumerist divide and Hall and Soskice's coordinated/liberal market economy dichotomy remains unclear because the two frameworks approach these political economies from wholly different vantage points—with Whitman focusing on the balance between producer and consumer interests as expressed in the law, and varieties of capitalism focusing on the capacity of producers to coordinate among themselves in the market. However, combining Whitman's emphasis on the law with insights drawn from VofC's emphasis on producer-group coordination, we can pinpoint two features of the American political economy that differ not just from continental Europe's coordinated market economies but also from fellow liberal market economies as well.[17] I argue that these two features, together, paved the way for the rise of the Amazon economy.

The first is the uncommonly congenial (for large retailers) legal regime, starting already in the late nineteenth century with the American embrace of what in comparative perspective was in fact a wholly unique approach to competition policy and jurisprudence (or what in the United States is called antitrust). In that period, a severe economic downturn and overcapacity across key markets caused wages and profits to plummet, and everywhere, producers and workers alike sought to stabilize markets by organizing to defend themselves against "ruinous" competition through coordination and

---

17. Despite his dismissal of the conventional divide between common-law and civil law traditions, Whitman does not compare the United States with fellow common-law countries such as the United Kingdom, but instead contrasts it to two continental countries—Germany and France.

collective self-help. Among its peers, the American judiciary was uniquely hostile toward the new associational forms that emerged in this period. The effect of this stance on the interest group landscape was momentous, because, as the legal scholar Sanjukta Paul points out, "antitrust law decides where competition will be required and where coordination will be permitted" (Paul 2020a: 382). And, as she emphasizes, the choice of which forms of coordination to permit and which to prohibit has always been profoundly political (Paul 2020a).[18]

Of particular importance in the present context are the different approaches that Europe and the United States took in the early industrial period with respect to what Paul calls horizontal coordination—that is, coordination or cooperation between competitors or potential competitors in a market (Paul 2020a: 383). In Europe, national legislation historically sanctioned these efforts at coordination and collective self-help. Such permissiveness gave rise to cartels, but it also provided a more hospitable context for the emergence of centralized labor unions and trade associations that would come to define Europe's more coordinated variety of capitalism (Thelen 2020; Foster and Thelen 2023, 2024). More important still were the radically different stances on the two sides of the Atlantic toward horizontal coordination among *nondominant actors*, including farmers, workers, and small businesses—all of which were consistently harassed by the courts in the United States. By contrast, in Europe, and even where explicit legislation was lacking, courts often exercised forbearance toward such arrangements. This applies not just to Europe's coordinated market economies; British courts, too, recognized and sometimes enforced agreements that under American law were being condemned as anticompetitive conspiracies operating in restraint of trade (Thelen 2020).

In what Skowronek has called America's "state of courts and parties," the federal judiciary in this period assumed an outsized role in shaping the national economy (Skowronek 1982; Bensel 2000). Its uniquely uncompromising approach to such forms of horizontal coordination famously

---

18. Paul's work is crucial for the way she disentangles distinct forms of coordination: coordination within the bounds of the firm (firms as "collections of contracts" that are protected from antitrust scrutiny by conventional understandings of property rights), vertical coordination (involving firms in "adjacent" markets, i.e., at different levels in the production and distribution chain), and horizontal coordination (cooperation between competitors or potential competitors in a market) (Paul 2020a: 383). Paul's core argument is that American antitrust has operated as a powerful "sorting mechanism to elevate one species of economic coordination [especially coordination within the bounds of the firm] and undermine others [especially coordination among nondominant actors beyond the boundaries of the firm]" (Paul 2020a: 378).

interfered with the development of unions (Forbath 1991; Hattam 1993). But as we will see, the courts also played a role in defeating the worker (and/or small-retailer) cooperative associations that thrived in many parts of Europe as alternatives to large private retailers, as well as in hobbling other organized interests—trade associations (especially of small manufacturers), small merchants, and other organized business groups—that elsewhere placed various constraints on the growth of big retail.

Second, and again different even from America's fellow common-law countries, mass retailers in the United States also benefited from a fragmented regulatory landscape that divided authority not only across different arenas (courts and legislatures) but also across different levels of government (federal, state, and local). In the late nineteenth and early twentieth centuries, the central government's weak administrative powers afforded large retailers the opportunity to scale up quickly, unmolested by the kinds of legislative restrictions imposed on their counterparts in Europe. State-level governments in the United States possessed more tools to regulate business in this period, and in fact Gerstle suggests that they enjoyed "a staggering freedom of action" to limit the rights of private actors to safeguard public welfare (Gerstle 2016: 56–57; Zackin 2013). However, the laws that individual states passed were often wildly divergent, and their limited jurisdictional reach was no match for mass retailers that—based not least on the head start the courts had given them—were soon operating on a national scale.

Large retailers were able to exploit the fractured regulatory landscape of the American political economy to undermine enforcement of whatever rules subnational governments devised, engaging in venue arbitrage to avoid or mitigate their impact. In fact, retailers leveraged regulatory differences across jurisdictions to inspire competition among states and localities—for sales tax revenues, for jobs and investment, and for access to low cost goods—thus fueling a deregulatory race to the bottom. And as they grew in scale and scope, America's large retailers assembled an ever-growing coalition of supporters who came to rely on these companies in various ways and who could therefore be mobilized to defend them in subsequent political battles with would-be regulators.

A Framework for the Study of American Retail Capitalism

One of the challenges—also one of the joys—of studying the political economy of American retailing is that the relevant conflicts play out across a wide range of venues and levels of governance, far wider than existing political-economic frameworks encompass. As Bart Watson (2011: 17–18) observed: "Retailers are among the most connected actors in the economy. . . . Politically, they must manage relationships ranging from international trade organizations and national regulators down to municipal governments. Within national economies, they connect with consumers, suppliers and producers, manufacturing firms, and wholesalers . . ." These multiple connections generated the tensions and conflicts whose outcomes shaped the retail landscape over time. Large retailers did not just battle smaller competitors in the market (and in politics), they also engaged in highly consequential struggles in the early twentieth century with manufacturers over "the right to cut prices" (as Macy's, for example, put it). They tussled with federal regulators in the legislature and the courts and also with municipal governments over such issues as taxation and store hours. Tracing the politics of retailing thus demands a wider-angle lens than most existing political-economic frameworks have on offer.

In recent collaborative work, Jacob Hacker, Alexander Hertel-Fernandez, Paul Pierson, and I proposed a general framework for analyzing the American political economy that guides the analysis in this book (Hacker et al. 2022: chap. 1). A first component of that framework involves a recognition of the way in which distributional and power conflicts play out *across distinct levels and arenas of governance*. As we will see, efforts at the subnational level (whether by state or by municipal governments) to regulate large retailers often stood in conflict with one another and with the rules operating at the national level. This fractured regulatory landscape is precisely what allowed national retailers to engage in venue arbitrage, working around states and localities with stricter rules and playing different jurisdictions off one another as they grew in scale and scope.

Conflicts played out not just between different levels of governance, but also across different arenas. Alongside national and state legislatures, courts are a key site of contestation within the American political economy (Rahman and Thelen 2022). Although legal scholars and students of American political development have long understood the importance of law and the courts in the development of American capitalism (Skowronek 1982; Bensel 2000; Forbath 1991; Pistor 2019, Fishkin and Forbath 2022), political scientists interested in distinct varieties of capitalism have overlooked the role of the judiciary almost entirely. Among the omissions the current study addresses is the importance of competition (antitrust) law. Indeed, in retrospect it is astonishing that comparative political economists, myself included, have spent decades debating the varieties of capitalism framework—which places the issue of coordination at the center of the distinction between coordinated and liberal market economies—while paying virtually no attention to cross-national variation in competition regimes (for a more fully elaborated discussion, see Foster and Thelen 2024).[19] This gap is glaring because, as Paul has emphasized, "antitrust law's core function is to allocate coordination rights to some economic actors and deny them to others" (Paul 2020a: 382). Competition policy—and the courts generally— thus figure prominently in the analysis below—shaping the interest group landscape and intervening in ways that tipped the balance of power among large and small retailers and between manufacturers and mass retailers in consequential ways over the entire century.

Tracing the origins of the Amazon economy also involves an analysis of shifting *coalitional alignments*, another of the foundational elements of the framework that Hacker, Hertel-Fernandez, Pierson, and I lay out (Hacker et al. 2022). The cleavages and conflicts that shaped and reshaped American retailing ran along a number of different fault lines: small versus large retailers, mass manufacturers versus low-cost distributors, retail employers versus unions. As the chapters to follow show, the complex interdependencies among these actors produced a changing geometry of alliances over time, often in response to evolving macroeconomic conditions. To take just one example, America's large brand manufacturers were locked in conflict with low-cost retailers over pricing in periods of high consumer demand, but they made peace with them during economic downturns when they found themselves saddled with large surpluses.

Regional divisions also figure centrally in the analysis below. Whereas in Europe conflicts in the evolution of retailing were generally played out along lines of class (labor unions versus employer associations) or among competing producer group interests (e.g., "traditional" versus "modern" retailing), sectional differences were far more pronounced in the United States (Bensel 2000). Regional alignments did not follow a single unitary logic: southern states sided with mass retailers on issues of pricing but fought them tenaciously on issues of taxation. The analysis below also features some stunning regional reversals. Southern states that were at the forefront of the populist opposition to chain stores during the 1930s would in the 1960s provide the congenial regulatory context in which the largest of them all (Walmart) could grow to dominance.

---

19. Hall and Soskice do mention antitrust in passing in the introduction to *Varieties of Capitalism*, but political economists working in that tradition failed to follow up on that clue.

Finally, understanding the origins of the Amazon economy requires *a developmental perspective* that appreciates the way in which outcomes and power relations are forged through conflicts over time within and across these multiple institutional venues. Historical sequencing plays an important role in the politics of distribution, for, as we will see, early victories in the courts provided America's large private retailers with opportunities unavailable to their European counterparts to grow unimpeded by alternative retailing models and countervailing political forces. Capitalizing on this head start, America's large retailers quickly grew to national scale and from there engaged in regulatory arbitrage to avoid—or directly challenge—whatever obstacles they faced within America's fractured regulatory landscape. Crucially, America's large low-cost retailers also picked up allies as they grew in scale and scope—farmers who came to rely on them to help unload periodic surpluses, capital-intensive mass manufacturers who came to appreciate the predictability they offered by ordering in advance and in large volume, and developers and local politicians who came to see them as valuable assets for local economic growth. Above all, American consumers got hooked on large chains as a go-to source of low-cost goods. America's large retailers understood the power of these alliances and dependencies and actively weaponized them in their ongoing battles with regulators at all levels.

An analysis of the American political economy through the lens of distribution holds lessons for both comparative political economists and students of American politics. For the former, the present study points to the importance of the courts as a hitherto neglected arena of contestation with the political economy. Beyond this, the present study also brings into view a new set of actors—large low-cost retailers—that have clearly left an important mark on the shape of American capitalism. While it is commonplace for comparative political economy scholars to code the United States as exemplifying a "consumption-driven" growth model, few have paused to consider where this model came from. For such a model to prevail, someone had to have been pushing this outcome, and the present analysis points to the very active and consequential role that mass retailers played in promoting it.

For Americanists, my hope is that the present study can denaturalize aspects of the American political economy that we often take for granted as the natural outcome of market forces. Without situating the United States in a broader international perspective, the highly unusual features of American capitalism frequently fade from view. The comparative analysis of the evolution of retailing in the chapters to follow brings these features into focus, serving as a window on the distinctiveness of the American political economy across multiple realms, from the central role of the judiciary in shaping the landscape of organized interests, all the way down to the role of local authorities in the politics of zoning and shopping hours that have defined the spatial and temporal contours of American retailing.

Outline of the Book

I develop my argument loosely by chronology, tracing the evolution of American retailing through three broad phases and with attention in each to the ways in which the United States compares to other advanced democracies. Part II analyzes the origins of a consumerist political economy in the late nineteenth and early twentieth centuries. Chapters 2 and 3 trace the construction of a mass market in the late nineteenth century, a monumental undertaking in which large mail-order companies benefited from state-sponsored suppression of potential competitors (especially working-class and other consumer cooperatives) even as they opportunistically repurposed public infrastructure for private ends. Chapter 4 then turns to the explosive growth of chain store retailing alongside the expansion of consumer credit in the interwar period, developments that were facilitated by the politicization of consumption and prices in the 1910s and 1920s and judicial forbearance in the face of regulatory arbitrage.

Part III of the book documents the political backlash and mobilization that flared up against ascendant retailers in the interwar war period and during the Depression. Chapter 5 focuses on political battles in which brand manufacturers fought large low-cost retailers for control over pricing. It documents how—very different from Europe—the federal judiciary intervened early in conflicts over price maintenance in ways that tilted the balance of power toward price-cutting retailers. Chapter 6 then considers the populist backlash against chain stores in the context of the Great Depression. Compared to the battles over pricing, these conflicts featured a different set of alliances, organized primarily along regional lines and between large retailers and small merchants. But by this time, mass retailers had assembled a formidable coalition of supporters that could be mobilized to come to their defense.

Part IV of the book turns to the postwar period, when the government's full-throated embrace of a consumption-driven growth model further empowered large retailers. Chapter 7 considers the role that the government came to assign to mass retailers to countervail the powers of the country's oligopolistic producers in a period in which heightened antitrust enforcement (often directed at large manufacturers) frequently redounded to the advantage of low-cost distributors. Chapter 8 tracks the rise, in this context, of a new group of highly disruptive discounters whose strategies of "Schumpeterian rule-breaking" (Teupe 2019) coincided with (and hastened) legal changes that sanctified the emerging consumer welfare standard.[20] Chapter 9 compares the resulting features of contemporary American retailing to the European model along several dimensions. It highlights differences in the recent evolution of competition laws, as Europe has taken a far stronger stance than the United States against "abuse of dominance" by powerful firms and platforms; it explores differences in the level of protection offered to retail workers on the two sides of the Atlantic; and it traces the politics that have driven differences in the spatial and temporal parameters of shopping in Europe and the United States.

Part V concludes by examining the turn to e-commerce and the way in which American retailing has shaped the political economy as a whole. Chapter 10 considers the extent to which Amazon represents a departure from or a continuation of the previous trajectory of American retail capitalism. Despite some important differences in the business model, Amazon's political playbook is strikingly similar to that of its predecessors. Most importantly, the company's strategy continues to rely on leveraging its market strength to squeeze suppliers and workers in ways that have contributed directly to the low-cost, low-wage trap we observe today. Chapter 11 pans out to consider how American retailing has shaped a growth model that relies on consumption even as it generates and exacerbates inequality. Through all three phases examined in this book, large retailers accumulated a growing support coalition as they expanded. Over time, policymakers, too, came to rely on them to soften the sharp edges of American capitalism, making it possible for a growing number of groups to participate (albeit on radically different terms) in the country's consumption-driven growth model while allowing the government to dodge the income redistribution that would otherwise have been required to sustain it.

---

20. For a general argument about the role of the creative use of law and the courts in promoting gradual institutional change, see Streeck and Thelen 2005; also Pollman and Barry 2017 on "regulatory entrepreneurship," and Teupe 2019 on "Schumpeterian rule-breaking" as a mechanism through which firms avoid or break laws strategically in an effort to shift the legal boundaries over time (2019: 186).

PART II

American Retailers in the Making of a Consumerist Political Economy

2

Clearing the Field

THE FATE OF CONSUMER COOPERATIVES

With justification, economists argue that large American retailers benefited from the country's vast domestic market. Consumer markets, however, do not emerge spontaneously, for as a large literature in political economy has taught us, markets are politically constructed, which is also why the forms they assume and the kinds of actors they support vary cross-nationally. In this and the following chapter, I show that America's large retailers did not simply discover and exploit a vast homogenous market, they created it. And they did so with considerable help from government and the courts.

The rise of retail capitalism in the United States received an early boost with the demise of potential competitors in the mass-retailing space, competitors that flourished throughout Europe, including in America's closest liberal market economy and common-law cousin, Britain. In Europe, agricultural and especially working-class consumer cooperatives founded in the nineteenth century not only survived, they thrived and grew to become major players in the retail landscape in the early twentieth century. In the United States, by contrast, similar ventures foundered in a fractured and uncongenial regulatory landscape in which the legal status of cooperative ventures was unclear and actively contested. Powerful (state-based) banking interests deprived consumer cooperatives of opportunities to secure the kind of funding that had allowed their European counterparts to grow and thrive, and agricultural cooperatives organized around joint purchasing and marketing were often harassed by the courts in the late nineteenth and early twentieth centuries. Cooperatives of all sorts were viciously attacked in the South, where they sought to deliver Black farmers from the grip of local company stores that were operated by previous slaveholders in ways designed to keep them in a state of semiservitude.

Entrepreneurial retailers moved into the void and grew by appropriating public infrastructure to serve their own private commercial ends. In particular, the mail order retailers who catered to the country's rural population (the vast majority of Americans in the late nineteenth century) repurposed the US postal system not only to deliver catalogs and goods but also to function as a critical financial intermediary. Without the government-sponsored mail order system, rural Americans—almost always unbanked—would never have tasted the fruits of the consumer goods Sears and other large retailers were offering them.

America's agrarian population was famous for its distrust of large "foreign" (nonlocal) firms. But farmers welcomed the arrival of Sears, which delivered them from the bland and limited range of (heavily marked-up) goods on offer at the local general store. Black consumers in the South, who faced racism and discrimination in local retail markets, benefited from the opportunity to order anonymously and at fixed, listed prices. Mass retailers recognized the political value of the large and loyal consumer base they had cultivated and actively mobilized them in the political battles they faced. Rural constituencies in sparsely populated states wielded outsized political power as a result of the country's malapportioned federal institutions, and this proved invaluable to large retailers as they sought to extend their market and political power at the turn of the century.

The First Mass Retailers: The United States in Comparative Perspective

In the nineteenth century, there was no mass retail market—not in Europe, not in the United States. Outside a few major urban centers, consumers relied on local merchants who in turn depended on various suppliers to provide the goods. In these small general stores, selection was limited to say the least: basically consumers could buy what shopkeepers happened to have in stock. Prices were far above those in urban markets, due both to the lack of competition and to the length of the distribution chain—with wholesalers, brokers, distributors, drummers,[1] and local shop owners all collecting a share of the final price (Barron 1997: 164). Local merchants on both sides of the Atlantic often extended credit informally to their customers—for example, by allowing them to run a tab and pay later. But they were not above deploying sketchy techniques such as selling diluted goods (e.g., flour mixed with powdered plaster, milk mixed with water) or manipulating weights by placing a thumb on the scale (Korf 2008: 12; Hilson 2017: 61, Jefferys 1954: 4–5).

Beyond the local general store, consumers on the American and European periphery could rely on the occasional visits of traveling salesmen for some goods. Roving peddlers typically sold smaller wares, often exotic items like jewelry or fancy clocks (Barron 1997: 159–60). These itinerant salesmen gave consumers access to goods otherwise unavailable to them. But buyers had to beware. Untethered from the communities they served, peddlers often defrauded unsuspecting consumers with cheap and shoddy goods before moving on to the next town. In general, given the spotty access to a limited range of goods, one can hardly speak of a consumer market throughout much of the nineteenth century.

The grip over local consumer markets of small merchants and the distributors who supplied them took on different forms in different contexts, but it was pervasive, and, in both Europe and the United States, it inspired the search for relief through collective self-help. In Europe, groups of workers or farmers often joined forces to found cooperative associations to challenge local monopolies by providing their members with a lower-cost source of more reliable and unadulterated goods (Purvis 1992: 107). By pooling resources, they could ensure quality and secure better prices by purchasing in higher volume, cutting out the middlemen and selling directly to members. Consumer cooperatives in Europe were almost always linked to some kind of credit institution or savings union that provided capital to support their operations and to finance expansion. Thus, beyond acting as an alternative wholesale distributor, consumer cooperatives in Europe often integrated in both directions, producing their own goods to reduce prices and maintaining their own retail outlets to reach a widely dispersed clientele (Hilson 2017: 136–37).

Such cooperatives appeared across Europe in the nineteenth century, establishing a foothold throughout the continent and in the Nordic

---

1. Drummers were traveling salesmen sent by manufacturers to generate orders from merchants in distant markets. To attract the attention of prospective buyers, they beat a drum—hence the phrase "to drum up business" (Harris and Larson n.d.). Whereas peddlers sold goods they themselves had purchased, drummers acted as intermediaries, carrying samples and taking orders on behalf of manufacturers.

countries.[2] But they also flourished in countries that share the United States' Anglo-Saxon roots and common-law traditions, including Canada, Australia, New Zealand, and Britain (for an overview, see Hilson et al. 2017; Spicer 2022). Only in the United States did consumer cooperatives fail to get off the ground at this time, though not for lack of trying. Small farmers' cooperative ventures for joint purchasing and marketing were especially prominent in the latter part of nineteenth-century America, but worker-based consumer cooperatives were also launched in this period.

The Grange, famous in American history as the main organization through which American farmers sought to advance their economic interests and to channel their political grievances, organized cooperatives to secure higher prices for their members' crops and to provide them with essential goods at lower cost (Goodwyn 1976: chap. 2; Schneiberg et al. 2008; Schneiberg 2013). The Farmers' Alliances that succeeded the Grange in the 1880s pursued the cooperative project even more vigorously. In these efforts, they also joined forces with the Knights of Labor—at the time the most powerful labor organization in the United States—in a short-lived alliance that sought to bridge sectional, class, and racial divides and to bring urban and rural constituents together behind the construction of a "cooperative commonwealth" (Goodwyn 1976: xv, xii; Gourevitch 2015).

Unlike in Europe, however, these efforts at collective self-help were met not by state support or even forbearance, but often by active state suppression, falling victim to problems generated by a hostile judiciary, a fractured regulatory landscape, and intense racial animus. As consumer cooperatives in America foundered, private retailers exploited public infrastructure to fill the resulting void.

Cooperatives in Europe

Across Europe, cooperatives emerged to challenge local merchants, large producers, and wholesalers by providing an alternative source of high-quality goods at lower cost.[3] Space does not permit a full analysis of the

2. See Hilson et al. 2017 for accounts of the cooperative movements in France, Belgium, Germany, Austria, Portugal, Spain, Italy, and Switzerland, as well as the Nordic countries. Furlough and Strikwerda (1999) also contains chapters on consumer cooperatives in Sweden, Denmark, Germany, France, and Britain, among others.

3. European cooperatives would later do a great deal to modernize and rationalize retailing and distribution—for example, through the adoption of self-service and centralized warehousing, and, later, even the introduction of hypermarkets (Jonsson 2017: 642–43; Ekberg 2017: 707).

various cooperative movements that sprang up in Europe in the nineteenth and early twentieth centuries. However, a brief review of developments across a diverse range of political economies—Scandinavia, Germany, and the UK—can help to identify key characteristics that these countries shared and that distinguish all of them from the United States.

Scandinavia is perhaps best known for its consumer cooperatives, which flourished especially in the closing decades of the nineteenth century and which still command a significant share of the retail market today.[4] Throughout the Nordics the cooperative movement was both a site of democratic engagement and "a driver of economic modernity and efficiency" in the retail market (Hilson 2017: 121, 138). In the nineteenth century, Scandinavia was, like the United States at the time, sparsely populated, with a population largely involved in agriculture for export. Thus, as in the United States, the history of consumer cooperation was "closely intertwined with that of agricultural co-operation" (Hilson 2017: 122). Farmers banded together into producer cooperatives, often attached to rural credit and savings institutions, to boost their power in the market though joint processing and marketing, as well as through joint purchasing of agricultural equipment and supplies (Hilson 2017: 122). Meanwhile, bourgeois liberal reformers sought to promote cooperation among industrial workers as a means to forestall working-class radicalization and social unrest in a period of economic turbulence. Although organized labor movements initially viewed such ventures with deep skepticism, they soon came to embrace cooperative principles and began to promote their own independent cooperative ventures (Peel 1937: 167; Christiansen 1999: 235–37; Aléx 1999: 247–49).[5]

Crucially, Nordic cooperatives enjoyed stable legal status from early on, which allowed them to coordinate among themselves and to acquire capital to expand their operations (Bonow 1938: 175; Peel 1937: 173). As Bonow points out for the case of Sweden, the state gave cooperatives wide latitude to operate and to achieve economies of scale (1938: 175). Consumer cooperatives proliferated especially in the 1890s, coordinating first on a regional and then national level. In Denmark, a merger of two previously independent regional cooperative federations in 1896 formed a unified central organization (Hilson 2017: 129). In Sweden, similarly, independent

4. Swedish cooperatives account for about 20 percent of the retail grocery market and are significant players in other sectors of retail as well. See also Christiansen 1999 on Denmark and Aléx 1999 on Swedish cooperatives.

5. In 1907, the Scandinavian Labor Congress passed a resolution that expressly encouraged workers to join cooperative societies (Hilson 2017: 131).

cooperatives merged in 1899 to form a single overarching association—the Swedish Cooperative Union and Wholesale Association (Kooperativa förbundet or KF)—that coordinated the strategies of hundreds of local co-ops (Bonow 1938: 172–73, 175).[6] In 1918, ongoing informal cooperation across the national peak organizations of the Nordic countries was formalized through the formation of a joint purchasing society for the entire region (Nordisk Andelsförbundet, or NAF) (Hilson 2017: 129).

The economies of scale in purchasing and marketing achieved through joint action allowed Scandinavian cooperatives to dominate the retail landscape. In Sweden, for example, some estimates suggest that consumer cooperatives accounted for more than a third of sales in the food retail sector in the 1930s and 1940s (Hilson 2017: 138).[7] Already by the end of the 1920s, the national cooperative federation (KF) had also become the country's largest wholesaler, with 20 percent of the market (accounting for 2 percent of GDP), and it continued to grow to achieve turnover equivalent to 6 percent of GDP a decade later (Jonsson 2017: 646).[8] By 1930 one in ten Swedes belonged to a cooperative society (Jonsson 2017: 646).

Their size and scale allowed the cooperatives to operate more efficiently than small independent retailers, and at far lower cost. These features also gave them tremendous purchasing power that they leveraged to reduce wholesale prices (Bonow 1938: 177) and to challenge monopolistic producers by integrating backward to launch their own production in select product lines.[9] While these effects earned cooperatives the opprobrium of the wholesalers and independent retailers with whom they competed, Swedish manufacturers often appreciated the efficient distribution chain they provided (Peel 1937: 175–76).

The growth of German cooperatives in the nineteenth century shares crucial similarities to the Scandinavian experience. Here, too, the early worker cooperatives originated in a bourgeois movement to promote collective

6. Individual local co-ops retained their autonomy, but within the federation they became part of a tightly structured hierarchy of representation in which elected assemblies at the local, district, and national levels presided over the federation's operations, including an elaborate system of inspections and auditors (Peel 1937: 173–74).

7. Their dominance is perhaps even better assessed at the local level, where turnover per cooperative sales point was significantly higher than the average turnover per enterprise in private trade (Bonow 1938: 176).

8. Jonsson provides growth figures for Swedish cooperatives, which expanded from 360 shops in 1908 to 4,849 by 1930.

9. Bonow (1938: 179) gives the example of galoshes, where Sweden's cooperatives launched their own production in order to break the monopoly of a prominent manufacturer.

self-help in the face of accelerating social and economic change. Dr. Hermann Schulze-Delitzsch, a Prussian reformer and member of the liberal Progress Party, was the driving force behind the founding, in 1864, of an overarching federation to coordinate the activities of local cooperatives across all the (at that time, independent) German states (Börsche and Korf 2003; Fairbairn 1999).[10] While Schulze-Delitzsch organized mostly in urban areas, a rival initiative launched by the social conservative F. W. Raiffeisen focused on rural communities (Fairbairn 1999: 273–75). As in Sweden, socialist workers' associations were initially skeptical of all such efforts (Belschner 2013; Martens 2015: 7). The German Social Democratic Party initially opposed consumer cooperatives as counterproductive to the movement's goals. But the party would eventually warm to cooperatives over time as they came to be seen as contributing to the well-being of workers and useful as a tool for training the working class in managing enterprises (Fairbairn 1999: 283–84; Bösche and Korf 2003).[11]

As a member of the Prussian parliament, Schulze-Delitzsch had also spearheaded the creation of a legal framework to recognize and stabilize cooperative ventures (Guinnane 2012: 227). The first such law, the Prussian *Genossenschaftsgesetz* in 1867, which was subsequently adopted as imperial German law in 1871 after the country's unification, granted cooperatives a legal status on par with that of a joint stock corporation (Martens 2015: 6).[12] German cooperatives proliferated, especially in the 1890s, growing from 263 in 1890 to 568 by 1900 (with more than 500,000 members) and on to 1,500 consumer co-ops with 2.25 members by the eve of World War I (Feil 2013). By 1914 cooperatives were "ubiquitous" in Germany, and in many rural areas they provided "the only practical access to larger markets for capital, inputs and products" (Guinnane 2012: 212). Berghoff's figures suggest that cooperative membership in Germany soared to 3.6 million and encompassed approximately 20 percent of all German households by 1927 (Berghoff 2012: 131).

---

10. The name of this association is one of those unmanageable German formulations: *Der Allgemeine Verband der auf Selbsthilfe beruhrenden deutschen Erwerbs- und Wirtschaftsgenossenschaften* (loosely: General Association of Work and Economic Cooperatives That Are Based on the Principle of Self-Help).

11. See also Furlough and Strikwerda (1999: 16–17) on cooperation between consumer cooperatives and labor unions and the socialist party in Germany after 1910.

12. Their capacity to recruit members and to raise capital to fund their activities (including production) was further enhanced by an imperial law passed in 1889 that allowed for the creation of cooperatives with limited liability.

As in other European countries, consumer cooperatives in Germany often also served as savings institutions where members could deposit small amounts of money that could then be invested in the development of the cooperative or to create production facilities (Schweikert n.d.). Similar to Sweden, cooperatives coordinated among themselves to scale up through joint purchasing and distribution of consumer goods for members. In 1894 representatives from ninety-four consumer cooperatives organized to establish an overarching purchasing agent, the Grosseinkaufsgesellschaft deutscher Consumvereine mbH (GEG), which grew mightily in the following years. By 1914 there were over thirty-four thousand registered co-ops with 6.4 million members, and cooperatives had become a "significant part of banking, retailing, and agrobusiness" (Guinnane 2012: 211). The GEG had begun establishing its own production facilities in 1910, and by 1933, it owned fifty-four production plants outright in key industries—from food to construction to clothing (Bösche and Korf 2003).

Worker-based consumer cooperatives did not survive the Nazis, having been taken over by the National Socialist Labor Front in 1941 (Schweitzer 1946: 105; Furlough and Strikwerda 1999: 22). Although some were refounded after the war, they never fully recovered, and they now play a minuscule role compared to their Swedish counterparts. What survived better than worker cooperatives were retailer cooperatives composed of independent merchants who had banded together to confront larger competitors through joint purchasing and advertising (Banken et al. 2021: 200–201). Two of Germany's largest grocery chains today—Rewe and Edeka—are examples of this. Both were established a century ago, when local grocer cooperatives composed of small retailers combined to form an overarching national organization (Wortmann 2020).[13] Unlike the worker cooperatives, these small-merchant cooperatives threw their lot in with the National Socialists and operated unmolested throughout the Nazi period (Bludau 1968; Wein 1968: 160n and 179; Kretschmer 2006: 164). They then quickly reemerged after the war to become major players in the food sector, and to this day, they command the top two shares of the German

---

13. Edeka grew out of a purchasing cooperative among small retailers dating back to the late nineteenth century, with thirteen local cooperatives joining forces in 1907 to establish a central purchasing cooperative. In the meantime, the number of independent retailers who are part of the Edeka cooperative association has grown to about 3,500 (*Frankfurter Allgemeine Zeitung*, April 26, 2023, p. 19, "Bald keine Pampers mehr bei Edeka"). Rewe, established in 1927, was similarly composed of local grocers' cooperatives that grew together into an overarching national cooperative (Wortmann 2020: 7).

food retail market (as of 2021, Edeka's share was 27.2 percent, Rewe's was 20.6 percent).[14]

Cooperatives did not flourish just in these so-called coordinated market economies; they also grew in many liberal market economies, including New Zealand, Australia, Canada, and especially the United Kingdom (Spicer 2022). As Chandler points out, the earliest and most successful cooperative retailing and distribution networks took root in Britain, the country whose institutions and legal traditions arguably resemble most closely those in the United States. In fact, Britain is widely seen as the birthplace of the modern cooperative movement (Hilson 2017: chap. 3). In the late nineteenth century, the British cooperative movement was a major player in the national retail market and also represented the largest distribution network in the world (Purvis 1992: 107; Chandler 1962: 257).

Britain's earliest cooperatives were founded in the 1830s by Chartists and utopian Owenite socialists in response to the economic upheavals in the context of industrialization. Here, too, many of the early supporters were middle-class reformers who saw cooperatives as important both for the alleviation of poverty and as a vehicle for moral uplift among workers. And while the earliest such initiatives failed, the idea survived and subsequent efforts proved more durable. The most famous and resilient of these emerged from the Rochdale Society of Equitable Pioneers (founded in 1844), which resolutely embraced "practical reformism" and political neutrality (Hilson 2017: 62). British historian G.D.H. Cole's figures suggest that British cooperatives enrolled 350,000 members in 1873, and this number rose to over a million by 1891 and to over 3 million by 1914 (Hilson 2017: 66). From there, membership continued to grow, to 9.3 million in 1945 (Secchi 2017: 530).

James Jefferys's study documents the growth of British cooperatives in the decades surrounding the turn of the century (Jefferys 1954). His estimates and figures suggest that the cooperatives' share of total retail sales rose from around 2–3 percent in the 1870s to between 6 and 7 percent in 1900 and to between 7.5 and 9 percent by 1920—an impressive share, given the extreme fragmentation of the retail market into literally hundreds of thousands of small shops (Jefferys 1954: 18–19; Purvis 1992: 107).[15] These figures

---

14. See Statista, "Market Share of the Leading Companies in Food Retail in Germany from 2009 to 2022," https://www.statista.com/statistics/505129/leading-companies-in-food-retail-germany/.

15. The figures for 1900 and 1920 cover the share of cooperative sales of the "main commodity groups," which include food and household goods, confections, reading and writing goods, and clothing and footwear (Jefferys 1954: 19, table 1). Jefferys also provides more fine-grained

also understate the dominance that cooperatives enjoyed in specific (more remote or heavily working-class) localities, where they often commanded close to 75 percent of the market in the 1890s and 1900s (Purvis 1992: 118).

As elsewhere, the survival of the cooperatives would not have been possible without the support of the government. Cole emphasizes the importance of legal recognition by the national government and the stable legal foundation for cooperative development that this provided (Cole 1944). Christian socialist sympathizers played a critical role in securing legislation to clarify the status of the cooperatives through their support for the Industrial and Provident Societies Act of 1852, which recognized them as commercial societies (Purvis 1992: 112–13). More important still was the subsequent amendment to this law, passed a decade later. The 1862 act not only sanctioned cooperatives but also expressly allowed them to hold shares in other societies—thus making possible the formation of a cooperative federation (Hilson 2017: 65).

The 1862 law inspired three hundred individual cooperatives to establish, in the very next year, an overarching Cooperative Wholesale Industrial and Provident Society (later known simply as the Cooperative Wholesale Society, or CWS). The CWS was able to pool purchasing and distribution on a broad basis, and it grew rapidly to become the world's largest retail operation. The same size and scale also allowed it to integrate backward to invest in its own production facilities across a range of sectors (Chandler 1990: 257–60; Purvis 1992: 129; Webster et al. 2017: 563). Further legislation in 1876 allowed the CWS to extend its operations beyond wholesaling and manufacturing operations to include services such as banking and insurance (Purvis 1992: 107; Hilson 2017: 66; Secchi 2017).

Although it only began trading in 1864, by 1890 the CWS had already grown into "a commercial giant" (Webster et al. 2017: 563). As the largest distribution organization in the world at that time, the CWS exploited economies of scale to deliver low prices to their primarily working-class constituents. Through its own banking department, it extended loans to local cooperative societies to purchase land and construct new retail outlets (Webster et al. 2017: 364). Webster notes that by the turn of the twentieth century, the CWS was also "a sophisticated corporate body with . . . a well-developed

---

breakdowns of the cooperative share of each of these commodity groups for the period 1900–1950, with comparisons to other types of retailers, including what over time became their main competitors, "multiple" (chain) retailers (1954: 77–79, tables 20–23). In general, the cooperatives held their own against the multiple shop retailers in food and household goods across the entire period, but they lost ground in confections, reading and writing goods, and clothing and footwear.

managerial structure" and with an impressive international supply network (2012: 898). It owned factories all across Britain and became a major producer of a wide range of its own branded goods—food products, household goods, shoes, and clothing—and later one of Britain's largest producers of pharmaceuticals and consumer durables such as radios and vacuum cleaners (Webster et al. 2017: 563–64). The CWS also established production facilities abroad in select products (such as tea) and controlled an impressive supply network throughout the former colonies and in Europe, transporting goods through its own shipping lines (Webster et al. 2017: 560).

Cooperatives continued to dominate the British retail sector in terms of food and household goods through the interwar period, until 1930 when multiple shop retailers (chain stores) began to catch up by offering a more attractive range of products and engaging in vigorous advertising (each type of business commanded between 12.5 and 14 percent of the market) (Jefferys 1954: 77, table 20).[16] Nonetheless, the cooperatives continued to innovate, pioneering the introduction of self-service in Britain in 1942 (Wilson et al. 2013: 279). They saw their share of retail trade peak in 1951 at 12 percent (17.1 percent of food retail) (Wilson et al. 2013: 277) before falling into decline relative to private competitors such as Sainsbury's and Tesco, which were engaged in aggressive consolidation and expansion (Wilson et al. 2013: 277 and 279–80).[17] Although British cooperatives never regained their previous dominant position, they remain a player on the retail market (with between 5 and 10 percent of market share) after surviving a hostile takeover bid that prompted deep structural changes in the 1990s to improve operations and reorient toward an emphasis on ethical trading (Wilson et al. 2013: 290–91).

Cooperatives in the United States

The urge to engage in collective self-help to address the economic dislocations of the late nineteenth century was no less present in the United States; indeed, immigrants from Europe often brought the cooperative model with them (Patmore 2017: 512; Spicer 2022: 155). However, unlike their counterparts across the Atlantic, American consumer cooperatives failed to thrive,

---

16. British cooperatives eschewed advertising in the interwar period on the belief that it encouraged its working-class constituents "to spend beyond their means" (Wilson et al. 2013: 278).

17. Successful defense of local autonomy by individual member societies impeded structural change and rationalization of operations, even as postwar affluence undermined the traditional cooperative strategy of catering to working-class consumers with solid if uninspired goods.

foundering on an uncongenial legal regime, restrictive state banking laws, and racial animus. Their failure in the late nineteenth century cleared the field and allowed large private retailers to emerge as the country's first mass retailers.

Some of the earliest American cooperatives emerged in working-class areas of New England, but the more important and widespread of such ventures were founded by small farmers in the Midwest and West (Patmore 2017: 512).[18] Agrarians in the United States faced extreme hardship in the closing years of the nineteenth century. They paid dearly for consumer and industrial goods, which were protected by high tariffs, while the prices for their own goods were determined by commodity brokers and international competition (Prasad 2012). Agrarians were also at the mercy of the railroads and express companies that monopolized distribution routes, the Eastern banking interests that controlled access to credit, and the wholesalers and the small merchants who controlled local retail markets.

As in Europe, the response to shared economic hardship was organization and efforts at collective self-help. In this spirit, small farmers in Minnesota founded the Patrons of Husbandry (better known as the Grange) in 1867 as a vehicle to advance the political and economic interests of American farmers. By the early 1870s regional Granges had been established in several states and the movement had become a significant force channeling the grievances of the country's rural population (Sanders 1999). Prominent among the activities the Grange chapters undertook was the founding of cooperatives to reduce farmers' dependence on wholesalers, distributors, and middlemen through joint purchasing and marketing, as well as through the establishment of cooperative stores to provide local populations with essential goods. As Patmore summarizes, Grange-sponsored Rochdale stores sought to "remove middlemen and bring consumers, farmers, and manufacturers into 'direct and friendly relations'" (Patmore 2017: 509). In the American context, the "boundaries between agricultural or producer co-operatives and consumer co-operatives became blurred" as agricultural cooperatives "extended their activities into general retailing" (Neunsinger and Patmore 2017: 738).

Although the Grange itself fell into steep decline in the 1870s, it "left its imprint on subsequent labor and farmers' organizations," including, crucially, the Farmers' Alliances that succeeded it (Sanders 1999: 108). The structure of the Farmers' Alliance reflected the deep sectional, partisan, and racial divides that characterized American politics in the postbellum

---

18. See Leikin (1999) on the history of working-class cooperatives in the United States.

period. The alliance was split into three separate regional associations—an integrated northern organization and two separate (white and Black) organizations in the South. Despite their many differences, the three associations were united in their opposition to the domination of concentrated Eastern financial and industrial interests and in a vague shared vision of an economic order in which people could "[win] for themselves control over their own individual lives" (Goodwyn 1976: xv). It was a vision they pursued through their efforts to organize cooperatives and one that formed the core of the farmer-labor alliance that fueled the Populist movement of the late nineteenth century. As Goodwyn puts it: "The cooperative movement recruited American farmers, and their subsequent experience within the cooperatives radically altered their political consciousness. . . . [It] provided the foot solders of Populism" (Goodwyn 1976: xviii).

In his account of the American cooperative movement, Goodwyn emphasizes especially the role of Charles Macune, leader of the Texas Farmers' Alliance, who conceived of a "multi-sectional cooperative movement as a vast structure of radical economic reform" (1976: xix). Tapping into the frustrations and anger of poor farmers, Macune and his followers spread the gospel of cooperation, speaking a language that farmers understood (1976: 73). Under Macune's leadership, "earnest farmer-lecturers [set off] on continent-spanning journeys . . . in the most massive organizing drive by any citizen institution of nineteenth-century America" (Goodwyn 1976: 88). Armed with materials and model charters, alliance lecturers traveled to instruct farmers on how to establish cooperative institutions for buying and selling, and they advised them of the "advantages of electing one of their own number as a business agent" to run the operation (91). The campaign unfolded over five years and "carried lecturers into forty-three states and territories and touched two million American farm families; it brought a program and a sense of purpose to Southern farmers who had neither, and provided an organizational medium for Westerners who had radical goals but lacked a mass constituency" (88).

William Lamb, Macune's more radical frenemy in the Texas Farmers' Alliance, was especially important in reaching out across class lines to forge an alliance with the Knights of Labor in establishing "the Farmers' Alliance and Industrial Union."[19] Lamb and his allies were "forever enjoining the

---

19. Lamb saw the value of a coalition between the Alliance and the Knights at a time when the latter was beginning to organize railway workers in a battle to take on the powerful Jay Gould. Thus, in 1886 Lamb famously signed on to lend the Alliance's support to the effort, arguing that

nation to 'remember the industrial millions'" who shared with the agrarians both an intense animosity toward the industrial and financial monopolies of the Northeast and a vision of an alternative economic model anchored in cooperative principles (Goodwyn 1976: xxii; Sanders 1999: 35). The idea resonated with the Knights of Labor, whose own vision and strategy from the start had included the organization of worker and producer cooperatives as part of the organization's 1869 constitution (Gourevitch 2015: 7).

While the Grange had organized white farmers in the West and Midwest, the Knights of Labor attempted to forge a broader alliance across lines of class, race, and gender (Gourevitch 2015; Spicer 2022: chap. 6). The latter's organizing campaign in the South directly challenged the brutal crop lien system that held poor (particularly poor Black) farmers there in a state of permanent debt and semiservitude (Goodwyn 1976: 26–27; Nembhard 2017).[20] In the postbellum South, the power exercised by local merchants went far beyond their monopoly over the local retail trade. Southern merchants (often themselves the large landowners) not only controlled access to virtually all necessary goods and supplies, they also dominated the distribution channels through which agricultural goods were marketed.

These merchants extended credit to desperate farmers, but on outlandish terms that often exceeded 100 percent annually, while taking a lien on the farmer's future crop for security. At harvest time, their control over distribution also allowed them to dictate the price that farmers would ultimately receive for their crops (Goodwyn 1976: 26). The income from the crop invariably fell short of the debts accumulated over the course of the year, which were then carried over and mortgaged against the following year's crop—leaving farmers in a perpetual state of indebtedness. "The man with the ledger became the farmer's sole significant contact with the outside world. Across the South he was known as 'the furnishing man' or 'the advancing man.' To Black farmers he became, simply, 'the Man'" (Goodwyn 1976: 28). As Goodwyn puts it, "Once a farmer had signed his first crop lien he was literally in bondage to his merchant as long as he failed to pay out" (1976: 28). The Knights of Labor's cooperative campaign in the South was designed to free poor Black farmers from the grip of the crop lien system by establishing cooperative distribution channels to allow them to market their own goods, and by setting up cooperative stores to provide them with

---

"we think it is a good time to help the Knights of Labor in order to secure their help in the near future" (Goodwyn 1976: 59).

20. See especially Spicer (2022: chap. 6) and Hild (1997: 298–99) for an account of some of the Knights of Labor's organizing efforts in the South.

an alternative to the company store (Knupfer 2013: 16–17; Nembhard 2017, Du Bois 1907; Spicer 2022: chap. 6).[21]

Legal and Political Obstacles to American Cooperatives

While the farmer-labor alliance that powered the Populist movement achieved a measure of political influence (Sanders 1999; Prasad 2012), the cooperative ventures they launched fared far less well, running headlong into unrelenting opposition from bankers, a hostile judiciary, and—in the South—intense racial hatred and violence (Goodwyn 1976: 110; Gourevitch 2015). Indeed, in the late nineteenth century it was the futility of their own efforts at collective self-help in the market that led the leaders of the Farmers' Alliance to turn to the political strategies that fueled the rise of the Populist Party (Goodwyn 1976; Postel 2007).

The European experience reviewed earlier points to the central importance of legal recognition and access to credit in allowing cooperatives there to expand and thrive through federation. National enabling legislation in Europe had clarified the legal status of cooperatives and allowed local branches to coordinate among themselves to enhance their purchasing power. Through their connections with savings unions of various sorts, European cooperative associations were able to expand operations into wholesaling and even production of essential goods.

In the United States, by contrast, no such national legislation existed to sanction and stabilize the kinds of joint marketing and distribution that stood at the center of the cooperative project (Spicer 2022: 156).[22] Crucially, the capacity of cooperatives to secure credit was thwarted in this period by banking interests and by restrictive federal and state regulations that prevented the entry of potential competitors such as credit unions (Wolters 2022: chap. 1).[23] The power to charter and regulate banks lay with the state governments, where influential local bankers and landed elites

21. Du Bois's study of Black cooperatives counted 103 still in operation in 1907, most operating on a local level selling groceries, meats, and other necessities (1907: 149ff).

22. In the 1860s and 1870s some *individual states* did pass legislation specifically allowing for cooperative marketing and distribution; for example, an 1865 Michigan law allowed the establishment of cooperative stores and was amended in 1875 to include agriculturalists as well. Pennsylvania followed suit in 1868, Minnesota in 1870, and Wisconsin and Kansas later, in 1887 (Goldberg 1928: 273).

23. Not until 1909 did the first state (Massachusetts) pass legislation allowing the formation of credit unions. And while other states followed, credit unions never became a major force (peaking in 1930 at 0.5 percent of the credit market).

successfully defended their turf throughout the nineteenth century (Wolters 2022: 52–61).[24] The inability of American cooperatives to secure funding for operations and investment from existing (state) chartered banks hobbled all efforts to expand (e.g., into wholesaling) that had proved so crucial to the growth of their counterparts in Europe.

Agricultural cooperatives whose activities included joint marketing also encountered resistance in the courts, particularly as the changing legal climate in the 1880s exposed them to potential prosecution under common-law prohibitions against contracts or conspiracies "in restraint of trade."[25] State courts in this period took varied positions on this question, based on their own interpretations of the common law, and, as Hanna points out, "the answer of one state may not be the answer of its neighbor" (Hanna 1930: 163–65; J.H.E. Jr. 1941: 675; Vaheesan and Schneider 2019: 28).[26] While some courts condemned the activities of farmers' marketing cooperatives as price-fixing or stifling competition (USDA 2002: 67–69), others gave forbearance, seeing these efforts as legitimate attempts on the part of farmers to "protect themselves against unfair prices and a vicious market" (J.H.E. Jr. 1941: 675; Hanna 1930: 164). However, even in states where cooperative activities were not expressly prohibited, their legal status was deeply ambiguous, which itself operated to dampen cooperative formation and growth.[27] "Apprehensive that the mere formation of a cooperative would be considered a combination and conspiracy in restraint of trade, as some

24. Though widely dispersed, bankers coordinated their lobbying activities through the American Bankers Association (founded in 1875) and put up furious resistance to national legislation as well—defeating efforts in the 1890s by Postmaster General John Wanamaker to introduce a postal savings system along the lines of many European countries (chap. 4; Wolters 2022).

25. On the shifting political and legal understandings of which types of contracts between parties were "natural" and therefore legally enforceable and which were "unnatural" and thus condemnable by the law, see especially Roy 1997: 190–91.

26. The common law—in both Britain and the United States—had generally evolved in such a way as to permit "partial restraints" (essentially, restraints limited in space and time and considered "reasonable"), while condemning "general restraints on trade" (see Hanna 1930: 160; Cassidy 1896: 13–17, 19–20). But as this language itself makes clear, the line between the two was deeply ambiguous, so that in the absence of clear statutory guidance as in Britain, it was entirely up to the courts to decide.

27. As Isaacs noted in 1928, "Cooperative marketing [had] found its way into the legal digest in the garbled form of an exception to an exception. The rule is freedom of contract; the exception pertains to restraint of trade; and the exception to the exception is the freedom of farmers to combine in cooperative societies"—which, as he went on to note, is not the same as a rule, so that, early on, this gave rise to considerable constitutional ambiguities (1928: 394).

state courts had already held, cooperative associations pressed for legislative exemptions" (Maurer 1952: 434–35).[28]

Moreover, and as noted in chapter 1, the federal judiciary in this period was generally hostile toward such forms of horizontal coordination and highly skeptical of exceptions for farmers. Thus states that had legislation exempting agrarian organizations and cooperative marketing arrangements from antitrust enforcement often saw their laws struck down by the Supreme Court either as restraints on trade or as violations of the equal protection clause of the Fourteenth Amendment (Hanna 1930: 175–81; Hanna 1948: 488; USDA 2002: 67–69). In 1897, for example, a federal court had declared unconstitutional a Texas law that exempted agricultural producers from some of the provisions in its antitrust laws on these grounds. The text of the decision acknowledged the contributions of farmers to society and economy, before proceeding to ask: "Yet what is there about all that to entitle him to the privilege of combining in restraint of trade as to those articles he produces, while his neighbors, the store-keeper and the mechanic, are precluded therefrom" (Hanna 1930: 176n76).[29]

Even where state laws were not challenged, the overall fragmentation of the legal landscape governing cooperatives—with some but not all states enacting legislation protecting their activities—severely limited the ability of cooperatives of all sorts to scale up.[30] The paradoxical impact of the American competition regime on American cooperatives deserves to be underscored: in the late nineteenth century, farmers had risen up to oppose large corporate monopolies, "enthusiastically aiding in the passage of state antitrust laws and the Sherman Act" only to find "that their first feeble attempts at cooperative action were held to be illegal, while the enlargement of business units continued with only minor setbacks" (Hanna 1948: 488).

A report from the US Department of Agriculture (USDA) recounting the history of the cooperative experience in this period puts it this way: "Agricultural producers were between the proverbial rock and the hard place in their relationship to State antitrust law. Without an exemption, efforts to do business on a cooperative basis were subject to challenge as an illegal conspiracy to restrain trade. And State efforts to provide special antitrust

28. A report by the US Department of Agriculture notes that "even unsuccessful prosecutions [of cooperatives] disturbed producers" (2002: 86).

29. Five years later, the Supreme Court invoked the same justification when it held that the Illinois Trust Statute of 1893 (exempting agricultural cooperatives) violated the Constitution by extending to farmers privileges denied to other actors (Tobriner 1928; Goldberg 1928: 275–76).

30. On the variation across states, see the cases cited in Maurer (1952: 431n8).

protection for farmers to market their products on a cooperative basis were stymied by court cases striking down such provisions as invalid under the 14th Amendment to the US Constitution" (USDA 2002: 70).

If farmers' marketing cooperatives in the Midwest were having trouble, the obstacles confronting the Knights of Labor in its efforts to promote joint worker/farmer cooperatives in the South were even more daunting. The Knights' organizing efforts had fallen on particularly fertile ground in the South, where farmers were eager to escape the crop lien system. But they also encountered violent resistance there. Black cooperatives faced ongoing vigilante harassment and violence. Hild suggests that southern whites were likely more concerned about the Knights' demands for higher wages and the right to form cooperatives than their demand for labor reform, because the former posed a more direct threat to the cheap labor supply on which they depended (1997: 303). The fate of the cooperative campaign in the South was sealed with the demise of the Knights of Labor itself. The Haymarket massacre of 1886, and the less well-known Thibodaux massacre of Black cane workers in Louisiana the following year, dealt a fatal blow to the organization, which saw its membership plummet by 90 percent by 1900 (Spicer 2022: 169).

With the decline of the Knights of Labor in the late 1880s, the idea of a broader cooperative movement uniting producer and consumer cooperatives would also perish (Patmore 2017: 510–11). And after the collapse of the populist People's Party a few years later, the Farmers' Alliances narrowed their sights, abandoning worker interests to focus exclusively on securing federal legislation exempting their own producer cooperatives (Sanders 1999: chap. 5). These efforts were partly vindicated in the Clayton Act of 1914, which exempted farm cooperatives from antitrust laws (Vaheesan and Schneider 2019: 29). However, even after the Clayton Act, the legal status of agricultural cooperatives remained somewhat vague and contested (USDA 2002; Guth 1982).[31] As Guth notes, the ambiguities in the Clayton Act had "left farmer marketing groups in an antitrust limbo" (1982: 68; see USDA 2002: 60–67 on the legal uncertainty even after 1914).

In 1922 the Capper-Volstead Act—described by Guth (1982: 68) as "the culmination of a decade's controversy over antitrust restraints on cooperative activity"—finally relieved farmers' joint marketing arrangements

---

31. Section 6 of the Clayton Act gave its blessing to coordinated action by farmers and workers so long as their combinations were "lawfully carrying out" objectives that were "legitimate," though courts still prosecuted some of them for "unlawful" (i.e., coercive) behavior (USDA 2002: 75; 83–84).

from the restraints of antitrust (Maurer 1952: 438). Cooperative marketing arrangements among independent farmers did emerge and thrive as regional rural producer cooperatives such as Land O'Lakes (founded in 1921) took advantage of the changing legal landscape (Schneiberg 2011: 1413). Between 1920 and 1928 most states adopted legislation that specifically allowed farmers to form marketing cooperatives, and such laws were upheld by the Supreme Court in 1927 (Spicer 2022: 146).[32]

But even if producer cooperatives were granted relief, any retailing and distribution functions had long since atrophied with the demise of the earlier worker-farmer alliances. Consumer cooperatives that could challenge large private distributors never revived. The joint marketing functions that American farmers had ultimately successfully defended did not directly challenge private retailers. On the contrary, they mostly operated as important suppliers to private companies such as A&P, which by the early twentieth century had already achieved towering dominance in grocery retail.[33]

Voluntary small-retailer cooperatives operating along the lines that had developed earlier in Germany also emerged in the United States and thrived for a time (Moreton 2006: 77–78). One of the earliest such chains was launched in 1922 under the name "Red and White Stores," but the largest and most successful such venture was the Independent Grocers Alliance (IGA), founded in 1926 (Spellman 2016: 156–58).[34] Independent grocers who joined the IGA cooperative paid the joint (regionally specific) wholesaler a fee for purchasing and distribution services and in return benefited not just from the discounts achieved through joint purchasing but also IGA advertising materials and sales campaigns. Other such voluntary chains existed in the United States in the 1930s (Spellman 2016: 159).[35] But Red and White and many of the other regionally based voluntary chains succumbed

32. Congress established a foundation for such activities with the Cooperative Marketing Act of 1926, and it also offered additional assistance in 1929 with the passage of the Agricultural Marketing Act, which established a loan fund to assist struggling farmers. The funding was directed toward farmer cooperatives, but it was not available to Black farmers who lacked their own cooperative agricultural organization (Spicer 2022: 147).

33. By 1930, A&P had opened just under sixteen thousand stores across the country and commanded nearly 25 percent of market share in its operating areas (10 percent nationally), https://en.wikipedia.org/wiki/A%26P.

34. As in so many other aspects of American political development, some of these voluntary associations reflected deep racial animus. Thus, for example, white-run retail cooperatives typically excluded Black and also often Jewish grocers, prompting the formation of separate associations (Spellman 2016: 159–61).

35. For examples, see Hearings Before the Committee on the Judiciary, House of Representatives, 74th Congress, 1st Session, July 10, 11, 17, 18, 19, 1935: 114–18 especially.

decades ago; IGA still survives in some small towns. And, in any event, all such operations were completely overshadowed by private retailers, first by A&P and later by grocery giants Kroger and Walmart.

Consumer cooperatives fared worse. The idea enjoyed a brief renaissance of interest in the 1930s in the wake of the Great Depression, and in 1936 President Franklin D. Roosevelt went so far as to appoint a "Commission for the Study of European Cooperatives" (an initiative that private retailers and wholesalers immediately denounced as un-American). But interest, including Roosevelt's own, waned quickly. With the 1938 election looming, the president released the commission's report only "after much prodding from commission members" (Deutsch 2010: 117). And it was not until 1940 that American consumer cooperatives secured the same legal rights as their European counterparts. By this time, however, powerful private corporations had long since captured the retailing space that cooperatives in Europe occupied—serving an emerging mass market by building an infrastructure for the mass distribution of consumer goods. To use a rural metaphor, by the time the status of American cooperatives was clarified, the cows had long since left the barn.

3

Mail Order Retail as
the "Farmer's Friend"

In the United States, then, it was not consumer cooperatives but rather large
private retailers that knit together the country's widely dispersed population into a single mass consumer market. In food retailing, A&P opened
its first shop in 1865 and grew to dominate the grocery sector, while mail
order giants Montgomery Ward and Sears & Roebuck launched operations
to bring an ever-expanding range of goods to consumers outside the urban
core. Whereas European cooperatives typically grew from the bottom up,
forming networks among local and regional branches, large American retailers grew from the top down. This means that the triumph of large mail order
retailers involved overcoming significant logistical challenges—above all,
finding ways not just to reach far-flung customers but to manage financial
transactions with a clientele that was almost entirely unbanked. Large private retailers also had to win over a population that was famously distrustful
of distant business interests with whom they had often found themselves in
a highly asymmetric relationship of dependence.

America's mass mail-order retailers overcame these hurdles by deploying
public infrastructure for private ends, and in the process they cultivated the
country's rural population as a loyal base of consumers that they could later
mobilize in battles with their opponents. While the geographic dispersion of
the rural population made the expansion of a mass consumer market more
difficult, the *political* geography of the United States endowed the farmers and rangers on the country's vast frontier with outsized power within

the country's distinctive federal system (Sanders 1999). Thus, even as large retailers cultivated the agrarian population as a loyal customer base, they also secured a powerful political ally.

Winning Rural Consumers Over

Aaron Montgomery Ward played a particularly important role in winning the allegiance of the country's large rural population. The company he founded in 1872 was the first mail-order operation to make serious inroads with the rural consumer (Barron 1997: 164). Having grown up in the Midwest and started out as a traveling salesman and dry goods retailer, Ward was intimately familiar with the customers he hoped to court. His greatest contribution was to win the trust of rural consumers who—after years of being fleeced by traveling salesmen and fraudulent advertisers—were understandably reticent to send their hard-earned money to an unfamiliar and distant company. As their own cooperatives were foundering, Montgomery Ward stepped in as a ready alternative, and a strong partnership developed (Barron 1997: 168–69).

Ward built his business by forging a close bond with farmers and their organizations, particularly the Patrons of Husbandry (aka the Grange). Montgomery Ward & Co. was founded in 1872, just five years after the Grange got its start, and the company began modestly—a single-sheet listing of items of practical value to the rural population. Advertising his business as "the Original Grange Supply House," Ward presented himself as an ally in farmers' political and economic fights with the country's great monopolies, traveling to Grange meetings to introduce himself and to make his case in person.[1] His business model relied on purchasing goods directly from manufacturers that could then be sold exclusively by mail to consumers—thus cutting out the wholesalers and agents who otherwise mediated the sale. Ward not only embraced the farmers' goals; he claimed them as his own: "to do away with the middlemen as far as possible" (quoted in Barron 1997: 167; Latham 1972: 15). He encouraged Grange business agents to bundle orders to secure more favorable rates on shipping, and he offered special payment conditions to local Grange chapters that submitted orders collectively.[2]

---

1. Ward commissioned the production of special "Granger hats," which were featured in one of the company's early catalogs and sold for $1.25 each (Latham 1972: 12).

2. Rates on freight orders—cheaper than express rates—all carried a hundred-pound minimum charge, no matter the actual weight (Latham 1972: 13). Freight orders normally had to be paid in advance (unlike express orders that could be sent on a cash-on-delivery basis), but

Ward relished the role of defending his customers against rapacious monopolies. In one episode in 1893, for example, his company publicly took on the Sugar Trust, running an ad in *The Farmers Voice* under the headline "The 1893 Sugar Famine—Granulated Sugar Famine Everywhere. We are fortunate in having a small supply of granulated sugar, and are glad to be able to accommodate our patrons. During the month of September, we will furnish our patrons with 20 pounds of granulated sugar for one dollar . . . will it help *you* any: We hope our supply will last. At any rate, we will do the best we can for you" (Latham 1972: 27). Such strategies infuriated sugar producers, who sought to control prices. Nevertheless, Ward persisted, and two years later, after the Supreme Court cleared the Sugar Trust of federal antitrust charges, the company ran the following ad in the same magazine: "No trusts! The various trusts in the country say: 'Montgomery Ward & Co. cannot have our goods for the reason that they will not demand the prices we make.' The goods we purchase we pay spot cash for. The goods belong to us; we claim the right to dispose of them as we wish" (and went on to offer different grades of sugar to its customers at discounted prices) (Latham 1972: 27).

As Ward himself readily acknowledged, the farmers' clubs played a significant role in the company's rapid growth (Latham 1972: 12). The country's agrarian population had responded to Ward's outreach enthusiastically. Indeed, from the perspective of rural consumers, mail order was a godsend. It offered them a wider selection of goods at much lower prices. It introduced competition into local retail markets, where local merchants operated as small monopolies. And, perhaps mostly revolutionary of all, Ward directly addressed the deep distrust that had been caused by the rampant fraud that had been visited upon the rural population by the unscrupulous peddlers and advertisers who had come before. He did so in part by adopting an iron-clad return policy.[3] The company's 1875 catalog thus featured the following assurance: "We guarantee all our goods. If any of them are not satisfactory after due inspection, we will take them back, pay all expenses, and refund the money paid for them" (Latham 1972: 12).

But if Montgomery Ward pioneered the mail order space, it was Richard Warren Sears who mastered the landscape. Sears's path into the mail order

---

Montgomery Ward allowed orders that carried the Grange seal to be paid after the goods had shipped (Latham 1972: 11).

3. While a few urban department stores offered money-back guarantees on goods they sold, Montgomery Ward was the first national mail-order house to adopt this policy (Latham 1972: 12–13).

business began in 1886, when he worked as a freight agent in Minnesota.[4] It was common at the time for wholesalers that wished to expand their markets to ship products to nonexistent recipients in hopes that local station agents would accept (and pay for) the goods at a discount and then sell them on the company's behalf. Sears received such a shipment (of watches) from a Chicago company and promptly sold them down the line to other freight agents, offering to split the profits for all that they sold. The plan succeeded, and it was not long before the ambitious young Sears quit the job to build a thriving watch business of his own, bringing in Alvah Roebuck (a watchmaker by profession) to service the products.

As Sears & Roebuck grew, the company followed Montgomery Ward in catering to the needs of the country's rural population with an ever-wider range of product offerings. The catalogs of both firms focused on items such as cream separators and saddles that addressed the specific needs of their rural base. While Ward's strategy relied heavily on personal outreach, Sears engaged in what we now think of as public relations—sponsoring trade fairs, building livestock arenas, producing farm safety films, providing college scholarships for promising rural youths, and establishing other educational initiatives (Emmet and Jeuck 1950: 622–47). Sears founded the radio station WLS in Chicago to broadcast vital agricultural information (weather, farm prices) to its customers on the prairie (WLS for "World's Largest Store") (Emmet and Jeuck 1950: 624).[5] In a context that lacked basic communications infrastructure, Sears sold a do-it-yourself local phone system to facilitate communication among neighbors in sparsely populated regions that were of no interest to the country's phone companies (Koenen 2002: 57).

Beyond the PR, however, Sears abandoned Ward's down-to-earth approach and increasingly deployed a more flamboyant style, one that earned him the moniker "the Barnum of merchandising" (Barron 1997: 175). Whereas Ward had built his reputation on quality and reliability, Sears was all about advertising and price. He engaged in aggressive advertising aimed at driving competitors out with volume sales at rock-bottom prices. Sales campaigns for specific products often produced a flood of orders, causing huge backlogs and delays. But Sears, who "believed devoutly in the attack," refused to take his foot off the pedal (Emmet and Jeuck 1950: 65). By the early twentieth century there were few items you could not buy from Sears— musical instruments, wigs, pumps, guns, corsets, ostrich feathers, and all

---

4. This paragraph draws on Emmet and Jeuck 1950: 25–27.
5. The station, sold in 1928, still exists. (I grew up in South Dakota listening to it.)

manner of household goods from meat hooks to toothbrushes. Motorized buggies were added to the catalog in 1909, and starting in 1908 you could buy an entire prefabricated house from Sears—shipped to you in parts, with all holes pre-bored and millwork complete—along with a construction manual to guide the assembly (Cooke and Friedman 2001).[6]

In rural areas cut off from much of the cultural life of the city, the arrival of the Sears catalog was an event, and a source of entertainment for the whole family. And Sears's aggressive distribution strategy made sure that the catalog was ubiquitous. As almost every chronicler of this company has noted, in the late nineteenth century the Sears catalog was in more households than any book other than the Bible (Fuller 1964: 254). As had been the case with Montgomery Ward, citizens in America's rural areas felt they had a personal connection to Sears, as exemplified in a letter to the company in which a farmer explained that he would have written sooner but "a mule kicked me and broke my arm" (Emmet and Jeuck 1950: 171; Weil 1977: 29–30).

The company was also a fixture in the rural South, despite furious resistance from southern merchants.[7] The catalog was wildly popular in the South, so much so that Georgia's populist (and white supremacist) governor would later famously declare that "the poor dirt farmer ain't got but three friends on this earth: God Almighty, Sears Roebuck and Gene Talmadge" (Emmet and Jeuck 1950: 254). But in the early days, and for Black consumers especially, Sears was a game changer. The catalog gave them the ability to order anonymously and at fixed, listed prices after decades of suffering at the hands of "the Man" and as they continued to experience discrimination in local stores.

The Sears catalog was critical in forging a mass consumer market and in enlisting the country's rural population as loyal customers and political allies for large retailers as they expanded. More than merely of commercial importance, the catalog also served as a tool of education and socialization. For the large immigrant populations living west of the Mississippi, the catalog included order instructions in German and Swedish, assuring their customers that "we have translators to read all languages." Many immigrants learned to read English by poring over the catalog. More generally, the company made purchasing easy for rural populations characterized by high levels

6. Some of these houses are still standing today, many of them in small towns in Illinois.

7. The company's opponents sought to take advantage of racial animus by circulating race-baiting rumors that Sears (or his partner Roebuck) were Black (Emmet and Jeuck 1950: 151).

of illiteracy. "Don't be afraid you will make a mistake . . . Tell us what you want in your own way, written in any language, no matter whether good or poor writing, and the goods will be promptly sent to you" (Sears Catalogue 1908: 1). Customers were told that they could use the order form, or "any plain paper" to submit their order (Emmet and Jeuck 1950: 86).

In sum, mail order companies played a central role in the process through which America's "republic of producers" would give way to citizen-consumers (Cross 2000: 2). By tying remote populations into national consumer trends, the Sears wish book extended—and homogenized—the American consumer market. Introducing a huge number of otherwise widely dispersed consumers to an ever-wider range of mass-produced goods at lower prices convinced American farmers—who were otherwise firmly opposed to big, distant companies—that these large retailers were, as the original Montgomery Ward catalog had declared, "the farmer's friend."

Logistics: Leveraging Public Infrastructure

As brilliant as the early mail-order wizards of the nineteenth century were, Ward's and Sears's successes would not have been possible without a rather large assist from the government. Just as the railroad companies benefited tremendously from government land grants (alongside coercion and violence to displace Indigenous populations), so too did mail order retailers benefit from—and exploit—the publicly funded infrastructure the government created. The railroad network itself was a necessary precondition (Carpenter 2001a: 98–101; White 2011). Beyond that, no state agency was more important to the success of mail order and mass consumption than the United States Postal Service.

Others have detailed the precocious development of the US postal network—a network whose reach into remote areas was decades ahead of Europe's network (John 1995).[8] Just as railroads provided the infrastructure for the flow of goods, the postal system was critical in forging connections between widely dispersed communities by facilitating the flow of information—"an unprecedented volume of newspapers, letters, and other kinds of information through time and over space" (John 1995: 3). As John notes, the postal system stood at the center of a "communications

---

8. Already by 1828, the United States had established seventy-four post offices for every one hundred thousand inhabitants, compared to just seventeen per one hundred thousand in Great Britain and four per one hundred thousand in France (John 1995: 5).

revolution" with consequences "as profound . . . as the subsequent revolutions that have come to be associated with the telegraph, the telephone, and the computer" (John 1995: vii). From the start, the US government saw the postal system as crucial to maintaining a link between the central government and its far-flung citizenry.[9] For this reason, the government had long subsidized the distribution of newspapers and other materials that were seen as important to keeping the population informed on the issues of the day (John 1995). But while John emphasizes the effect of the US postal system on American *citizens*, the impact on Americans as *consumers* was no less momentous.

Although government subsidies were designed to promote the circulation of educational materials such as literary magazines and government news, merchants of all sorts immediately seized on the opportunity to tap into the lower rates customarily charged to such publications, buying ads in newspapers and magazines (especially women's magazines) (Fuller 1972: 125–26). More resourceful entrepreneurs found ways to package their marketing as journals, which resulted in "an entirely new kind of magazine whose plain purpose was to advertise the products of assorted businesses" (Fuller 1972: 134–35). By the 1850s "circulars and advertisements of all kinds were dumped into the mails" (Fuller 1972: 126). Postal legislation in the 1870s brought more order to the system—among other ways, by developing different classes of mail—but since mail order magazines were considered important to the dissemination of knowledge, they continued to enjoy a privileged rate (Emmet and Jeuck 1950: 60).

The postal service thus provided large American retailers with a crucial, subsidized connection to rural consumers. More important still, these retailers enlisted postal officials as critical intermediaries in their *commercial transactions* with customers. The key link here was the money order system the post office had introduced in 1864 to allow Union soldiers to send and receive money safely and to accommodate "urbanites who were . . . looking for a safe way to send money through the mail" (Fuller 1972: 70).[10] This service proved critical to the growth of mail order because it provided companies with a secure means to transact with their rural consumers. In order to place an order, the customer obtained a money order from the

9. As one indication of the importance attached to the postal system, Benjamin Franklin was appointed as the country's first postmaster general.

10. The money order system addressed the problem of robberies of the stagecoaches that carried the mail (Fuller 1972: 247). Previous fixes, such as registered letters, had mostly simply drawn the attention of robbers (p. 249).

local postmaster to make the sale. While not fail-safe (forgeries were still possible), money orders were a tremendous improvement because they allowed for financial transactions to be accomplished through the mail without cash.[11] The instructions included in the 1908 Sears catalog convey how centrally the US Postal Service (USPS) came to figure in relations with the company's customers: "If you live on a rural mail route, just give the letter and the money to the mail carrier and he will get the money order at the postoffice [*sic*] and mail it in the letter for you" (Sears Catalogue 1908: 1).

The importance of this intermediary function had only grown as Montgomery Ward and Sears both embraced the practice of allowing customers to inspect the goods they received and send them back if they were not satisfied (Barron 1997: 169). Sears had matched Montgomery Ward's return policy and featured its "Send No Money" policy prominently. Buyers deposited the money at the post office at the time of the order, and the payment was released to the company only when the goods were picked up and accepted by the customer (in the case of rejection, the goods were sent back and the money order destroyed). Large retailers thus effectively used the post office as a credit intermediary, relying on it to mediate financial transactions with their widely dispersed and unbanked rural clientele. As mail order grew, so too did the number of money order transactions. Fuller documents a huge increase in the use of money orders corresponding to the growth of mail order retailing in the closing decades of the nineteenth century, noting a rise in the value of money orders issued from $34 million to over $114 million between 1870 and 1890 (1972: 248).

In short, entrepreneurial retailers enlisted the postal service to play a starring role in the expansion of the consumer market in America's vast frontier. The services it provided subsidized the growth—in scale and scope—of the mail order companies through which farmers accessed a wider array of goods at lower prices than ever before. It was only a matter of time before local merchants would feel the effects of the competition and the USPS would become an epicenter of conflict between local merchants and big retail, a conflict in which rural consumers would side decisively with large retailers.

---

11. Other postal reforms in the 1870s and 1880s had introduced oversight of the mail through the large-scale employment of special agents and inspectors (see especially Carpenter 2000). Railway clerks and special agents replaced stage contractors with government employees, a move that both enhanced efficiency and rooted out fraud caused by "unscrupulous mail-order businesses and advertisers" (Carpenter 2000: 129).

Weaponizing Consumers

Although residents of cities enjoyed at-home mail delivery beginning in the 1860s, until 1896 there was no such thing as door delivery of rural mail. All the transactions that linked rural customers to mail order retailers—distributing the catalogs, securing money orders, mailing the order forms, receiving the goods—occurred in local post offices.[12] The local post office, however, was not the institution we think of today, but instead typically a sideline within the general store of a local merchant. So long as the mail order companies were offering a limited range of goods, the postal sideline did not directly compete with the local retailers. On the contrary, these merchants had benefited from the way the postal service brought customers into the store (Bush 1906). But the growth of mail order and the expansion of selection introduced tensions into the relationship.

These tensions erupted into full-scale political conflict starting in 1889, when President Benjamin Harrison appointed John Wanamaker as postmaster general. For scholars interested in state building, Wanamaker is best known as a zealous and highly effective reformer who did a great deal to enhance the efficiency of postal operations and root out the patronage-based corruption that had spread through the postal service after Andrew Jackson's election in 1829.[13] But Wanamaker was also a highly successful retailer with strong ties to the Republican Party.[14] Known as the "merchant king" (Emmet and Jeuck 1950: 13), he ran a large department store in Philadelphia, one that also included a significant mail order operation. In fact, he bragged that his company had "the fastest and most satisfactory Mail Order Service in the country" (quoted in Emmet and Jeuck 1950: 168). Although his company was well known in urban areas for bringing European fashion to American cities, Wanamaker also cultivated a customer base in rural areas, advertising heavily in farm journals as well.

---

12. Larger orders flowed through the express companies because of weight limits imposed on postal traffic. However, companies went to great lengths to remain under the USPS's four-pound limit—including by shipping garments that exceeded that weight limit in halves, along with a needle and thread to stitch them together when they arrived (Latham 1972: 13).

13. Postal reformers had already begun to address some of these issues in the 1870s and 1880s before Wanamaker took office. For example, postal inspectors directly employed by the government had been put in place to monitor efficiency and prosecute fraud (see especially Carpenter 2000; also Zulker 1993: 104).

14. Wanamaker had served as a hugely successful fundraiser and treasurer for Harrison's presidential campaign. Indeed, his efforts "revolutionized" campaign financing, enhancing the power of business interests in politics (Ershkowitz 1999: 84).

Whether inspired by self-interest or personal conviction (likely a combination of the two), Wanamaker wanted the post office to play a greater role in the country's economy (Carpenter 2000: 128).[15] In any event, one of the primary goals he pursued as postmaster general was "to increase the powers of the government so that all people would enjoy greater access to the goods and pleasures of modern life" (Leach 1993: 182). And in this, his most important contribution was to catalyze a movement to introduce at-home delivery to the rural population, known as rural free delivery or RFD (Carpenter 2000). Although the project was not realized during his short tenure (1889–93), Wanamaker's agitation for RFD was decisive in setting in motion the dynamics that drove this project—and its successor, parcel post—forward (Carpenter 2001b: 117; Zulker 1993: 100–13).[16]

Wanamaker confronted fierce opposition, especially from the country's four most powerful express companies, which otherwise controlled the transportation of goods in both directions (Barron 1997: 182–83). However, he managed to persuade Congress to allocate a modest $10,000 for a small pilot project in 1891. From there Wanamaker proceeded to orchestrate public pressure to build on its success, "shrewdly cultivat[ing] agrarian support through [his] ties to farm leaders and presses" (Carpenter 2000: 139–40). Working with the National Grange, the National Farmers Congress, and state Farmers' Alliances, Wanamaker "summoned rural communities to petition Congress to grant the POD [Post Office Department] experimental funds to enlarge the program" (Carpenter 2000: 140). These groups came through, organizing a "massive petition drive" in 1891 and 1892 (Carpenter 2000: 140).[17]

Wanamaker was completely open about the war on peddlers and small retailers he was unleashing. Accusing them of deceiving and overcharging customers, he sought to stake out the "moral high ground" on the issue, convinced as he was that consumers were better served by the more efficient operations of large retailers like himself (Ershkowitz 1999: 61, 72). The initial success of RFD and the subsequent campaign for parcel post heightened the conflict by activating its opponents. Thus, in the 1910s, the express companies were joined in their opposition by the recently founded Retail and

15. Zulker's rather fawning biography attributes it to altruism while, however, noting that his detractors "accused him of trying to advance sales in his own clothing business through low-cost delivery" (Zulker 1993: 105).

16. As one congressmen later (1916) remarked: "Rural delivery made possible parcel post" (quoted in Fuller 1964: 227).

17. The petition was a powerful tool in this period especially among rural constituencies (see Theriault 2003; Blackhawk et al. 2021; and Carpenter 2021 for an earlier period).

Wholesale Association, which brought together a broad range of commercial interests—wholesalers, distributors, and local retailers—that stood to lose business with the introduction of parcel post (Barron 1997: 183; Fuller 1964: 213–15). The epicenter of opposition formed in 1911 in Chicago (perhaps not coincidentally, where both Sears and Ward were headquartered) with the founding of the American League of Associations, which was established "for the specific purpose of fighting a rural parcel post" (Fuller 1964: 215).

The proponents of parcel post, however, were themselves a formidable force by now. Beyond having mobilized agrarians, Wanamaker used his ties to influential Eastern commercial interests to enlist their support as well. Although his own mail order operation was not as big as that of Marshall Field's or Sears & Roebuck, his reform proposals as postmaster general had resonated with all large retailers who sold goods nationally or who had an interest in expanding their markets (Ershkowitz 1999: 89). Macy's, for example, had a significant mail order operation, starting in the 1870s (Hower 1946: 148).[18] The problem they faced was that the "costs for sending merchandise through the mails were almost prohibitive. Packages [domestic packages] were limited to four pounds at sixteen cents per pound; meanwhile, international agreements allowed packages of up to eleven pounds to be sent overseas at a rate of twelve cents per pound" (Ershkowitz 1999: 89). Improved and lower-cost postal service was Wanamaker's "most notable effort to aid business" (Ershkowitz 1999: 89).

Retail titans such as Rowland Macy thus stood alongside farmers' organizations and emerging consumer groups such as the National Consumers League in support of the reforms. A Postal Progress League formed, supported by prominent political-economic interests from across the United States—publishers, labor leaders, media (advertising) companies, consumer groups, agrarians, and, of course, mail order retailers (see Carpenter 2000: 151–52 for a list of important boosters).[19] Already in 1905 the Postal Progress League was lobbying Congress with a program that would lead "straight to the adoption of a domestic parcel post with practically *no limit as to weight*" [italics in original] (*Dry Goods Reporter* May 20, 1905: 9).[20] The idea was

18. The company would, however, end the operation in 1912 to focus on its brick-and-mortar outlets (Hower 1946: 333).

19. The league was supported by Sears and Montgomery Ward alongside "all the large urban retailers with significant mail order divisions—Macy's, Wanamaker's, Altman's, Siegel-Cooper's" (Leach 1993: 183).

20. The league had also announced plans "to concentrate its energies upon a measure . . . authorizing the rural carriers to transport merchandise in packages of all sizes up to 200 pounds

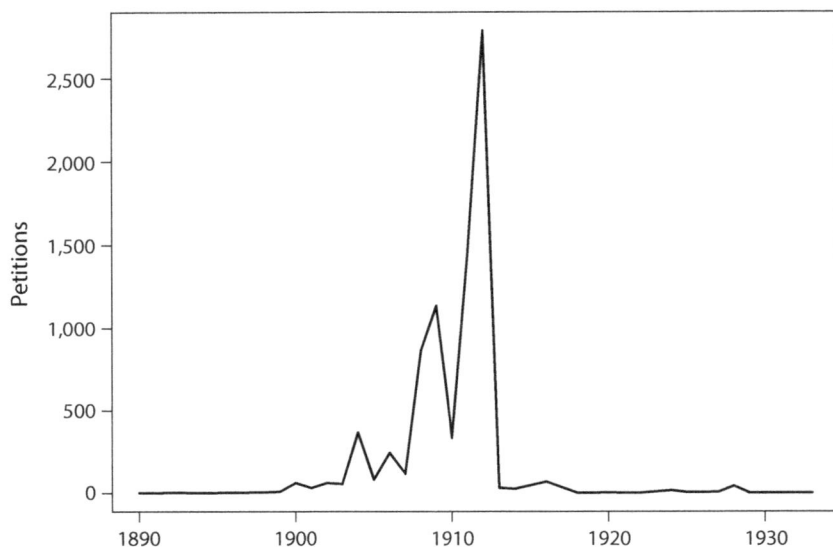

FIGURE 3.1. Parcel Post petitions over time, 1890–1933. Own calculations based on Petitions Database.
Source: Blackhawk et al. 2020.

to do "for the rural dwellers what the trolley and telephone have done for suburban dwellers—bringing them in touch with the advantages of urban life" (*Dry Goods Reporter* May 20, 1905: 9).

Proponents and opponents alike mobilized massive petition campaigns directed at their congressional representatives. As figure 3.1 shows, the flow of petitions hit a first peak in 1909 (1,134 petitions) and rose steeply again in 1911 (to 1,438) and 1912 (2,783) as Congress considered specific bills. Among petitions relating to parcel post over the entire period from 1890 through 1912, the overwhelming majority (2,928 out of a total of 4,220, or just under 70 percent) came from western and midwestern states.[21] Farm groups came down overwhelmingly (96 percent) in support of parcel post, while a signifi-cant majority of petitions from business and merchant groups (57 percent) expressed opposition.[22]

---

at rates ranging from 1 cent for an eight ounce parcel up to 25 cents for the 200 pound limit" (*Dry Goods Reporter* May 20, 1905: 9).

21. Own calculations based on Blackhawk et al. 2020. Not included in these figures are the 1,055 petitions in which no state was listed.

22. These figures reflect only those petitions (a total of 1,967) that were submitted by petition-ers who identified a clear interest or constituency and therefore could be reliably coded. Thus,

Montgomery Ward and Sears tried to keep their heads down through these conflicts, as the issue was controversial in the rural communities they served. Rural consumers resented the higher prices local merchants charged, but in the West and Midwest, these shopkeepers were sometimes neighbors who had helped families through hard times by extending credit informally (Barron 1997:183; Emmet and Jeuck 1950: 187–88). Both companies refrained from publicly taking sides, allowing the Postal Progress League, other reformers, and the farmers' organizations to take the lead. But it was an ugly fight, one in which local merchants and their allies resorted to bigoted slander and libelous claims. It reached a fever pitch with campaigns to reward local residents who turned in catalogs for public bonfires (Barron 1997: 185). Mail order companies had originally broken into the rural market by positioning themselves as the farmers' allies in the fight against northeastern monopolies. Now, however, local merchants sought to persuade their neighbors that it was Montgomery Ward and Sears who were the enemies—new "mail order trusts" that threatened the fabric of the rural community (Barron 1997: 176–78; 184).

Congressional Debates on Parcel Post

Between 1890 and 1910, organized opposition to the introduction of parcel post services prevented the issue from receiving a congressional hearing. New York senators Chauncey Depew (general counsel and later president of one of the lines controlled by railroad magnate Cornelius Vanderbilt) and Thomas Platt (president of the United States Express Company) led the effort to block parcel post bills (Fuller 1964: 205). However, large gains by progressives in the 1910 election, alongside Depew's defeat and Platt's retirement, cleared the most important hurdles (Fuller 1964: 205–6, 218). The congressional hearings that were held over the next two years clarified the coalitions by mobilizing interest groups on both sides of the issue. The ensuing debates pitted express companies, wholesalers, and small merchants against a formidable coalition that included farmers' organizations, urban retailers, postal reformers, and women's groups organized around consumer interests.

included in the count for farmers' organizations were petitions from a "National Grange," a "Local Grange," "Patrons of Husbandry," "Farmer's Club," "Convention of Fruit Growers," "Horticultural Society," or the like. Those coded as representing businesses or local merchant groups included petitions from a "Board of Trade," a "Commercial Club," a "Chamber of Commerce," "Businessmen of [town name]," store owners, and similar groups.

OPPOSITION TO PARCEL POST

Express companies, which clearly stood to lose their regional monopolies in parcel delivery, led the opposition (*Parcel Post* 1912, George: 1161–200; *Parcel Post* 1912, Johnson: 1214–32). They were joined by a contingent of local merchants who also saw parcel post as an existential threat and who activated their organized lobbyists, including the Retail Grocers' Association (which claimed more than one hundred thousand individual members) and the National Retail Hardware Association (with a membership of fourteen thousand firms across thirty-four states) to make their case in Washington (*Parcel Post* 1911, J. Green: 404; *Parcel Post* 1911, Corey: 589). Representatives of independent retailers drew on their experience with rural free delivery, which had already hurt small businesses. S. R. Miles of the National Retail Hardware Association, for example, testified that rural free delivery in Iowa had bankrupted over eight hundred country merchants who had served as local postmasters and whose stores had relied on mail pickups to draw farmers to town and to drive sales of goods (*Parcel Post* 1910, Miles: 197). Representatives of small stores predicted even greater losses from parcel post. In his congressional testimony, Charles Underhill of the Retail Hardware Merchants of Massachusetts predicted a devastating 25 percent decline in sales for small stores under parcel post (*Parcel Post* 1910, Underhill: 243). George Green of the Illinois Retail Merchants' Association similarly warned of the death of independent retailers as consumers shifted purchases of high-margin products to catalog houses (*Parcel Post* 1910, G. Green: 255).

Downplaying the higher prices they charged, small merchants sought to frame their competitive disadvantage as the result of the sensational and even deceptive advertising tactics of the mail-order houses. For instance, a representative of the National Association of Retail Druggists argued that catalog photography was misleading consumers about the products' quality and appeal (*Parcel Post* 1910, Richardson: 305). John Green, of the National Association of Retail Grocers based in Cleveland, was clear-eyed about the situation when he dejectedly acknowledged that small merchants could not possibly compete with goods from urban centers on quality, at least in the minds of consumers (*Parcel Post* 1911, J. Green: 433–44).

Small retailers argued that competition with mail order houses would have catastrophic knock-on effects for small-town life in general. Willard Richardson of the National Association of Retail Druggists insisted that farmers benefited from traveling to the post office because the town center provided social and educational opportunities (*Parcel Post* 1910, Richardson:

301). The local store also provided the farmer with a market to sell his own produce (*Parcel Post* 1910, Richardson: 306). Schools, churches, and civic organizations also tended to locate near the town retail hub. As one representative from the American League of Associations put it: "The small town is not only a social and trading center for the farmer and his family; it is a training ground for young men" (*Parcel Post* 1911, Moon: 369). Independent merchants warned that the demise of small-town stores spelled trouble for the entire country. Edward Moon, of the American League of Associations, argued that "parcel post will work serious injury to the retail merchants, villages, and small towns of the United States, and in that way will deplete or destroy these towns, a result which will prove a serious injury to the Nation itself" (*Parcel Post* 1911, Moon: 366).

When it came time to vote, opposition to parcel post came overwhelmingly from Republican legislators, and while about thirty from the North abstained, not a single northern Republican in the House voted in favor of the final amendment to the appropriations bill that authorized parcel post.[23] Some focused on the cost of the new government services, swayed by the claims of wholesalers who maintained that the government could not compete with the express companies—especially on shorter, city-to-city routes that represented the most profitable hauls—and would therefore drag the postal service into perpetual deficits (*Parcel Post* 1910, Maxwell: 275–76). Testimony of other critics suggested that the government would also have to subsidize the longest hauls to the most obscure areas with revenue from shorter hauls—forcing it to offer worse rates than the express companies (*Parcel Post* 1911, Clark: 700).

Other legislators anchored their opposition to parcel post in an expressed commitment to the general principle of limited government. For instance, a representative of the American League of Associations swayed some with the argument that "the Government should not further engage in enterprises in competition with its citizens" and charged that "our Government has already approached the halting line of socialistic and paternalistic legislation" (*Parcel Post* 1911, Moon: 546). In a similar vein, a merchant from Mount Vernon, Ohio, testified that parcel post, if enacted into law, "would be contrary to the genius of our institutions, because it proposes to undertake the

---

23. Voting record available at https://www.govtrack.us/congress/votes/62-2/h184. However, some northern Republicans attempted to thread the needle by supporting limited implementations of parcel post. For instance, David Foster of Vermont and William Bennet of New York each introduced legislation that would limit parcel delivery to areas within existing rural-free-delivery routes.

carrying of merchandise thus coming into competition with the people who are supporting the Government" (*Parcel Post* 1910, Bogardus: 178).

SUPPORT FOR PARCEL POST

But support for parcel post was broad and deep. Although the parcel post bill was sponsored by New York Democrat William Sulzer and pulled in some support from other northern Democrats, the supporting coalition consisted overwhelmingly of Democrats from the South and West. Legislators from rural districts responded to farmers whose organizations turned out in force to testify in support of the bill. These included the Farmers' Educational and Cooperative Union (representing three million members across twenty-nine states, strongest in the South), the Farmers' National Congress, the Farmers' National Committee on Postal Reform, and state Granges from Connecticut, Pennsylvania, Maine, Kentucky, Colorado, South Dakota, Oregon, and Washington (*Parcel Post* 1910, Shuford: 82; *Parcel Post* 1910, Stahl: 25; *Parcel Post* 1911, Creasy: 815).

By far the most common argument these groups advanced was that parcel post would provide a greater variety of goods at lower cost to farmers. A. C. Shuford of the Farmers' Union argued that parcel post would provide his members a wider range of products than could be stocked in a country store and thereby function "indirectly [as] a means of education; it would throw them [farmers] nearer in touch with the outside world" (*Parcel Post* 1910, Shuford: 87). W. T. Creasey of the Pennsylvania State Grange argued that farmers would benefit from cheaper goods as a result of parcel post, pointing out that under the parcel post's "zone" system—in which the postal rate depended in part on the distance the package traveled—local merchants would still enjoy a cost advantage over distant mail-order houses (*Parcel Post* 1911, Creasy: 816–17). Several speakers drew special attention to the lack of locally available goods in the South and the ways in which southern farmers would benefit from parcel post (*Parcel Post* 1910, Shuford: 110–12).

Farm representatives and congressmen alike often lashed out at the express companies, often in quite caustic terms. For instance, Francis B. Harrison, a Democratic congressman from New York, began his testimony by arguing: "I have long regarded the express companies as the most burdensome incumbrance in modern life. Economically, they are parasites; and socially, they are the greatest obstruction to modern progress and comfort" (*Parcel Post* 1911, Harrison: 79). Harrison condemned the express companies—which relied on the railroads to transport goods across long distances—as greedy middlemen who inserted themselves between consumers and railroads but performed no useful function. Indeed, some witnesses suggested that the express companies were conspiring to thwart any hope of government competition. For instance, W. T. Creasey of the Pennsylvania State Grange argued that the express companies might agree to cede the unprofitable hauls to the government and compete only on profitable hauls, dooming parcel post to failure (*Parcel Post* 1911, Creasy: 818–21; *Parcel Post* 1911, Hampton: 866).

Agrarian groups were joined in their advocacy for parcel post by urban retailers (led by E. W. Bloomingdale of the eponymous department store), women's clubs, and the Postal Progress League—which, as pointed out above, enjoyed the support of all the large retailers "with significant mail order divisions" (Leach 1993: 183). Bloomingdale spoke for a group of New York retailers (including Bloomingdale's, Macy's, Lord & Taylor, Saks, and others) who argued that parcel post was crucial to giving more citizens access to urban department store inventories (*Parcel Post* 1910, Bloomingdale: 164–67). All these interests were bundled together by the Postal Progress League into an umbrella organization that also represented shippers, publishers, and newspapers and included among its members labor leaders Samuel Gompers of the American Federation of Labor (AFL) and John Mitchell of the United Mine Workers (Carpenter 2000: 151). The Postal League's James Cowles assured Congress that parcel post services could be run economically without a deficit to the government (*Parcel Post* 1910, Cowles: 335–37).

Women's organizations also testified in favor of parcel post. The National Consumers League, a powerful organization of reformist middle-class women launched in 1899, was a particularly prominent advocate. Other women's groups also showed up in support, including the Equal State Suffrage Association, the Stanton Suffrage Club of Washington, and the Women's Single Tax Club of Washington. These groups tended to frame their arguments in terms of the impact of parcel post on farm wives who ran households. For instance, Florence Etheridge of the Stanton Suffrage Club argued that parcel post would bring lower costs and more competition to local merchants, making it easier to run the household on a shoestring budget (*Parcel Post* 1911, Etheridge: 757–58). Mrs. Charles Craigie—the president of the Brooklyn Public Library—testified that parcel post would make the lives of suburban wives and families easier as well. Craigie argued that suburbanites had cultivated tastes for expensive and high-quality goods that local merchants simply did not carry; without parcel post, husbands would have to pick up these goods as they commuted back to the suburbs (*Parcel Post* 1911, Craigie: 780–81).

THE OUTCOME

In the end, then, rural consumers and their allies sided decisively with parcel post and, by extension, with the large retailers on whom they had come to rely. Local merchants were hurt by their association with the wholesalers and express companies that had long victimized struggling farmers. In the House of Representatives, the bill, which passed 144 to 85, relied almost entirely on the votes of Democratic members from across all regions (against resistance from northern and western Republicans, the latter mostly representing the interests of independent merchants), as shown in figure 3.2.

On January 1, 1913, John Wanamaker himself ceremoniously mailed the first parcel post package to President William Howard Taft from Philadelphia's central post office (Zulker 1993: 106; Ershkowitz 1999: 90).[24] As Daniel Carpenter notes, the US Postal Service had "wrested control of parcel post delivery from the nation's express companies, rendering them obsolete in the parcel market in under a decade" (2000: 122).[25] Parcel post ushered in a "golden age" of mail order (Emmet and Jeuck 1950: 187; Fuller 1964: 205; Ershkowitz 1999: 90). In under ten years, weight limits for packages were raised, in stages, to fifty pounds and beyond in some zones (Fuller 1964: 254). As Fuller summarized: parcel post "pulled the stopper out of the transportation system, sped the farmer's merchandise over steel rail and rural routes from Chicago directly to the farm, and revolutionized the farmers' buying habits" (1964: 252). In the very first year of parcel post, Sears's orders increased fivefold and Montgomery Ward's threefold (Fuller 1964: 254). "Never before had the farmers had such a convenient method of breaking the rural merchants' monopoly of their trade and they wasted no time taking advantage of it" (Fuller 1964: 252).

24. Wanamaker's was also the first store to provide free parcel post delivery to customers (Zulker 1993: 64).

25. On the link between the postal system and the railroads in the early twentieth century, including Wanamaker's role in the Railway Mail System, see Carpenter 2001a: 98–101.

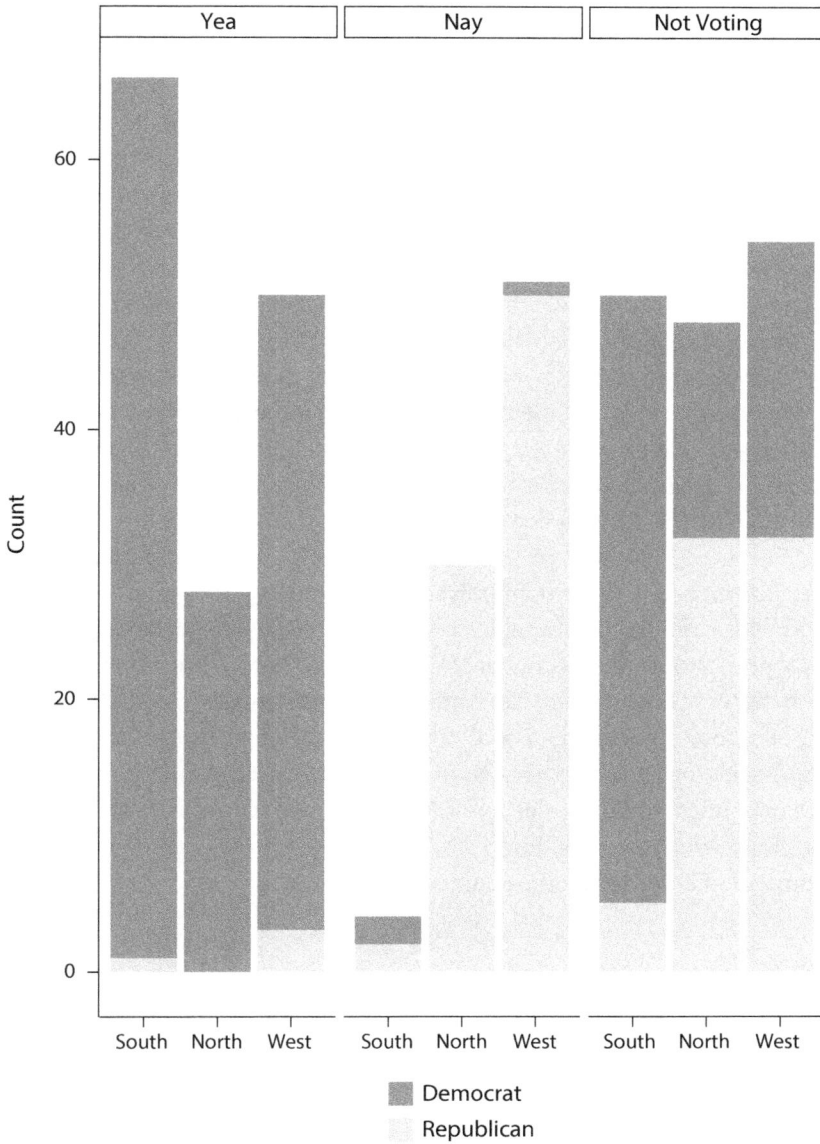

FIGURE 3.2. Parcel Post (H.R. 21279) votes by region, House of Representatives. *Source:* House of Representatives, House Vote no. 184, 62nd Cong., 1912, "To Amend a Motion to Recommit to the Committee on the Post Office and Post Roads . . ." https://www.govtrack.us/congress/votes/62-2/h184.

Conclusion

Summarizing the previous two chapters: in this first phase in the creation of a mass market in the United States, the fragmented political-economic landscape and the unsettled legal status of cooperatives played key roles in suppressing the kind of consumer co-ops that thrived in other countries, and helped clear the way for private mail-order retailers to actively exploit and repurpose public infrastructure to win over the country's powerful agrarian population. Alongside the railroads, the USPS provided the network through which increasingly standardized goods flowed to the country's vast rural population. While parcel post served as a subsidized means to distribute the catalogs and the goods, the government-sponsored mail order system provided the crucial tool for managing the financial transactions. Appropriating public infrastructure for private ends, mail order retailers knit together consumers across a vast continent.

Farmers who otherwise battled "big business" did not experience large retailers such as Sears as oppressive. On the contrary, they welcomed their growth for the way it liberated them from colorless local retail markets, high-priced town merchants, and fraudulent peddlers to bring them a world of exotic new consumer goods. And they enthusiastically joined forces with postal reformers and urban retailers to break the chokehold of the express companies and middlemen who had long tormented them. In this way, a broad political coalition—of agrarians, progressive consumer associations, and Eastern commercial interests—paved the way for a nationwide consumer market served by the country's largest retailers.

4

Social Peace and Democratic Participation through Consumption

The previous chapters documented large retailers' conquest of rural America, an outcome much facilitated by the demise of agrarian and working-class cooperative distribution arrangements that flourished in Europe, as well as by the ability of large private retailers to leverage public infrastructure to thrive and grow. This chapter turns to developments in the Progressive Era and the interwar period, highlighting the role that mass retailers played in promoting the growth of a distinctly consumption-oriented political economy.

I begin by considering the continuing impact that America's distinctive antitrust regime had on the broader political-economic landscape and, with that, on retailing and distribution. American courts played a critical role in paving the way for the triumph of large retailers by disarticulating nascent class-based producer-group organizations that developed in Europe and that would serve as important countervailing forces to the advance of large retailing there. On both sides of the Atlantic, intensified industrialization in the late nineteenth century had heightened distributional conflicts not just between labor and capital, but also between "traditional" and modern industry, and between small and large firms in many sectors. Governments (whether democratic or predemocratic) all faced the same general problem of how to manage and channel these new conflicts so as to maintain social peace.

The farmers discussed in the previous chapters were not the only ones who turned to collective self-help in this period; the Long Depression at the turn of the century had inspired similar efforts by firms and workers as well. In Europe, the state and the courts recognized and sanctioned these emerging forms of horizontal coordination. In fact, national governments often facilitated such organization, and social peace emerged through producer group representation and accommodation. This does not mean that there was no conflict; indeed, conflicts between organized workers and associations of employers were especially epic across all of Europe (Freyer 1992: 20). But conflicts of interest *within* producer groups (e.g., between large and small firms or between skilled and unskilled workers within particular sectors) came to be worked out internally, while struggles *between* groups with opposing interests (e.g., labor and capital, export-oriented and domestic industries) were fought by increasingly centralized and encompassing organizations (Freyer 1992: 20). In the United States, by contrast, the courts often interpreted producer-group coordination of the sort that was becoming common in Europe as anticompetitive acts of collusion. These efforts at collective self-help thus often met with the same reception as the cooperatives discussed in the previous chapter, frequently running afoul of the Sherman Act's prohibition against horizontal coordination.

In the American context, then, producer organizations and identities withered, and progressive reformers instead channeled the search for social peace toward consumption. America's leading retailers enthusiastically signed on to this program, presenting themselves as ready allies with progressive forces that viewed consumption as a distinctly American formula for social integration and democratic engagement. In the war and interwar period, the country's premier retailers eagerly partnered with the government to manage wartime shortages and to combat postwar inflation, endearing themselves to an ever-widening base of grateful consumers. In the subsequent period large retailers in fact jumped out ahead of the government to fuel spending through advocacy, innovation, and regulatory arbitrage.

The Role of the Courts in Shaping the Interest Group Landscape

On both sides of the Atlantic, the economic turbulence of the late nineteenth century had sent wages and profits into a steep downward spiral, setting in motion vicious cutthroat competition among firms and provoking intense industrial strife. Everywhere, firms sought to stabilize prices by organizing to defend themselves against ruinous competition through coordination and collective self-help. The divergent legal regimes governing competition policy played a central role in shaping the interest group landscape that emerged this period.

America's small producers often banded together in the nineteenth century in response to increasing industrialization and the nationalization of markets (Roy 1997). Like their European counterparts, these producer groups drew on older forms of (local) associationalism (Spillman 2012, 44–45). And similar to their European counterparts, they sought to mitigate market volatility in this period by engaging in efforts to stabilize competition through information sharing and, in many cases, price and production agreements (Roy 1997: chap. 7; Spillman 2012: 41–47; for an example, see Galambos 1966: 35, 37).

Different from Europe, however, these nascent trade associations struggled to survive let alone thrive, because the courts coded many of their coordinating activities as operating "in restraint of trade" and therefore illegal. By contrast, under American antitrust law there was no conspiracy or collusion where all these coordinating functions occurred within the context of a single company. Thus, large firms avoided antitrust prosecution by internalizing coordination functions—merging with their former rivals and swallowing up smaller competitors that could not survive in the era's ultracompetitive markets. In these ways, competition policy in the United States weakened the country's trade associations while strongly promoting a dramatic increase in industrial concentration (Lamoreaux 1985). As Sanders (1986: 159) points out, in 1899 alone over one thousand companies had vanished, subsumed into larger corporations through mergers, and just a few years later more than one hundred industrial sectors were dominated by a single firm.

By contrast, courts in Europe applied an expansive understanding of the principle of freedom of contract that included recognizing agreements that under American law were considered anticompetitive (Gerber 1985: 5). In this way, Europe's more permissive competition regimes encouraged and often actively reinforced coordination among firms within industries.[1] Judicial forbearance toward these forms of cooperation in Europe tolerated cartels, but it also supported the flourishing of the dense associational landscape of producer group politics (trade associations, employer organizations, and labor unions) that we now associate with coordinated capitalism.

---

1. For an extended comparison of the United States and Germany, see Thelen 2020; on Scandinavian cartels, see Lapidus 2013; Gerber 1998: 155–63.

Europe's distinct approach to competition policy was a choice, not an oversight. Lawmakers often explicitly considered—and rejected—the United States' version of antitrust in the late nineteenth century. They saw the Sherman Antitrust Act's prohibition against horizontal combinations as detrimental for the way it encouraged monopoly power while allowing cutthroat competition among firms to go unchecked. Indeed, coordination among firms (of all sizes) was viewed as highly desirable to prevent the growth of large US-type monopolies and to protect against the "ravages of hyperindividualism" (Nörr 1995: 7; Richter 2007: 207–10).[2]

As Gerber points out, in interwar Europe, cartels were widely viewed as "unavoidable, or even necessary, outcomes of modern economic development" (1998: 159). While "specific cartel conduct might have harmful consequences for consumers, labor or other elements of society . . . cartels as an organizational form were assessed positively—as a means of stabilizing economic conditions, promoting the rationalization of industry, and enhancing the competitiveness of domestic industries" (Gerber 1998: 159–60). These convictions guided policy in Europe well into the post–World War II period: Sweden, for example, passed its first legislation on antitrust only in 1953 and Germany's 1956 competition law continued to allow for certain forms of coordination among small- and medium-sized firms on many issues.[3]

Even in Britain, America's closest European (and common-law) cousin, trade associations grew unencumbered throughout the early twentieth century and the interwar period, taking an active role in managing competition among their members (Mercer 1995: chap. 2). As Letwin (1954: 379) points out, British law on combinations in restraint of trade had become "narrow and ineffective" by the late nineteenth century. Especially after Parliament legalized labor unions and expressly sanctioned collective bargaining in 1875 with the new Combination Act (an act unmatched in the United States until many decades later), English courts came to the view "that employers

---

2. As Freyer put it, business self-regulation in Europe "facilitated a degree of cooperation between large and small business, which helped to protect the latter," whereas in the United States "both the law and the market fostered conflict between the two business groups" (Freyer 1992: 8).

3. Previous laws (in Germany in 1923 and in Sweden in 1925) had given the state more oversight over cartels to prevent their engaging in "abusive" practices, but the laws were not designed to suppress the cartels themselves (Jackson 2001: 135; Feldenkirchen 1992: 259; Kessler 1936: 681–82; Lapidus 2013; Gerber 1998: 155). The 1923 German law, for example, had included procedures to adjudicate disputes that arose among cartel members or between them and outsiders (Thelen 2020). After WWII, the German government broke up many of the big cartels, but a new competition law had to wait until 1956, and even then the law contained exemptions for some forms of horizontal combination (see chapter 9).

should not be denied rights granted to workers [and] matched the new legal power of the latter with a solicitous concern for employers' combinations" as well (Letwin 1954: 379). Thus, despite the shared common-law tradition, the British approach to regulating the market "encouraged the alteration of old doctrines to create a more flexible rule of reasonableness which permitted family firms to adopt loose rather than tight anticompetitive business structures" (Freyer 1992: 20)—that is, horizontal, interfirm coordination as opposed to intrafirm coordination in Sanjukta Paul's terms.

While American trade associations and unions were navigating a legal landscape that was singularly hostile to these sorts of arrangements, British competition policy up to World War II exhibited a "marked preference for self-regulation by business," including affording firms more freedom to coordinate among themselves to defend their interests in the market (Mercer 1995: 2; Dobbin 1994: chap. 4). In addition, and again in sharp contrast to the United States, the British government also played an active role in promoting industry-level collective bargaining in the late nineteenth and early twentieth centuries in an effort to mitigate class conflict and reduce interfirm competition (Howell 2005: chap. 3, 55–58, 66–69). Government support for producer cartels[4] in Britain persisted until 1948, when the Monopolies and Restrictive Practices Act was passed (Mercer 1995: 4).[5]

The different interest-group landscapes that emerged in the early twentieth century had important implications for the cleavages that structured political-economic contestation in this period. Politics in Europe at the turn of the century were very much focused on competing *producer* identities and ideologies as channeled through contests among organized producer groups. Class conflicts featured prominently, as powerful employer associations came together to battle labor unions that were themselves often organizing on broad industrial lines. Meanwhile, artisanal associations, farmers, and organizations of small shopkeepers—surviving remnants of previous guilds—were also organizing to struggle against industrial interests in an effort to defend traditional rights and privileges.

In such contexts, consumption was typically far from the center of the political agenda. As De Grazia notes, in Europe in the 1920s, "it was rare to hear consumption spoken of outside the cooperative movement" (2005:

---

4. As an aside: the term "cartel" was not necessarily deployed as an epithet in Europe in this period; it was simply descriptive.

5. The rather weak 1948 law was replaced by stronger legislation in 1956 (Mercer 1995: chap. 7).

118–19). In fact, retailing and consumption patterns in Europe, if anything, *reflected and reinforced* producer group identities and class divisions. As outlined in chapter 2, in many parts of Europe, union-affiliated cooperatives served the working classes with a limited range of standardized essentials. Meanwhile, the grand urban department stores catered to upper-class demands for luxury, variety, and choice (Jefferys 1954: 32–33; Logemann 2008: 525; De Grazia 1998: 68–69, 155).

Political parties in Europe almost always organized along lines that mapped onto the dominant producer group cleavages (Martin and Swank 2012), with socialist (or in some cases reformist) left-wing parties aligned with unions. Business interests were typically represented by one or more conservative parties (some representing "traditional" interests, others advocating on behalf of "modern" large-scale industry). Farmers and/or small businessmen (shopkeepers, artisans) often wielded outsized political power because they were seen as critical to political stability, "a healthy core, sandwiched between rich and poor," a bulwark against social democracy on one side and "unbridled" markets on the other (Berghoff and Köhler 2019: 103).

In Europe's producerist political economies, government policy subordinated consumer interests and consumer protection issues to producer group interests in the late nineteenth and early twentieth centuries. In Germany, for example, the imperial government passed a series of laws that were advertised as protecting consumers but in fact were aimed at heading off destructive competition among producers (Hähnel 2021: 211–21). These included trademark protection laws (1874 and 1894) shielding brand manufacturers from cheap "knockoff" imitations and laws against "unfair" "cutthroat" competition (*Gesetze zur Bekämpfung des Unlauteren Wettbewerbs* [1896, 1909]) (Hähnel 2021: 223–25; von Stechow 2002).[6] The political parties associated with traditional sectors thus fought on two fronts: against the advance of modern industry and against nonproducers ("unproductive elements" of society; "nothing-but-consumers") (Nonn 1999: 222). In Europe, the left-wing defense of "consumer interests" centered on worker cooperatives offering low-priced goods to the working class, while the right pursued an alternative, nationalist version of "consumer politics" based on buying domestically produced goods, combined in times of economic crisis with efforts to "mold housewives' shopping and cooking habits" to adjust to shortages (Reagin 1998: 242).

---

6. For example, these laws included protection against obfuscation of quality (*Qualitätsverschleierung*), misleading advertising, and defamation of a competitor (*Geschäftsehrverletzung*) (von Stechow 2002).

The Triumph of Consumption over Class in the United States

The interest group landscape in the United States was wholly differ-ent because of the court's intolerance for these forms of producer group organization and coordination. Whereas conflicts in Europe were chan-neled through relatively well-organized producer groups, those in the United States could not be channeled in the same way. Partisan politics also did not cleave neatly along class lines, but instead along regional lines that reflected the radically different models of political-economic growth that characterized the American North, South, and West. As Sanders sum-marizes, in the United States national politics revolved around geographic divisions in which "the pull of region diminished the counterpull of class" (Sanders 1999: 5). Chapter 3 underscored the importance of these sectional divides in structuring conflicts over parcel post, and subsequent chapters will consider their impact on discount retailing in the 1930s and the 1960s. The remainder of this chapter, however, sets the scene by focusing on the ways in which the absence of strong producer group organization allowed for the emergence of a consumerist alternative in the first years of the twen-tieth century.

As David Thelen (no relation as far as I know) has argued, the Progressive Era marked an important transition, one characterized "by a new conscious-ness of citizens as consumers rather than merely producers" (D. Thelen 1972; quote is from Tedlow 1981: 38). At the same time that mass retailers such as Sears were consolidating a nationwide mass market in standardized goods, early progressives were casting about for ways "to reintegrate a society that industrial capitalism had divided into competing producer-oriented classes and interest groups" (D. Thelen 1972: 2). Social movements increasingly began to center their appeals on citizens' shared identity as taxpayers and consumers (D. Thelen 1972: 2). The populist farmer-labor movement of the 1870s and 1880s had rallied around traditional republican values of prop-erty ownership and self-reliance, but in the wake of its failure, progressives promoted a new definition of democracy centering on consumption—what Leach calls a "democratization of desire" (Leach 1993: 5–7). American exceptionalism was no longer portrayed as a republic of rugged independent producers and jacks-of-all-trades; instead, "Americans came to understand spending as a form of citizenship" (McGovern 2006: 3).

Thus, even as Europe's socialist unions were waging pitched battles with organized employers over control of the shop floor, America's ascendant

AFL unions were embarking on what Glickman calls a "consumerist reconstruction of working-class identity," abandoning demands for a new economic order and instead latching on to the notion that full citizenship involved a right to consume (Glickman 1997: xiii). As vicious attacks on unions and the advance of mass production techniques eroded their control at work, American workers "turned to consumption, not as a pathetic substitute for, but as a logical fulfilment of their desires for autonomy, on or off the job" (McGovern 2006: 12). Already in 1893, the AFL's powerful leader, Samuel Gompers, articulated an explicitly consumerist orientation: "The prosperity of a nation, the success of a people, the civilizing influence of an era, can always be measured by the comparative consuming power of a people" (Glickman 1997: 97).

By this metric, American workers (more precisely: a subset of skilled white male workers) were doing well in comparative perspective. Purchasing power in the United States increased by 23 percent between 1913 and 1929, as compared to a European average of just 5.5 percent (De Grazia 2005: 106). Consumption of household equipment far outstripped that in Europe at the time. A 1928 study of Berlin revealed that fewer than half of all households had electricity, and of these, only 0.5 percent had washing machines (compared to 76 percent of all US homes with electricity, of which 26 percent had washing machines at this time) (Reagin 1998: 245). As Jacobs points out, the "American standard of living" to which labor aspired was one defined by consumer comforts—"a six-room house with indoor plumbing, a separate parlor, and dining room, multiple bedrooms and a library" (Jacobs 2005: 51). In the face of intense and violent employer opposition (actively supported by court injunctions), class consciousness in the American context "moved from the shop floor to the store front," as union leaders campaigned for a "living wage," defined by Gompers as one that would prevent the breadwinner from becoming a "non-consumer" (Glickman 1997: 77).[7]

A new class of professionals, above all those employed in the booming advertising industry, promoted these developments and actively fueled

7. Many of the views articulated by American unions were deeply exclusionary and often explicitly laced with racism and sexism because, in their view, greedy capitalists were not the only threat to workers achieving the American standard of living. The leaders of America's skilled male blue-collar unions often saw their members as threatened by other groups—women, immigrants, and Black workers—who "degraded" work by accepting lower employment standards (Glickman 1997: 85). As De Grazia emphasizes, the "populist consumerism" of skilled American (male) workers in this period was not at all incompatible with bloody class struggles (2005: 99). But they perceived theirs as a two-front battle, not just against their employers but also against what they saw as their "contemptable competitors in the labor market" (see especially Glickman 1997: 85–91).

these aspirations, deploying new "scientific" methods to track and influence consumer behavior. Tapping into American political traditions, they "cast spending as a specifically *American* social practice, an important element of distinct national identity" (McGovern 2006: 5).[8] They portrayed "consumers as sovereign rulers of a democratic marketplace," exercising independence and choice by "voting" through their spending choices (McGovern 2006: 67, chap. 2; Pope 1983: 11–12).

During the Red Scare of 1919–20, advertisers leaned in to the message that consumption was the alternative to socialism and could serve "as a means of soothing worker discontent"—essentially a message of unity through mass consumption of the same nationally advertised consumer goods. Although never realized in practice, the "democratic promise" of America's emerging consumer culture "suggested that everyone—regardless of age, class, gender, or race—was entitled to desire whatever they pleased" (Jacobson 2004: 2). Thus settled in what De Grazia calls a "peculiarly American notion of democracy, that which comes from having habits in common rather than arising from equal economic standing . . . or [from] recognizing diversity and learning to live with it" (2005: 2–3).[9]

Other groups also rallied around the unifying language of consumption in the Progressive Era. Women had famously entered American politics as fierce advocates of consumer interests even before they enjoyed the right to vote (Sklar 1998; Wolfe 1975: 379). Led by the formidable social activist Florence Kelley, they founded a National Consumers League (NCL) that served as a powerful force behind the passage of the Pure Food and Drug Act of 1906[10] (and, as we saw in the previous chapter, the league was also centrally involved in the battles over parcel post). The consumer league's state organizations now formed "a part of the wider Progressive Era phenomenon of reform-minded 'club women' putting their wealth, political connections, and elite educations to the task of social uplift" (Haydu 2014: 637).

Though Kelley herself was a socialist, the league was overwhelmingly made up of middle- and upper-class women whose main project reached more patronizingly across class lines. Through its "white label" campaign,

8. Italics in the original. Advertising, as Pope emphasizes, was "a method of rivalry well suited to a wide range of oligopolistic consumer markets" (Pope 1983: 61).

9. The issue of social peace in this period was also tied up in debates over immigration, since some groups saw immigrants as a threat to social peace. Many of the women's clubs in this period directed their efforts at changing the consumption habits of immigrants so they would become more "American." I thank an anonymous reviewer for emphasizing the importance of this to me.

10. See Carpenter 2001a on the role of mid-level bureaucrats (Harvey Wiley in particular) in assembling the coalition behind the Pure Food and Drug Act of 1906.

the NCL sought to promote "ethical consumption" by educating middle- and upper-class shoppers and encouraging them to spend their dollars exclusively on goods produced under safe and healthy working conditions (Haydu 2014: 629; Vose 1957).[11] League leaders viewed consumers as an important "third force" in modern society; in the words of NCL leader Maud Nathan: "When consumers organize, as capital and labor have organized, their power will be greater than either of the two forces. The consumer will be in a position to dictate terms" (Wolfe 1975: 380). And they were convinced that all three groups—workers, employers, and consumers—could "live harmoniously with their various needs fulfilled" (Wolfe 1975: 380–81).

Progressive political theorists and pundits, similarly, saw consumption as a distinctly American way of bridging class, regional, and racial divides to secure social peace (Wolfe 1975; Leach 1993: 5). Influential journalist and public intellectual Walter Lippmann envisioned a movement capable of ending "the scourge of class conflict by recharacterizing every member of American society as a member of a single class, the class of consumers" (Whitman 2007: 361). Lippmann's fellow political commentator (and cofounder of the *New Republic*) Walter Weyl also embraced consumption as a "unifying economic force" with the power to overcome all the various cleavages that divided Americans—urban versus rural, labor versus capital, lender versus borrower (Whitman 2007: 361). "The consumer," argued Weyl, "is undifferentiated. All men, women and children who buy shoes (except only the shoe manufacturer) are interested in cheap good shoes" (Whitman 2007: 361).

The strand of progressivism represented by public intellectuals such as Lippmann and Weyl "encouraged Americans to confront the impersonal world of big business and centralized markets not as members of traditional communities . . . but rather as enlightened, empowered consumers" (Sandel 1996: 221). In a context marked by class conflict and rising costs, a politics organized around "bringing prices down could thus unite Americans in a single national interest, putting an end to the particularisms of the producer orientation" (Whitman 2007: 362). "Market replaced polis in a new communal public life characterized not by geography, religion, or politics,

---

11. Relations between the NCL and organized labor were chilly to say the least. The AFL unions saw the league's white label campaign as operating at cross-purposes to its own union label drives. But the deeper source of tension lay in the fact that AFL unions were not concerned with the women and immigrant workers at the heart of the NCL campaigns and saw their participation in the labor market as exerting downward pressure on the wages of their own members (see especially Haydu 2014).

but by spending" (McGovern 2006: 5).[12] De Grazia suggests this orientation informed foreign policy as well, citing a 1916 speech by President Woodrow Wilson to a Detroit convention of the World Salesmanship Congress in which "America's most renowned foreign policy idealist" could be heard exhorting his listeners to "go out and sell goods" to convert others "to the principles of America" (De Grazia 2005: 1–3).

Mass Retailers and Progressive Politics

This was an agenda that the country's mass retailers could embrace. "Merchant elites . . . attached themselves to Progressive coalitions in alliance with feminist groups, consumer movements, labor organizations, and government that spoke in the name of the consumers' interests" (De Grazia 2005: 144). Well before Ford's famous "Five-Dollar Day," large retailers were espousing mass consumption as a solution to labor strife and an alternative to socialism (Jacobs 2005: 50–51). Edward Filene, doyen of Boston retailing, paid above-market wages to his own unskilled, mostly female workforce and spoke out in favor enhancing the purchasing power of consumers generally. In some ways, Filene's rhetoric and advocacy went further than the AFL's demand for a "living wage," since the AFL was mostly advocating for its skilled white male workers and was often working at cross purposes to progressive groups concerned about the condition of women and immigrants (Haydu 2014: 640).[13]

Mass retailers benefited from the turn toward consumerist politics, especially when a surge in prices in 1910–13 elevated pocketbook issues to the top of the political agenda (Jacobs 2005; Macleod 2009). Taking a page from the populist playbook, critics placed the blame for high prices on "greedy middlemen, speculators, and trusts" (Macleod 2009: 366). Recently founded consumer groups such as the National Anti-Food Trust League heaped criticism on the country's monopolistic producers and wholesalers (meatpackers Armour and Swift came in for particularly vitriolic attacks).

12. In 1929, two other prominent progressive thinkers, theorist John Dewey and the economist Paul Douglas, would found a third party, the League for Independent Political Action, to advocate specifically for the consumer. They saw a convergence in "the interests of consumers in the economy and voting citizens in a democracy" (Cohen 1998: 116–17).

13. Filene himself testified on behalf of minimum-wage legislation for women (Jacobs 2005: 64). Forbath (manuscript in progress) suggests that the Filene brothers (A. Lincoln and Edward) were sympathetic to the cause of garment workers and the International Ladies Garment Workers Union in part because of a shared Jewish ethno-cultural identity.

But they also blamed inefficient distribution networks as well as the local grocer or butcher who "put his thumb on the scales" (Macleod 2009: 377). Editorials portrayed neighborhood grocers "not as community pillars but as extortionists and profiteers" and railed against inefficient modes of distribution (Deutsch 2010: 47, 50).

Consumer prices were further politicized when inflation hit during World War I (Jacobs 2005). In Europe, governments in this period turned to organized producer groups to help them manage wartime shortages and steer production and distribution—moves that invariably strengthened producer group organization. In the United States, by contrast, the government enlisted consumers and mass retailers to assist in its campaign against inflation. After President Woodrow Wilson appointed Herbert Hoover to lead a newly established US Food Administration, Hoover wasted no time in tapping the country's vast network of women's clubs to support his home-front war on waste and inflation. Women's clubs that had previously mobilized to improve working conditions for women and immigrants now "became acutely sensitive to the problem that inflation presented to their middle-class members and to the working class" (Jacobs 2005: 55). Organized women fanned out across the country to expose merchants whose prices exceeded the US Food Administration's "fair prices" list and to organize boycotts to bring them in line. As Jacobs summarizes: "The administration's denunciations of manufacturers, middlemen, and merchants as war profiteers and its creation of a state oversight apparatus to monitor wages and prices validated and encouraged grassroots activism at the market and on the shop floor" (2005: 65–66).

Mass retailers were only too happy to offer their support to the government's campaign. Hoover—raised as a Quaker and trained as an engineer—brought his intensely held convictions for thrift and efficiency to the job, and these were values that resonated deeply with mass retailers. Under his stewardship, the US Food Administration had "reinforced the perception of local shops as bastions of higher prices" (Jacobs 2005: 62; Howard 2015: 41). Mass retailers eagerly signed on to Hoover's war on waste and inefficiency "because they saw themselves as the vanguard of modern distribution" (Jacobs 2005: 61). And as we saw in the previous chapter, mass retailers such as Montgomery Ward had spent the past decades battling small merchants and railing against the wholesale "trusts"[14] while themselves perfecting

14. As noted in the previous chapter, Montgomery Ward had taken on the Sugar Trust in 1893 in a very public dispute, siding decisively with consumers (Latham 1972: 27).

efficient distribution networks that translated economies of scale and scope into the lower prices that Hoover valorized and that consumers craved.

During the war, prominent retailers thus rushed to collaborate with Hoover in his conservation efforts. Filene actively led the effort to organize retailers in support of Hoover's initiatives, and his manager, Louis Kirstein, would work alongside Sears's Julius Rosenwald in assisting the government in requisitioning food, clothing, and shoes (Jacobs 2005: 61). The retail giant A&P, which dominated the grocery sector, had already begun launching "economy stores" that sold a more limited range of items at low cost, and by 1916, the company had set up 3,500 such operations (Macleod 2009: 377). A study conducted in Chicago in the 1920s found that residents did not necessarily view large retail chains as undermining community; indeed, many saw them "as a tool for making their communities stronger," not least because their efficiency and low prices often gave these retailers "the aura of being somehow progressive" (Deutsch 2010: 51).[15]

Hoover would also continue to work closely with large retailers in his capacity as secretary of commerce after the war. Among other initiatives, he would continue to promote rationalization and product standardization, thus helping to hasten and solidify the reorientation of competition away from product diversity and toward price (Dunlavy 2024: chap. 5). In his view, the War Industries Board had done an excellent job eliminating "these endless variations" in manufactured goods, and after the war, he advocated continued product simplification and standardization to reduce the cost of consumer goods (Dunlavy 2024: 71). Hoover also pushed Congress to establish a national Census of Distribution (on par with the population census), based on his conclusion that the sharp downturn the economy suffered in 1921 was primarily a function of overproduction and inefficiencies in distribution. He pressed the Chamber of Commerce to convene the First National Distribution Conference in 1925 (De Grazia 2005: 140). And in 1929 the United States became a pioneer in conducting an annual nationwide census on distribution (most of Europe would follow only much later, in the 1950s and after). Hoover showered the Bureau of Foreign and Domestic Commerce with resources. The bureau, which published business surveys, saw its budget increase from a mere $100,000 to over $8 million between 1921 and 1930 and its staff increase from 100 to 2,500 in the same period (Leach 1993: 359, 364–66).

---

15. And the chains did, of course, deliver lower prices, for as a 1930 study in Chicago showed, chains were able to charge around 10 percent less than the independents (Deutsch 2010: 52).

Some mass retailers had been keen to align themselves with progressive forces in other ways, including by distancing themselves from the kind of class warfare that the large manufacturing concerns were waging on organized labor in the opening years of the twentieth century. Florence Kelley and the NCL had previously called out department stores for exploiting the young women they employed, but in the early twentieth century some large retailers went out of their way to cultivate reputations as caring employers. Big department store owners joined Kelley in her campaign against child labor. For example, John Wanamaker aligned himself publicly with the NCL's white label campaign (Sklar 1998: 31). Kelley acknowledged the efforts of these prominent retail magnates in a 1910 speech at the opening of a new Gimbels in New York City, in which she praised "the cooperation in this movement extended by the heads of the great retail concerns in many centers" (Leach 1993: 181).

Almost no other large retailers followed Filene's lead in welcoming organized labor (indeed, they were typically rabidly anti-union) but many devised some of "the most elaborate welfare programs in the country" (Leach 1993: 118–20; McQuaid 1976).[16] And as minimum wage legislation for women workers was being debated, many large retailers "jumped ahead of their states" in paying their female employees a weekly minimum wage of eight dollars, often also enhancing workplace amenities (lunch rooms, locker rooms, training programs) as part of an effort to burnish their public images (Howard 2015: 47, 49–50). Concerned to project a softer public image, they found that it "was in their interest to give the impression that they . . . were the true populists and that consumption, not production, was the new domain of democracy" (Leach 1993: 117).

In addition, and different from Europe, American department stores were doing all they could to blur class divisions within the consuming public as well, innovating ways to allow shoppers at different income levels to all "shop under the same roof" (Leach 1993: 78). Many of them set up "bargain basements" in the early years of the twentieth century, areas of the store where working-class consumers could find affordable goods. These practices had been introduced in a few Chicago department stores already in the 1880s, but Filene's of Boston was especially famous for steeply discounting goods. The company's policy of "automatic" price markdowns institutionalized a strategy based on low margins and high turnover. Established

16. Emmet and Jeuck devote a full chapter to Sears's corporate welfare programs (chap. 9); on Wanamaker's personnel policies, see Leach 1993: 120–21.

in 1909, Filene's "automatic bargain basement" discounted goods at a rate of 30 percent each week, donating whatever was left after thirty days to a local charity (De Grazia 2005: 132). The success of this venture prompted other major department stores (e.g., Wanamaker's and, in a different way, Marshall Field's) to follow suit (Leach 1993: 78–79). Macy's did not have a separate bargain basement but it, too, was famous for slashing prices on select items to attract middle- and lower-income customers (Jacobs 2005: 31; Hower 1946: 332).

In sum, different competition regimes in the late nineteenth century generated important differences in the political-economic landscape, as Europe's more permissive competition policies facilitated the formation of strong producer group associations, while America's stricter antitrust rules actively disarticulated emerging producerist organizations and helped redirect the search for social peace away from producer-group accommodation and toward a consumerist alternative. Europe's producer group politics centered on the accommodation of competing organized interests, at the expense of higher prices for consumers. Political economic conflicts in the United States, by contrast, featured large retailers battling monopoly producers in the name of efficiency, while social reformers argued for social peace through consumption. Large retailers would play a key role in promoting levels of consumption in the 1920s that stood out in comparative perspective. And consumer credit would figure prominently in their strategies.

Retail and Credit-Fueled Consumption in the Interwar Period

Consumption did indeed take off in the United States in the interwar period, with the result that Americans—especially middle- and upper-class Americans—were enjoying household conveniences such as washing machines and vacuum cleaners long before their European counterparts. One reason for this is the expansion of installment selling on a scale unmatched in Europe (Logemann 2008: 529).[17] Automobiles were destined to dominate installment purchasing by the late 1920s, but installment credit in fact goes back much further. Manufacturers such as Singer Sewing Machine Company

---

17. Martha Olney's figures show that household debt began increasing in the opening years of the twentieth century (doubling between 1900 and 1920 from levels in the 4–6 percent range to 10 percent of household income; cited in Calder 1999: 18–19). The Federal Reserve did not begin tracking consumer debt until 1928, when it increased rather steadily from $6.5 billion that year to $45 billion by 1958, stalling only briefly in the Great Depression (Calder 1999: 9).

and McCormick (farm implements) were selling "on time" already in the nineteenth century (Calder 1999: 158–64). Particularly in rural areas, this was simply the only way to sell big-ticket manufactured goods in a context in which farmers could not pay for things until after the harvest (Calder 1999: 160). Installment selling (or "hire purchase" selling) was also well known in Europe at the time, having been introduced to Britain and Germany by Singer in the 1860s (Koenen 2002).

Unlike the manufacturers who worked through agents, the retailers who engaged in installment selling in this period were often sketchy operations that extended credit on outrageous and predatory terms. In the United States, most observers agree that retailers trading in factory-made furniture were pioneers in installment selling (Cox 1948: 62). In the late nineteenth century, so-called borax houses that offered low-quality furniture at high interest rates (disguised behind "easy" weekly payments) had given installment purchasing a bad name (Calder 1999: 57). But working-class families often had no other way to pull the funds together to furnish their homes, and so installment credit on such items became widespread.[18]

The diverging trajectories of credit financing in the United States and Europe is a topic that has received extensive attention in the literature and need not be reviewed here (Trumbull 2014; Logemann 2008; 2012b).[19] For present purposes, the key point is that consumer credit in Europe in the interwar period remained closely associated with poverty and inability to pay, while in the United States "motives of convenience and services to the customer" began to take root already in the interwar years (Logemann 2011: 539–40). In what follows, therefore, I wish simply to emphasize key differences to Europe and the central role played by large American retailers in promoting credit and lending legitimacy—indeed, luster—to credit-based consumption in this period.

SAVINGS OR CREDIT FOR THE MASSES?

Mass consumption requires mass purchasing power, based either on savings or credit. With industrialization, the rapidly expanding urban working classes became untethered from their families and communities—and financially left to their own devices. In both Europe and the United States,

18. Calder reports that an 1899 study of Boston retailing revealed that half of the city's furniture dealers sold on installment (1999: 56).

19. For a more detailed analysis of the evolution of credit in the United States specifically, see Carruthers 2022; Calder 1999; Hyman 2011; Hyman 2012.

predatory loan-shark lenders were quick to capitalize on the misfortunes of working-class families who fell on hard times, whether through unemployment, sickness, or just bad luck. Charitable institutions emerged in the nineteenth century to provide opportunities for the lower classes to put away small amounts of savings (earning modest interest) to encourage frugality and to protect the working poor from such loan sharks. In Europe, these initiatives served as a model for the creation of state-sponsored institutions to facilitate consumption through savings. In the United States, similar arrangements were blocked by banks and southern landowners, redirecting the efforts of philanthropic interests toward making credit available to the masses on less onerous terms. Thus credit, rather than savings, emerged in the United States as an important device for sustaining consumption in the interwar period, and American retailers played an active role in promoting its expansion (Hyman 2011: chap. 4; Hyman 2012: chap. 4).

Philanthropic institutions aiming to shield the working class from predatory loan sharks emerged in the industrializing urban hubs in the United States and Europe—London, Paris, and the American Northeast. Like their counterparts in Europe, the purpose of institutions such as the Philadelphia Savings Fund Society and the Provident Institution for Savings in the Town of Boston (both established in 1816) was to "encourage and promote industrious and provident habits among the poor; and to bring within the reach of every industrial person, the great advantage of public security and interest for small sums of money, without much expense of time or trouble" (Wolters, 2022: 31).

Given the tenuous incomes of their clientele, these arrangements were fragile to say the least, and many collapsed within a few years of their founding. However, European governments viewed them as a model to be emulated, and in the latter half of the nineteenth century they began to use their networks of post offices to provide basic financial services to their populations. In 1861 Britain became the first country to implement a postal savings institution, followed by France (1875), Italy (1875), the Netherlands (1881), Austria (1883), and Sweden (1884), with Germany bringing up the rear in 1909.[20] With the founding of postal savings, access to basic financial services

---

20. The best account of the flourishing (Europe) and failure (United States) of postal savings is by Lukas Wolters (2022), and I draw heavily on his account here. One possible explanation for the delayed introduction of postal savings in Germany is the early establishment of credit unions and savings banks (Sparkassen) as widely used alternatives. Schulze-Delitzsch, the bourgeois social reformer from chapter 2 who was instrumental in founding German's first consumer cooperatives, also pioneered the establishment of credit unions. These so-called people's banks allowed

for the lower classes diverged dramatically from that in the United States, as the number of savers grew rapidly and steadily, attracting hundreds of thousands of depositors year after year. In France and the United Kingdom, for example, millions of citizens had opened postal savings accounts by the turn of the century (Wolters 2022: 37).

These developments were not lost on American policymakers, and the precocious growth of postal services in the United States (already described in chapter 3) would have made the country a prime candidate for such a system to thrive. Nor did postal savings lack for advocates in late-nineteenth-century America. Unions (both the Knights of Labor and later the AFL) were strongly in favor of the introduction of a postal savings system, as it would facilitate worker savings, protect the laboring classes from loan sharks, and provide a counterweight to the power of private capital (Wolters 2022: 49). Farmers, too, were strongly supportive. The Greenback and Anti-Monopoly parties of the 1880s had included postal savings among their demands, and in the 1892 election the Populist Party—keen to limit the power of the country's financial capitalists—included in its platform the demand "for the safe deposit of the earnings of the people and to facilitate exchange" (Wolters 2022: 51).

Postmasters general, beginning already in the 1860s, looked upon the European postal savings systems with envy and repeatedly advocated for institutionalizing one in the United States as well. John Wanamaker, the retail magnate cum postmaster general who (as we saw in chapter 3) had been so successful in advancing parcel post, was a strong advocate, and he lobbied heavily in favor of postal savings during his tenure at the head of the USPS (Wolters 2022: 48). However, like his predecessors, Wanamaker's exhortations fell on deaf ears. A total of eighty bills calling for the introduction of postal savings (most sponsored by progressive Republicans in rural districts in the West and South) were introduced to Congress between 1873 and 1910, but all of them failed, foundering on ferocious resistance from an alliance of state unit bankers and southern landowners bound together by a shared desire to protect local privilege and thwart any centralization of power in the federal government (Wolters 2022: 51).

---

members to pool resources to create a common fund from which members could draw to cover expenses on a short-term basis. While the institutions Schulze-Delitzsch established were designed specifically for the urban working class, a constituency with low but regular income, Friedrich Wilhelm Raiffeisen created parallel institutions for the rural population. By 1913, over two million Germans belonged to credit unions (and Raiffeisen banks exist to this day).

Banks in the United States were chartered to operate within individual states, and so state bankers (organized into the powerful American Bankers Association) were keen to defend against the encroachment of a new financial center in Washington, DC.[21] Large landowners, for their part, opposed any system that would interfere with the role they played in controlling credit that, as we saw earlier, they used to maintain a system of racial domination and to reinforce their control over dependent sharecroppers. Both also worried that a national postal savings system would drain financial resources out of the regional economy and toward the Northeast.

When advocates of postal savings finally broke through in 1910, the system that emerged from the legislation in that year was so heavily compromised that it was effectively designed to fail. The American version of postal savings specifically kept capital local and in fact operated essentially as an appendage of local banks. Among other provisions, "a minimum of 65 percent of all deposits [to the US postal banking system] had to be offered as low-interest loans to local commercial banks" (Wolters 2022: 68). Earnings on postal savings deposits were set at a low level to allow local banks to make a substantial profit off of them, which also of course rendered them unattractive to depositors (Wolters 2022: 68). While there was a flurry of deposits in the two years immediately after the introduction of the system, the number of clients quickly fell off. The peak, in 1917, was a mere 670,000 account holders (a level that Britain had achieved in 1866 and France had achieved in 1885) and slumped to insignificance thereafter (Wolters 2022: 156–57, table A5). As the number of depositors declined, tens of thousands of postal savings banks (intended to be self-sufficient) were also forced to close, with the heaviest casualties in the South. As postal banking continued to grow in Europe, it stagnated in the United States at a negligible level—leaving most of the working poor, as before, unbanked and without access to even the most basic financial services.

AMERICAN RETAILERS AND CONSUMER CREDIT

The failure of postal savings in the United States left the country's growing urban working classes even more dependent on credit than their European counterparts and thus even more at the mercy of predatory lenders. Given the considerable expense associated with administering small loans combined with the high risk of default, commercial lenders were completely uninterested in

21. This account draws on the analysis in Wolters 2022: 52–61.

extending credit to individual consumers. But the existence of urban workers, who now lacked the usual financial fallbacks of family and community, meant that demand for small loans to provide support in emergencies was robust.

Most states had usury laws but did not enforce them vigorously, so it was easy for small lenders to avoid prosecution through various legal maneuvers (e.g., exorbitant fees that hid the interest) (Hyman 2011: 14–15). Moreover, enforcement depended on victims themselves bringing charges, a highly unlikely prospect given the clientele. Predatory lenders were thus free to deploy sketchy techniques, extending credit at high rates against property or garnishing wages.[22] Without recourse to other sources of credit in times of need, the urban working class was forced to accept whatever deals were on offer. In 1911, fully one in five workers borrowed from illegal lenders at some point in the year (Calder 1999: 118).

In the opening years of the twentieth century, sharp disparities in the terms on which the wealthy and the poor were able to secure credit and the predatory terms inflicted on the latter offended the sensibilities of American progressives and attracted the attention of prominent philanthropic foundations (Carruthers et al. 2012; Calder 1999). One strand of philanthropic work—spearheaded by Edward Filene, the progressive retail magnate we encountered earlier in this chapter—sought to promote the establishment of credit unions that would allow people of modest means to draw on a common pool of resources to finance purchases.[23] Consistent with the emphasis of some progressives on consumption as the key to social peace and prosperity, Filene saw credit unions as an important support for mass buying power (McQuaid 1976: 90). Articulating his logic in congressional testimony before the passage of the Federal Credit Union Act, Filene blamed the depression in the late nineteenth century in part on the failure of banks to extend the loans needed to support the purchasing power the economy needed:

> While the masses are so short of buying power that they cannot consume the products of our improved machines, a large section of the population is still hoarding money individually or putting it in banks where it is not being constructively employed. It can not be constructively employed,

---

22. Credit was often extended against future wages (the practice was called "salary buying," and failure to repay put debtors in peril since the creditors could approach their employers who might then fire the worker [see especially Bittman 2021]).

23. Filene became enamored of the idea "after observing how credit unions in India, Europe, and Canada enabled communities to provide their members with low-interest loans" (Jacobs 2005: 86).

in fact, unless the masses have adequate buying power; and because it cannot be so employed, we have not only unemployment, but the fear of unemployment, both of which still further reduce buying and aggravate the whole situation.[24]

Filene was instrumental in pushing through the first state legislation permitting the establishment of credit unions—in Massachusetts in 1921—but this came over a half century after similar institutions had been set up in Europe. Over the next nine years, thirty-eight states passed similar enabling legislation, and in 1934 the Federal Credit Union Act exempted them (as nonprofits) from income tax. However, credit unions never came to play the same role in the United States, as banking interests were again able to secure restrictions on their functions and membership. In particular, credit unions were not permitted to offer the full range of banking services and are still limited in size by a requirement that members share a "common bond of association," typically a shared employer or a common locality (Spicer 2022: 147–48).

Another strand of philanthropic work—more fruitful in the end—was led by the Russell Sage Foundation. The foundation was initially drawn to the credit union idea but quickly pivoted to efforts to reform small-loan lending (Carruthers et al. 2012; Calder 1999). The foundation's Department of Remedial Loans sponsored studies that showed that the application of existing usury laws was bound to drive legitimate actors out of business, leaving the field to illegal lenders. On the basis of this research, and working together with a newly created association of small-loan brokers who had an interest in bringing the sector out of the shadows,[25] the Russell Sage Foundation developed model legislation that called for a monthly interest rate of 3.5 percent (42 percent annual interest) to allow small lenders to operate openly and profitably (Carruthers et al. 2012; Anderson 2008). They then also set about promoting this model legislation in the states in an effort that eventually resulted in a total of thirty-four states adopting some version of the legislation over the next two decades.

But America's large retailers did not wait for the progressive reformers (or for that matter, banks) to solve the consumer credit problem.[26] As Car-

---

24. Testimony of Edward Filene, "Investigation of Economic Problems," Senate Committee on Finance (1933), p. 1142, https://congressional-proquest-com.libproxy.mit.edu/congressional/docview/t29.d30.hrg-1933-fns-0002?accountid=12492.

25. The Association of Small Loan Brokers, founded in 1916.

26. Banks in the United States were slow to extend credit to consumers and mostly demurred until the 1940s.

ruthers notes, as early as the late nineteenth century, American department stores were extending credit for a growing share of nondurable goods. By 1880, over half of the sales of Chicago's Field, Leiter & Co. (predecessor to Marshall Field & Co.) were made on credit (Twyman 1954: 129; Carruthers 2022: 306n23). (By contrast, Germany's major department stores remained firmly attached to cash sales and introduced installment plans only in the 1950s [Logemann 2011: 544].) Large American retailers pioneered the establishment of specialized credit departments that collected information on the purchasing and payment histories of individual consumers.[27]

In the interwar period, American retailers expanded credit not just through their own credit departments but also by exploiting "wide gaps in [the] regulatory armor" (Nugent and Henderson 1934: 102) through increasingly aggressive installment selling, which at the time was not covered by existing usury laws (Hyman 2011: 107). Indeed, installment credit was more important to the development of the American political economy than small-loan lending; in fact, in the 1920s, small loans were often used to pay off installment debt because only the latter was secured against property that consumers would lose if they failed to pay on time. However, installment credit—unlike small loans—completely eluded all regulation. And the key players driving its massive expansion were not progressive reformers or state legislators but manufacturers and retailers (Hyman 2011: 107–13).

Sears and other established mail-order houses had traditionally frowned on credit sales of all sorts, seeking instead to impress on customers that installment purchasing was a bad deal compared to the low prices they could offer on a cash-only basis. However, they faced competition not just from borax houses but also from more reputable competitors who recognized the attractions and got in the game. Thus, for example, Spiegel, a direct marketing dry-goods retailer founded in 1865 by a German immigrant, Joseph Spiegel, previously counted as a high-quality (cash-only) retailer. Under pressure from the likes of Sears, whose ever-expanding inventory was cutting into its sales, Spiegel's company distinguished itself by offering installment credit, promising customers "all the time you need to pay"

---

27. As credit was a central element in retail competition, the biggest retailers kept the information for themselves. Over time, however, the expansion of credit sales they inspired also explains the early institutionalization in the United States of what would grow into a national credit rating system. Organizations that emerged in the late nineteenth century to serve local retailers created national associations such as the National Association of Credit Men (founded in 1896) and the National Association of Retail Credit Agencies (1906) (Carruthers 2022: 7).

(though they mostly enforced a twelve-month limit), with the costs of credit embedded in marked-up pricing (Calder 1999: 175).

These developments were enough to bring Sears around to installment selling. Thus, in 1911, the company abandoned its "cash-only" policy and by 1917 was aggressively advertising "no money down" for a select but expanding range of goods. Sears's earlier "send no money" promotions had not represented a departure from its long-standing cash-only policies; it had just been a catchier way to advertise its usual cash-on-delivery policy. But the expansion of installment terms offered by other firms put pressure on Sears, as requests from its customers to purchase goods on credit rolled in (Emmet and Jeuck 1950: 264). By 1910 Sears had concluded that "it would be unwise to refuse terms any longer" (Emmet and Jeuck 1950: 265). With that, the company began (initially quietly without fanfare) offering a select group of goods on "easy monthly payment" terms—resulting in a huge surge in sales (the company sold three times as many pianos in that first year, for example).

Thus, well before bank-based consumer lending, sales finance corporations, credit ratings, and all the rest, retailers were competing with one another to make it easier for middle-class Americans (and working-class Americans with relatively stable incomes) to buy things on time. Already in 1917, Sears was inserting credit order blanks into every catalog it sent out, and this "application" consisted of just three questions: the length of time at the customer's current address, the customer's occupation, and two references (Emmet and Jeuck 1950: 268). The installment credit wave took off among large retailers, and, as Cox notes, "by 1920 even the most conservative retailers were beginning to sell on installments" (1948: 3).[28]

REGULATORY ENTREPRENEURSHIP AND
THE CREDIT EXPLOSION

While the sudden, sharp depression of 1920–21 prompted some to tighten credit (Sears, for example, scaled back the list of items offered on installment and introduced a slightly more elaborate credit questionnaire), it also provoked a great scramble among retailers for consumer dollars—and offering credit was a distinct advantage.[29] Indeed, after 1922, consumers were "engulfed in a sea of easy credit" (Leach 1993: 299). Lower-income families

---

28. Macy's was a notable holdout, insisting on cash-only sales until 1939 (Hower 1946: 404).

29. Louis Hyman's work is particularly important in illuminating the role of retailers and regulatory arbitrage in promoting credit purchasing in the interwar period (Hyman 2011: chap. 4; Hyman 2012: chap. 4).

were more likely to use installment plans to purchase durables such as furniture (and the poorest turned to installment even for semidurables such as clothing) (Cox 1948: 155–56), while middle- and upper-income families used them to acquire household conveniences their European counterparts could only dream of. By 1927, Sears was selling 15 percent of all goods on installment, with household equipment such as radios, refrigerators, and washers leading the way (Emmet and Jeuck 1950: 274).

Competition for sales to middle-class (skilled and salaried) workers drove a steady liberalization of the terms on which installment credit was being extended. A 1929 study by Rolf Nugent (director of the Russell Sage Foundation's Department of Remedial Loans) documented the trend toward ever-smaller down payments and longer repayment schedules. Between 1910 and 1929, the annual volume of retail installment purchases increased from $500 million to $7 billion. By 1925, Americans were purchasing 70 percent of their furniture, 75 percent of their radios, and 80 percent of their appliances on credit (Cross 2000: 29). Over the course of the decade, installment purchasing was no longer limited to goods such as vacuum cleaners and washing machines; it was also a means to acquire smaller items such as clothing and jewelry (Nugent and Henderson 1934: 93).[30]

Installment credit in the United States continued to grow in a legal gray zone, formally uncovered by prevailing usury laws that regulated interest rates on loans.[31] In an act of "regulatory entrepreneurship" (Pollman and Barry 2017), enterprising retailers exploited this gap to expand sales to consumers who had modest but steady incomes. Before the Uniform Small Loan Law, most small lending had spread illegally and underground. By contrast, retailer-sponsored installment credit expanded faster and openly despite the fact that installment pricing (which was higher—often far higher—than sales prices) was functionally equivalent to interest. Indeed, the expansion of installment credit depended crucially on active forbearance on the part of the judiciary, as state courts declined to apply usury laws to installment credit sales (Berger 1935; Hyman 2011: 31–32). The legal status of installment credit was explicitly tested at the Supreme Court, and in the case of

30. A study by the National Credit Retail Association in 1935 found that 90 percent of American department stores were selling at least some goods on installment (Cox 1948: 74).

31. By contrast, Germany had moved very early (in 1894) to attempt to regulate installment credit, partly at the behest of small retailers seeking to forestall competition (Logemann 2011: 533). Britain passed its first Moneylenders Act in 1900. It required that moneylenders register with the local magistrate, and, importantly, it gave courts powers "to dissolve agreements judged unfair," which many did, even before the more effective 1938 Installment Credit Act was passed (McFall 2016: 8).

GMAC v. Weinrich, the court offered no protection to the consumer because it assumed that this form of credit was flowing only to affluent borrowers for discretionary purchases (Hyman 2011: 32).

The same progressive reformers who were working tirelessly to bring the small-loan sector out of the shadows viewed the unregulated expansion of installment credit with alarm. Consumer loans were subject to government regulation (albeit, as noted, on terms with which the reformers took issue), but because of the way installment purchasing was linked to the sale of goods or services, it "had escaped any vestige of supervision" (Nugent and Henderson 1934: 101). After all, retailers had long extended credit informally—either to tide families over (as was the case with the rural merchants described previously) or as a courtesy (as in department stores that offered "open book credit" to preferred customers as a convenience so they could shop without carrying cash and then settle up at the end of the month) (Hyman 2012: 99–100; Nugent and Henderson 1934: 101). But the risk had traditionally been borne by the merchant. What was new was that installment sales now routinely included a price differential to cover the costs of the additional bookkeeping they required, and they came bundled as well with contractual provisions that allowed creditors to recover losses in the case of nonpayment, thus shifting the risk to the debtor (Nugent and Henderson 1934: 101).

Progressive reformers were especially concerned because the terms on which credit was being extended was widely divergent and mostly opaque (Cox 1948: chap. 12). Carrying charges were often stated in such a way that it was impossible for the consumer to know how much the credit was actually costing him. Over time, quoted rates came to cluster around 6 percent but with enormous variation in how this worked out in practice depending on the exact terms—which appeared in fine print if they appeared at all (Cox 1948: 118–21, 174–80, 193–94). It is a measure of the extent of controversy surrounding installment credit that in 1930, the National Forensic League had high school and college debaters across the nation arguing over whether installment credit was "socially and economically desirable" (Calder 1999: 111).

Debates notwithstanding, installment credit was already part of the retail mainstream (Calder 1999: 58).[32] For the lowest-income groups, installment

32. The results of a nationwide survey of retail credit carried out by the Department of Commerce at the request of the National Retail Credit Association suggested that over the years between 1925–27 installment sales in department stores increased by 16.8 percent, outpacing the growth in cash and open-book credit sales (though installment sales still accounted for a small part of their overall sales (under 6 percent) (Plummer 1930: 3).

buying had opened "the possibility of acquiring things which they would have wanted and could not otherwise have acquired because of the sheer self-denial necessary to save out of pitifully inadequate incomes the amount of the cash price." For consumers with larger and less precarious incomes, installment plans served more benignly as "an aid to their family budgeting" (Nugent and Henderson 1934: 99).[33] All income groups used installment credit, but those who relied on it most were neither the rich nor the very poor. Instead, they were primarily middle-income wage earners who could "offer as security for credit only the facts that they are earners and good moral risks [and cannot otherwise] obtain the kind of credit which depends in large part on property and social position" (Cox 1948: 404, see also table 56 on 400; Calder 1999: 57–59). And by the 1930s it was eminently clear that "installment selling is as much a part of American life as banking or steelmaking. It has been deeply woven into our economic fabric by many years of increasingly widespread use" (Nugent and Henderson 1934: 99).[34]

AMERICA TAKES VISA: US RETAIL AND REVOLVING CREDIT

This was not the end of the story, for competition in the 1920s also drove other forms of regulatory arbitrage as big retailers competed for middle-class dollars, introducing innovations that would result in the credit cards we carry today (on these developments, see Hyman 2011: chaps. 4 and 5; Hyman 2012: chap. 4). Already in the 1920s, some retailers began issuing so-called Charga Plates to a select group of preferred customers (Mandell 1990: xii).[35] The card's purpose—which complemented the open-book credit system already described—was to make it easy for employees to recognize the store's most prized customers. It was offered as a convenience to allow them to shop (and spend freely) without needing to carry cash (Mandell 1990: xii, 18).[36] A mark of preferred status, possession of such a card was associated with considerable prestige (Mandell 1990: 18), even if the expectation was

33. Economist Edwin Seligman's exhaustive 1927 empirical study of installment selling took an especially sanguine view of the massive expansion of this practice in this period (Seligman 1927).

34. Carruthers (2022: 306 n25) notes that by this time almost the entire retail sector relied on credit sales.

35. Produced in Boston by the Farrington Manufacturing Company, "these metal plates resembled the Army-issue dog tags and were, in fact, nothing more than reconfigured embossed-address plates" (Mandell 1990: 18).

36. The difference to Europe at this time was significant. In Germany and Britain, for example, the dominant form of credit was "trading checks," which carried stigma.

no different from that of regular open-book credit, in that customers were expected to pay the outstanding balance on their Charga Plate at the end of every month (Hyman 2012: 103).

Over the 1920s, intensified competition within an increasingly crowded retail market encouraged merchandisers to indulge open-account customers who did not pay the full balance on time. Why risk alienating your best and wealthiest clients? In what is one of the earliest precursors to today's revolving credit arrangements, Wanamaker's of Philadelphia adopted an explicit policy of allowing customers to repay their balances over four months (without interest) (Mandell 1990: 24). Other stores soon began offering similar flexibility but for a small price. For example, in 1938, Bloomingdale's introduced an extended payment plan called "permanent budget account." Under this plan, customers did not have to clear their balance every month, but "in return for this flexibility, the store would charge a small amount of interest" (Hyman 2012: 105).

Concerns about inflation during World War II prompted Roosevelt to rein in consumer spending by establishing some limits on installment purchasing through Regulation W under Section 23A of the Federal Reserve Act.[37] However, observant and opportunistic retailers simply expanded their use of open-book credit when they "realized that the government's regulations did not apply to this new kind of revolving credit" (Hyman 2012: 105). So, while some companies continued to collect the balance on their open-book credit at the end of the month, others instead adopted so-called option accounts in which a small interest fee was charged on the unpaid balance (Hyman 2011: 156–63).[38]

In other words, when confronted with government efforts to curtail consumer spending, big retailers found ways "to obey the regulation in name but to break it in practice" (Hyman 2011: 99). Over a very short period of time, revolving credit had largely replaced the installment purchase plans under which consumers had previously bought consumer durables such as furniture and appliances. Glancing forward: by 1949, 75 percent of major retailers offered revolving credit programs of one sort or another (Hyman 2012: 106). The postwar boom in consumer spending in the 1950s provoked such intense

37. The Fed established minimum down payments (typically one-third of the total price of the good) and maximum contract lengths (typically eighteen months) on installment purchases of a broad but finite set of consumer durables (see Hellerstein 1942 for the specifics and the list of consumer goods it covered).

38. They were called "option accounts" because they gave shoppers the option of paying off the entire balance or carrying over part of the debt (Hyman 2012: 111)

competition among retailers that the government finally stopped trying to regulate these practices, which by 1953 were "ubiquitous" (Hyman 2011: 130). By 1959, 88 percent of all department stores offered their customers revolving accounts (Ryan, Trumbull, Tufano 2011: 474).

To preview further: enormous demand for home furnishings and intensified competition for consumer dollars in the 1950s drove retailers to offer more credit, to more customers, and on ever-more generous terms. Large chain department stores angling for new customers no longer reserved special privileges for well-known, loyal customers. Instead, they took to sending their Charga Plates to new suburban homeowners as soon as they moved in (Hyman 2011: 149). These credit operations almost never made money (Hyman 2012: 119). Revolving credit accounts were expensive to administer; repossession of goods was clearly not an option (unlike with installment credit) since the credit was unattached to any specific item and because many of the "soft goods" sold in this way were inherently nonrecoverable. The point was not to make money on the credit services, but rather to bolster sales by getting your card in the hands of the customers most likely to spend—and as many of them as possible. After 1958, competition had stiffened to the point that most stores abolished all limits on their revolving credit accounts.

Banks and financial services companies followed the big retailers into the credit card business, providing the service to smaller retailers or discounters that did not have the resources to manage their own credit operations (Mandell 1990: xviii).[39] And while it took some time for the large retailers to give up their own cards,[40] the share of American families with retail store cards declined relative to those with bank cards over time (see the figures in Durkin 2000: 625).[41]

39. Bank of America (BankAmericard) was the first to initiate a credit card offering in 1958 and proceeded to flood American households with unsolicited credit cards, leading to widespread fraud and losses (Manning 2000: 84–85). But banks' early forays into the credit card business mostly flopped in this period (see especially Hyman 2011: 145–48). While a few that organized around travel and entertainment for businesspeople (such as Diners Club) survived, mostly the bank credit cards failed because department stores refused to honor them.

40. Mandell points out (1990: 92) that "bank cards were not honored at any of the larger retail chains" until the end of the 1970s (1990: 92). In 1981, a study found that of the one hundred largest department stores in the country, only forty-eight took bank cards (Mandell 1990: 101). Sears held out longest, until 1993 (Manning 2000: 83).

41. Although American credit card companies would make some headway in Europe, the main card in use there—the EC Card—is in reality a debit card linked to a bank account, not a credit instrument as in the United States (Knacke 2008, 2011). Consumers in some countries actively resisted the encroachment of American credit card companies. In Germany, for example,

Conclusion

The early decades of the twentieth century were crucial for anchoring a consumerist political economy in the United States. Europe's more permissive competition regime had encouraged the formation of associations—of farmers, workers, and firms—and in this way, facilitated the emergence of a politics that, in the interwar period, came to center on contests among organized producer groups. In the United States, by contrast, the judiciary's strict stance against horizontal coordination frustrated emerging producerist organizations. In this context, a growing chorus of voices—including organized labor, women's groups, social reformers, advertisers, philosopher-pundits, philanthropists, and politicians—began to see consumption as the key to bridging the country's class, regional, and racial divides.

Mass retailers participated in—and benefited massively from—this consumerist turn. Indeed, they played a starring role in the Progressive Era project of seeking social peace through consumption. They signed on as enthusiastic allies in government efforts to rein in wartime inflation and to combat waste and inefficiency through "rational," "modern" distribution methods. And they actively promoted the growth of consumer credit well before banks ventured into this area. Exploiting regulatory gaps and legal gray zones, large retailers innovated new forms of credit as they sought advantage in the intensely competitive environment of the 1920s. Yet even as some large retailers flourished by incorporating credit into their competitive strategies, other, low-cost retailers who shunned credit would also thrive in the United States in this period. These are the developments to which I now turn.

"protesters marched in the street in opposition to Citibank's proposal to bundle discount rail and Visa cards in 1995; the program was interpreted as an arrogant attempt to impose credit cards on people who did not want them" (Manning 2000: 301). Europeans generally carry far less plastic than their American counterparts—one or two per person in Europe versus, on average, four in the United States. See "Credit Card Declined Codes: What Do They Mean?" November 7, 2019, Dual Payments, https://shiftprocessing.com/credit-card/; Patrick Whatman, "Credit Card Statistics 2022: 65+ Facts for Europe, UK, and US," December 1, 2021, Spendesk, https://www.spendesk.com/blog/credit-card-statistics/.

PART III

Contestation and Opposition to Emergent Retail Capitalism

5

Low-Cost Retailing and the Battles over the "Right to Cut Prices"

At the same time that large department stores were offering Americans the opportunity to purchase consumer goods on increasingly attractive install-ment credit terms, emerging new discount chain stores were finding other ways to promote mass consumption through cash purchases at rock-bottom prices. Grocery chains were especially prominent, and the oldest, the Great Atlantic and Pacific Tea Company (A&P, founded in 1859), was by far the largest. By 1930 it commanded fully 40 percent of the food market (Schrag-ger 2005: 1013). Indeed, with 15,737 outlets across the country, A&P was the fifth-largest corporation in the United States (Luchsinger and Dunne 1978: 51; Schragger 2005: 1013). Besides A&P, however, drugstore and variety store chains also proliferated rapidly in the interwar period. Among the most important companies to emerge at that time in the United States—some of which are still around today—were Woolworths (variety), Kresge (variety), Walgreen Drug, J. C. Penney (dry goods), Piggly Wiggly (groceries), and Kroger Grocery and Baking Co., to name a few.[1]

---

1. In 1886, there were just two chains with five stores. By 1912 the figure had risen to 177 chain store companies with 2,235 outlets, and by 1929 it was 1,500 companies with almost 70,000 outlets (Leach 1993: 273).

Many of the large discount chains that would rise to dominance in the interwar period were founded in the late nineteenth or early twentieth centuries, but they expanded rapidly after 1921 by launching operations in smaller towns in the South and West, areas where other large urban retailers had no presence. Chain store retailing in the United States accelerated between 1920 and 1930, when the number of outlets rose dramatically, from 30,000 to 150,000 (Schragger 2005: 1020).[2] In this same stretch of time, the share of national retail sales captured by the chains rose from 4 percent to 20 percent (by 1933, to over a quarter) (Moreton 2009: 19; Schragger 2005: 1013 and 1020; Strasser 1989: 222; Palamountain 1955: 7). Woolworths almost doubled its number of outlets between 1919 and 1929, by which time the company was second only to General Electric in total turnover (De Grazia 2005: 165). In dry goods, J. C. Penney (founded in 1902) also grew spectacularly, positioning itself as a lower-cost department store tailored to the budgets of Americans of modest income.[3]

In Europe, where small merchants were both better organized than in the United States and had powerful political allies, chain stores encountered more effective resistance, and variety discount chains (five-and-dimes) were the object of some of the most intense regulation (De Grazia 1998: 74). By the mid-1930s, variety chains accounted for just 7 percent of retail turnover in Britain, 1.3 percent in France, and 1.5 percent in Germany, compared to 23 percent in the United States (De Grazia 2005: 170). A key reason for this disparity is that the politics that accompanied the arrival of the chains played out very differently on the two sides of the Atlantic.

Conflicts in Europe, as in the United States, centered on two issues: resale price maintenance arrangements, and special taxes and restrictions on large retailers. In accounts of the United States, these two conflicts are often treated together because they overlapped in time, but distinguishing them is important because each involved a different political coalition and the conflicts over each of them followed a different logic. Among other reasons, this is important for unraveling why the South took radically different positions on the two issues—siding with chains over resale price maintenance but bitterly opposing them in the conflicts over taxation. This chapter and the next lay out the issues and the coalitions and elaborate the causes and consequences of America's distinctive trajectory.

2. See especially Lebhar 1959: chap. 3, which documents this growth.
3. Lebhar (1959: 53) provides growth figures for all the major chains.

Resale Price Maintenance in Comparative Perspective

Resale price maintenance (RPM) is a practice though which manufacturers commit retailers to charge a specific (usually minimum) price for their products. In the interwar period, such arrangements were often promoted by producers of patented goods who wanted to protect the reputation of their brands; fixed prices (and guaranteed margins) also incentivized retailers to carry their products. From the perspective of brand manufacturers, discounters' cut-rate pricing policies blurred the difference between higher-quality goods and lower-priced alternatives, thus devaluing the brands that these producers (along with the high-priced ad men they worked with) had carefully cultivated. While they understood that lower prices might produce a temporary bump in sales, the result over time would be a decline in demand as consumers lost confidence in the quality claims of the brand (Allender 1993: 221–23; Kanter and Rosenblum 1955: 328; *Yale Law Journal* 1959).

Related to this, low-cost retailers threatened the distribution networks these manufacturers relied on to reach consumers by causing small independent outlets to drop their products in the face of price competition they could not match. Small manufacturers of specialized or niche goods were especially dependent on the existence of a broad network of outlets since big discount retailers virtually by definition carry only those products that already have proven broad market appeal (Allender 1993: 226). But even the largest manufacturers worried that they might find their trade "in the hands of powerful and aggressive mass merchandisers" with monopsony power to push them around (Pope 1983: 95–96). Heavy reliance on a few big retailers to get their goods to customers renders manufacturers vulnerable to holdup; as Allender notes; "it is in the trademark owners [*sic*] interest to distribute its products through many small retailers, each without significant bargaining power" (1993: 227).

Small independent merchants also benefited from resale price maintenance arrangements since RPM provides relief from price competition generally, including, of course, the intensified price competition that invariably accompanies the entry of larger, more efficient retailers. Larger rivals lose their cost advantage if all retailers are bound by RPM to charge the same price for a given product. In this sense, RPM arrangements in the interwar period often reflected—or created—an alliance of interests between small independent retailers and brand manufacturers of trademarked goods against large low-cost retailers advocating for "the right to cut prices" (Seligman and Love 1932: 90). This period thus saw not just battles between small retailers and their larger and more efficient rivals; it also featured the unfolding of an important tug-of-war between brand manufacturers and cost-cutting retailers. This was a conflict in which struggles over resale price maintenance would play an important role and one in which America's large low-cost retailers would ultimately prevail.

The politics of RPM in the United States in the interwar period diverged sharply from those in Europe, and for reasons that can be traced both to differences in market conditions (product and labor markets) and to the vastly different legal regimes governing RPM in this period. In general, periods of high consumer demand give power to producers in the producer-distributor relationship since distributors are essentially competing for supplies. Economic downturns flip the scales, as manufacturers (especially those with high fixed costs) rely on their distributors to carry and push their products and often need to offload surpluses. Depending on how and by whom they are enforced, RPM arrangements can affect this logic and these relationships, and that is where different legal regimes come into the picture. Europe and the United States were mirror images of one another in the first half of the twentieth century. In Europe's coordinated market economies, minimum price resale agreements were perfectly legal into the post–World War II period. These agreements were also imbricated in a broader pattern of coordination (described in chapter 4) among well-organized producer groups, and this is why they often continued to be enforced informally even after the legal protections around them were lifted.

In the United States, by contrast, RPM was *per se* illegal in interstate trade beginning in 1911, and price-cutting remained a problem for most brand manufacturers even after a large number of states legalized the practice in the late 1930s. The analysis below makes clear that the meaning and valence of resale price maintenance is heavily context-dependent and hinges not just on market dynamics but also, crucially, on the structure of the industry (degree of organization and coordination among producers, retailers, and workers). It also underscores how the effectiveness of laws governing RPM depended on the strength of other institutions that either undermined (United States) or supported (Europe) the ability of countervailing interests to enforce such laws.

RESALE PRICE MAINTENANCE IN EUROPE

In Europe, resale price maintenance arrangements were legal, widespread, and collectively enforced through trade associations until well into the postwar period (e.g., until 1964 in the United Kingdom, 1974 in Germany).

Courts in Europe saw no problem with such arrangements. Consistent with the more permissive competition regimes described in earlier chapters, they supported RPM by holding "steadfastly" to the principle of freedom of contract, including by recognizing agreements that under American law were considered anticompetitive (Gerber 1985: 5). And in line with the general producerist orientation of the law, courts in Europe were not so much concerned with ensuring low prices or even "fair and open competition" (after all, cartels were ubiquitous) as they were with the question of whether prices were "justified" in terms of affording both producers and distributors a reasonable (but not excessive) profit (Froelich 1939: 449).

In Europe, then, RPM was part of the broader pattern of "organized" capitalism described in the previous chapter. However, RPM arrangements were not just legal in Europe's coordinated market economies, but also in Britain, a fellow liberal market economy and one that shares America's common-law tradition. The organizational vehicle through which these arrangements operated there was the British Proprietary Articles Trade Association. This organization, founded in 1896, brought together manufacturers, wholesalers, and retailers who jointly administered and policed a list of protected prices on trademarked goods (Yamey 1952; Grether 1934: 620–21). The way it worked is that manufacturers set the prices at which they wanted their products sold. Retailers then monitored prices, notifying the association when they learned of price-cutting by any of their competitors. The association would then collectively enforce the manufacturer's price by putting the offending retailer on a "stop list," which obliged all association members to stop supplying that vendor (Grether 1934; Grether 1939: 335).[4]

Such practices were not even questioned until 1919, when David Lloyd George's government responded to postwar price inflation by appointing a Standing Committee on Trusts in 1920 to "inquire into and report on certain trades or industries" (Rees 1922). The committee, however, proved "generally sympathetic to the system of price maintenance" (Shaw et al. 2000: 1981). It argued that in times of excess demand, fixed retail prices dampened inflationary pressures and tended "to ensure to all classes, including labour employed in manufacture and distribution, a fair rate of remuneration for the services respectively performed by them" by preventing "speculating middlemen" from capitalizing on market fluctuations to capture rents that were really due to consumers, traders, and manufacturers (Yamey 1966:

---

4. Producers could also appeal to the courts to issue an injunction or sue for damages.

255). In times of excess supply, the committee reasoned, producers would be forced by competition to adjust their prices anyway.

As on the continent, British courts gave primacy to firms' broad freedom of contract, and violation of price stipulations in agreements between manufacturers and dealers (including RPM contracts) were subject to a right of action (Grether 1934: 621). Moreover, because Britain's system of "collective laissez faire" recognized firms' "right to combine" in defense of trade interests, the courts also recognized the right to organize secondary boycotts to enforce these restrictive agreements (Grether 1934: 621).[5] Mercer notes that, in this period, "the trend of legal judgements was 'to assist rather than put down restrictive arrangements.' Resale price maintenance agreements were sometimes held enforceable in the courts, while traders damaged by stop lists or boycotts could expect little help from the courts" (Mercer 1995: 48).

Two further government committees charged with looking into the state of competition in Britain (in 1929 and 1931) similarly saw no need to interfere with the rights of producers in this area, nor any case "for immediate legislation to restrain possible abuses resulting from combines" (Mercer 1995: 48; Yamey 1966: 256). In both cases, the committee reports concluded that the disadvantages of RPM (e.g., cost to consumers) did not justify government intervention to depart from the status quo, which had its own advantages (e.g., mitigating destructive price competition, protecting quality goods) (Grether 1934: 622). Commenting in 1932 on the difference between the rather sanguine view prevailing in the UK compared to the heated discussion of RPM unfolding in the United States at that time, Scottish economist D. H. MacGregor noted that although RPM arrangements had come under review twice in Britain since the war, the committees "have not found anything in it which would be worth special legislation. . . . it is here regarded as an interesting aspect of competitive practice in which there is nothing to get excited about" (MacGregor 1932: 455). Parliamentary debates on legislation proposed in 1937 that was intended to restrict the growth of large retailers (including, notably, the cooperatives) included worries about the potential impact that monopsony power in the retail market could have on British manufacturing (Shaw et al. 2000: 1984).

Historians disagree on whether small retailers or manufacturers were the instigators for RPM in Britain. Yamey and Jefferys both suggest that

---

5. The issue of contention was not the right to enforce prices but only the methods of enforcement.

retailers led the way (Yamey 1952; 1966: 251; Jefferys 1954: 38). Tracking the evolution of RPM in three sectors, Yamey argues that traditional retailers canvassed manufacturers "intensely," urging them to adopt RPM, and sought to nudge them into action "by diverting sales to brands which were price-maintained from brands which were not" (Yamey 1966: 251). Jefferys also argues that retailers led the charge but notes that, in the context of fierce price competition in the late nineteenth and early twentieth centuries, manufacturers were not particularly hard to persuade: "[Though the] most vociferous pressure for the introduction of such a system came from the retailers, the manufacturers and wholesalers would not appear to have been unduly reluctant" (Jefferys 1954: 38). Mercer (1995) contests the claim that retailers were the instigators and suggests instead that manufacturers were the ones who took the initiative. Either way, all agree that the alliance between producers and distributors was crucial to the success of these arrangements.

What is also uncontested is that RPM remained pervasive in Britain and indeed expanded dramatically in the interwar years (Jefferys 1954: 53–54; Grether 1934: 635). A report commissioned by the Home Office Committee of Inquiry into Proposals to Amend the Shops Act estimated that the share of consumer spending represented by goods under RPM agreements rose from between 2 and 3 percent in 1900 to 38 percent by 1938 (Kay et al. 1984: 16).[6] The expansion of RPM tracked the growth of British trade associations: "This important increase in the extent of [RPM] was accompanied by a growth in the numbers and representativeness of trade associations in the distributive trades. These associations were often directly or indirectly concerned both with the agreements as to the prices and margins involved in any system of resale price maintenance and with the enforcement of the agreed practices" (Jefferys 1954: 54). Mercer provides figures on the number of trade associations and the reason for their formation. About one-third of trade associations that were founded in Britain over the period up to 1950 were formed at least in part to maintain prices (Mercer 1995: 24; table 2.8).

British cartels were far less formalized than their counterparts in other European countries (German cartels, for example, often had a supervisory committee or sales agency) (Mercer 1995: 31–32). But, as in Germany,

---

6. Jefferys's estimates are a bit lower; he suggests that the share of total consumer expenditure represented by goods under RPM agreements rose between 1900 and 1938 from about 3 percent to nearly 30 percent (1954: 53–54). Yamey (1966: 253) also cites a rough estimate that between 27 and 35 percent of all consumer goods in the UK in 1938 were sold at manufacturer-recommended prices.

enforcement through trade associations was nonetheless quite effective. A 1949 Board of Trade report "concluded that collective resale price maintenance had 'turned price maintenance from a reasonable means of preventing damage to well-known quality brands . . . into a comprehensive system for regulating and policing entire industries'" (Mercer 1995:18–19). A survey of industrial trade associations in the 1950s (conducted by the research group Political and Economic Planning, or PEP) found that "price fixing was the raison d'être" of British trade associations (Mercer 1995: 23).

Despite the impact on consumers, the Conservative Party—which was close to industry—was largely on board with these arrangements, spooked as they were by Britain's chronic problems of overproduction and declining international competitiveness. The Labour Party was more critical of price maintenance, but it was also cross-pressured. The cooperatives that served the working class wanted RPM abolished. Since many producers refused to supply them (viewing the cooperative dividend as a form of price-cutting), the cooperatives saw RPM as a conspiracy against working-class consumers (Mercer 1995: chap. 8). However, the Labour Party was also sensitive to fears articulated by the trade unions that ending the practice would trigger widespread unemployment among shopworkers, with negative knock-on effects for working conditions generally. The unions also worried that any attack on price maintenance (as "price-fixing") could easily escalate into an attack on their own collective rights to set wages and working conditions (Mercer 1995: 156, 171).

Independent retailers and brand manufacturers both benefited from RPM. The most authoritative study of British retailers (by Jefferys) suggests that the overall result was to shift the terms of competition from price to quality, in both products and retailing services. "In trades where practically all the products were manufacturer-advertised or price-maintained . . . the large-scale retailers had no alternative but to sell the same goods at the same prices as competing retailers" (Jefferys 1954: 93). Small merchants could ride on the coattails of the manufacturers' own advertising while their large competitors were deprived of the opportunity to undercut them on price. Hence, to the extent that manufacturers "were successful in securing a demand for their products, and in so far as the small-scale rather than the large-scale retailer stocked and sold the articles, the development of manufacturer branding, advertising and price fixing tended to operate to the advantage of the small-scale retailer" (Jefferys 1954: 93). Since "large-scale retailers in the interwar years no longer had a significant selling-price advantage over the small-scale retailers," competition centered more on service (though large retailers could also gain an edge by securing the best locations and offering perks such as credit) (Jefferys 1954: 82 and 97).

It was not until 1956 that Britain passed legislation (the Restrictive Practices Act) that made collective enforcement of fixed resale prices illegal. But this law also strengthened the hand of the manufacturer in his individual efforts at enforcement as compensation for the elimination of collective enforcement (Yamey 1966: 274). Previously, individual manufacturers could turn to the courts to enforce their resale prices only against those distributors with whom they themselves had a contract, but the new law gave "the manufacturer the right to enforce his resale price condition against any distributor who 'acquires the goods with notice of the condition' as if he had been a party to the contract of sale with the manufacturer" (Yamey 1966: 274, 277). RPM thus lived on in Britain for another few years, as individual manufacturers enlisted select retailers as outlets for their goods, assuring them of high margins in exchange for upholding the manufacturer's prices.

In 1964 that version of RPM was eliminated with the passage of the 1964 Resale Prices Act. This law marked a more profound change, for it prohibited RPM entirely, though with some goods exempted. However, whereas exemptions from the 1956 law could be granted to take account of the interest of shopkeepers or shopworkers, the 1964 bill allowed exemptions only where they operated to the benefit of consumers (Yamey 1966: 290–91).[7] After 1964, all forms of RPM gradually faded in Britain (Mercer 2017).

RPM was also prevalent and in fact even stronger in Europe's coordinated market economies. In Sweden, for example, RPM was "allowed to develop perfectly freely" until the mid-1950s (Trolle 1966: 103; Kjølby 1966). Trolle notes that "by far the most widespread form of [RPM] in Sweden was that in which the supplier—normally the producer—determine[d] fixed prices which the retailer must neither exceed nor fall below" (1966: 105). Enforcement involved the same kinds of arrangements described by Grether for the UK—either producers joining together to set and enforce the prices for their goods, or retailers coordinating with one another to decide the prices at which goods were sold—supported by agreements with producers "to ensure that the prices thus determined were respected, if necessary by withholding supplies" (Trolle 1966: 105).

---

7. Yamey, himself an opponent of all restraints on greater efficiencies in distribution, remained unimpressed, for, as he noted, local governments still exercise controls over the establishment and extension of shopping centers and sites, which he sees as another factor constraining the development of more efficient distribution in Britain (Yamey 1966: 298).

Such arrangements ran up against collective action problems in periods of intense competition (as, for example in the 1920s), but RPM "developed rapidly" after 1931, when the government passed a law against "unfair competition" (Trolle 1966: 107) While policymakers had declined to bow to pressure from trade associations to include in this law prohibitions on unfair price competition specifically, the government implicitly sanctioned the defense of prices through collective action by firms themselves (Trolle 1966: 107–8). By the start of World War II, "practically all branded goods of importance were sold under [RPM]" (Trolle 1966: 108). During the war, government-imposed price controls worked in tandem with existing RPM arrangements and indeed expanded them beyond branded goods (Trolle 1966: 108–9). Consumers and retailers alike grew accustomed to uniform prices, and in 1945, a "uniform price board" was established "in anticipation of a postwar revival of competition." This board, which included representatives of all the important trade associations, policed and enforced prices by withholding supplies from retailers who undercut the prices of goods under RPM (Trolle 1966: 109).[8]

RPM was ruled unlawful in Sweden in 1954, but even then manufacturers and distributors were still free to suggest resale prices so long as it was clear that these were not mandatory and binding. Firms were also free to coordinate informally around recommended prices, and indeed retail and trade associations often encouraged compliance by distributing these recommendations to their members (Trolle 1966: 140).[9] As Trolle notes, the purpose of the new law "was not to prohibit restrictive trade practices as such, but primarily to remove any possible injurious effects of such practices" by making sure that no legal obstacles stood in the way of competitors who wanted to enter the market or to reduce prices on existing lines (Trolle 1966: 103, 142). While the prices were entirely voluntary after 1954, studies by the Price and Cartel Office indicated that adherence was nonetheless high (sometimes as high as 70–90 percent for the products included in the studies) (Trolle 1966: 141).

The story for Denmark is similar. There, RPM had originally been initiated by producers, though retailers soon discovered the benefits it held for

8. In the late 1940s, in industries featuring a large number of branded goods such as pharmaceuticals, photographic equipment, and the like, the share of goods under RPM was around 80 percent; for groceries (where, for example, cooperatives were active and did not participate in RPM) it was lower, between 35 and 45 percent (Trolle 1966: 110).

9. Nonmembers such as consumer cooperatives, department stores, mail order houses, and discount retailers were free to ignore these guidelines (Trolle 1966: 141).

them as well, especially in periods when intense competition veered into cutthroat pricing (Trolle 1966: 149). Danish firms had been so enamored of the advantages of these arrangements that they had successfully pressed for a law (the Competition Act of 1912) to go beyond simply allowing manufacturers to protect standard pricing (through collective bans and black lists) by rendering price-cutting illegal (Kjølby 1966: 150). Though that particular law did not survive (it was modified in 1918 and then reversed in 1926), the courts continued to support RPM contracts so long as they were not seen as entrenching dominant producers (Kjølby 1966: 150). As Kjølby points out, the obligation to observe contractual terms and conditions, including prices, "could be imposed separately by the individual supplier in his contract with the various dealers, or they could be imposed collectively by several suppliers. Sometimes such arrangements were combined with agreements between the retail trade associations and the suppliers' organisations on concerted action to be taken against price-cutting resellers" (1966: 150).

Such arrangements remained legal in Denmark until 1955, at which point a new Monopolies and Restrictive Practices Control Act rendered enforced observance of prices illegal. Boycotts and refusals to supply were now out of bounds, but, as in Sweden, suggested or recommended prices were still legal as long as compliance was voluntary. But here too, coordination through trade associations often supported high levels of compliance even after the legal protections for RPM were lifted. While empirical evidence is scant, Kjølby cites a government study of the grocery trade, where compliance in Denmark was 85 percent and in Sweden 90 percent (in Norway 95 percent) for a majority of goods included in the study (Kjølby 1966: 166). Writing in the mid-1960s, Kjølby—himself a critic of RPM—found it "disturbing" that it had "aroused surprisingly little discussion" that "the ban on [RPM] is undermined by widespread compliance with manufacturers' price recommendations" (Kjølby 1966: 167).

In Germany as well, RPM was legal throughout the early twentieth century and indeed until 1974, when a new competition law rendered most such arrangements illegal (Gesetz gegen Wettbewerbsbeschränkung, or GWB).[10] Fixed consumer goods pricing had first appeared toward the end of the nineteenth century, initiated by manufacturers and producers of branded goods.[11] Brand manufacturers founded the Trademark Protection

---

10. Books are still under RPM in Germany.

11. The earliest examples include stone construction sets for children (1880s) and Karl August Lingner's Odol mouthwash (1893). The latter is still sold today (Logemann 2012a: 90–91).

Association (*Markenschutzverband*) in 1903 to defend (via joint boycotts) retail prices (Seligman and Love 1932: 492), but price maintenance arrangements were also organized and enforced by sectoral trade associations (Kühnert 2009). The country's first cartel law in 1923 did not ban resale price maintenance arrangements, though it did provide for government oversight and mechanisms to intervene where organized business activities were seen as endangering economic life or social welfare.

It was only under the occupation after World War II that the Allies (specifically the Americans) sought to prohibit these arrangements as part of a broad decartelization policy. Even then, however, intense lobbying by the Trademark Protection Association secured an exemption for RPM under Germany's first postwar competition law, passed in 1956. This new law did require companies to register their prices with a newly founded competition authority (Bundeskartellamt), and that agency had the power to enforce against "abusive" practices (Teupe 2016: 258). But RPM itself remained legal until 1974, when it was banned in its entirety in the second reform of the anticartel law (2. Kartellgesetznovelle) (Epple 2014: 175–86). As in Scandinavia, however, informal compliance (e.g., based on price lists distributed to retailers) often continued after the legal ban (Trumbull 2006a: 153). In 1975, the Bundeskartellamt investigated these practices but ultimately concluded that "protection of brands and distribution, not protection of the consumer, is . . . still the predominant criterion for interpreting the [new competition law]" (Trumbull 2006a: 153).

RESALE PRICE MAINTENANCE IN THE UNITED STATES

The situation in the United States in the early twentieth century was radically different because the kinds of strategies that shored up RPM in Europe ran afoul of prevailing antitrust laws. Coordinated enforcement involved arrangements that the courts viewed as collusive acts in restraint of trade, and, as such, they were *per se* illegal. While small American manufacturers struggled to carve out a space for themselves in highly competitive consumer markets, the country's largest manufacturers turned to heavy advertising to defend their brands (Seligman and Love 1932: 12–13). Unlike their smaller counterparts, they could maintain a diverse distribution network by refusing to sell to price-cutting retailers while also cultivating a loyal customer base that was admonished to "accept no substitutes." Enforcement of prices, however, was entirely up to individual manufacturers and involved lengthy and expensive legal battles. Thus, in the United States, RPM largely failed to help small producers and retailers and mostly devolved into a protracted conflict between oligopolistic manufacturers and large low-cost retailers over what the latter considered their "right to sell cheaply" (Hower 1946: 353; Seligman and Love 1932: 90).

As discussed previously, the Supreme Court's interpretation of the Sherman Act had already weakened trade associations among small manufacturers (Spillman 2012; Thelen 2020), and the court was also decisive in suppressing RPM arrangements by interpreting such contracts as horizontal combinations operating in restraint of trade. Already in 1906, a circuit court had invalidated an agreement among drugmakers and retailers that established "an elaborate system of surveillance to stop price cutting"—that is, exactly the kind of arrangement operating in a range of sectors in Britain (Pope 1983: 96). Around this time as well, the American Publishers Association (APA) was locked in a battle with Macy's, which was ignoring the APA prices, sometimes going to great lengths to evade them.[12] Confronted with an association boycott, the retailer went on the offensive against what it called the "book trust" and ultimately prevailed in 1913, when the Supreme Court held that the publishers' association had formed a combination in restraint of trade (Hower 1946: 356).[13]

The landmark Supreme Court case in this area came earlier, however, in 1911, in *Dr. Miles Medical Co. v. John D. Park & Sons Co.* The dispute involved a small producer of a popular patent medicine that had sought to bind retailers to minimum resale prices for its goods as a way to protect the value of its carefully cultivated brand. Lower-level courts had previously upheld Dr. Miles's price protection plan, for example, in 1903, when the New York Court of Appeals "unanimously ruled that doing away with price competition among dealers was not in restraint of trade because there was no evidence of coercion or fraud" (Phillips Sawyer 2018: 98).

Based on these precedents, Dr. Miles Medical Co. confidently brought suit against John D. Park & Sons, a major wholesale drugstore that was advertising the company's products at a heavy discount, using them as "loss

---

12. The company set up a private checking account for the head of its book department to source titles from out-of-town wholesalers, retailers, or buying agents (Hower 1946: 357).

13. An earlier decision, in 1908, waged by Macy's against book publishers, had established that the publishers holding copyrights could neither fix the price at which their books were sold nor combine with others to do so. See "Publishers Cannot Fix Price of Books; R. H. Macy & Co. Win Victory in Highest Court for Which They Have Fought Six Years," *New York Times*, June 2, 1908, https://www.nytimes.com/1908/06/02/archives/publishers-cannot-fix-price-of-books-rh -macy-co-win-victory-in.html.

leaders" to attract customers into the store. However, Park's lawyers creatively invoked previous judicial interpretations of the Sherman Act to argue that the Dr. Miles company had essentially "created a horizontal 'combination between dealers' inimical to free competition" (Phillips Sawyer 2018: 101). The Supreme Court sided with Park & Sons, finding that "the effect [of the price protection plan] was market coercion—and that Dr. Miles's property right in the secret-processed good did not protect it from antitrust prosecution" (Phillips Sawyer 2018: 102). Henceforth, the court would apply a *per se* rule that "prohibited any contract in interstate trade that affected prices between a manufacturer and either its wholesalers or retailers, regardless of that contract's economic or political effects" (Phillips Sawyer 2018: 104).[14]

It was not just small specialty firms such as Dr. Miles that felt the effects of this ruling. Many of the country's premier mass producers of consumer goods had invested heavily in branding and advertising as a strategy for locking in a steady stream of repeat demand for their products, and the prohibition on RPM in interstate trade came at precisely the moment that large mass producers were investing heavily in national branding. Standardization was central to these strategies, since the whole point of these campaigns was to promise guaranteed quality and a guaranteed price ("satisfaction guaranteed"—see Strasser 1989: 270–72). Brand manufacturers perceived themselves to be highly vulnerable to the dual problems of brand dilution through loss-leading strategies and product substitution with lower-priced alternatives.

Among the large retailers, Macy's was one of the more notorious price-cutters, and the company wore this label as a badge of honor.[15] The company had never shied away from the fight for what it called "price freedom" or "the right to cut prices," trumpeting (also somewhat exaggerating) its opposition to RPM in its newspaper and magazine advertisements: "Macy's is the only store that fights combinations designed to uphold high prices" (Hower 1946: plate opposite p. 335, underline in original). The company repeatedly initiated vicious price wars with competitors that often centered precisely on branded merchandise because this focused the consumer's attention on the price difference they offered for identical goods (Hower 1946: 287–88, 350).

14. A subsequent case, in 1913, *Bauer v. O'Donnell*, pitted a retail druggist (O'Donnell) against a German producer of patented medicine, and the Supreme Court's ruling reinforced and extended the prohibition against RPM (Pope 1983: 96).

15. Indeed, the company's signature boast was that by dealing exclusively in cash and sourcing directly from manufacturers, it was prepared to beat all competitors on price (Hower 1946: chaps. 2 and 11).

As early as 1888 some manufacturers were already refusing to sell to Macy's because of its policy of underselling competitors (Hower 1946: 242). The retailer doubled down on these practices in the early twentieth century and, as a result, had trouble securing supplies from a number of firms including Inger-soll (watches) and Gillette (razors), among others (Hower 1946: 357–58).

On the other side of these conflicts, America's largest name-brand manufacturers (e.g., Procter & Gamble, General Electric, Campbell Soup, National Biscuit) were key players in the movement to introduce legisla-tion to legalize RPM in the interwar period. "By fixing the price at which wholesalers and retailers sold their brands, national advertisers hoped to get their products on as many dealers' shelves as possible, induce shopkeepers to offer customer services, combat price-cutting mass merchants, and associate their products with a set, stable price" (Pope 1983: 94).

Their ability to act on these preferences routinely fell afoul of the law, however. For example, between 1911 and 1913, manufacturers had asked the Bureau of Foreign and Domestic Commerce (and later the Federal Trade Commission) to "arbitrate a disagreement between mass retailers and manufacturers over which group had the right to control the resale price of goods," a dispute in which the bureau sided with mass retailers defending their freedom to cut prices (Leach 1993: 179). After a 1913 ruling denied the right of manufacturers to set resale prices even on patented items, large retailers were jubilant: "The time is close at hand . . . when there will be no manufacturers' brands, but the public will walk into our stores, look over the stock and choose goods on their merits as they appear to them. . . . We ourselves—the retail trade—will do all the advertising" (Pope 1983: 97).

The Fair Trade Movement

Opposition to the outcome of the *Dr. Miles* case inspired the formation of a movement against the court's restrictive stance on RPM and efforts at col-lective self-help more generally. Opponents of the ruling coined the more positive term "fair trade" and demanded that the courts assume a more nuanced stand with respect to associations of small independent produc-ers, similar to the "rule of reason" it was applying to large vertical combi-nations (Phillips Sawyer 2018: 18–19). The movement had some powerful supporters, including future Supreme Court Justice Louis Brandeis (Berk 2009). Brandeis was a fierce opponent of monopoly power and a strong advocate for reframing antitrust to allow workers and small independent firms to coordinate their activities to defend themselves collectively against destructive competition and monopoly power. He had long disagreed with the binary distinction the courts were drawing "between the permissible vertically integrated corporations and the impermissible nonintegrated trade associations" (Phillips Sawyer 2018: 108; Paul 2020a).

Brandeis was well aware of how Europe's competition regimes approached the question of horizontal coordination among firms. His positive views of what he called "regulated competition" were influenced by developments in Germany and Denmark, which "promoted competition through producer, retailer, and laborer associations" and which, as just discussed, allowed for (in many ways, encouraged) coordination within the context of trade associations (Berk 2009: 27, 60–61). Brandeis was deeply sympathetic to the plight of small business, both small manufacturers who struggled against industrial behemoths and independent retailers who saw their livelihoods threatened by the volume retailers. But, as Berk emphasizes, his views are not reducible to a simple defense of petit bourgeois interests. He "admired the inventors of brand-name, trademarked consumer goods . . . and his most creative work as an attorney involved fashioning collaborative relations between small and large firms" (Berk 2009: 41–42).

Resale price maintenance fit into the Brandeisian vision because he was convinced that regulated competition, policed by the state, would stabilize markets and serve consumer interests by steering competition toward quality and service. "By cultivating confidence among manufacturers, retailers and consumers, it made a market for innovation" by removing opportunities for "predatory competition" by low-cost mass retailers (Berk 2009: 57). Thus, Brandeis was less concerned about preserving small retail than defending against unfair competition that undermined manufacturers' incentives to uphold quality and to innovate (Brandeis 1913; Berk 2009: 59).

Brandeis was not so naive as to believe that RPM would not result in somewhat higher retail prices, but he also did not share the consumer-oriented views of other progressive reformers such as Weyl and Lippmann (McCraw 1984: 136). His primary concern, rather, was for the fate of small producers, embracing what Whitman (2007) calls a producerist ideology of the sort that (as we saw in the previous chapter) was more prominent in Europe than in the United States. For Brandeis, the health of American democracy hinged on citizens' active participation in the political economy, not as consumers but as producers, whether farmers, merchants, or entrepreneurs (Sandel 1996: 236). He defended resale price maintenance by drawing attention to actors other than consumers. In hearings before the

House of Representatives Committee on Interstate and Foreign Commerce in 1915, he readily conceded that the consumer "should get a good article at the lowest price that he reasonably can, consistent with good quality and good business," but he went on to insist that "there is another interest that the public has . . . [which includes] the dealer and his clerks and the producer and his employees. We are all part of the public and we must find a rule of law that permits a business practice which is consistent with the welfare of all the people" (Winerman 2003: 35). In addition, and despite his optimistic belief in the virtues of local democracy and the wisdom of Americans as citizens, the famed "people's lawyer" actually took a rather dim view of American consumers, seeing them as "easily manipulated by advertising" (Rosen 2010).

The fair trade movement gained a footing in the government with the establishment in 1914 of the Federal Trade Commission (FTC), whose early leaders were sympathetic to the plight of small firms and sought to assist them to "enhance and organize" competition rather than suppress it (Berk 1994; 1996). Brandeis played a key role in promoting the establishment of what Berk calls "developmental associations" through which small firms would be educated in cost accounting and would engage in information sharing and monitoring to steer competition away from volume and price and toward innovation, improvement, and competition based on quality (Berk 1994). It was largely through Brandeis's influence that the FTC and, later, the Supreme Court itself would eventually come around to a more relaxed approach to information-sharing among firms, even while continuing to draw a red line at anything that smacked of price-fixing.

Efforts at bolstering the role of trade associations got a boost in World War I (during which more trade associations were also founded) as part of the government's wartime production controls (Galambos 1966: 66). After the war, trade associations cooperated with the FTC to initiate "trade practice conferences"—forums for members of an industry "together to set competitive and accounting standards and then to foster cost-based pricing before the vicious circle of price fixing and prosecution occurred" (Berk 1996: 383). As then-FTC chair Nelson Gaskill put it, the trade conference "implies a transition from the accepted conventions of free competition . . . a willingness to surrender somewhat of individual liberty for the benefit of the whole. *It recognizes the individual self-interest as bound up in a community of interest*" (Berk 1996, 384; italics in original).

However, the FTC and the courts were at odds with one another from the outset. As Gerstle (2016) has pointed out, the early administrative state that was being constructed in this period did not displace the courts but instead grew up around and on top of the preexisting court-based policymaking regime (Skowronek 1992). The situation was full of tension, as the judiciary viewed the emerging bureaucracy with deep suspicion and sought to defend its own privileged position in the governance of economic activity. Whether or not one agrees with Howard's (2015: 43) assessment that the courts were working "on behalf of mass retailers" in their rulings against RPM in this period, it is certainly the case that they were operating on the basis of a rather different notion of what it meant to defend free markets—one that was uniquely intolerant of all forms of horizontal (interfirm) coordination and thus in some ways far more interventionist than their European counterparts.

Even after Brandeis himself was appointed to the Supreme Court in 1916, subsequent legal wrangling in the area of RPM, if anything, muddied the waters. In 1919, Brandeis had provided a key vote in a case brought by the Department of Justice against Colgate Company for refusal to sell to distributors that it knew to be deviating from its price lists. The government claimed that this was a violation of the Sherman Act along the lines of *Dr. Miles*, but a narrow (5 to 4) majority on the court joined Brandeis in emphasizing instead the idea that the company's agreements did not obligate its dealers to resell at specific prices. Ultimately, the court decided the matter on long-standing common-law precedents that held that private companies are free to deal with whichever parties they choose. However, just three years later, Brandeis found himself in a minority dissent on what he, at least, considered a virtually identical case (*FTC v. Beech-Nut Packing Company*, 1922) in which the court curtailed the right of refusal to sell that had been established under *Colgate* (Seligman and Love 1932: 71–74).

In contrast to Europe, the United States in the early twentieth century was characterized by tremendous legal uncertainty as to whether (or what forms of) RPM might survive legal scrutiny. Companies tried different ways of circumventing the laws, but over the course of the interwar period, courts narrowed their room for maneuver so that firm after firm dropped the effort as they "began to feel the curb placed upon their actions by the courts" (Seligman and Love 1932: 28). By 1931, the only unambiguously legal way for manufacturers to control their resale prices was through the use of agency sales (essentially consignment sales) (Seligman and Love 1932: 87). This was obviously not an option for many of the household items (personal hygiene items such as toothpaste, or over-the-counter remedies such as Alka-Seltzer) that some fair trade manufacturers produced.

The Legislative Battle for Resale Price Maintenance

In light of the Supreme Court's mostly skeptical view of RPM, fair traders took their campaign to Congress. The first attempt to legalize RPM at
the national level was undertaken in 1914, and similar legislation was proposed, but defeated, in each of the next fifteen congressional sessions (Rose
1949: 42). Congressional testimony from the most promising among these
legislative efforts—the Stephens-Ashurst bill of 1917[16]—provides a picture of
the coalitions that formed on both sides of the issue, as well as a sense of the
uphill battle faced by fair trade advocates, particularly in a context in which
prices had become politicized and consumers were mobilized.

Like their European counterparts, America's independent merchants
would have benefited from the legalization of RPM, for this would relieve
them of the price pressures of larger and more efficient retailers. But with the
notable exception of the National Association of Retail Druggists (NARD),
small retailers were woefully disorganized.[17] While small merchants would
provide the public face for the battles over RPM in the American context,
the real firepower (and financing) behind the movement in this period
came from mass producers of heavily advertised brand-name goods such
as Procter & Gamble (Pope 1983: 95–96). A study by the Chamber of Commerce later released in 1929 confirmed that "manufacturers advocating fair
trade were larger, more profitable, and heavier advertisers than their opponents" (Pope 1983: 102).

However, in a context marked by enormous distrust of large industrial
concerns, the support of such players was a political liability. Thus, the Fair
Trade League's secretary Edwin Whittier presided over a strategy that
actively downplayed their role, "keeping the manufacturers' interest sub-
merged" and instead emphasizing the interests of small merchants as more

---

16. H.R. 13568, "A Bill to Protect the Public against Dishonest Advertising and False Pretenses
in Merchandising" (see US Congress House Committee on Interstate and Foreign Commerce
1917).

17. Palamountain (1955: 83n79) gives figures from a 1941 study by the Temporary National
Economic Committee that revealed that only eighty-five of the 1,311 trade associations in operation organized retailers despite the fact that retailing accounted for almost half (42.9 percent)
of all business operations. NARD was an outlier. It was founded in 1898 in the context of early
efforts to regulate pharmaceuticals, and this group was RPM's most powerful and prominent
proponent. In 1915, Brandeis submitted a list of 143 national, state, and local associations of retailers, wholesalers, and manufacturers who favored RPM—and those representing retail druggists
outnumbered all others by a wide margin (more than twice as many as the next-largest group,
jewelers [FTC 1945: 40]).

likely to generate public support for the cause (Pope 1983: 100–1; FTC 1945: 45). Minutes from a 1915 meeting of the Fair Trade League suggest that elevating the role of small retailers was specifically designed to win the support of the largely Democratic Congress based on the view that "if they [legislators] thought this legislation was for the benefit of the manufacturers we would not get it but if it was for the benefit of retailers we would get it" (FTC 1945: 45; Pope 1983: 101). The same arguments and rationale came up time and again at the 1915 meeting: "Our strongest point in Washington is protection for the small man against being driven out of business, and the public welfare" (FTC 1945: 46).

The terms on which the RPM campaign was waged in the United States reveals important differences to Europe. Across the Atlantic, RPM was straightforwardly justified in the interest of avoiding ruinous competition among producers, a framing that was not perceived as particularly problematic. In the United States, by contrast, proponents of fair trade sought to thrust consumer interests to the fore with legislation whose stated objective was "to protect the public against dishonest advertising and false pretenses in merchandising."[18] The claim behind this somewhat convoluted language was that discount retailers were taking advantage of gullible consumers by seducing them into frivolous purchases with promised bargains, a framing that put them on the side of the public (FTC 1945: 45). But the minutes from the 1915 meeting suggest that this rhetoric also raised eyebrows among others: "I am skeptical about the consumer arguments. . . . I don't like the sham in it" (FTC 1945: 46).

Meanwhile, the mere prospect of congressional action in this area had prompted a countermobilization by large retailers who were far better organized than small merchants. Rowland Macy spearheaded the founding of the National Retail Dry Goods Association in 1911 to organize his fellow retailers against any such initiatives. The association repeatedly pounded the message that price maintenance arrangements would only protect inefficient small retailers. Spokesmen for major retailers (including Macy's, J. L. Hudson, Jordan Marsh, Filene's, and Marshall Field's) "depicted price maintenance proposals as hostile to competition and unfair to bargain-conscious consumers" (Pope 1983: 103; Yamey 1966: 20). In congressional testimony, Edmond Wise, a New York lawyer representing large retailers,

---

18. Advertisers themselves had long sought to clean up untruths in advertising, which they thought gave the entire industry a bad name. But they also viewed advertisements that offered substitute products for much lower prices than their clients' branded goods to be unfair or at least amoral.

disputed claims that these companies were using discounted goods to dupe customers into purchasing other goods at higher prices in testimony that dripped with sarcasm: "Of course the people of the United States, and especially the women, are such hopeless ignoramuses that they need the intervention of this committee to come in and protect them. The shoppers of the United States are such fools that, when they come in and see a Gillette razor advertised below $5, they will go and buy their household supplies at a very much higher figure at that place" (*Regulation of Prices* 1917, Wise: 10–11).

Wise bolstered his testimony with a long annex that drew invidious comparisons to Europe. Noting the stark differences not just to continental Europe, but to Britain as well, he documented how the common law on antitrust had diverged dramatically from that in the United States. English courts, he argued, had become far more tolerant of combinations—"the necessary effect of which is to enhance prices" (*Regulation of Prices* 1917, Wise: 60). "As a result, combinations, which in this country would clearly come within the provisions of the Sherman Antitrust law, have grown up unmolested" (*Regulation of Prices* 1917, Wise: 60). The English approach tolerates control of markets and prices "in the belief that in trade every evil will find its own corrective in the absence of any governmental restraining influence. American public policy is radically opposed to this view" (*Regulation of Prices* 1917, Wise: 61).

J. M. Barnes, head of credit at Marshall Field's, also railed against the proposed legislation, charging that the bill's promoters were "mostly large and wealthy manufacturers whose wonderful success under present conditions fully demonstrates that the manufacturer does not need additional legislation in order to prosper" (*Regulation of Prices* 1917, Barnes: 79). Percy Straus (vice president of Macy's, which by this time was the world's largest department store) showed up claiming to represent the interests of consumers: "I feel I am in closer touch with the consumer than any other individual kind of merchant" (*Regulation of Prices* 1917, Straus: 114). He particularly emphasized the impact of RPM on prices: "If, by legislation, we make the most efficient sell merchandise at the same prices as the least efficient, we necessarily add to the cost of merchandise to the consumer" (*Regulation of Prices* 1917, Straus: 115).

Women's groups also provided testimony against the measure. Miss Mary Wood of the New York Federation of Women's Clubs derided the claims of fair trade proponents for their characterization of women as gullible consumers easily swayed by misleading advertising. She insisted instead that "the average purchasing woman has sense enough to know an inferior

article when she handles it or sees it before her and has it in her hands"
(*Regulation of Prices* 1917, Wood: 285–86). She lampooned the suggestion
that farm women were overly inconvenienced by the need to wait for products to arrive from distant sellers who offered lower prices than local stores:
"Perhaps that woman has waited 20 years for that stove or that washing
machine, and she certainly can afford to wait three weeks for it; and she gets
it at a less [*sic*] price. You do not find the farmer's wife complaining" (*Regulation of Prices* 1917, Wood: 286). Here again the comparisons to Europe cast
the latter in an unflattering light: "There is now a growing tendency in this
country to-day . . . to impose upon this great American people ideas and
influences and laws, so-called social legislation which serves very well in
some countries over there whose area is so small that you could dump them
in some of our large States and never know they were there" (*Regulation of
Prices* 1917, Wood: 287).

Debates in the context of subsequent efforts to pass national legislation
legalizing RPM in the mid-1920s point to growing disparities between small
manufacturers and larger producers, with the latter overall enjoying more
success in navigating the uncertain legal climate surrounding RPM. Congressional representatives from the more industrial Northeast and Midwest
complained that small manufacturers were disproportionately disadvantaged by the inability to control their pricing (*Price Regulation for Trade-
Marked Articles* 1926, Clarke: 21). Large manufacturers of popular products
could still exert some control over their prices by refusing to sell to cut-
price distributors or, in the case of some consumer durables, by adopting
an agency system of distribution (along the lines already practiced by the
automobile industry, for example, and which had cleared Supreme Court
scrutiny in 1926 in *United States v. General Electric*).[19]

Small manufacturers did not have the same capacity to maneuver around
the legal obstacles through national advertising or through their own distribution channels. One of the sponsors of the RPM bill that failed in 1926,
Clyde Kelly, a Republican from Pennsylvania, complained that it was unfair
that *Dr. Miles* prohibited small manufacturers from enjoying the same protections as large retailers such as Sears, which were marketing private-label
goods, and large producers such as Ford and General Electric, which were
able to fix prices by selling exclusively through agents (*Price Regulation for*

19. In ruling for General Electric (GE) in this case, the Supreme Court upheld the company's
right to require Westinghouse (to whom GE had licensed its right to manufacture and sell its light
bulbs) to sell at prices that GE fixed (a practice that the Department of Justice had considered to
be in violation of antitrust laws, hence the case against GE).

Trade-Marked Articles 1926, Kelly: 4). The American Fair Trade League's W.H.C. Clarke echoed these sentiments when he pointed out the fundamental inconsistency in allowing price-fixing *within* large enterprises and not *between* small ones: "If I own a chain of stores or agencies I may maintain the price on everything that I sell, whether it be branded goods or bulk goods, but if I do not own that long line of chain stores or agencies I cannot even maintain the price on the branded goods by contracts with independent men" (*Price Regulation for Trade-Marked Articles* 1926, Clarke: 22).

Repeated attempts throughout the 1920s to legalize RPM at the national level were defeated, for, as Pope points out, members of Congress (whose constituents were on a spending spree in this period) were mostly unsympathetic to the entreaties of RPM advocates (1983: 103–4). They were reluctant to encroach on retailers' freedom to determine their own prices, and they were especially unwilling to deprive consumers of the lower prices the chains offered: "It was quite difficult, if not impossible, to persuade consumers that merchants needed to be protected by law from offering them lower prices" (Pope 1983: 104). In 1913, the *New York Times* reported that "popular sympathy is with the price cutters" (Pope 1983: 104), a view later confirmed in a 1928 FTC survey of almost two thousand consumers that found that nearly three-quarters opposed RPM legislation (Pope 1983: 104). Indeed, public sentiment against fair trade had grown steadily, right alongside the growth of the chains themselves, through the 1920s. The FTC again polled consumers in 1929 and found that a majority of all occupational groups (*nota bene*: other than those involved in manufacturing) opposed legalizing RPM contracts (Howard 2015: 46).

The Depression and Its Impact on the Fair Trade Campaign

National legislation lifting the ban on RPM came closest to passing in 1931 in the midst of the Great Depression, when it gained a majority in the House (before dying in the Senate) (*Harvard Law Review* 1933: 1195). But the vote on this bill (the Capper-Kelly bill) is revealing of the way the Depression had shifted the lines of conflict. Southern consumers, who, as we saw in chapter 3, welcomed the advance of large mail-order companies, stood firm against the industrial North and Midwest in opposing RPM, which they saw as raising prices and lining the pockets of northern industrialists. But the more industrial northern states were now joined by representatives from the West in support of fair trade. In these states, independent pharmacists

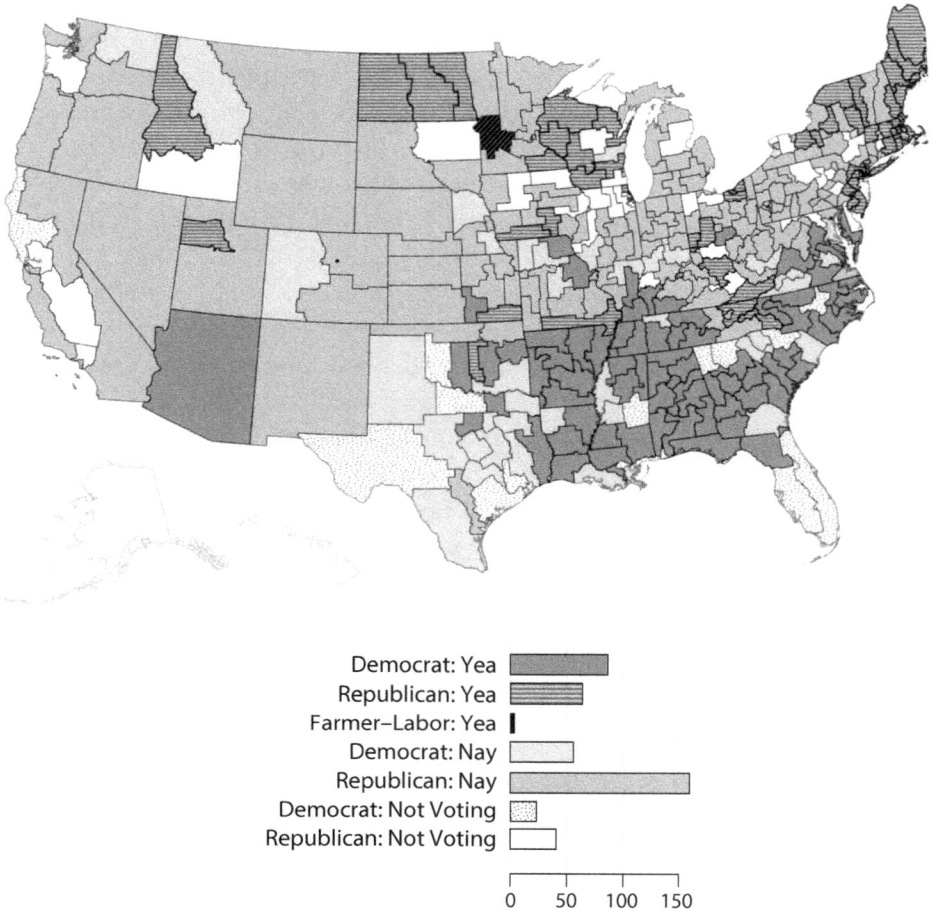

FIGURE 5.1. Vote on recommitting the RPM bill.
Source: House of Representatives, House Vote no. 80, 71st Cong., 1931, "To Recommit to Committee on Interstate and Foreign Commerce . . ." https://voteview.com /rollcall/RH0710080.

had waged a particularly vigorous campaign, characterizing the legislation as crucial to shoring up independent merchants who faced increasing competition from the low-cost chains that were now expanding rapidly into their regions. While there is no recorded vote on the bill itself, a procedural measure to recommit the bill (essentially delay or kill it) was subject to a recorded vote on January 29, 1931 (see figure 5.1). The defeat of this motion (146 to 211) moved the bill forward in the House (so a "no" vote here is a vote to move forward with the bill, while a "yes" vote indicates opposition to the measure).[20] It appeared that Congress was poised to overturn the *Dr. Miles* decision and legalize RPM.

Opposition to the measure had come from the usual corner—large department and chain stores—but they were now joined by southerners and some farm groups who feared the power that large manufacturers would wield in a regime of RPM, which, in the meantime, was increasingly controlled by powerful oligopolistic producers. A representative from the American Farm Bureau Federation argued that the bill would heavily impact farmer households, which had experienced falling incomes as the prices for agricultural commodities collapsed (*Capper-Kelly Fair Trade Bill* 1932, Gray: 208–17). Higher prices of household goods would only deepen the misery of these financially strapped households. Representatives of rural areas voiced deep resentment at the idea of giving large manufacturers powers to fix their prices. John Nelson, a Republican from Maine, opposed the bill as government overreach and anticonsumer, calling it "the most objectionable sort of class legislation" because it was so transparently "in the interest of the producer" (71 Cong. Rec. H3487 1931).

Southern Democrats—precisely the constituency that, as we will see in the next chapter, were otherwise at the core of battles to tax chain stores—were on the same side as large retailers in the conflicts over Capper-Kelly, providing notable *opposition* to the legalization of RPM through national legislation. Many expressed the fear that the practice would simply allow northern industrial interests to dictate prices (see statement by T. Jeff Busby of Mississippi, 71 Cong. Rec. H3490–91 1931). Representative George Huddleston of Alabama denounced the proposed legislation as a "fraud" that would hurt consumers while turning retailers into "agents" of big northern manufacturers (71 Cong. Rec. H3503–04 (1931). As they stared down defeat in the House, two Southern Democrats offered amendments to the Capper-Kelly bill to mitigate its impact. One amendment excluded necessities such as meat and flour from the bill's coverage, another allowed retailers to cut prices below the manufacturer-set minimums with ten-days' notice to the manufacturer.[21] Georgia Representative Cox spoke at length in opposition to the Capper-Kelly bill during the 1932 Senate hearings, arguing that "what the manufacturer in this case is inviting the Congress to do is to simply put

---

20. The final vote on the actual legislation, then, was the mirror image—with 210 in favor and 147 against (*Baltimore Sun*, January 30, 1931).

21. "Price Fixing Bill Passed by House," *Baltimore Sun*, January 30, 1931. For the amendments, see 71 Cong. Rec. H3536–7 1931; 71 Cong. Rec. H3540 1931.

shackles on the hands of the retailer and give him the key" (*Capper-Kelly Fair Trade Bill* 1932, Cox: 195). He contended that smaller retailers would be hamstrung without the ability to discount seasonal or unpopular items (in a depression, it was a huge problem for small merchants to pay their bills when consumer demand fell). Ohio Representative Robert Crosser predicted that Capper-Kelly would make the retailers into "an order taker" for manufacturers (71 Cong. Rec. H3496 1931).

As noted, Capper-Kelly was never brought to a vote in the Senate. In the meantime, the passage of the National Industrial Recovery Act (NIRA) in 1933 took the edge off pressures for federal fair trade legislation by suspending the enforcement of antitrust laws and calling on businesses to draw up industry rules governing wages, prices, and business practices in order to halt the downward spiral in employment. In the process, and as Laura Phillips Sawyer underscores, the fair trade movement also underwent a significant transformation as NIRA was captured by the large corporations that the government invited to participate in defining these "codes of fair competition" (2018: 277).

The Depression did not just decimate small merchants; it also had a devastating impact on small producers. Between 1925 and 1933 the share of manufacturing assets held by the largest one hundred firms rose from 34.5 percent to 42.5 percent (and by then the largest two hundred corporations accounted for nearly one-half—49.5 percent—of all manufacturing assets) (Niemi 1980: 336). With small manufacturers in crisis, the system of trade conferences that the FTC had cultivated in the 1910s and 1920s to facilitate information-sharing and cooperation also essentially "collapsed" (Seligman and Love 1932: 35) as small firms either went under or dropped out of their trade associations for lack of money to keep up with dues. Membership in the National Association of Manufacturers, the most prominent trade organization, plummeted from a previous high of 5,350 to under 1,500 by 1933 (Tedlow 1976: 29).

Large corporations came to the financial rescue of many of these beleaguered associations, but they also took over the leadership. For example, Robert L. Lund, CEO of Lambert Pharmaceuticals (best known for its popular mouthwash, Listerine) took the helm of the National Association of Manufacturers in 1931. A prominent member of the informal but highly influential "Brass Hats" group of big industrialists, Lund proceeded to centralize the organization and bring it under the control of corporate giants (Tedlow 1976: 29–30). Brady reports that all of the organization's directors between 1933 and 1937 came from just eighty-nine member firms, and approximately 5 percent of all members accounted for nearly half of the organization's contributions, putting them in a position to set the policy for the organization as a whole (Brady 1943: 211–12). In this context, the "vision that Brandeis and the . . . fair traders had promoted to preserve and support individual proprietors and industry-based substantive rules of fair exchange had morphed into a system controlled by corporate capitalists, by large-scale industrial firms" (Phillips Sawyer 2018: 261–62).

The Depression had also brought a truce between large producers and mass retailers. Big manufacturers that had ramped up production in the go-go years of the 1920s suddenly found themselves saddled with high fixed costs and found it useful (or necessary) to turn to discounters to unload their surplus (Palamountain 1955: 192). While retailers of all sizes suffered from plummeting demand, the large chains held their own better than smaller independent merchants because of the lower prices they offered to cash-strapped customers (Craig and Gabler 1940: 103). Between 1929 and 1933, the share of sales by independent department stores dropped from 48.8 to 43.9 percent, while variety (five-and-dime) stores increased their share from 14 to 17.5 percent and chain department stores from 11.2 to 15.6 percent (Craig and Gabler 1940: 103, based on Census Bureau figures).

In most sectors, the biggest firms on both the production and distribution sides benefited from the price stability afforded by the National Industrial Recovery Act, while small manufacturers and merchants were not as lucky. Small producers relied on inputs from larger companies that now exercised greater control over their prices. And even with fixed prices, small retailers' margins were thin because they had higher operating costs than large distributors (Bean 1996: 76). So while mass manufacturers and lean retailers benefited, small producers and independent retailers still struggled.[22] Moreover, cooperation under the pressure of the Depression and the auspices of the recovery act had inspired a growing "rapprochement between national advertisers and mass marketers" in the 1930s. Desperate to unload goods in a period of sagging consumer demand, many of the country's largest producers "realized the futility of opposing the growth of mass marketing institutions" (Pope 1983: 105).

---

22. In response to bitter complaints, FDR appointed a National Recovery Review Board to investigate charges of monopoly price-fixing. The board was dominated by two critics of big business (Clarence Darrow and Lowell Mason) and would ultimately conclude that minimum prices did help independent retailers but hurt small manufacturers because they were forced to pay higher prices on supplies under price maintenance and because it deprived them of the ability to compete on the basis of price (Bean 1996: 72).

The Depression had also sensitized some mass merchandisers to the possibility that it was perhaps both "impolitic" and "unprofitable" to fight brand manufacturers through combative product substitution and that "too aggressive price cutting was dangerous" for them as well (Pope 1983: 105; Seligman and Love 1932: 166). Intense price competition in the early years of the Depression had given some discounters a taste of their own medicine. For example, when his large drug chain was challenged by deep discount ("pine board") drugstores, Charles Walgreen came out in favor of legalizing resale price maintenance in 1932, and he brought other big players such as George Gale of Louis K. Liggett and Malcolm Gibbs of Peoples Drug with him (Lebhar 1959: 107; Palamountain 1955: 240). Grether notes that the Depression had "created new [alignments] of interests . . . [as] in some instances the better entrenched, large-scale firms became willing to compromise and accept a modicum of price control" generally supporting price floors to eliminate "dramatic, spectacular, deep loss leader price cutting" (1939: 9). As skeptical observers pointed out, in these years, all the fair trade laws did was "provide the chains with an excuse to avoid price cutting long enough to weather the depression" (Luchsinger and Dunn 1978: 53; Phillips Sawyer 2018: 308).

In general, the more that large-scale manufacturers and retailers appropriated the fair trade message, the more the original "fair trade agenda became distended and discredited" (Phillips Sawyer 2018: 308). Given that the point of the National Industrial Recovery Act was to halt the downward spiral of production and wages to address soaring unemployment and to give labor a seat at the table, its designers "had been prepared to tolerate price increases" to the extent that they were needed to cover a larger wage bill (Brand 1988: 116–17). But the government lacked the authority and administrative capacity to define and enforce "fair prices," and efforts to do so brought an allergic reaction from business to the entire machinery of the "regulatory state" (Brand 1988: 102–4). Public and labor support drained away as prices rose but without the gains being passed on to workers or consumers.

State-Level Fair Trade and the Miller-Tydings Act of 1937

Fair trade would almost certainly have perished when the 1931 Capper-Kelly bill died in the Senate had it not been for the efforts of organized pharmacists who took up the battle within state legislatures, where they enjoyed considerable success. Compared to all other trade associations at this time, pharmacists were uncommonly well organized and powerful both in the market and in politics (in the words of Hollander, "an amazingly effective political operation" [1966: 68]). The cohesion and the power of pharmacists as a group owed a great deal to their strong shared professional identity (in fact, most did not think of themselves as merchants at all).[23] Their role as trusted professionals lent them outsized power in local and state politics, especially since they wrapped their advocacy of RPM in the language of consumer protection.

Pharmacists also wielded a great deal of power in the market as a result of features of the sector itself. Retailing generally is characterized by easy entry (as well as high failure rates and constant churn). By contrast, pharmacology is a lifelong career and entry into the sector was limited by licensing requirements, thus generating far more continuity over time. The National Association of Retail Druggists (NARD) had been founded in 1898, and by 1906 it was "powerful enough to enforce a 'Tri-Partite Agreement' among drug manufacturers, wholesalers, and retailers" that established uniform retail prices, enforced through blacklists and boycotts (Palamountain 1955: 94). One example of NARD's extraordinary clout was a successful boycott of Pepsodent, a major toothpaste manufacturer that had withdrawn from its fair trade contracts in 1935. NARD mobilized druggists to drop the product or, often, to simply bury it under the counter. So effective was the action that the company did not just capitulate, it was also pressed to donate $25,000 to the association for use in its legislative campaign on behalf of fair trade (Palamountain 1955: 238–39; Wilcox 1971: 701–2; Hamilton 1975: 257; Fulda 1954: 192–93).

Commerce committee hearings made it clear that it was now pharmacists (not manufacturers) who were pushing fair trade (Fulda 1954: 180–81). Indeed, if anything, the former were often nudging reluctant producers into setting prices. In the hearings, a lawyer for the Illinois Pharmaceutical Association said that "the fair trade movement is a retailers' show with a manufacturers' sign or label over it" (Fulda 1954: 180, 208–9). In a reversal from the 1910s and 1920s, Seligman and Love suggest that by the 1930s, retailers were at the core of the RPM movement: "Far from price maintenance being a device forced by the manufacturer upon the retailer, we have found, on the contrary, that movement is more commonly the result of an attempt on

---

23. Pharmacology developed as a distinct profession at the turn of the century alongside other professions such as lawyers. The American Pharmacists Association was founded in 1852 and played a role in the Progressive-Era campaign for Pure Food and Drug laws.

the part of retailers to force the device upon the manufacturers" (1932: 198). Manufacturers, they find, were divided. Many were lukewarm or neutral, and some who professed to be in favor are "secretly opposed and brought into line only through the efforts of their distributors" (1932: 199, 213, 221). Seligman and Love themselves concluded that more manufacturers would benefit from RPM "if they really knew their own interests" (1932: 210). Writing in 1939, Grether noted that "one of the most marked aspects of the evolution of the movement for resale price regulation has been that retailers and wholesalers have displaced manufacturers as active sponsors," suggesting as one possible reason "the rapid progress of large scale retailers . . . and a growing public attitude of skepticism regarding the intrinsic qualities of many popular brands in relation to their alleged virtues . . . [that] have tended to make many manufacturers much more wary about assuming the burden of price control" (Grether 1939: 260, 261).

The pharmacists' state-level fair trade campaigns yielded fruit in 1931, when the California legislature legalized price maintenance contracts. This was followed up two years later by an amendment that made minimum-price agreements binding on nonsigners (i.e., on any retailer with knowledge of another retailer's agreement with the manufacturers; see Phillips Sawyer 2018: chap. 5). The state-level campaigns for fair trade got a boost in 1936, when the Supreme Court confirmed the constitutionality of these laws as a legitimate exercise of state police power—a measure to stabilize prices to ensure reasonable profits in a time of economic emergency.[24] By 1938, forty-three states had fair trade laws on the books, many of them copies so true to the model legislation that NARD had developed that they included the same typos (Grether 1939: 19; Kreps 1940: 1111; Humbach 1966: 148). By June 30, 1938, all but five states (Texas, Missouri, Vermont, Delaware, Alabama) had passed fair trade laws.

Capitalizing on growing hostility to President Franklin D. Roosevelt's centralizing initiatives (and on the enduring popularity of appeals to "states' rights"), NARD also led the effort to secure congressional approval for a new law, the Miller-Tydings Act of 1937, which exempted price maintenance contracts from prosecution under federal antitrust rules if they were lawful under *state-level* laws. According to Palamountain, "The *NARD Journal* for 1936 and 1937 reads like a file of battle orders. At one time one thousand communications were ordered sent to each member of the committee

---

24. The case was *Old Dearborn Distributing Co. v. Seagram-Distillers Corp.* (1936). The court, however, continued to prohibit RPM arrangements in interstate trade.

considering the bill; at another time each druggist was commanded to write a letter a week to his Representative and Senator; in the latter stages of the bill's consideration 'a constant barrage of letters and telegrams and letters' was ordered" (Palamountain 1955: 243–44). While collective enforcement was still banned, contracts or agreements prescribing minimum prices for the resale of branded products sold and shipped in interstate commerce would henceforth be legal so long as such products were "in free and open competition" with goods in the same class.[25]

The Miller-Tydings Act of 1937 was never voted on as a separate measure. It was instead attached to a must-pass appropriations bill to avoid a threatened veto by FDR, who worried about consumer backlash and who—along with his Department of Justice—opposed RPM. The chain-store-dominated National Retail Dry Goods Association, the American Home Economics Association, the National Grange, and the Mail Order Association of America all expressed opposition, albeit in more muted tones than before (FTC 1945: 61). Upon grudgingly signing the bill, FDR ordered an investigation of RPM practice and effects. The resulting report, published in 1945, confirmed the central role played by pharmacists in pushing the fair trade agenda and also pointed out the reluctance on the part of manufacturers in many fields to place their products under price maintenance unless their competitors also did so (FTC 1945: LV). The report also found that manufacturers who sold products through different types of dealers (e.g., discount and department stores) also "generally hesitate to maintain a uniform minimum price for all types of dealers because to do so may entail loss of volume from one or more of the different dealer groups" (FTC 1945: LV).

American RPM in Comparative Perspective

Despite the passage of the Miller-Tydings Act of 1937—and the entrenchment of fair trade laws in the vast majority of states—conflicts over resale price maintenance were by no means over. Indeed, as we will see in chapter 7, these conflicts flared up again in the 1950s and 1960s, when booming consumer demand intensified competition in retail markets and as a new

---

25. "The Act is expressly limited in its application to those states whose statutes or public policy permit vertical resale price maintenance agreements" (and where the good is resold or delivered). Specifically, "a price agreement made, therefore, in a non-fair-trade state is valid if the resale occurs in a fair trade state" so long as the commodity is "in free and open competition with commodities of the same general class" (see *Harvard Law Review* [no author listed] 1937: 342; and *District of Columbia Revenue Act of 1937*, Pub. L. No. 314, 50 Stat. 673 (1937).

group of discounters entered the fray. However, at this point it is helpful to pause to consider important differences between the European and the American versions of RPM in this period. Two stand out.

The first is the difference between collective and individual defense of prices. In Europe, RPM was part of a broader system of managed capitalism, one in which price maintenance was monitored and enforced by relatively strong trade associations that included both large and small producers. In the United States, by contrast, decades of legal prohibitions against RPM and other forms of coordination had limited the ability of small producers to protect their interests throughout the entire interwar period, and the Depression had in fact produced another massive wave of industrial concentration.

Miller-Tydings provided legal cover for RPM contracts in fair trade states, but it also made clear that the *collective* defense of prices was still legally out of bounds (Hollander 1966: 71–72, 81; *Harvard Law Review* [n.a.] 1937: 342–43). Individual defense was possible, but this confronted producers with a dilemma if they chose to go it alone. Grether's study of fair trade in the late 1930s found that one reason manufacturers in many branches shied away from price maintenance was that they had "learned from bitter experience that if one of them attempted to stabilize prices alone he would be holding the umbrella for competitors whose brands were price free" (Grether 1939: 276).

Voluntarism stabilized RPM where retailers were organized (as in pharmaceuticals) and where all the major interests (both producers and distributors) were in favor or could be kept in line, à la Pepsodent (Lebhar 1959: 108).[26] Where such conditions did not prevail (i.e., in most of the consumer retail market), individual manufacturers could seek to defend their prices, but these firms had to bear the cost of the investigation and litigation. This involved lawyer fees, court charges, and other expenses that made it prohibitively expensive for all but the largest producers.[27] As Bean points out, in 1954 only 1.4 percent of small manufacturers (less than $1 million in annual sales) were engaged in price maintenance practices (Bean 1996: 209n84).

---

26. Indeed, the Pepsodent example gives an indication of what an outlier the pharmacy sector was. Customers were inclined to defer to the authority of pharmacists in their purchasing behavior, producing a situation in which independent pharmacies' informal boycott of the company's product forced Pepsodent—a popular and powerful brand—to reinstate its price maintenance policies. In almost every other sector, the incentives—in the context of intense competition—were to lower prices.

27. *Yale Law Journal* (1959) contains an extended discussion of the difficulty of enforcing RPM arrangements though litigation; see also Fulda 1954: 202–6. See also chapter 7 for an extended discussion.

A second key difference from Europe is that the Miller-Tydings Enabling Act was just that—an enabling law. It did not overturn the *Dr. Miles* decision that had outlawed RPM at the national level, but instead left it to states that wished to opt in to fair trade to write (and seek to enforce) their own rules.[28] In this sense, Miller-Tydings had never given advocates a particularly strong tool: it simply allowed interstate commerce for goods under state-level price-maintenance contracts, so long as these goods were "in 'free and open competition' with similar goods on the market" (Howard 2015: 183). The result was a fractured regulatory landscape that invited venue arbitrage.

To preview developments recounted in greater detail in chapters 7 and 8, discount retailers would display "considerable ingenuity and persistence" in working around state fair trade laws by, for example, "obtaining their supplies of price-maintained merchandise through complicated and unorthodox channels, such as the trans-shipment of goods from one retailer to another" (Hollander 1966: 84; Howard 2015: 112). The trade journal *Chain Store Age* featured articles on how to do this. Small discount retailers often simply ignored or evaded the rules in the knowledge that producers were not likely to find it worth their while to challenge them in court, while major players such as Sears aggressively replaced fair trade goods with their own private brands. In 1937 (the year Miller-Tydings was passed), the fall and winter Sears catalogs encouraged customers to "Buy Sears Own Guaranteed Products, at prices not fixed under any State Laws," noting that the prices on its own products "always represent Sears' savings in distribution passed on to you" (Grether 1939: 246). Montgomery Ward's advertising similarly highlighted the lower prices for Ward's private-label products, placing them alongside the branded goods with higher prices, emphasizing "You Don't Have to Pay Them" (Grether 1939: 246).

Macy's and "hundreds of thousands of other distributors nationwide" made strategic calculations as to whether to abide by the prices or flout them (Howard 2015: 185). As one discounter put it, "If we think the manufacturer is serious we stop," while another described the fair trade laws as "somewhat of a headache" and the cases brought against his firm as "harassment lawsuits" (Howard 2015: 184). It was impossible for fair trade producers to investigate each and every pricing infraction, so they rationally focused on the largest violators. But discounters could also fight back in court, claiming discriminatory treatment or arguing that the producer had "unclean

---

28. Grether provides a summary of the specifics of state fair trade laws as of 1939 (1939: Appendix A p. 403ff).

hands" (i.e., was engaging in discriminatory enforcement) for allowing other retailers to undercut their pricing unmolested. In fact, some large retailers perfected such strategies, proactively collecting evidence of price-cutting by other merchants in anticipation of suits so they could launch an immediate countersuit (*Harvard Law Review* 1955: 320–21).[29]

The more porous regulatory and enforcement regime in the United States meant that the share of goods under fair trade never reached the levels seen in Europe. Precise figures are lacking, but most sources suggest that at its peak in the early 1950s, the share of goods under RPM amounted to between 4 and 10 percent of total retail sales in the United States (Herman 1959: 586). The practice was heavily concentrated in a few sectors, led (unsurprisingly) by the pharmaceuticals sector, which alone accounted for almost one-half of all fair trade manufacturers (45.7 percent).[30] Other goods—notably, household appliances—accounted for a smaller but still significant share of fair trade products (appliances made up approximately 13.6 percent of fair trade goods in 1954) (Herman 1959: 586).

Discounters actively courted consumers and the public at large. Differences in state-level rules allowed cut-price retailers like Macy's to turn the tables on fair trade advocates by publicizing the higher prices consumers were paying in fair trade states as a way to stir up public pressure against price maintenance (Howard 2015: 112). Indeed, the most prominent discounters who violated fair trade laws "embraced the fame their lawbreaking brought them" (Howard 2015: 187). In general, by the end of the 1950s, "retailers who have generally chosen to ignore fair trade and seek profits through a larger volume of cut-price sales—have been propelled into increasing preeminence" (*Yale Law Journal* [no author listed] 1959: 170, 168; Rose 1949: 52).

Conclusion

America's large retailers, and the country's low-cost retailers in particular, enjoyed a massive head start over their European counterparts, thanks not least to the interventions of the Supreme Court in imposing an early federal ban on resale price maintenance. In Europe, small producers and retailers alike were partly shielded from the advance of low-cost competition

---

29. The laws' deterrent effects were similarly weak because damages, while "theoretically available and often requested," were rare in the extreme and the injunctions that were issued were "frequently violated" (*Harvard Law Review* 1955: 321).

30. Drugs, cosmetics, and drug sundries and the like made up 42 percent of all sales of fair trade merchandise in 1954 (Herman 1959: 585).

throughout the interwar period. In sharp contrast to the United States, national courts gave forbearance toward resale price maintenance contracts, and these arrangements were often shored up by strong trade associations that could collectively police and enforce them. Those chain stores that did gain a foothold in this period grew up in an environment organized around RPM on branded goods and adapted to it.

In the United States, by contrast, price maintenance came much later and had to be imposed on "well established, powerful, large scale retail interests," many of whom had already developed private brands fully capable of competing with leading manufacturers (Grether 1934: 644). With RPM banned at the federal level, proponents of fair trade—led by organized pharmacists—mobilized at the state level, where they enjoyed considerable success. Yet advocates of RPM in the United States faced the daunting challenge of explaining to a mobilized consuming public why they should suddenly be denied the lower prices that mass retailers were offering them (Pope 1983: 104). Producers confronted a dilemma that low-cost retailers were quick to exploit by loudly condemning the practice as anticonsumer and by finding ways to evade the law. As Howard puts it: "In this struggle over control of the postwar retail market, discounters and opponents of fair trade from within the department store industry succeeded in part because they had shoppers on their side" (2015: 187).

6

Backlash

CONFRONTING THE "CHAIN STORE MENACE"

Running parallel to the battles over fair trade in the late 1920s and especially 1930s were efforts to slow down the chains in other ways, in particular by limiting the ability of large retailers to extract from suppliers discounts that were unavailable to smaller competitors (price discrimination) and by taxing chains at higher rates relative to competitors (chain store taxation). In the United States, conflicts over price discrimination and chain store taxation were both spearheaded by the same fierce advocate, Texas Democrat Wright Patman, and both were directed primarily (and rather explicitly) at what at the time was the country's largest chain, the massive grocery retailer A&P.

Conflicts over these two issues are linked together—and distinct from the conflicts over resale price maintenance discussed in the previous chapter—by the very different political coalition that they inspired. Whereas the battles over price maintenance pitted small retailers and brand manufacturers of all sizes against discount retailers, conflicts over price discrimination and chain store taxation pitted small merchants and large retailers against one another, with mass manufacturers sometimes siding with mass retailers. These issues also gave rise to regional cleavages that were distinct from those surrounding resale price maintenance, as Patman's battles against chain stores generated almost all their support in the South and West, areas in which populism enjoyed a renaissance in the Depression.

Resistance by independent merchants to the intrusion of new low-cost chain stores was by no means restricted to the United States. In Europe, coalitions of organized merchants and manufacturing interests successfully lobbied for a variety of measures (some more effective than others) aimed at slowing the rise of large retailers. In the United States, however, similar initiatives were blocked or delayed by the courts until deep into the 1930s. And while the resurgence of populism during the Depression resulted in a flurry of state legislation to rein in the chains, large retailers in the United States had already grown to such a size that they were able to exploit the fractured regulatory landscape to evade or minimize their impact, using the same playbook of regulatory arbitrage and rule-breaking that weakened fair trade. And as the Depression dragged on, appeals to stifle the growth of low-cost retailers became an increasingly hard sell, as the latter assembled an ever-expanding political-support coalition of groups that had come to rely on them.

Moreover, the very measures that slowed the advance of the chains in Europe in some cases accelerated their growth in the United States. As in the case of consumer credit and fair trade, American retailers developed strategies to work around existing regulatory constraints that resulted in innovations that further magnified and consolidated their power. In the case of credit, as we saw, revolving credit was a means to elude government restrictions imposed on installment selling (which itself had expanded in a legal gray zone). In the case of discount chains, low-price retailers countered regulations limiting price discounts with extreme cost reductions through other means, above all labor streamlining (pioneering and vastly expanding the self-service cash-and-carry methods that are now ubiquitous) (Levinson 2011: 211). And faced with state laws attempting to impose additional tax burdens, they minimized their obligations by pioneering large-scale supermarkets that American zoning laws did nothing to prevent and that municipal governments were often only too eager to welcome.

The next sections consider how parallel conflicts over chain stores and discount retailing were channeled and resolved in Europe compared to the United States.

Political Contestation over Low-Cost Retailing in Europe and the United States

In interwar Europe, where cooperatives were a significant force in the retail landscape, conflicts over chain stores were deeply entwined with broader class politics, as the cooperatives posed the greatest threat to small merchants. Where social democracy was strongest, working-class-based cooperatives survived and thrived. Elsewhere, however, right-wing political coalitions defended small merchants as a bulwark against socialism. As De Grazia summarizes: "Faced with the choice between allying themselves to the new retailing and a new middle-class constellation and consolidating their base in old retailing backed by a reactionary political coalition, most governments choose the latter" (2005: 177).

Sweden provides an example in which social democracy enjoyed significant strength already in the interwar period and where cooperatives survived best. Small merchants had organized among themselves in 1908 (and joined with wholesalers in 1918) to form the Swedish Retailer Association (S. K.). Since their most important rival was the Swedish Cooperative Union and Wholesale Association (KF), one of the core demands by organized merchants called for taxation of consumer cooperatives (Håkansson 2000: 8). "The problem for the S. K. was that the KF represented something new in Swedish retailing: a co-ordinated flow of goods through a joint control of wholesaling and retailing" (Håkansson 2000: 9).

The country's highly successful and powerful cooperative organization was subject to ongoing attacks by independent retailers. Social Democrats in parliament sided with the working-class cooperatives and deemed restrictive measures to be unnecessary and discriminatory. But conservative parties, aligned with independent merchants, sought additional taxes as well as enhanced restrictions on entry to the trade. The strength of social democracy in Sweden (the Social Democratic Party was the largest party in parliament in the interwar period, capturing 104 of 230 seats in the legislature in 1932) allowed consumer cooperatives to survive and to position themselves as a countervailing force to discipline the power of large manufacturing concerns.[1]

In Germany, by contrast, traditional interests were historically far more powerful and united (including against social democracy) than in Sweden. Here, local merchants had organized themselves into defensive alliances (*Schutzverbände*) in the imperial period, flooding state and local parliamentary representatives with petitions to curb the power of emerging large competitors, whom they accused of degrading German culture ("Entwürdigung des deutschen Kulturs") and undermining social order by weakening a strong conservative pillar against socialism (Spiekermann 1994: 34; Banken

---

1. In the United States, John Kenneth Galbraith would point to the role of cooperatives in Scandinavia as an example for the United States (see chapter 7).

et al. 2021: 201). Joining forces under a national association, the Zentralverband Deutscher Kaufleute und Gewerbetreibender (ZDK), independent merchants had scored some victories in the late 1880s and 1890s, including securing additional taxes on large retailers of all sorts across a number of German states (Coles 1999: 284–85).[2]

By the turn of the century, however, the ZDK's calls for assistance from the government began to give way to a reorientation toward self-help through collective action.[3] In the grocery trade, smaller merchants copied the model of cooperative self-help already well known on the right (e.g., in the artisanal *Handwerk* sector; Thelen 2004: chap. 2). Taking advantage of favorable laws, including a cooperatives act from 1889 that "allowed the formation of limited liability cooperatives without a minimum equity," smaller retailers joined together without fear of losing everything if the enterprise failed (Wortmann 2021: 459). The ZDK vigorously promoted the formation of purchasing cooperatives among small merchants, which essentially copied the formula pioneered by large retailers and cooperatives in order to secure cheaper supplies and compete more effectively (Spiekermann 1994: 143; Leopold 1917). The year 1907 thus saw the founding of the Verband deutscher Kaufmännischen Genossenschaften, which formed the basis for the purchasing cooperative known today as Edeka (currently one of Germany's four largest grocery chains) (Kiehling 1996: 23). By 1923, Edeka had already grown to include thirty thousand member-retailers (Wortmann 2021: 459). Another of today's big-four grocery chains, Rewe, was founded later, in 1927, but on a similar model, when 8,500 grocers joined forces in a similar retailing cooperative (Banken 2021: 487).

Druggists and department stores followed this model in pursuing a "progressive" *Mittelstandspolitik* that aimed to support collective self-help as an alternative to protectionism (Leopold 1917: 4). Between 1918 and 1923 the number of purchasing cooperatives (*Einkaufsgenossenschaften*) tripled (Kiehling 1996: 23). Combining forces allowed independent retailers to

2. In Germany's largest state, Prussia, taxes were levied only on stores that offered "more than one of four clearly defined groups of goods (which were periodically updated)" and had sales over 400,000 marks a year. "The taxation bands were set by the state and started at a 1 percent levy on sales over 400,000 marks rising to 2 percent on sales over 1 million marks" (Coles 1999: 285). Although it was called "the department store tax," it applied to a wide range of large-scale operations that included the chain stores (*Filialgeschäfte*), but also consumer cooperatives and mail order retailers (Coles 1999: 285).

3. Among other reasons, the taxes they had secured were not proving to be particularly effective and may even have backfired by encouraging large players to consolidate (Spiekermann 1994: 144–59).

compete with their larger rivals (Spiekermann 1994: 143) while also transforming their interests in ways that led them to oppose additional taxes on large retail (Spiekermann 1994: 163–64; Leopold 1917: 7–8). Kurzer summarizes these developments, noting that the locally based protectionist organizations that had prevailed during the Great Depression of 1873–96 were gradually overtaken by (and by 1918, largely replaced with) trade associations and purchasing cooperatives (Kurzer 1997a: 56).

Germany's merchant cooperatives survived and indeed thrived after the collapse of the empire and the transition to democracy. They turned their lobbying activities toward efforts to curtail the growth of other large competitors, including both working-class cooperatives and newer "single-price" discount stores that emerged in the 1920s (Kurzer 1997a: 56).[4] They benefited directly from the rightward shift in the political climate over the short life of the Weimar Republic, and they profited from Nazi agitation against Jewish retailers (some but by no means all of the country's largest private retail stores were owned by Jewish entrepreneurs).[5] Once in power, the National Socialists passed a "Law for the Protection of the Retail Trade," which, among other things, restricted the entry of new establishments that authorities did not perceive to be "reliable" (Wortmann 2021: 456–57; Banken 2021: 489–93). Small merchants had also cheered in 1930 when the government imposed special taxes on all department stores and consumer cooperatives with total annual turnover of over one million reichsmarks. Two years later the government followed up with an "emergency decree" that prohibited the establishment of new single-price stores in any city with a population over 100,000 (Banken 2021: 489).

Hitler entirely liquidated the working-class-based cooperatives, while the merchant cooperatives such as Edeka and Rewe accommodated themselves to the new regime.[6] Although Hitler did not follow through on promises he had made to small merchants to eliminate large-scale retailers altogether, his government did prohibit new department stores from being created and existing ones from expanding (Berghoff 2001: 171). Some of the restrictions that were imposed during these years in fact survived well into the

4. The first of the "one price" discounters, Ehape, was founded by Leonhard Tietz in 1926; Karstadt also founded a unit price sister Epawe (Einheitspreis Aktiengesellschaft Warenvertrieb) in 1926, and Woolworths arrived in Germany in 1927 (Banken 2021: 486–87).

5. *Reichsgesetzblatt* (GBl) 1, p. 121. Chains owned by leading Jewish retailers, such as Tietz and Karstadt, were targeted for "Aryanization" by the Nazis (Banken 2021: 490).

6. See, especially, Detlef Grumbach, "Aus der Not geboren," Deutschlandfunk, November 20, 2007, https://www.deutschlandfunk.de/aus-der-not-geboren-102.html.

post-WWII period, as some "proof of competence" was still required to open a retail establishment (for retail trades other than groceries until 1965 and for groceries until 1972 [Wortmann 2021: 457]).[7]

The story is different in Britain, where large retailers, including chain stores or multiples, generally encountered less legislative resistance than their counterparts in other parts of Europe.[8] Partly this was a function of the electoral system, for Britain's two-party system did not make room for a separate party to channel right-wing lower-middle-class militancy as on the continent (Hosgood 1992: 285; Chang et al. 2011). In addition, though, the main political parties were themselves cross-pressured on the issue. Conservatives were torn between defending traditional shopkeepers and promoting more "modern" forms of retail. Labour, for its part, had an interest in supporting the cooperatives (which, as in Sweden, were among the largest chains), but party leaders were also fearful that any attack on small merchants would drive unemployment up, pressing the wages of all down (Mercer 1995: 171).

The one significant attempt to impose greater restrictions on the growth of large retailers, the Shops Bill (Retail Trading Safeguards Bill), introduced in 1937, failed. The proposed legislation was designed in such a way as to limit the spread of the multiples and cooperatives by requiring a license to open any new shop, with applications considered by one of eleven regionally based Retail Trade Commissions (Shaw et al. 2000: 1984). The bill's sponsor, Conservative MP Harold Balfour, was rabidly anticooperative, and, with the legislation, he sought, in his own words, to check the "uncontrolled growth of co-operative and multiple stores which are at present helping rapidly towards the extinction of the independent shopkeeper" (*Parliamentary Debates* 1937: 1206–7).

But the Balfour bill failed on the second reading, and parliamentary debates suggest that conservatives were split on the issue. Some factions of the Tory Party sided with small shopkeepers, whom they regarded as bastions of local communities. Others, however, argued on behalf of large-scale retailers on efficiency grounds. Labour MP Rhys Davies noted, no

7. This could be fulfilled either through completion of a retail apprenticeship followed by two years of experience in the trade or through five years' experience.

8. They did encounter some difficulties in siting their shops, largely as a result of lack of space and town planning controls that limited the number of shops in the main shopping areas (Jefferys 1954: 90). Some of the low-cost retailers that had popped up across the Atlantic were not homegrown but rather American transplants. Woolworths, for example, launched operations in Europe in 1909, starting with Liverpool (De Grazia 2005: 166).

doubt with some pleasure, the spectacle of "the small capitalists disagreeing with the big capitalists" (*Parliamentary Debates* 1937: 1245–46). For its part, the Labour Party opposed the bill, not just because the cooperatives would be hurt but also on grounds of their belief that unions would have an easier time organizing big shops than myriad small retailers (*Parliamentary Debates* 1937: 1244–46).

Despite this and other calls to regulate large retailers, the British state demurred throughout the interwar period (Shaw et al. 2000: 1982). In the case of the Balfour bill, chain stores (organized into the Multiple Retailers Federation) argued alongside the Board of Trade against regulation; both clearly saw Britain's future as lying with large enterprises (Shaw et al. 2000: 1985). Moreover, the legislation did not distinguish between large national chains and smaller regional networks of stores—and independents of the latter type joined national chains in opposing state regulation, fearing that they themselves might be held back by it (Shaw et al. 2000: 1987).

THE ANTICHAIN CAMPAIGNS IN THE UNITED STATES

In Europe, conflicts over the growth of the chains generated cleavages that ran along lines of class, particularly in those countries in which working-class or consumer cooperatives occupied an important role in the retail sector. In the United States, by contrast, the antichain campaigns had a strongly regional character, anchored primarily in the South. This poses a puzzle, since, as we saw in the previous chapter, the South was firmly aligned with low-cost retailers in the battles over fair trade. The paradox vanishes, however, when we consider the very different implications of these conflicts for the regional political economy prevailing in the American South.

Simplifying only slightly: struggles over fair trade were fundamentally about the ability of northern manufacturing interests—now under increasing pressure from organized labor to share the rents—to impose (high) prices in the South, a demand wholly at odds with a southern political economy still very much organized around low-wage agricultural production. However, the advance of chain stores into the South also posed an existential threat to local elites and to the racial order they were protecting. Chains challenged not just local merchants but also the entire local economic infrastructure attached to them, including, among many others, the local printers who produced their advertising and the local bankers who carried their accounts (Levinson 2011: 135). The resurgence of southern populism in the 1930s was thus highly selective: upholding the right to cut prices, as championed by the anti–fair traders against the interests of (northern) brand manufacturers, while vehemently opposing the intrusion of "foreign" chains operating in direct competition with local business elites.

The man who figured most prominently in the antichain campaigns of this period was Texas Democrat Wright Patman. Patman was an, ahem, colorful and controversial figure in American politics—celebrated by some as America's "last populist" (Stoller 2019: viii) and condemned by others as a racist.[9] But either way (or, actually, both ways), Patman's antimonopoly convictions were deeply interwoven with a desire to protect a regional political economy premised on low wages.[10] Elected to represent one of the country's most impoverished congressional districts (a previous stronghold in the Farmers' Alliance movement at the turn of the century), Patman carried the populist banner in a crusade against chain stores and, in particular, A&P—which was by far the dominant player in the grocery sector (Levinson 2011: chap. 14).

Patman had plenty of allies in his crusade against the chains. In 1929, fellow populist Huey Long, the governor of Louisiana, famously proclaimed that he "would rather have thieves and gangsters than chain stores in Louisiana" (Fulda 1951: 1051). Alabama Senator Hugo Black joined the chorus in 1930 with a fiery speech against the chains: "We are rapidly becoming a nation of a few business masters and many clerks and servants . . . A wild craze for efficiency in production, sale, and distribution has swept over the land, increasing the number of unemployed, building up a caste system, dangerous to any government" (quoted in Moore 2017: 148).[11] The Ku Klux Klan chimed in with antisemitic and anti-Catholic tropes, denouncing chains as a "Little Group of Kings in Wall Street" that threatened "to pauperize native-born white Protestants" (Moreton 2006: 70). But the "chain store problem" was also widely debated outside the South. In fact, just a year after

9. Of course, in the peculiar political context of the American South at that time, the two are not mutually exclusive. As Gabriel Winant (2020) points out, Patman was one of the signatories to the 1956 Southern Manifesto that condemned the Supreme Court's decision in *Brown v. Board of Education*. At the same time, and as Young (1996: 58–59) notes, Patman was generally on the liberal side of the political spectrum in the South, and many Black voters supported him in elections as the lesser evil (see also Caughey 2018).

10. Patman thus supported the passage of the Taft-Hartley Act that sharply circumscribed the rights that organized labor had won in the 1930s (Winant 2020).

11. Moreton emphasizes that the populist critique of the chains in the South was infused with a strong strain of racism and also patriarchy—the fear of a loss of manly independence and relegation "to the lifelong status of a 'helper,' classed by one outraged observer alongside such effeminate professionals as typists, stenographers, and secretaries" (2006: 71).

focusing on the issue of installment selling, the National Forensic League's debate question for 1931 asked whether chain stores were "detrimental to the best interests of the American public."[12]

Anti–chain-store arguments resonated, especially in the South and West, where populist sentiments still ran strong. The Depression had wiped out scores of small businesses and rekindled antipathy toward Wall Street and northern interests generally (Ryant 1973: 208). The chains' rate of growth had slowed in the Depression, but their low prices allowed them to increase their share of total retail sales, reaching a peak of 25.2 percent in 1933 (Palamountain 1955: 160). As Palamountain notes, the Depression thus "added to the economic distress of independents and intensified their fear and hatred of the chains, whose price appeal was sharpened by the slash in consumer income" (Palamountain 1955: 160).

Grocery chains (A&P in particular) came in for especially intense criticism. Not only did A&P enjoy economies of scale that gave it an efficiency advantage, its size also allowed it to extract price concessions from suppliers that gave it a further edge over local merchants.[13] Moreover, absent any real presence of financial or industrial concerns in these regions, A&P was one of the only obvious targets for populist antimonopoly sentiments. Critics railed against chains for draining revenues out of local communities, devastating local businesses, sucking the life (and wealth) out of the communities they entered, and lining the pockets of "foreign" (northeastern) elites (Ryant 1973: 221).

Price Discrimination: The Robinson-Patman Act of 1936

Independent merchants were already experiencing intense pressure from chain stores as the latter expanded into the South and West in the 1920s, but the Depression clearly intensified their distress as consumers flocked

12. Resolved: That chain stores are detrimental to the best interests of the American public. See National Federation of State High School Associations, "National Debate Resolutions," https://www.nfhs.org/media/1018339/past-resolutions.pdf.

13. The entire debate over price discrimination—both then and now—centers on the degree to which the advantages that large retailers hold are due to economies of scale or greater bargaining leverage. Most observers acknowledge that it is a combination of both factors, although the opinions tend to follow the observer's beliefs about whether the Robinson-Patman law that would emerge from these debates in the 1930s (and that remains on the books today) was a good idea or not (I thank Erik Peinert for emphasizing this to me). The contemporaneous debates, discussed in this chapter, reflect this pattern, with detractors and supporters of A&P and large retailers generally emphasizing one or the other of these two factors.

to the chains for their lower prices. Patman's stature and seniority in Congress allowed him to secure approval for a congressional investigation (under his chairmanship) of the trade practices of large retailers in 1934. The hearings before the committee in 1935–36 provided a golden opportunity—and a very public platform—for him to elevate the issue of the "chain store menace."[14]

Under his leadership, the committee presided over a heavily choreographed process that spotlighted price discrimination, and within the food sector in particular.[15] Witnesses testified that the large grocery chains were coercing suppliers into granting generous terms against the threat of launching their own competing sources of supply. The price concessions, secret rebates, and favorable terms they were able to extort, it was alleged, allowed these chains to sell at prices that were ruinously low, driving smaller competitors out of business. A&P came in for special scrutiny and opprobrium based on testimony that the company "had been receiving on an annual basis $6 million in off-the-invoice discounts and another $2 million a year in brokerage fees on its purchases" (Macintyre 1960: 333).

Wholesalers and small retailers in the food sector rallied around Patman's call for legislation to redress the inequities they saw in these arrangements. By purchasing directly from producers and selling directly to consumers through their retail branches, the chains were performing the wholesaling functions that small merchants (unable to secure supplies directly from manufacturers) had to pay wholesalers for. Large food retailers (such as A&P) were able to claim significant brokerage fees that lowered the cost of their supplies.[16] They could also sometimes extract advertising advances in exchange for promises to aggressively market a producer's goods (e.g., through prominent placement in the retailer's advertising or a prime location in the store).

Defenders pointed to the efficiency gains from economies of scale and scope: because they bought in such large quantities and in predictable volumes (with orders typically submitted well in advance), chains offered mass producers key advantages and cost savings by allowing them to run expensive machinery on a more continuous basis. Their size alone was thus

14. See Hearings Before the Special Committee to Investigate American Retail Federation, House of Representatives, 74th Congress, 1st session (June 5, 6, 25, 27, 28; July 9, 10, 1935).

15. As Edwards notes, the Robinson-Patman law that would ultimately emerge was "developed both by the Congress and by the Federal Trade Commission with the food industries primarily in mind" (1959: 621).

16. A&P regularly demanded (and received) brokerage commissions "on the ground that its field buying agents eliminated the need for the use of brokers by its suppliers," a strategy that policymakers viewed as "price concessions masquerading as brokerage" (Edwards 1959: 102, 108).

a significant source of leverage over suppliers. For example, Strasser cites investigators writing for *Printers Ink* as early as 1914 describing how large retailers demanded and often got leniency on credit because "once they have tasted the chains' money it is twice as hard to refuse" (2006: 47). And large retailers could use their power to extract concessions, for, as Levinson notes: "The possibility that A&P might refuse to stock their products or relegate them to the top shelves was enough to bring even the biggest grocery manufacturers into line, making sure that A&P got better deals than anyone else" (2011: 105).

Patman viewed such discounts as predatory and destructive of independent businesspeople and the communities they served. The National Industrial Recovery Act (NIRA, May 1933 to May 1935) had provided temporary relief from the price pressures exerted by the chains. Large wholesalers had been able to participate in setting the prices to which the chains too were bound, and NIRA codes for the food industry specifically had included a number of provisions that were designed to limit the ability of large chains to secure supplies for lower prices (Edwards 1959: 11). However, as soon as the Supreme Court struck NIRA down, prices fell and A&P profits again soared (Levinson 2011: 149–50).

The end of NIRA and the publicity around the congressional hearings on price discrimination reignited opposition to the chains. Patman's campaign got an enormous boost from the efforts of the owner of a popular radio station in Shreveport, Louisiana, W. K. "Old Man" Henderson, who used his platform to broadcast a steady stream of tirades against the "foreign" intruders (Ingram and Rao 2004: 450). Henderson also helped Patman gain national attention for his cause when the National Conference of Independent Businessmen assembled 1,500 of their members in Washington, DC, in March 1936 for what they called the "March of the Little Men" (Levinson 2011: 164).

Building on the growing momentum, Patman forged an alliance with Arkansas's Democratic senator Joseph Robinson to craft legislation to deal with the chain store issue. Together they whipped up support in Congress for what became the Robinson-Patman Anti-Price Discrimination Act of 1936. Based on a draft that the US Wholesale Grocers' Association had provided (Evans 1936: 143n21; Edwards 1959: 22), the bill was rather transparently directed against A&P, so much so that it was informally dubbed the anti-A&P bill. A key goal of the legislation was to reinstate some of the protections for small retailers and wholesalers that had expired when NIRA was declared unconstitutional. Specifically, the bill sought to prohibit wholesalers and manufacturers from supplying goods to "preferred" customers at reduced prices (Hawley 1995: 251–54).

Hustled onto the legislative calendar on the eve of the 1936 election (the first hearings, before the House Judiciary Committee, were in July 1935), the Robinson-Patman Act sailed through Congress. But the legislation that emerged was vaguely worded and difficult to interpret and thus did not always have the intended effects. Support for the bill, though largely from small merchants and wholesalers in the food industry, was bolstered by the well-organized pharmacists who also felt threatened by the intrusion of chain stores (both grocery and drug chains) in the sale of household beauty aids and cosmetics. These groups faced a formidable array of opponents that included not just the chains themselves but also consumers and some manufacturers. In fact, as Edwards notes in a 1959 report evaluating the Robinson-Patman Act, "With the sole exception of the National Association of Retail Druggists, all business interests outside the food industries opposed the bill in both [congressional] hearings" (1959: 24).

COALITIONS AND DEBATES

The opposition to the Robinson-Patman bill was spearheaded, unsurprisingly, by the chain stores. Similar to the battles over mail order described in chapter 3, in which Sears and Montgomery Ward kept a low profile, A&P also sought to stay out of the fray, likely out of concern for alienating the rural populations they served. However, a representative of Chain Food and Grocery Stores (an association of fifteen grocery chains, including the country's second-biggest private chain, Kroger Grocery and Baking Co. of Cincinnati) did testify, complaining that the bill "penalizes efficiency in distribution" (*To Amend the Clayton Act* 1935, Silliman: 174). The vice president of the Independent Grocers Alliance Distributing Company, or IGA—a large voluntary (as opposed to corporate) chain of independent grocers, and the second-biggest purchaser of grocery products after A&P—also testified against the bill, emphasizing that the wording was vague and the provisions in it were also likely unconstitutional (*To Amend the Clayton Act* 1935, Ungaro: 115–17). In later hearings before the Senate Judiciary Committee on a related bill (Borah Van Nuys, discussed below), representatives of agricultural marketing cooperatives expressed frustration and dismay. After finding a way to distribute their products so as to "[eliminate] all necessity for the middleman" by selling direct to chain stores, and feeling "satisfied with what they have been willing to pay us," they saw the proposed legislation as removing the advantages they had gained through coordination (*Price Discrimination* 1936, Thompson: 93–94).

Chain retailers outside of the food sector were overall less well represented in the House hearings, but Robert E. Wood (president of Sears, which in the 1920s has grown well beyond mail order to become a major department store chain) laid out the general logic of the efficiency argument. He readily conceded that independent merchants pay more than Sears for manufactured goods, but he maintained that his company allowed manufacturers to bridge lulls in demand through advance orders of large quantities: "We give him straight runs on his machines, and he can sell to us at a lower price and make a larger profit and yet give the consumer a low price" (*To Amend the Clayton Act* 1935, Wood: 89).[17]

A number of suppliers to the chains also testified against the bill. The lawyer representing the Associated Grocery Manufacturers of America (which organized the country's leading manufacturers of food and grocery products) took pains to assure congressional representatives that his association was in principle all in favor of prohibitions on "unfair" price discrimination. But the organization opposed the Robinson-Patman Act as contradicting prevailing antitrust laws and interfering with legitimate competitive pricing anchored in higher-efficiency operations (*To Amend the Clayton Act* 1936, Dunn: 431–41). In a similar vein, individual large food manufacturers such as General Mills expressed opposition to the bill (Levinson 2011: 162). The president of the Lehigh Valley Cooperative Farmers Association also objected to the legislation, emphasizing the central importance of the chains in getting their goods to market ("We have found from experience that the chain stores offer a mighty good outlet for farm products") (*To Amend the Clayton Act* 1935, Boger: 124).

Producers of perishable goods (e.g., dairy) were keen to defend their ability to offer chains a discount. Karl King, whose company sold vegetables though various distribution channels, including chains (he reported that two-fifths of his company's total volume went to the largest chains), argued that it would be impossible for companies like his to avoid awarding price differences to different buyers (*To Amend the Clayton Act* 1935: 118–19). A representative of the International Association of Ice Cream Manufacturers similarly emphasized the impracticality of the proposed legislation and the importance

---

17. Representatives of smaller chains argued similarly (e.g., William Eden of American Stores Co. Inc. of Philadelphia [*To Amend the Clayton Act* 1935: 147–49]), objecting to why his chain should have to pay brokerage fees for services that his company itself already provided (by having eliminated the wholesaler).

of the chains as an efficient outlet for his product (*To Amend the Clayton Act* 1935, Hibben: 164–66). In the later Senate hearings, Vermont's maple sugar manufacturers claimed that the chains were crucial to helping them deal with unanticipated surpluses (*Price Discrimination* 1936, Adams: 46).

The National League of Women Voters came out against Robinson-Patman, as did the women's clubs of Chicago and Cleveland, calling it a women's issue because of the way it would impact household finances (Levinson 2011: 163). Virginia Huntley Morrison represented the Community Roundtable of Illinois "to speak in behalf of the housewives of our State," arguing that "we are not concerned whether the independent merchants or the chain stores get the business, just so the housewife gets the most in quantity and the best in quality for her dollar. Therefore, we are opposed to any legislation that would increase the cost of foodstuffs" (*Price Discrimination* 1936: 90). She strenuously objected to the Robinson-Patman bill on grounds that "it would force the chain stores to buy through other wholesalers and middle men . . . that would increase the cost of living, and that is our objection to these bills or any legislation that would do this" (*Price Discrimination* 1936: 90).

Despite opposition, Robinson wielded his power as Senate majority leader to forgo Senate hearings on the Robinson-Patman bill by arguing that it had been sufficiently vetted in the House. Yet clearly there were concerns in the Senate, enough to prompt William Borah (progressive Republican from Idaho) and Frederick Van Nuys, a Democrat from Indiana, to propose an alternative piece of legislation (the Borah-Van Nuys bill). Having been denied the chance to debate the Robinson-Patman bill before the Senate Judiciary Committee, witnesses testifying in the hearings on the Borah-Van Nuys proposal instead took the opportunity to vent their objections to the Robinson-Patman bill. Although, given the political climate, witnesses saw some legislation as virtually inevitable, most argued for the alternative Borah-Van Nuys bill as the "lesser evil" (*Price Discrimination* 1936: 38, 102).

Evans's contemporaneous account of the Borah-Van Nuys hearings suggests that of the twenty-seven witnesses who testified, all either preferred Borah-Van Nuys or found it "less objectionable" than the Robinson-Patman bill (Evans 1936: 145). Unlike the Robinson-Patman proposal, which some saw as "[running] contrary to the spirit of the Clayton Act and contrary to what we have found to be in the public interest" (*Price Discrimination* 1936, Sammons: 33), the Borah-Van Nuys bill did not seek to alter the Clayton Act, but rather to deal with specific abuses that this previous legislation had not anticipated. Thus, for example, the proposal would still allow volume discounts under some circumstances even as it imposed heavier (criminal) penalties against illegal discounting (*New York Times* 1936, "Chain Store Bill Reported to House"). Rather than explicitly prohibit price concessions, Borah-Van Nuys foresaw criminal prosecution of discriminatory treatment through "concessions which are *collateral* to price, such as discounts, rebates, allowances and service charges" and this only "in respect to goods of 'like grade, quality and quantity'" (Evans 1936: 172–73, my emphasis). Although the penalties were harsher, the modifications attached to the language of the prohibitions was designed to effectively limit their impact (Evans 1936: 175).

For many witnesses, another of the attractions of the Borah-Van Nuys proposal was that it was seen as overall clearer than the Robinson-Patman bill. Indeed, a great deal of the testimony in the Senate judiciary hearings centered on clashing interpretations of what the Robinson-Patman legislation would and would not proscribe. There was considerable uncertainty on this, and much time was spent simply trying to get clarity on what the various provisions in the bill actually meant.[18] One witness (Benjamin Marsh, executive secretary of the People's Lobby) testified in favor of the Borah-Van Nuys bill in large part "because it is so drawn that you can make a fair guess at what it means" (*Price Discrimination* 1936: 113).[19]

Only later in the deliberations did manufacturers from industry at large weigh in. They voiced concerns about Robinson-Patman as they contemplated how it might affect their own operations. A representative from the National Association of Manufacturers observed how the popular debates and previous hearings had created the impression that the bill would mostly affect grocery chains, so that manufacturers in other sectors had given "very little attention . . . to the effect of this bill." But once it became clear that it would affect the ability of sellers to grant quantity discounts, he reported that manufacturers in his association were "definitely opposed" to the bill (*To Amend the Clayton Act* 1935, Sargent: 236–37). Thus, much of the testimony on the Borah-Van Nuys bill was actually concerned with Robinson-Patman, and "much of it came from manufacturers and mass distributors who opposed these bills" (Edwards 1959: 26).

Small manufacturers testified to the way the chains allowed them to scale up production to achieve higher volume (*Price Discrimination* 1936, Klein: 41); other producers argued that they had to have leeway to sell at

18. See Senate Judiciary Hearings, 74th Congress, second session on S.4171, March 24 and 25, 1936: 30, 34, 53.

19. For a contemporaneous account of what the bill allowed and prohibited, see Evans 1936.

different prices to unload products in order to cover their operating costs (*Price Discrimination* 1936, Jungbluth: 53); still others argued that small manufacturers need the chains for the service they provide in advertising their products (something they themselves are not in a position to do) (*Price Discrimination* 1936, Dunn: 73). A New York–based textile manufacturer testified that it was entirely due to mass distributors that his firm was able "to keep over 200 looms in continuous production for 6 years. . . . if we did not have the benefit of the continuity and large-scale purchases of these mass distributors, we would have difficulty in supplying these proponents [of the legislation] with merchandise within a very wide percentage of prevailing prices" (*Price Discrimination* 1936, Rose: 125).

Congressional deliberations to reconcile the bills that emerged out of the House and Senate resulted in vague legislation containing myriad exceptions, which, as detailed below, would later complicate enforcement (Moreton 2009: 19; Lebhar 1959: 226). It did not help that the conciliation committee that was charged with reconciling Robinson-Patman with the Borah-Van Nuys bill essentially merged the two (Evans 1936: 146; Rowe 1962). The original draft of the Robinson-Patman bill had sought to prohibit any and all price discrimination—that is, no differences in price for goods could be offered regardless of differences in quantity ordered (Cohen 1965: 715). The final version of the bill banned price discrimination for commodities "of like grade and quality" regardless of quantity but with exceptions for "differences in the costs of manufacture, sale or delivery" or if concessions had been "made in good faith to meet an equally low price of a competitor" (Cohen 1965: 715, 717n16).

The rather baroque language of the final legislation rendered the interpretation and enforcement of the law an ongoing problem. The first empirical study of the impact of Robinson-Patman, published by the Brookings Institution in 1959, criticized the "haphazard way in which the bill was developed," suggesting that this created "unusual difficulties in ascertaining the intent of Congress from a study of the legislative history" (Edwards 1959: 28). A few years later another empirical study of the law's impact called the final compromise "a masterpiece of obscurity" and a "bizarre mating of the two divergent proposals" with the result that it was left to the courts to resolve their overlaps and incongruities (Rowe 1962: 19, 458).

However, despite or perhaps because of its many ambiguities, Robinson-Patman had become something of a legislative juggernaut. The Senate added some amendments, but when it reached the House it passed overwhelmingly (290 to 16). Few politicians had been willing to defend the chains, particularly in the West and South in an election year. FDR had tried to avoid taking a stand, cross-pressured as he was by his need to mollify the southern wing of his Democratic Party with an election looming while also attending to the interests of northern workers and consumer groups (mostly women's groups) who had testified against the bill and who appreciated the ability to purchase lower-cost goods (Levinson 2011: 163). Filene and others warned the president against endorsing the bill on grounds that it would cut into the purchasing power of consumers at a critical moment (Jacobs 2005: 162). But Roosevelt had no appetite for inviting a challenge from a Huey-Long-type populist, so he not only signed the bill but invoked the legislation in his 1936 campaign speeches in the South to hold his electoral coalition together (Sparks 2000: 258–59).

THE IMPACT OF ROBINSON-PATMAN

Ambiguities aside, Robinson-Patman clearly had an impact. The law forced "a substantial change in [A&P's] buying practices," above all by depriving the company of concessions it had previously received in the form of brokerage fees (Edwards 1959: 110, 623). The company's stock price also took an immediate hit and its market share declined (Levinson 2011: 165). But A&P did not retreat to passivity. The company "held meetings of its buyers to make sure" they understood the law and produced a manual on how to comply with it (Edwards 1959: 108). But the manual also "set forth ways of obtaining low prices without violating the law" (Edwards 1959: 109). These included, among other tactics, buying the entire output of a particular commodity or of a particular seller, or having the supplier produce goods specifically for A&P that were of "substantially different grade or quality" from those they sold to other distributors (Edwards 1959: 109; Hawley 1995: 267).

A sort of cat-and-mouse game thus unfolded in which A&P lawyers sought ways to exploit the loopholes in the law and avoid legal liability. As another example, A&P added amendments to its standard contract through which suppliers who paid the company an advertising commission or received a volume discount were required to "certify that it [the manufacturer] was not engaging in illegal price discrimination" by explicitly stating that it was willing to conclude the same agreement "'with any other purchaser similarly situated on proportionately equal terms'" (Levinson 2011: 173). The FTC viewed such provisions with skepticism, but an investigation yielded mixed results, upholding some of A&P's advertising allowances and quantity discounts but also finding that the company had indeed violated the law in other ways (Levinson 2011: 173–74, 200). In the biggest case, the Department of Justice charged the company with "having extracted anticompetitive discounts from its suppliers and for having sold to consumers at discriminatory (predatory) prices" (Wrigley 1992: 737). The suit dragged on for seven years and though the government ultimately won (the conviction was also upheld on appeal in 1949), the fine ($175,000) was modest given the company's size and dominance (on the suit see Levinson 2011: 228–34, 242–49; Wrigley 1992: 737).

Moreover, as Jacobs notes (2005: 162) the price advantage the chains had over the independents was only partly a function of the discounts they secured; it was also lower operating costs (Edwards 1959: 628). Thus, A&P pivoted toward a laser focus on achieving price advantage by further reducing its operating costs. The chain drastically reduced the number of stores in operation (by 27 percent in the three years immediately following the bill's passage) (Levinson 2011: 171). The company began a strategy of launching far fewer (but much larger) stores, more lightly staffed by moving toward centralized checkout, with employees simply restocking rather than servicing customers. By 1941, two-thirds of the stores that had existed in 1937 had been shuttered, but sales grew because turnover at each of these larger, more efficient outlets increased fourfold (Levinson 2011: 210).

In some ways, the bigger casualties of the Robinson-Patman Act were the cooperative retail chains. Voluntary chains and cooperative associations of wholesalers or independent grocers such as IGA and Red and White were composed of small companies that sought through "joint ownership or franchise control of a private brand" to compete "more effectively against manufacturers' national brands and against the private brands of corporate chains" (Edwards 1959: 117). Combining forces to purchase jointly was a means both to match the purchasing power enjoyed by large private chains and to "obtain merchandising assistance such as a corporate chain could render to its outlets but an individual store could not provide for itself" (Edwards 1959: 117–18). The prohibitions against payment of discounts "in lieu of brokerage" that were written into the Robinson-Patman Act were clearly targeted at A&P. However, the courts also applied these provisions to voluntary cooperatives in ways that undercut the advantages they had sought to achieve through joint purchasing (Edwards 1959: chap. 5, 122–30). As Edwards summarizes:

> The law has curbed not only the practices of the powerful but also the practices of others designed to furnish protection against the powerful.

Flexible adjustments designed to give independent small concerns some of the buying advantages of the chain stores have been struck down where . . . they gave brokers the status of buyers and where, as in the cases involving voluntary chains, they gave associations of independent merchants power comparable to that of the great buyers. The capacity of the independent to protect himself has been weakened. . . . In checking the growth of voluntary groups and encouraging vertical integration, the law may have assisted the powerful in ways that will become more significant with time (1959: 626–27).[20]

Section 2(c) of the law prohibited sellers from making payments to brokers who were effectively agents for the buyer in the transaction (as in the case of A&P's own brokerage operations), but it also affected the cooperative brokerage services of independent food stores since they, too, were operating as agents of the buyers, albeit as a collective.

At the end of the day, Patman's effort to rein in price discrimination by dominant actors was successful in achieving results, even if it was hardly debilitating for big retailers like A&P. And while Robinson-Patman had clearly put a big dent in A&P's profits, it had also awakened a giant. When the Department of Justice later launched a civil antitrust case aimed at breaking A&P up, the company struck back with a massive public relations campaign, mobilizing its consumer base by placing ads in every one of the country's two thousand daily newspapers and in five hundred weeklies and sending scores of representatives out on national speaking tours (Levinson 2011: 244). According to Levinson, the company spent fully one-seventh of its after-tax profits in just three months in 1949 in a media blitz (2011: 244). One ad, running under the headline "Don't Let Anybody Fool You!" ominously warned, "These Things Will Happen If The Anti-Trust Lawyers Have Their Way" and ticked off a series of dire consequences, including higher prices (*New York World-Telegram*, December 1, 1949: 13; *Wall Street Journal*, December 2, 1949: 7).[21] In what was perhaps its most memorable advertisement, the company lampooned the government's goals by placing a

---

20. Three years later, Rowe reached the same conclusion, arguing that the act not only failed to help small retailers, it actively "victimized its intended small business beneficiaries," among other ways, by "prohibiting the receipt of lower prices by joint buying groups formed by independent distributors to compete with mass buyers" (1962: 501).

21. Another ad, running under the headline "Isn't America A Wonderful Country!" featured clippings from other grocers who took A&P's side in the government's antitrust suit and expressed gratitude for the "fine sportsmanship of many of our competitors all over the country" (*Wall Street Journal*, November 10, 1949: 6).

picture of the Empire State Building alongside text saying: "It's Far Too Big. It Ought to be Seven Buildings" (Levinson 2011: 244; Stoller 2019: 171–72).

Levinson notes that winning consumers to its side was "an easy feat," given that the prices that chain grocers offered were 10–15 percent lower than elsewhere (Levinson 2011: 191–92). In the course of the PR campaign, the Department of Justice found itself swamped with 2,900 letters from concerned consumers (Levinson 2011: 243–46). Two national polls suggested overwhelming support for the chain (Levinson 2011: 245). Figures 6.1 and 6.2 record results from surveys conducted on the government's case against A&P. When asked whether they agreed more with the company or with the government on this issue, those who had an opinion in the case sided decisively with A&P, with 45 percent agreeing with A&P and just 24 percent agreeing with the government (figure 6.1). A separate poll asked whether respondents thought A&P should be broken up, and again public opinion was strongly on the side of the grocery chain, with 60 percent opposing such a move and only 24 percent in favor (figure 6.2).

By 1950, company CEOs George and John Hartford had landed on the cover of *Time* magazine (Levinson 2011: 245). The accompanying article featured a sympathetic account of how "the familiar red-front A&P store is the real melting pot of the community, patronized by the boss's wife and the baker's daughter, the priest and the policeman" and lavished praise on the company for keeping food prices low. Commenting on the support A&P enjoyed when confronted with antitrust suits, the article noted that the "average US housewife did not need to look any farther than her pocketbook to know where she stood" (*Time*, November 13, 1950).[22]

The government dropped its most ambitious goals in the suit, though it did force A&P to close its produce brokerage. Wrigley argues that despite the fact that the settlement "imposed certain minor disadvantages on [the company's] purchasing operations . . . in effect, it was a major victory for A&P and an early sign that the concerns of the 1930s and their legislative legacy were fading" as the antitrust authorities' focus began to turn away from price discrimination toward mergers (Wrigley 1992: 738).

The impact of the Robinson-Patman legislation continued into the early postwar years and, as we will see in the next chapter, it continued to generate cases—and criticism and controversy—until the late 1960s, when enforcement went into steep decline. But before we turn to these developments, I

---

22. See "Red Circle and Gold Leaf," *Time*, November 13, 1950, https://content.time.com/time/subscriber/article/0,33009,821397,00.html.

From what you have heard or read, with which side do you agree, the United States Government or the A&P (food store in the government's lawsuit against them)?

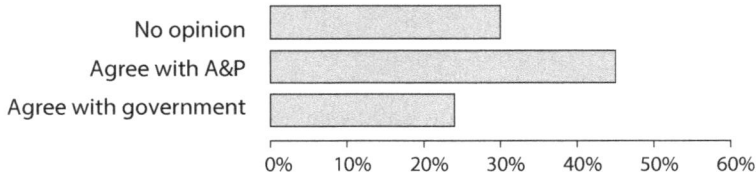

FIGURE 6.1. Support for government vs. A&P in lawsuit, 1949.
Source: Gallup Poll no. 449, version 3 (Cornell University, Roper Center for Public Opinion Research, 1949).

The government is asking to have the A&P broken up into a number of smaller companies. Do you believe the A&P should have to break up, or not?

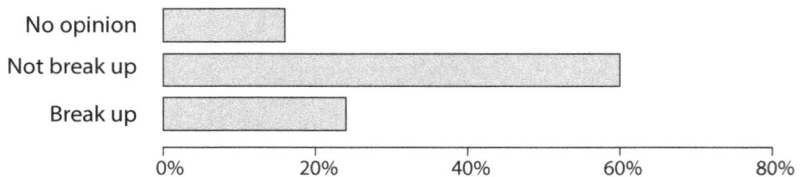

FIGURE 6.2. Support for breaking up A&P, 1949.
Source: Opinion Research Corporation Poll, October 1949, Question 34. USORC. 49NOV.R27 (Cornell University, Roper Center for Public Opinion Research, 1949).

will show how the other prong of Patman's efforts to debilitate chain stores— this time, through taxation—was far less successful. The chain store taxation movement initially enjoyed a populist wave of enthusiasm, to which large retailers responded by mobilizing their allies to come to their defense. Unlike with the price discrimination act, Patman failed utterly in his efforts to pass a national chain-store tax.

Chain Store Taxation

As noted earlier, a second front in the war on "the chain store menace" sought to weaken large retail chains through additional taxation. Efforts to impose special taxes on these companies resulted in a flurry of *state* laws in the depths of the Depression. However, like the Robinson-Patman Act, these measures slowed but certainly did not halt the chains' advance.

Indeed, if anything, they again inspired innovation resulting in larger and more efficient operations through reorganization in the direction of greater consolidation (De Grazia 2005: 145; Levinson 2011: 210; Ryant 1973: 219). Moreover, here again, the fragmentation of the regulatory landscape invited venue arbitrage, since not all states passed chain store taxes, and the level of tax varied widely across those that did. By 1938, this situation had prompted Patman to embark on an effort to impose a *national tax* on chains. This initiative would backfire spectacularly in the face of significant opposition from a wide range of political economic groups that, over time, had become dependent on the chains.

The main line of cleavage in the chain store taxation wars ran between small independent merchants and large retailers, with manufacturers mostly on the sidelines. But, as in the parallel battle over price discrimination, there was a strong regional component to the fight, which was centered again in the South and Midwest.[23] As Moore notes, of the 260 antichain organizations active in 1930, a minority (31) were located outside these two regions and almost three-quarters (69 percent) were located in towns with populations under ten thousand (2017: 149).

On the taxation question, chain store opponents faced an uphill struggle, initially in the courts and then in Congress. Missouri was the first state to attempt to impose additional taxes on chains, in 1923, and by 1927, fifteen states had taken up the issue (Schragger 2005: 1028–29). However, the state laws that did get passed were frequently struck down in court, based on a strong aversion to any intervention in the market that smacked of legislative favoritism (Schragger 2005: 1030–31).[24] Equal protection arguments were regularly invoked in cases involving antichain legislation—for example, in Kentucky (1925), Maryland (1928), and North Carolina (1928) (Schragger 2005: 1033–34). The Supreme Court took up the issue in 1928 and ruled against chain store tax laws in Pennsylvania and Kentucky on these grounds. Against the backdrop of the court's long-standing defense of unfettered markets, "chain store taxes looked a lot like many other forms of discrimination against out-of-state corporations" (Schragger 2016: 183).

Prospects for taxing the chains brightened, however, in 1931 when the Supreme Court relaxed its stance on the issue (*State Board of Tax Commissioners v. Jackson*). In that year, a narrow court majority (including

23. Opponents of chain stores comprised a wild stew of different actors and motives, including progressives like Brandeis and Robert LaFollette; populists like Huey Long and Wright Patman; Black leaders; and the Ku Klux Klan (Schragger 2005: 1014).

24. Lebhar 1959: chapter 7 has a long discussion of various cases; see especially 120–23.

Brandeis in concurrence) upheld a state tax passed in Indiana that levied higher licensing fees on chain stores (*New York Times*, May 19, 1931; Schragger 2005: 1038). Like other states at this time, Indiana was desperate to raise revenues, and the state government planned to use the funds from the chain store tax on schools (*New York Times*, May 19, 1931). In its decision, the court now held that there was no "iron rule of equal taxation" and argued that "the fact that a statute discriminates in favor of a certain class does not make it arbitrary if the discrimination is founded upon a reasonable distinction, or if any state of facts reasonably can be conceived to sustain it."[25] The court's majority reasoned that the fact "that there are differences and advantages in favor of the chain store is shown by the number of such chains established and by their astonishing growth" (*New York Times*, May 19, 1931).

Over the next six years (1931–37), twenty-six states followed Indiana's lead in passing some kind of enhanced taxation on chain stores—typically some form of graduated license law under which the tax assessed increased in proportion to the number of outlets (Hawley 1995: 261; Schragger 2005: 1029). A 1939 article in *Business Week* (July 8, 1939: 28), reproduced in table 6.1, provides an inventory of the twenty-seven states—mostly in the South and Midwest—that had passed chain taxes to that point, and it includes as well repeals and court rulings against such laws to that point (twenty were still on the books at the time the article appeared). The table records the variation in the level of taxes across states, which Palamountain attributes to differences in the motives behind the laws. While some states were simply trying to level the playing field to allow independent merchants to compete, others wanted to eliminate the chains altogether (Palamountain 1955: 165–67). Indiana imposed some of the mildest taxes, while states such as Louisiana (Huey Long's stomping ground) and Texas (Patman's home state) enacted the most severe taxes (Ryant 1973: 212; Palamountain 1955: 167–68).

The 1931 *Jackson* decision had given chain store opponents a welcome win, but it turned out not to signal a clear shift in jurisprudence on this issue. The court proceeded to address five more chain store tax cases between 1931 and 1937, issuing a series of mixed decisions (Schragger 2005: 1040–41). One of the most famous of these, *Louis Liggett v. Lee* (1933), involved a class action suit brought by thirteen chain stores against a Florida law that imposed greater taxes on companies with operations in more than one county. In a 5–4 decision, the court ruled the Florida tax to be "unreasonable and arbitrary," prompting one of Brandeis's most powerful dissents

25. State Board of Tax Commissioners v. Jackson, 283 U.S. 527 (1931).

TABLE 6.1. State Chain-Store Tax Laws as of July 1939

State	Date enacted	Maximum fee in US dollars	Base number of stores for maximum fee
Alabama	1935	112.50	21
Arizona	*1931*	*25.00*	*21*
California	*1935*	*500.00*	*11*
Colorado	1934	300.00	25
Florida[1]	1935	400.00	16
Georgia	1937	200.00	41
Idaho	1933	500.00	20
Indiana	1933	150.00	21
Iowa	1935	155.00	51
Kentucky	*1934*	*300.00*	*50*
Louisiana[2]	1934	550.00	501
Maine	*1933*	*50.00*	*26*
Maryland	1933	150.00	21
Michigan[3]	1933	250.00	26
Minnesota[4]	1937	350.00	151
Mississippi	1936	300.00	41
Montana	1937	200.00	5
New Mexico	*1934*	*Tax on gross receipts*	
North Carolina	1935	250.00	202
Pennsylvania	*1937*	*500.00*	*501*
South Carolina	1930	150.00	30
South Dakota	1937	150.00	50
Tennessee	1937	Tax on floor space	
Texas	1935	750.00	51
Vermont[5]	*1933*	*Tax on gross receipts*	
West Virginia	1933	250.00	76
Wisconsin	1937	100.00	26

Note: Italics indicate that a law has been repealed or declared unconstitutional.
Source: Business Week, July 8, 1939: 28.

[1] Florida, Mississippi, and Idaho do not have graduated taxes like other states. Instead of having lower rates, say, for the first ten stores and higher taxes for the next ten and so on, up to the maximum, these states assess all stores in a particular size classification at the same rate.

[2] Louisiana and South Dakota tax stores on the basis of the number of stores operated throughout the whole country rather than just those within the state.

[3] Michigan also has a graduated tax on chain counters, leased departments, etc. Maximum is $25 for each counter over twenty-five.

[4] Minnesota also has a graduated tax on mail order chains. Maximum is $1,200 for each establishment over eleven.

[5] Vermont's law, before repeal, was held unconstitutional.

(Schragger 2005: 1049–54). Taken together, the cases reflected a deep tension on the court between the views of antimonopoly progressives and those of opponents of any form of "special interest" legislation that could be seen as protecting one class of economic actors over others (Schragger 2005: 1042). The court thus vacillated through the 1930s on chain store taxation, deeply ambivalent and divided. The problem, as Schragger puts it, was how to protect small dealers "while simultaneously aiding consumers, who benefited from the efficiency brought by large-scale producers" (2005: 1058).

In any event, the chains' response to these state laws had often been to adjust their strategies to minimize whatever new obligations were imposed on them, and in ways that reduced employment and further enhanced their efficiency advantages. Since taxes were based on the number of outlets, many embarked on consolidations, resulting in an overall decline in chain store units across the country, from 151,712 in 1928 to 123,195 in 1939 (Ryant 1973: 219). As noted above, A&P pursued an aggressive consolidation strategy, replacing scores of small outlets with larger (and more labor-saving) supermarkets in this period; in fact, the number of separate A&P stores dropped by over half between 1930 and 1940 (Ryant 1973: 219; Brown 2019).[26] But the reduction in the number of chain outlets did not result in a commensurate decline in sales, and the chains' share of total retail business actually rose over these years from 20.3 percent to 21.7 percent (Ryant 1973: 219). As De Grazia summarizes, "Far from obstructing the pace of growth of large-scale modern retailing, the American regulations acted like modern forest husbandry," clearing away old methods and encouraging new growth. The "net effect was to accustom business, state policy and the public to never-ending, head-spinning newness in the retail trades" (De Grazia 2005: 145).

With the chains engaging in regulatory arbitrage and intense innovation and consolidation to work around states' chain store taxes, Patman launched a last-ditch effort in 1938 to impose a *federal* tax on chains. Dubbed the "death sentence bill" by its opponents and the "community preservation bill" by advocates (Moreton 2006: 68), Patman proposed a graduated tax "so high that it would effectively end chain stores" (Brown 2019). Chains with fewer than ten stores would be exempt, but beginning with the tenth outlet, chains would pay $50 for each store up to fifteen. This dollar amount would increase progressively until it reached $1,000 for every outlet over five hundred. The total would then be multiplied by the number of states in

---

26. See also Deutsch (2010: 140–41), who notes that other chains also responded to the taxes by reducing the number of stores and increasing the size of each of them.

which the chain had operations. Lebhar worked out the effect the tax would have had on several big chains: Woolworth Company (with net profits of $28 million in 1938) would have been on the hook for $81 million, and A&P (with twelve thousand outlets across forty states) would have had to pay more than $471 million (Lebhar 1959: 247).

But the fervor behind the chain store tax movement had already begun to burn out. On July 7, 1939, the *New York Times* reported that chain tax proposals had been defeated in twenty-six state legislatures ("either by direct action or by letting the measures die with adjournment"), and state chain taxes were ruled unconstitutional in three further states: Kentucky, Pennsylvania, and New Jersey ("Chain-Tax Proposals Killed in 26 States This Year," *New York Times*, July 7, 1939). The *Business Week* article cited above (also from July 1939) reported that the chains were "particularly encouraged . . . by their remarkable success so far [that] year in sidestepping new state tax laws and in erasing others from the statute books" (1939: 29). Figure 6.3 charts the course of chain store taxation for the entire period from 1927 to 1941. It registers the passage of such laws as well as annulments by courts and legislative repeals. It shows that, outside the South at least, the energy was clearly draining away, as initiatives for new taxes were being defeated in some states, while other states that had previously adopted taxes now repealed them.

Chains had mounted major public relations campaigns "to combat charges that [they] were monopolies that undermined the prosperity of communities," fighting back with extensive advertising of their contributions to local economies and encouraging local managers to assume leadership positions within the local business associations (Deutsch 2010: 78). In a California referendum on a chain store tax proposal, big retailers had waged a massive campaign, enlisting their employees to participate in get-out-the-vote actions and poll-watching and urging citizens to vote "no" to defeat the tax (under the motto "vote NO and keep prices low"). Their efforts were rewarded with a resounding victory in which they won 64 percent of the vote (Schragger 2005: 1078; Lebhar 1959: chap. 11).

The chains used the same playbook five years later in Utah, at the tail end of the movement (Moore 2017: 150–59). When the Utah Senate passed a chain store tax in 1941, it was essentially dead on arrival, as Utah voters turned out to overturn the law in a referendum (the state's first). The debate in the legislature had already been uncommonly divisive and the governor had signed the law with reservations. Within hours of the signing, however, the Chain Store Association had launched a petition to force the referendum. The association's Utah chapter had already laid the groundwork to respond

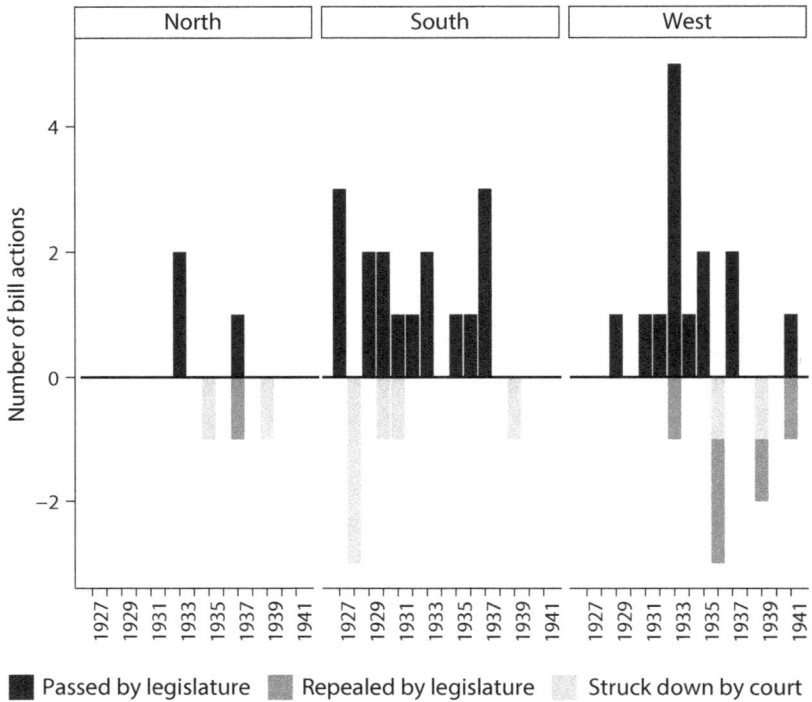

FIGURE 6.3. State-level chain store taxes (passed, repealed, and reversed), by region and year. Based on data from Ross, "Store Wars: The Chain Tax Movement," *Journal of Law and Economics* 29, no. 1 (1986): 125–37.

to any such legislation, beginning over a decade earlier by creating city advocacy groups anchored in women's circles. So they were ready to fight back in a vigorous campaign, arguing that they would pass the cost on to consumers and threatening that the tax could force them to leave the state entirely.

The chains further argued that they provided workers with better pay, and they courted the American Federation of Labor (AFL) by allowing the union to organize grocery workers. J. C. Penney argued plaintively that locals could be losing "an old friend" (Moore 2017: 159). Grocery chains warned more forebodingly that they would no longer be around to buy up surplus agricultural products from local farmers, and they courted groups like the Utah Beet Growers and the Dairymen with pledges to assist them in unloading surpluses in exchange for their support (Safeway did take care of a potato surplus) (Moore 2017: 151, 154–55).[27] And the chains unleashed

27. Chains (particularly A&P) had used this tactic repeatedly, courting farmers to great effect in Florida and Maine as antichain legislation was pending (Palamountain 1955: 174).

a huge blitz of newspaper and radio ads with the slogan "No. 2 is a tax on YOU," with No. 2 being the referendum (Moore 2017: 155–56). Utahans responded much the same as their counterparts elsewhere, rejecting the tax overwhelmingly (69 percent to 31 percent overall, with even bigger margins in rural areas, sometimes reaching 5 to 1 against) (Moore 2017: 158).

CHAIN STORES ENTRENCHED

In the end, Patman's federal tax proposal failed utterly (the Ways and Means Subcommittee that considered it declined to report it out to the full committee). Chain store critics by now faced concerted opposition not just from the American Retail Federation that represented the country's largest retailers, but from a growing and diverse coalition of chain store supporters that now included farmers, manufacturers, developers, and consumers, who, in the meantime, had all become fully invested (albeit for different reasons) in the success of the chains (Scroop 2008: 938; Watson 2011: 32).

The debates over the national tax provide a window on the broad base of support on which large retailers could now depend in their struggles with regulators in this period. Agrarians across the country had come to rely heavily on the chains as a reliable market for their crops (Moreton 2009: 22). Grocery chains had explicitly wooed farmers in the California referendum by helping peach growers deal with a surplus through an aggressive advertising campaign for canned peaches (Lebhar 1959: 237–38; 310–11). Thus, farm groups sent their representatives to Washington, DC, to support the chains in the congressional hearings on the chain store taxation bill. As the president of the American Farm Bureau Federation testified: "This great mass-producing industry of agriculture needs an efficient mass-distributing system close to consumers" (Lebhar 1959: 307–8). Representatives of the National Grange and the National Council of Farm Co-ops also testified on behalf of the chains (Lebhar 1959: 273). In fact, "no important agricultural group failed either to appear in person in opposition to the bill or to file formal resolutions condemning it" (Lebhar 1959: 318).

Manufacturers—including many of those that had tussled with the chains over pricing—now climbed on board as well. As noted in the previous chapter, once the Depression hit and they were confronted with problems of overproduction, they had made their peace with their mass-retailing counterparts. As Palamountain observed: "While some manufacturers had supported the Robinson-Patman Act because it improved their vertical relations with chain buyers, few wished to cripple or kill the chains" (1955: 179).

The country's mass-production industries, heavily capital intensive, benefited from the predictability that their relationship with the chains provided because the latter ordered in large volume and often with long lead times, which reduced costly interruptions in production and helped smooth out seasonal cycles. Only a few small manufacturers (themselves not dependent on the chains for distribution) testified in favor of the bill (Palamountain 1955: 179). J. Frederic Dewhurst, executive director of the Twentieth Century Fund, would later sum up the situation: "The high degree of specialization in American industry, simplification of design, and the lavish use of automatic power-driven machinery in turning out low-cost standardized goods would be impossible without the means of assuring mass consumption in a mass market . . . The distribution institutions and methods which make this possible—the mail order house, the chain store, the supermarket, installment buying, market analysis, national advertising and, whether we like it or not, even the singing commercial—are just as much a part of American technology as are radioisotopes and fork-lift trucks" (Lebhar 1959: 350).

The chains had won over other groups as well. Although most retailers had traditionally been hostile toward unions, organized labor came out against the Patman tax bill—both because the chains employed large numbers of workers and also because they provided working-class Americans with everyday necessities at low cost. The AFL had initially been skeptical of the chains until a 1938 study it had commissioned estimated that over three hundred thousand workers "owed their jobs directly to the chains" and a further one million jobs were indirectly attached to them as well (Ryant 1973: 219). The union most directly affected, the Retail Clerks International Protective Association, came out against the Patman tax out of concern for its expected employment effects (Ryant 1973: 218). Unions also viewed their prospects for organizing the big chains as rosier than unionizing hundreds of thousands of independent shops (Schragger 2005: 1079). In July 1939 *Business Week* reported that the AFL had adopted a resolution "condemning excessive taxation of chains, and the Congress of Industrial Organization thinks the same way. Labor's attitude is easy to explain: it can organize chains where it can't independents" (*Business Week*, July 8, 1939: 30). This view had gained traction in 1938–39, when the AFL concluded a collective agreement with A&P itself (Scroop 2008: 942).

State and local governments, along with real estate companies and developers, were also coming around to a favorable view of the chains. Realtors and developers viewed them as desirable tenants and assets for local development. The National Association of Real Estate Boards testified on behalf of chains, as did some state and city chambers of commerce (Palamountain

1955: 180). Changes in the financing of state and local government would also create cross-pressures for politicians at these levels (Deutsch 2010: 89–90). Before the 1930s, state governments were mostly financed through property taxes, but the Great Depression drove state and local governments to look for alternative sources of funding to make up for declining income and property tax revenues (Mehrotra 2022: 261). Thus, starting in 1931, states began to introduce sales taxes as an additional source of revenue. By 1937, such taxes had been introduced in twenty-six states as well as in New York City and Washington, DC, and they quickly became a major source of funding. In Illinois, for example, by 1933–34, the sales tax was the single largest source of revenue for the state— accounting for 23.9 percent of total revenue, a figure that grew to 42.8 percent by 1937–38 (Deutsch 2010: 90). With that, large retailers became a significant source of tax revenue there, meaning that "their success became more important to state government finances" (Deutsch 2010: 94–95).

As individual states grew dependent on consumer spending for their financing, they also learned that it was easier to enforce the new sales taxes on large retailers, both because they offered less resistance (they could absorb the costs more easily than small retailers) and because they already had the administrative capacity to comply with the recordkeeping that was now required. Again citing figures for Illinois: "More than 80 percent of the tax collected in 1937 came from only 14 percent of retailers in Illinois, a fact that researchers ascribed to 'the presence of mail order houses and many chains in this state'" (Deutsch 2010: 94–95). Thus, as the economy recovered from the Depression, state legislatures became increasingly ambivalent about their war on the chains (Schragger 2005: 1068). By 1938 four states had repealed their antichain tax laws, and others let theirs lapse (Schragger 2005: 1078).

Most important, perhaps, over a decade of growth had allowed the chains to build a large customer base that gladly accepted the low prices and convenience they offered (Moreton 2009: 19). Chains cultivated consumer support with a "strong public relations and propaganda drive. A&P alone bought space in 1,300 newspapers, and chain spokesmen, sometimes bearing deceptive labels, addressed thousands of women's clubs" (Palamountain 1955: 181). Organized women's groups had established themselves as the authoritative voice of American consumers, going back to their work on the Pure Food and Drug Act of 1906 and to Hoover's war on waste and inflation during World War I. They carried with them out of these earlier campaigns an intense cost-consciousness that the Great Depression in 1929 had only reinforced (Jacobs 2005). Whatever their sympathies for independent merchants, they were the ones who had to make household ends meet (Schragger 2005: 1075–76).

Consumer interests were represented in the congressional hearings on the Patman tax bill by women's clubs that showed up to "attack the bill as a threat to efficient and cheap methods of distribution" (Palamountain 1955: 181; Lebhar 1959: 278–80). Mrs. Ernest W. Howard (from the District of Columbia Federation of Women's Clubs) testified that the bill "would put an end to a system or method of distribution which justifies its survival by economies of operation and low prices to consumers" (Ryant 1973: 217).[28] As Ryant notes, the representatives of consumer interests who appeared before Congress to testify "were united in their opposition to the tax" (Ryant 1973: 217). A 1938 article in *Newsweek* noted that attitudes had shifted over time in favor of the chains "due in large part to the action of groups of consumers which have organized . . . to defend the chain store and themselves against measures that threatened to raise retail prices" (Ryant 1973: 218).

At the height of the antichain movement in 1937, a majority of the population favored some form of "special" tax on the chains in their states,[29] but a separate Gallup poll from the same year revealed that Americans were also overwhelmingly (60 percent) against prohibiting chain stores in their state.[30] Opposition to prohibiting the chains was especially strong in rural communities, where competition in the retail market was more limited than in urban areas (67 percent against prohibiting chains and only 23 percent in support).[31] In fact, it turned out that even those who favored some restrictions on the chains nonetheless shopped in them (Levinson 2011: 172, citing a *Fortune* magazine survey from January 1937: 154). Lower-income groups relied more on chain stores for their food than did prosperous consumers (nearly 56 percent of "poor" shoppers indicated that they bought "most" or "some" of their groceries at chain stores, as against just under 43 percent

28. These views were echoed by Mrs. Harriet Howe of the American Home Economic Association and Dr. Caroline Ware, a historian who chaired the social studies section of the American Association of University Women (Ryant 1973: 217).

29. In a 1937 Gallup poll, 56 percent of respondents answered "yes" to the question "Are you in favor of requiring chain stores in this state to pay special taxes?" (32 percent were against and 12 percent registered no opinion). Gallup Poll (AIPO) [05/26/1937–05/31/1937] Gallup Organization. Gallup Poll #1937–0084: Business/Supreme Court/Employment, Question 2. USGALLUP.37-84.Q01. Gallup Organization. Cornell University, Ithaca, NY: Roper Center for Public Opinion Research, 1937.

30. Gallup Poll (AIPO) [05/12/1937–05/17/1937]. "Would you favor prohibiting all chain stores in this state?" (60 percent responded "no," 30 percent responded "yes," and 10 percent expressed "no opinion"). Gallup Poll #1937–0082. Chain Stores/Military Spending/Movies. Question 1. USGALLUP.37-82.Q01. Gallup Organization. Cornell University, Ithaca, NY: Roper Center for Public Opinion Research, 1937.

31. Gallup Poll #1937–0082 and 0085.

Which do you think would be the best policy toward chain stores?

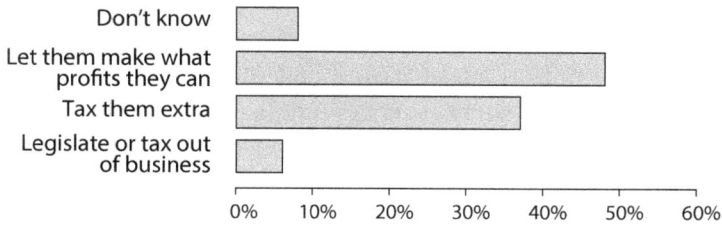

FIGURE 6.4. Position on best policy toward chain stores, 1938.
Source: November 1938 Roper Center Survey, Question 30, USROPER.38-003. RC7 (Cornell University: Roper Center for Public Opinion Research, 1938).

for prosperous shoppers) (*Fortune* 1937: 154). And price was the primary attraction for both groups ("overwhelmingly" for the poor but a "majority" for the prosperous as well) (*Fortune* 1937: 154).[32]

A survey just one year later, in 1938, during the heat of the chains' countercampaign against the Patman tax, again tapped public opinion toward the chains. Figure 6.4 records the results. When allowed to choose off a menu of options, nearly half of all respondents (48 percent) now answered that the chains "should be allowed to make what profits they can." Just over a third (37 percent) still said chains should be taxed extra, but a mere 6 percent said they should be legislated or taxed out of business—which was Patman's original objective (Levinson 2011: 200).

It is perhaps a measure of how isolated the opponents of chain stores had become that over a quarter of the testimony in favor of the 1938 "death tax" bill came from Patman himself (Palamountain 1955: 179–80). In general, it was all too little and too late, because by the time these measures were seriously considered, chains had grown to massive scale and assembled a broad and diverse coalition of support. As Schragger notes, at the end of the day "the chains won. Despite significant popular engagement and legislative successes, the anti–chain store movement failed almost completely to stop the chains" (Schragger 2005: 1014). Some states (predominantly in the South) held out, retaining their state chain store taxes after the Patman bill

32. In the 1937 poll, a small majority of "prosperous" shoppers indicated that they would favor taxing chain stores "enough so that they would have no advantage as to price over the independent grocer" (51.5 percent), a view not quite as widely shared among poorer respondents (48.6 percent). Of the prosperous, 36.5 percent were against such a tax, and 39.1 percent of poorer were against, with the remainder expressing no opinion (*Fortune* 1937: 154).

went down (Ryant 1973: 220).[33] However, despite the "widespread spontane-
ity" of the movement, Palamountain notes that "what is surprising is that a
circumstance in which so many people shared a common grievance produced
so little in the way of organization and lasting legislative results" (1955: 161). In
general, and as Ryant summarizes, opposition to the chains, "epitomized . . .
by the chain-store tax, came out of the South, grew national, and returned to
the South eventually to die" (Ryant 1973: 222).

Conclusion

In sum, in the United States, the political backlash against the chains that
developed in the 1920s and 1930s failed to halt their advance. The states'
fair trade laws discussed in the previous chapter, alongside the Robinson-
Patman Act of 1936, imposed some limits on the ability of large retailers to
exploit their dominance. However, as elaborated further in the next chapter,
enforcement was an ongoing problem and often proved ineffective. Meanwhile, the chain store taxation movement largely fizzled just a few years after
it first began gathering steam.

In general, state-level legislative efforts to shore up small merchants
were simply no match for retailers that were now operating on a national
scale. Through the interwar period, American mass retailers ran roughshod
over the county's fragmented regulatory landscape, and their very growth
allowed them to assemble a politically powerful support coalition. The
American public became increasingly comfortable with the retail giants so
long as they were delivering low prices; as Laura Phillips Sawyer notes: "In
the end, American consumers, through organized protests and individual
purchasing choices, abandoned popular antimonopoly sentiment—and only
on rare occasions have they looked back" (2018: 307–8).

Large, low-cost chains provided critical fuel to the development of the
American consumption model. Indeed, they had become entrenched and
popular fixtures in the political economy, a part of the infrastructure of the
lives of American consumers and producers alike. One of the ironies that
we will unpack in the chapters to follow is how and why the South—once
the heart of the chain store taxation movement—came to embrace the chains
as Sam Walton, its native son, presided over the growth of America's most
successful discount retailing empire.

---

33. Nine of the fourteen states that still had such legislation on the books in 1958 were southern states (Ryant 1973: 220)

PART IV

Retail Capitalism Resurgent

7

Postwar Paradox

LOW-COST RETAILING IN THE "GOLDEN ERA" OF AMERICAN ANTITRUST

The postwar period saw the full flowering of the American consumption-driven growth model. President Franklin D. Roosevelt had signaled the change already in 1932 when, in the midst of the Depression and renewed concerns over corporate power, he declared that the government should "think less about the producers and more about the consumer" (Whitman 2007: 346). The model that emerged was based on the formula that had begun to take shape in the 1920s: credit for the middle class and budget discounters for the rest. Lizabeth Cohen has chronicled the emergence of the "consumers republic" in the United States in the late 1940s and 1950s. Henceforth, "mass consumption . . . would not be a personal indulgence, but rather a civic responsibility" to support full employment and to raise the standard of living for all (2004: 113). Mass consumption would fuel demand for manufactured goods, increased productivity would then be rewarded with higher wages, and this in turn would boost purchasing power in a virtuous cycle of shared prosperity (Cohen 2004: 54–55). In this way, mass consumption promised to bridge the divide between labor and capital and generate greater income equality.

This chapter explores the politics surrounding low-cost retailing in a context characterized by rapid economic growth. Favorable macroeconomic conditions strengthened the country's newly incorporated unions, and growing membership translated into significant gains in wages and benefits. Robust consumer spending, fueled by the government's turn toward Keynesian economic policies, generated intense competition in product and retail markets. At the same time, concerns over growing industrial concentration prompted an important shift in government antitrust policy toward greater enforcement against anticompetitive practices, ushering in what has widely been seen as a golden era in American antitrust.

Yet even as the courts leaned heavily on dominant producers, they would also place a thumb on the scales in favor of a new brand of upstart low-cost retailers. Starting already in 1951, the courts handed down a series of decisions that eroded what was left of America's already shaky fair trade regime. Even before the rise of the Chicago school, they weighed in repeatedly on behalf of upstart hard discounters employing strategies of regulatory arbitrage and outright rule-breaking, and in so doing laid the foundation for the subsequent explosion of discount retailing.

Consumption and Retailing in the Immediate Postwar Period

Although mass purchasing power was a central element in America's postwar growth model, the US government had few tools available to it to maintain consumption while also holding inflation at bay. With many of their rivals in ruins after the war, America's great industrial corporations were more dominant than ever, reactivating worries about the overweening power they might hold over the economy. John Kenneth Galbraith, who served as a key economic adviser across the presidential administrations of Roosevelt, Truman, Kennedy, and Johnson, articulated this concern, noting that large manufacturers possessed the "power to control the prices the citizen paid, the wages he received, and [. . .] interposed the most formidable of obstacles of size and experience to the aspiring new firm" (Galbraith 1952: 109).

How to discipline these corporate behemoths and channel their considerable efficiencies toward the collective good? Direct government involvement in the economy (along the lines being pursued, for example, by Britain's Labour government in this period) was not an option in the United States, which (especially after the failed NIRA experiment) lacked both the state capacity and the political will to engage in central planning. For Keynesians like Galbraith the alternative was clear; private power would be countervailed by private power: "The long trend toward concentration of industrial enterprise in the hands of a relatively few firms has brought into existence not only strong sellers, as economists have supposed, but also strong buyers as they have failed to see. The two develop together, not in precise step but in such manner that there can be no doubt that the one is in response to the other" (111). Galbraith was convinced that the parallel growth of actors on "the opposite side of the market" (as he put it) could be counted on to "neutralize" the power of large producers: "As a common rule, we can rely on countervailing power to appear as a curb on economic power" (113). Direct government control or planning were neither necessary nor warranted; instead, the primary role assigned to the state was to assist in organizing such countervailing forces (151).[1]

What were these countervailing forces? Trade unions were clearly one such force. Keynesians saw the Wagner Act of 1935 as having removed the constraints on unions, empowering workers to stand up to powerful producers by demanding their fair share of the returns on increases in efficiency and productivity. By securing high wages, workers would not just lift themselves up; they would contribute to sustaining the consumer demand on which the entire growth regime rested. But what would prevent excessive and inflationary demands, and, relatedly, what would prevent organized labor and manufacturers from colluding to raise prices at the expense of consumers?

This is where large retailers came in: "One of the most important instruments for the exercise of countervailing power is the large retail organization. These by proxy are the public's main line of defense against the market power of those who produce or process consumers' goods" (Galbraith 1952: 141). Spurred on by competition with other retailers,[2] and situated as key intermediaries between producers and consumers, retailers "are required by their situation to develop countervailing power on the consumer's behalf" (117). "Thus, as in the labor market, we find the mass retailer, from a position across the market, with both a protective and a profit incentive to develop countervailing power when the firm with which it is doing business is in possession of market power" (118). Indeed, Galbraith saw in the country's large

1. As Galbraith put it: "The support of countervailing power has become in modern times perhaps the major domestic peacetime function of the federal government" (136). "Given the existence of private market power in the economy, the growth of countervailing power strengthens the capacity of the economy for autonomous self-regulation and thereby lessens the amount of overall government control or planning that is required or sought" (151).

2. Galbraith viewed retailing (in sharp contrast to manufacturing) as highly competitive, a sector in which even large firms were "constantly under the threat of an erosion of [their] business by the more rapid growth of rivals and by the appearance of new firms" (118).

retailers "an American counterpart of the consumer co-operatives which, in other countries, are viewed explicitly as an instrument for countering the power of the cartels," and he argued that cooperatives might well have played this function in the United States had it not been for the fact that the corporate chains simply got there first (Galbraith 1952: 126–27; 141).

In short, large retailers would no longer be attacked as scary would-be monopsonists; instead they would be welcomed as a crucial countervailing power (alongside labor) to sustain mass consumption by reining in the power of the country's large manufacturers. For Galbraith and other key economic advisers, large retailers were to be supported, not harassed as they had been by southern populists in the 1930s. Galbraith was sharply critical of what he considered the misguided antitrust suit that the government had brought against the A&P grocery chain in 1944 (chapter 6; Levinson 2011). To him, the A&P case reflected a massive failure "to distinguish between *original* and *countervailing* power [my italics] . . . [The company's] crime has been too vigorous bargaining, which bargaining was, effectively, on the consumer's behalf. . . . No explanation, however elaborate, could quite conceal the fact that the effect of antitrust enforcement, in this case, was to the disadvantage of the public" (Galbraith 1952: 142–43). Galbraith considered episodes such as this to be deeply counterproductive because they undermined the countervailing powers that large retailers wielded while leaving powerful producers and suppliers "undisturbed" (Galbraith 1952: 142).

Galbraith decried the entire lawsuit as an ill-advised fiasco, "a serious embarrassment to friends of the antitrust laws" (Galbraith 1942: 143). Moreover, as we saw in the previous chapter, the episode had also proved to be something of a public relations own-goal. The 1949 Gallup poll made clear that voters were well aware of the case and revealed that A&P enjoyed twice the level of support as the government (chapter 6; Levinson 2011: 245). By this time as well, Congress had also come around to Galbraith's view of A&P's prosecution "as an ill-conceived attack on consumers" (Freyer 1992: 298).

Galbraith took the same dim view of legislation, such as the Robinson-Patman Act discussed previously, that had sought to rein in the purchasing power of chain stores: "Even those who are unwavering in their belief in competition have been inclined to doubt whether this legislation does much to protect competition. What is not doubtful at all is that the legislation strikes directly at the effective exercise of countervailing power. To achieve price discrimination—to use bargaining power to get a differentially lower price—is the very essence of the exercise of countervailing power. In trying, with questionable effect, to preserve one of the autonomous regulators of the economy the government is seriously impairing another" (1952: 144). In short, in Galbraith's view, America's large retailers were decidedly not part of the problem; in fact they were part of the solution to monopoly power. The two countervailing forces—organized labor and large retailers—complemented one another, with labor's strength vis-à-vis manufacturers waxing in periods of robust demand for consumer goods, and large retailers winning the upper hand when demand dropped off (132–33).

Indeed, in the heady consumer markets of the 1950s and 1960s, events unfolded broadly in accordance with Galbraith's script. American manufacturers enjoyed unprecedented dominance, buoyed above all by virtually insatiable demand for the consumer goods that they were cranking out. As others have documented in great detail, postwar consumption was heavily underwritten by government policies that promoted homeownership (for white families), that guaranteed loans for home improvement, and that connected southern homes to the electric grid (Cohen 2003; Logemann 2012b; Calder 1999: 279–80; Thurston 2018).

Manufacturing was buzzing, and just as Galbraith had predicted, strong demand for labor provided a congenial context for unions in industry to organize and to claim their fair share of the productivity increases. Overall unionization peaked in the United States in this period (in 1954 at just under 35 percent), with the highest levels in manufacturing. Key industries such as automobiles and steel adopted coordinated pattern-bargaining, resulting in important gains for labor that set the tone for other sectors as well. The truce between large manufacturers and large retailers that had emerged in the depths of the Depression largely held, as large cut-price retailers such as Macy's laid off the price wars and settled into a less conflictual relationship with their suppliers. In fact, as we saw in previous chapters, many of the country's large retailers had themselves become involved in manufacturing, contracting with producers to manufacture their house brands (e.g., Sears and the producers of its Kenmore appliances).

As in other countries, unionization rates in the retail sector lagged far behind the levels achieved in industry, but even there organized labor made important gains. The Retail, Wholesale, and Department Store Union had had some success in organizing large retail chains (e.g., Macy's, Bloomingdale's), and, as noted in chapter 6, the United Food and Commercial Workers Union had made important inroads with large grocery chains (e.g., A&P, Kroger). Even those large retailers that remained vehemently anti-union were typically forced to pay competitive wages against the threat of unionization. Sears, for example, offered generous company benefits and famously featured career ladders that allowed hard-working frontline workers to advance in the corporate hierarchy (Jacoby 1986).

In this period, then, American manufacturers were powerful—in the market and in politics—but their power was countervailed (exactly as Galbraith had hoped) by relatively strong unions capable of claiming a share of the profits from increasing productivity. And while their European counterparts rebuilt their economies on the strength of rising exports, American manufacturers and the rising wages they paid fueled an unprecedented consumer boom.

Antitrust and the Rise of the Discount Retailers

There were undercurrents of trouble though. Galbraith's prescription for reining in the power of America's oligopolistic firms—confronting the growing might of manufacturing with the countervailing power of large retailers and unions—failed to anticipate that one of these countervailing powers would thrive and grow at the expense of the other.

On the labor side, one of the most consequential legacies of antitrust jurisprudence in the late nineteenth and early twentieth centuries had been to actively disarticulate the emerging sectoral associations (on both the labor and employer sides) that could have anchored more encompassing forms of collective bargaining (see chapter 2 and Thelen 2020 for an extended analysis). The Wagner Act of 1935 was, undoubtedly, a significant breakthrough. However, as other scholars have pointed out, because the battles over labor rights in the United States were fought in the courts and on the (for employers) more congenial terrain and language of individual rights, the settlement the Wagner Act institutionalized proved to be a flimsy foundation for guaranteeing labor's *collective* rights (Forbath 1991: 7–8; Andrias 2016: 1610–11). Already in 1934, business elites had organized to form an American Liberty League to claw back the property and corporate rights that they saw the government as having usurped in the context of the Depression. Just nine days after the Wagner Act passed, the league's National Lawyers Committee prepared a brief challenging the constitutionality of the new measure and offering "free legal counsel to those who wished to resist" (Shamir 1995: 67–68, 69).[3]

Of course the Wagner Act did survive the constitutional test, though in 1938 the Supreme Court expressly condoned employers' use of permanent replacement workers in the case of economic strikes. And as soon as the

---

3. The National Association of Manufacturers invoked this brief to urge noncompliance by its members.

Second World War ended, Southern Democrats and Republicans mobilized to secure the passage of the 1947 Taft-Hartley Act, which further undermined the fragile legal basis on which union gains would be possible—for example, by banning secondary strikes and boycotts, outlawing the closed shop, and holding unions liable for damages through industrial action. Southern states rushed to pass the "right to work" laws that Taft-Hartley allowed, providing American companies with an easy nonunion exit option and undermining union efforts to organize the South to this day.

Passed against intense union opposition, and over President Harry S. Truman's veto, Taft-Hartley also rendered union certification more difficult by eliminating card checks and other mechanisms though which unions could demonstrate majority support. Henceforth, unions would have to seek recognition, shopfloor by shopfloor, in elections in which employers enjoyed an explicit right to countermobilize (Goldfield 1987: 185). In 1951, the Supreme Court added an exclamation point by upholding Taft-Hartley's restrictions on collective action that targets multiple employers, thus ensuring that unions' strategic horizons would be limited to the firm level rather than aimed at broader sectoral, let alone class, solidarity. The prosperity of the 1950s and 1960s masked the weaknesses in the legal foundations of labor's power, but it would not be long before American unions were quite unable to perform the countervailing functions Galbraith had envisioned for them.

In the meantime, disruptive new discounters would enter the market, provoking what *Fortune* magazine would call an upheaval in retailing (Petrovic and Hamilton 2006: 112) and putting intense pressure on American manufacturing by challenging the cozy relations between distributors and producers. In the go-go years of postwar economic growth and high consumer demand, the balance of power between manufacturers and retailers shifted toward producers since distributors were essentially competing for inventory. Large manufacturers, more likely to be unionized than small ones, had an interest in maintaining prices that would allow them to pay union wages and retain a healthy profit for themselves. Courts, however, made it increasingly difficult for producers to maintain their prices. Antitrust jurisprudence would play an important role in tilting outcomes, for in the battles that ensued the courts would lean heavily on large manufacturers, while new low-cost retailers often found themselves on the winning side of court decisions upholding their right to cut prices.[4]

---

4. I am indebted to Louis Hyman for emphasizing the importance of the interventions of the courts in a series of cases in the 1950s, discussed in this chapter.

The seeds for these developments were planted already in the 1930s at the height of the Depression. As Peinert in particular has meticulously documented, the failure of NIRA and the public backlash it provoked—against both central government power and large corporations—had led to a major reorientation of antitrust policy (Peinert 2020: chap. 3; Peinert 2023). The theory behind the NIRA experiment had been that stabilizing prices would lead the country out of the Depression by stimulating investment, which would create jobs, which in turn would stimulate consumption. But NIRA had become a political liability even before the Supreme Court struck it down in 1935. In the previous year, a growing chorus of consumer groups, labor unions, and small business interests began denouncing the experiment as having failed to produce growth while allowing large producers to capture fat rents that they declined to pass on to workers and consumers.

Hard evidence had also accumulated to corroborate these impressions. In 1938 FDR and Congress had created a commission charged with assessing the impact of economic concentration on the economy. Chaired by the economist Leon Henderson, the Temporary National Economic Committee (TNEC) undertook an expansive investigation of the impact of "cartels, state fair trade laws, patents, and various other competitive practices" across a wide range of industries (Weber Waller 2004: 586). Their report, released in 1941, delivered a stark repudiation of previous efforts at price stabilization through NIRA. The committee found that it was the more *competitive* sectors, rather than those with stable pricing through industry codes, that showed superior employment and wage effects (Peinert 2020: chap. 3). One of its central recommendations called for the repeal of the Miller-Tydings Act, a recommendation that Congress declined to take up until much later, in 1975. However, the committee's report also called for a prohibition on large horizontal mergers unless specifically approved by the Federal Trade Commission. This recommendation would feed into the Celler-Kefauver Act of 1950, which strengthened restrictions on mergers and acquisitions (Weber Waller 2004: 586–87).

Responding to these findings, and to the widespread criticism of NIRA—from inside and outside government circles—Roosevelt reversed course on antitrust. He appointed Thurman Arnold to head the antitrust division of the Department of Justice (DOJ), and Arnold went on to launch a period of reinvigorated enforcement. Taking up his new job with verve, Arnold prosecuted almost as many cases during his short tenure (1938–43) as head of antitrust as the previous fifty years of antitrust combined (Weber Waller 2004: 583). However, he also transformed antitrust enforcement by redirecting its focus toward consumers, inspired in part by the results of a DOJ study of prices on food and prescription drugs that wound up pointing the finger at small merchants and pharmacists (the National Association of Retail Druggists, or NARD, in particular) (Sparks 2000: 359–61). In Arnold's words: in the past, antitrust laws were "designed to eliminate *the evil of bigness. What ought to be emphasized is not the evils of size but the evils* of industries which are not efficient or do not pass efficiency on to consumers . . ." (italics in original; Sandel 1996: 241).

This reorientation fit perfectly with the government's turn toward demand-driven growth in the postwar period. Arnold "conceptualized both cartels and monopolies as 'bottlenecks' on production and distribution, which kept the industrial production of America from reaching the consumer" (Weber Waller 2004: 579). He identified "four horsemen"—fixed prices, low turnover, restricted production, and monopoly control—as riding roughshod over the economy (Weber Waller 2004: 579). Thus, the impact of heightened antitrust enforcement in the immediate postwar period would fall unevenly on different actors in the political economy, imposing new constraints on large manufacturers but often enhancing the power of cut-price retailers. Over the next several decades the outcome of the dual conflicts detailed in chapters 5 and 6—between manufacturers and retailers over the price at which goods would be sold (fair trade) and between large and small retailers over the prices at which the larger competitors could purchase from suppliers (price discrimination)—would both break for low-cost retailers. The remainder of this chapter and the next chapter address these developments, each in turn.

FAIR TRADE IN THE POSTWAR PERIOD

Fair trade, already deeply unloved by FDR and his DOJ at the time the Miller-Tydings bill had come to the president's desk in 1937, was now completely out of sync with the government's new antitrust approach.[5] The DOJ had ramped up antitrust enforcement and was busy fearlessly taking on some of the biggest names in American industry, from Paramount Studios to the Pullman Company, as well as major steel and aluminum producers (Weber

---

5. Recall from chapter 5 that the DOJ and the FTC had both opposed the legislation in 1937, but FDR signed it because its proponents had attached it to a must-pass funding bill. And the TNEC report from 1941 had unequivocally called for the law to be repealed (Weber Waller 2004: 587).

Waller 2004: 588–91).[6] In cases that involved resale price maintenance, low-cost retailers were on the winning side, scoring key victories. As the courts eroded manufacturers' ability to defend their fair trade prices, they tilted the balance of power toward low-cost retailers. Three pivotal decisions stand out, and I discuss each briefly in turn.

A first, enormously important ruling was *Schwegmann Bros. v. Calvert Distillers Corp.* (1950–51) (Hyman 2012: 125).[7] The Miller-Tydings Act, it will be recalled, exempted from antitrust prosecution resale price maintenance (RPM) contracts that had been concluded in fair trade states even when products crossed state lines. The law was silent, however, on a key provision in many states' fair trade laws that held that RPM applied not just to the parties to the contract, but to any distributor who "willfully and knowingly sells the commodity below the prices established by such a contract, whether or not a party thereto" (Fulda 1954: 175). These so-called nonsigner clauses were critical to the effectiveness of fair trade laws since discounters, by definition, would not willingly submit to their terms.

The *Schwegmann* case involved a supermarket chain (Schwegmann Bros.) that was selling Calvert products in Louisiana (a fair trade state with a nonsigner provision) at cut-rate prices (Fulda 1954: 176–77). The district court, citing Miller-Tydings, had ruled in favor of Calvert, affirming the company's right to hold Schwegmann Bros. to the fair trade contract agreed by other retailers in the state even though the supermarket had itself not signed on to Calvert's pricing policy. The Supreme Court, however, reversed to rule in favor of the retail chain, arguing that Calvert's claim to hold noncontracting parties to the contracts it had with other distributors went beyond the exception the Miller-Tydings Act had allowed.[8] By making clear that

6. Arnold's first big case was against the big auto manufacturers, attacking the practice of requiring their dealers to use the companies' own financing operations to underwrite customers' purchases. In another huge and very public case, Arnold took on the motion picture industry. Major studios had exclusive deals with their own theaters, so if moviegoers wanted to see, say, *Gone with the Wind* they had to go to a Paramount theater (with thanks to Chase Foster for this example). Arnold's antitrust division attacked these practices as limiting competition and forced the studios to relinquish control over their theaters. Another enormous case was brought against Alcoa, which possessed a near monopoly on aluminum and bauxite (crucial construction inputs, and therefore hugely important in the postwar housing boom) and which was shown to be part of an international cartel engaged in illegal boycotting. And the list goes on (Weber Waller 2004: 589–91).

7. I thank Louis Hyman for directing my attention to this case and to emphasizing its impact on fair trade.

8. "The power of a contracting manufacturer and a contracting retailer to maintain a uniform price by imposing the price on non-contracting parties is a form of price fixing which is expressly

the nonsigner provisions were outside the protection of Miller-Tydings, the *Schwegmann* decision dealt fair trade a massive blow. Now any retailers who could get their hands on fair trade products could sell these goods at whatever price they wanted. The ink had hardly dried on the decision before Macy's (with its characteristic hyperbole) announced discounts on 5,978 "price fixed" items (Zipser 1951), though, as Fulda notes, the price wars were almost exclusively centered in New York City and did not last long (1954: 177–78).

Pharmacists again jumped into action and secured legislation (the 1952 McGuire Act) that reinstated the legality of enforcement against nonsigners in states whose fair trade laws allowed it.[9] But anxiety ran high among companies struggling to maintain prices. As one appliance manufacturer fretted, "We are afraid that there will be violent price wars with a few of the strongest, most financially powerful retailers and discount houses emerging in monopolistic position of dominance over the retailing of appliances. While price wars initially move a lot of merchandise, they also make it absolutely unprofitable for the great majority of dealers to continue handling the price-cut merchandise so the long-run effect of the weakening or destruction of the fair trade laws will be to develop retailing concentration and monopolies" (Allender 1993: 226).[10]

Despite the new legislation, the damage from the court's ruling had already been done. By 1954, the number of companies using price maintenance contracts had declined from 1,600 to 900, and the share of total retail sales involving price-maintained products was just 7 percent (Bean 1996: 81). A study of pricing for fair trade toothpaste (to take one prominent example) showed that prices fell in fair trade states after the *Schwegmann* decision and did not rebound after the McGuire Act passed (Bowman 1955: 857–58). Moreover, state courts were themselves now reevaluating nonsigner clauses, often

---

excluded from the protection of the Miller-Tydings Act." See *The Fair Trade Laws: Address by James M. Mead, Chairman, Federal Trade Commission, before the New York State Pharmaceutical Association,* June 11, 1951, https://www.ftc.gov/system/files/documents/public_statements/684181/19510611_mead_the_fair_trade_laws.pdf.

9. Congressional minutes from the debates indicate that NARD representatives were keen to enlist allies in their lobbying efforts: John Dargavel of NARD urged members of other associations to support the cause by encouraging "every friend of fair trade in the country" to write to their congressmen. Dargavel provided a list of justifications that they could adapt "so that you can present the case for fair trade in your own words" (*Minimum Resale Prices* 1952: 9).

10. From the US Congress, Senate Select Committee on Small Business, *On a Study on Fair Trade, Based on a Survey of Manufacturers and Retailers* (Report no. 2819), 84th Cong., 2d sess., July 27, 1956, p. 18.

striking them down either as a violation of property rights or based on a rejection of the argument that such clauses represented a valid extension of state police power (Hollander 1966: 71; Fulda 1954: 209–10). State legislatures were also rethinking their fair trade laws, particularly after 1955 when a federal antitrust advisory committee condemned such laws on grounds that they increased prices for the consumer (Levinson 2011: 252).

Table 7.1 provides details on when and for what reason state courts ruled against fair trade following the *Schwegmann* decision. By 1959, courts in seventeen states had nullified enforcement of nonsigner clauses, mostly on grounds of due process or improper delegation of police power.[11]

As state after state abandoned the nonsigner clauses in their fair trade laws, a "domino effect" took hold, "weakening the position of fair traders in other states" (Bean 1996: 86).

A second key Supreme Court decision (*Masters Mail Order v. General Electric*, 1957) blew another hole in fair trade by declaring that mail order sales consummated in non–fair trade states were exempt even when the purchaser lived in a fair trade state (Weston 1963: 80–83). The status of mail order under state fair trade laws was already on shaky ground. In 1950 a Circuit Court of Appeals had considered a case in which the Sunbeam Corporation sought to enjoin Wentling (a mail order retailer headquartered in Pennsylvania) from selling its electric razors below the fair trade price. At that time, the court ruled that Sunbeam was not entitled to protection against Wentling in interstate sales, but it did enjoin the mail order house from selling Sunbeam's razors below price within the state.[12] The case came back to the same court in 1951 (in a slightly different form) after the Supreme Court's *Schwegmann* decision, and this time the court handed down an unequivocal decision denying Sunbeam protection against below-price sales by nonsigners, in intrastate as well as interstate trade: "Our conclusion here is free from doubt. Sunbeam's rights under the fair trade act against a nonsigner are shown by the decision in the Schwegmann case. There are no such rights."[13]

---

11. It may be no coincidence that these developments followed closely the rollout of the US power grid (Lewis and Severnini 2017: 25, figure 1; Lebergott 1976: 280; Historical statistics of the US: 827). The share of farm households with electricity rose from about 50 percent to nearly 100 percent in the ten years between 1945–55. Once on the grid, rural households were keen to purchase appliances.

12. Sunbeam Corp. v. Wentling, 192 F.2d 7, (US Court of Appeals, 3rd Circ. November 1951), https://cite.case.law/f2d/192/7/.

13. Sunbeam Corp. v. Wentling.

TABLE 7.1. State Court Rulings against Fair Trade, 1951–58

Year	State	Reason
1951	Florida	Citing *Schwegmann Bros. v. Calvert Corp.*
1952	Michigan	Due process
1955	Arkansas	Deprivation of due process
1955	Georgia	Due process
1955	Indiana	In derogation of Indiana constitution
1955	Nebraska	Due process
1955	South Carolina	Due process
1956	Colorado	Deprivation of due process; improper delegation of police power
1956	Louisiana	Improper delegation of legislative power
1956	Oregon	Due process; improper delegation of legislative power
1956	Utah	Conflict with antitrust section of Utah constitution
1956	Virginia	Repealed by state antitrust law
1957	New Mexico	Improper exercise of police power
1958	Kansas	Improper delegation of legislative power
1958	Kentucky	Due process
1958	Ohio	Improper exercise of police power
1958	West Virginia	Improper exercise of police power

Source: Yale Law Journal 1959: 168–69. All of these cases, except for Virginia 1956, were rulings that "effectively eliminated fair trade by ruling that the crucial 'nonsigner' provisions . . . are violations of state constitutional guarantees" (169). The 1956 Virginia case "held resale price maintenance impliedly repealed by state antitrust laws" (169).

The Supreme Court itself took up the mail order exception in 1957 in a series of cases involving Masters Mail Order Co., a DC-based mail order firm. The District of Columbia was outside the reach of state fair trade laws, and Masters Mail Order was selling fair trade products at cut prices to buyers in fair trade states (*Yale Law Journal* 1959: 168). The court's decision in dual cases brought against Masters (one brought by Bissell Carpet Sweeper and the other by General Electric) confirmed that, the McGuire Act notwithstanding, mail order sales consummated in non–fair trade states were outside the scope of the laws that immunized state price maintenance legislation from federal antitrust (*Yale Law Journal* 1959: 168). The decision in the GE case sent Sears's and Ward's sales soaring ("Sears' Sales Set a High in Month" 1959: 68).

Third, and finally, three years later the Supreme Court further undercut fair trade in its pharma stronghold with its ruling in *United States v. Parke,*

David (1960) (Bean 1996: 82–83). In this decision, the court limited the scope of the so-called Colgate doctrine that had allowed manufacturers to refuse to supply retailers who violated their price policies (*Duke Law Journal* 1961: 122). The DOJ—acting on a complaint by a discount drugstore, Dart Drug—brought the case against a major drug manufacturer that the government contended had "induced and compelled" wholesalers and retailers to conspire with them to maintain prices, thus going beyond "the limited dispensation" the Colgate doctrine had allowed. In dissent, Justice John Marshall Harlan claimed that the court's ruling had "reduced the *Colgate* rule to a hollow shell, leaving the manufacturer with a theoretical right that was not legally enforceable" (*Duke Law Journal* 1961: 122). As Kenneth Dam put it in a debate with Robert Pitofsky, though the Supreme Court did not eliminate the Colgate exemption, it had "steadily tightened the noose" around it (Pitofsky and Dam 1968: 784).

Fair trade pricing had always been especially difficult to defend for the fast-moving toiletries and household goods that pharmacies carried alongside prescription drugs. As Pope notes, since the early twentieth century the advertising industry had always faced the problem of finding ways "to differentiate fundamentally equivalent products . . . and to cultivate brand loyalty through intensive publicity" (1983: 14). But for everyday household products such as toothpaste, consumers had trouble distinguishing the branded goods from other virtually identical (but less expensive) private brands.[14] Moreover, food chains had already begun selling some beauty and toiletry articles, a trend that increased rapidly in the 1940s. Fairly traded products commanded higher margins than groceries (in part because of pharmacists' defenses), and grocery stores like A&P were eager to use such sales to subsidize the far lower margins they secured on food items (Fulda 1954: 191).[15] The number of grocery stores selling such items increased from 37 percent to 70 percent between 1941 and 1950 (Fulda 1954: 191), prompting

---

14. Crest leaped ahead of the pack in toothpaste sales in 1960 after the American Dental Association endorsed a new formula that included fluoride (an innovation subsequently copied by other companies). See Harvard Business School, "How Crest Made Business History," January 17, 2005, https://hbswk.hbs.edu/archive/how-crest-made-business-history. The general issue, however, was one that Chase and Schlink's popular 1927 book *Your Money's Worth* discussed in the context of a critique of the fog of advertising. Sometimes the difference between something sold in five-and-dime stores and those sold at three to four times the price elsewhere was "only a trifling matter of finish" (82).

15. The margin on items such as branded toothpaste (e.g., Gleem) was around 33 percent, much higher than the usual 16–17 percent margin grocers were able to secure for food products (Fulda 1954: 192).

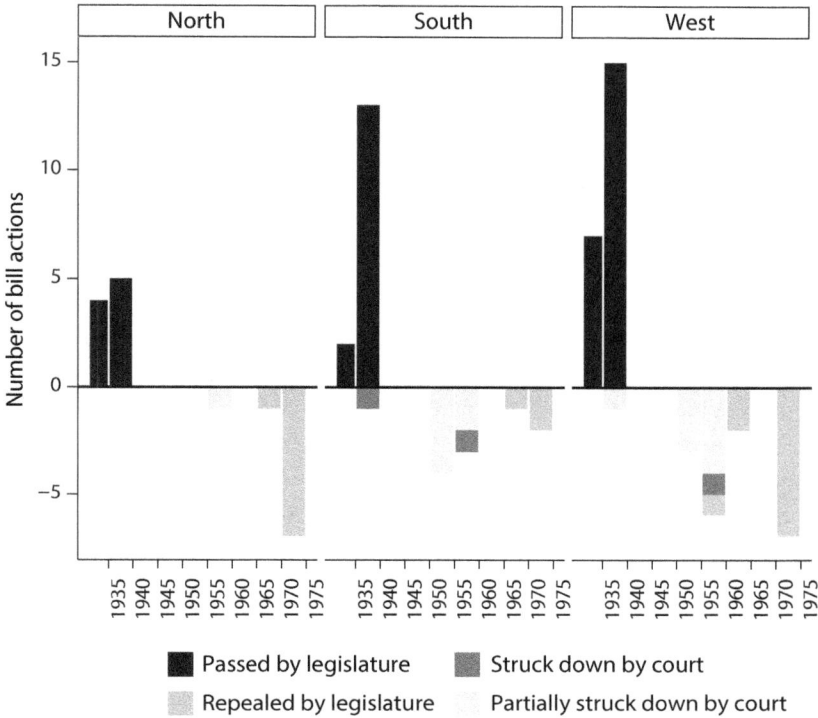

FIGURE 7.1. Fair trade legislation passed, repealed, and reversed, by region and year. *Sources:* FTC, 1945, "Report of the Federal Trade Commission on Resale Price Maintenance" (Washington, DC: US GPO), 67–123; *Fair Trade Laws: Hearings Before the Subcommittee on Antitrust and Monopoly of the Senate Committee on the Judiciary*, 94th Cong. 328–29 (1975, Appendix 1); Eileen Shanahan, "'Fair Trade' Laws Coming to an End," *New York Times*, December 13, 1975.

one congressman to suggest that druggists had been "hoisted by their own petard" because their successful defense of high margins had drawn more competitors into the game (Fulda 1954: 192n91).

Figure 7.1 documents the overall trajectory of state fair trade laws across the entire period, tracking their rapid expansion in the South and West in the 1930s and their later gradual collapse, either though legislative repeal or court action. The timeline ends in 1975 because in that year Congress passed federal legislation repealing the Miller-Tydings and McGuire acts, thereby ending the authorization for state fair trade acts altogether. But as the figure shows, by this time many of the states with fair trade laws had repealed these laws or seen them struck down in court, so that the 1975 federal law only affected a few states with such laws still on the books.

LAST DEFENSES OF FAIR TRADE IN THE UNITED STATES

The unique features of American fair trade—distinct, as we saw in chapter 5, from the European version, which rested heavily on collective enforcement in the market rather than individual enforcement in the courts—had long meant that resale price maintenance was not protecting small niche producers of high-quality goods in the United States. On the contrary, in the American context, resale price maintenance was a luxury that only the country's large mass manufacturers could afford. Numerous contemporary accounts emphasize the difficulty and expense associated with efforts to maintain prices (Senate Report 1956: 7, 21; *Yale Law Journal* 1959: 172–74, 177–78; Fulda 1954: 202–6). Beyond securing fair trade contracts with their various distributors, firms had to bring considerable resources to bear to monitor compliance, for example, by hiring shoppers to check the prices charged by retail outlets. Violators had to be pursued through expensive litigation that often resulted in protracted cases. Moreover, even when such litigation resulted in an injunction, the manufacturer had to bear the cost of policing to make sure that the injunction was actually observed, which it frequently was not.[16] One reason why is that the fines that violators incurred were often low, so low that retailers intent on lower pricing simply folded the expense into the cost of doing business (*Yale Law Journal* 1959: 188–89).[17]

All these maneuvers became even more expensive in the wake of these Supreme Court decisions and as the Colgate exception that allowed firms to attempt to control prices by refusing to sell to price-cutters was increasingly circumscribed by the court. Some producers had whole departments devoted to administering their fair trade programs, though for many more the task was more dispersed (Senate Report 1956: 5). Either way, monitoring, policing, litigating, and enforcing fair trade contracts was expensive. A Senate report from 1956 (based on a survey of manufacturing firms) quoted one company representative as saying that, although he could not provide an exact figure, "needless to say, the cost of enforcing our fair-trade program is quite considerable and a major item in our budget" (Senate Report 1956: 5).

16. Fulda, for example, cites a case in which General Electric sought an injunction against Macy's for selling its appliances below the list price. Macy's responded by coming back with evidence of widespread lack of enforcement, citing myriad sellers of GE products who continued to sell below price despite injunctions (Fulda 1954: 203–4).

17. For example, in one case involving Sunbeam products, the violator was charged a fine of just $500, alongside $750 to cover the court costs; another case involving GE products brought a fine of just $100; a Kodak case resulted in $400 for four violations, plus an additional $150 to cover the lawyer's fees (*Yale Law Journal* 1959: 188n123).

GE complained that it was impossible to monitor all of its thirty thousand fair trade contracts while at the same time pursuing three thousand lawsuits against companies that had violated them (Howard 2015: 186; Bean 1996: 83). The trouble and expense of defending prices often proved too much. Sheaffer Pen Company, for example, found that it was spending 4 percent of sales revenue on legal expenses attempting to defend their prices before giving up the effort in 1955 (Bean 1996: 82).

The one legally fail-safe avenue to price maintenance that remained open to brand manufacturers was an agency model. While agency or franchise arrangements were clearly not tenable for everyday goods such as toiletries and toasters that require little to no service, it was a viable option in sectors such as consumer electronics and home appliances where credit, trade-ins, and after-sales service were important (see Teupe 2016 on the role of franchising in the appliance industry). Household appliances were also just the kind of big-ticket consumer durables for which quality claims mattered a great deal, and big brand manufacturers of such products had invested heavily in advertising.

Leading producers such as General Electric and Westinghouse faced formidable rivals such as Sears, whose Kenmore line commanded a significant share of the household appliance market. By contracting directly with manufacturing firms to produce private brands sold exclusively at its own retail outlets, Sears had essentially turned its suppliers into agents of the retailer. In the 1950s and 1960s, Sears's competitors often responded by pursuing the same strategy in reverse—channeling sales through exclusive "authorized dealers"— turning independent retailers into agents of the producer.[18] Under franchise or agency arrangements, manufacturers granted their wholesalers or individual retailers exclusive distribution rights in exchange for control over key aspects of their competitive strategies, including prices. The attraction of such vertical arrangements was that they not only allowed firms to maintain prices, they also made it possible for them to exercise control without the legal, economic, and political expenses and responsibility associated with full ownership.

As a method of distribution, franchising was not new, having grown out of the practice of agency sales that had been pioneered by manufacturers like McCormick (farm implements) and Singer sewing machines in the

18. One result of this double shift, as Palamountain's figures suggest, was to squeeze traditional wholesalers, whose share of retail declined rather sharply between 1929 and 1939, from both directions (1955: 20–21). Seligman and Love refer to "the factory-owned chain" and "the chain-owned factory" (1932: 12) as alternative ways of ensuring coordination between producer and distributors.

mid-nineteenth century (Dicke 1992: chap. 1). And although automobile makers and petroleum refiners had operated a franchise system since the 1920s, the practice was not widespread in other sectors of retailing. (As one indicator: it did not show up as a separate entry in business periodicals until the late 1950s—e.g., the *Business Periodicals Index* started listing it only in 1958 [Dicke 1992: 2].) But with fair trade under attack, the model spread in the 1950s and 1960s, growing to encompass over a third of the total value of retail sales.

The rapid growth of franchising inspired a small cottage industry of business publications documenting its rise (Kursh 1969) and also promoting it as a new model. Many business publications heralded a "new frontier for small business," encouraging would-be entrepreneurs to "be your own boss" (Dicke 1992: 126). The "franchise boom" of this period (Kursh 1969) also unleashed an outpouring of writing evaluating its virtues and dangers. The American Manufacturers' Association heralded franchise arrangements as "partnerships for profit" (Curry 1966), even as other writers warned darkly that these arrangements were a "trap for the trusting" (Brown 1969).[19] And although franchising "was born to fill the need of small independent businessmen for professional assistance and group buying power in what [had] become a 'chain store age,'" dealers "stood in an awkward position: they enjoyed few of the personal benefits of small business ownership yet were still subject to most of its risks" (Pelletier 1969: 602; Dicke 1992: 47).

Whether franchising was the "last and best hope for the survival of small business in an economy dominated by big business" or "a cruel hoax, promising economic freedom but in reality only creating a new type of 'wage slave'" (Dicke 1992: 47) depended heavily on the economic context. The postwar boom of the 1950s and high demand for consumer goods had tilted the balance of power toward the producers, increasing costs as distributors jockeyed among themselves for access to inventory, even as competition from the likes of Sears (with its private-label products) narrowed independent retailers' room for maneuver with respect to the prices they could charge consumers. Beleaguered merchants could both guarantee themselves a steady source of supplies *and also* seek refuge from price competition by signing exclusive contracts with brand manufacturers who promised decent margins, albeit with strings attached. In the intense competitive market for consumer dollars of the 1950s, franchising contracts were often a "golden cage" (Teupe 2016: 237) that they were happy to enter.

19. Brown's book provided a number of strategies for franchisees to sue their franchisors, "making it appear to be a manual for lawsuits," according to one review (Pelletier 1969: 607).

This was a far cry from the devolution of power to small business that Brandeis's version of fair trade had sought to defend. As agents of large manufacturers, these independent merchants were able to secure a slice of the rents, but they also became appendages of the mass producers with whom they had thrown in their lots. They were thus subject to pricing and other decisions handed down from above—and all enforced against the (for them, existential) threat of withdrawal of the franchise.

Although franchise arrangements almost immediately attracted scrutiny under heightened antitrust enforcement, brand manufacturers heaved a sigh of relief when early legal contests found that the kinds of vertical restraints they were imposing were not *per se* illegal.[20] But both the legal and the market context were shifting around them—and large manufacturers turned out to be fair-weather friends. Some producers sought competitive advantage by essentially throwing their independent dealers under the bus. Sunbeam, for example, opted for increased sales volume through a mix of full price and discount outlets, and the company watched its sales soar in the 1950s (Hollander 1966: 86–87). Indeed, by this time, more and more manufacturers were following Sunbeam's lead, seeking increased sales by selling through both full price and discount stores.

These developments unleashed intense price competition among independent merchants ("list" became the price you'd be a fool to pay) even as new discount retailers began to capture a growing share of the consumer goods market. And as soon as competition heated up, the franchisee's cage became less golden. As a captive market for their suppliers, dealers often found themselves stuck with inventory they could not unload and tied to prices that could no longer be defended.

The "Distribution Upheaval"

The developments described above—and the decline through a thousand cuts of fair trade—were both cause and consequence of the entry of disruptive new players into the retail market during the postwar boom. These new players aggressively challenged the laws and norms of that period (a 1956

20. In Teupe's telling, an agreement in 1958 between Philco and the Department of Justice had created a legal gray zone within which vertical restraints could grow (2016: 214). A 1963 case (*White Motor Co. v. United States*) reaffirmed the legality of such arrangements. Just four years later, however, another case (*United States v. Arnold, Schwinn &Co.*) would reverse this by ruling that territorial exclusivity constituted a *per se* restraint of trade (Teupe 2016: 215). This would be reversed again in *Continental Television, Inc. v. GTE Sylvania, Inc.* in 1977.

Senate report refers to "the savage competition provided by discount houses" [Senate Report 1956: 3]). It was a new wave of discounters that defied manufacturer pricing, and the more such firms succeeded, the more they drew in competitors with business models premised on the same strategies.[21] The new discounters differed from traditional retailers and five-and-dimes on a number of important dimensions: above all, extremely low price markups (razor-thin margins); an emphasis on high turnover of merchandise; radically streamlined personnel (almost all self-service); and later, large nontraditional locations, often on the outskirts of towns and cities (Adams 2006: 214).

E. J. Korvette was an early mover in this space and one of the most pugnacious of the new discounters (Barmash 1981). Founded by the maverick young entrepreneur Eugene Ferkauf in 1948 as a small luggage store on the second floor of a Manhattan storefront, Korvettes grew rapidly to become the country's premier discounter in the immediate postwar period. Following a now-familiar general script, Ferkauf built his discount empire on regulatory arbitrage and outright rule-breaking. Catching the wave of consumer demand for appliances, Korvettes actively flouted manufacturers' prices to offer customers nationally branded merchandise at a steep (33 percent) discount—far lower than anyone else's prices (Barmash 1981: 12). Although it grew only to fifty-eight stores (mostly in the Northeast), Korvettes became famous as a go-to source for brand-name household appliances and furnishings (toasters, hair dryers, audio equipment, cameras, records, tapes, folding chairs, card tables, carpets, and similar items), all sold at "ridiculous prices" (Barmash 1981: 162).

Korvettes initially navigated a legal environment in which fair trade laws were still in force in many states by exploiting gray zones—for example, by posing as a membership club while distributing thousands of member cards and catalogs (Barmash 1981: 12). Spurned by manufacturers of branded goods, Korvettes was nonetheless able to secure merchandise through various circuitous routes. As it grew in size, Korvettes also grew bolder, actively flouting fair trade laws, virtually inviting lawsuits that enhanced its reputation with consumers by underlining the company's low prices. The company's hard-driving leaders were undeterred by the summonses and injunctions slapped on them by manufacturers. In 1956, Korvettes was facing thirty-five different fair trade lawsuits (Barmash 1981: 40). Sometimes the company simply dropped brands that complained and replaced them with others (Barmash 1981: 11). In other cases, it stood and fought. For example,

---

21. In a 1956 survey of manufacturers, the behavior of discount houses emerged as a major problem for firms attempting to defend prices (Senate Report 1956: 8, 21).

it prevailed in a suit against Parker Pen "on the ground that the producer hadn't made a case that it was properly enforcing its fair trade program"—that is, discriminatory treatment (or the "unclean hands") defense described in the previous chapter (Barmash 1981: 40).

Journalists were drawn to the company's audacious strategies, and the resulting coverage eliminated the need for advertising. As senior executive William Wilensky put it: "We . . . had a free advertising umbrella, our fight against the fair trade laws. . . . The publicity made us white knights and we got a lot of good will out of it" (Barmash 1981: 24). The strategy cost the company some suppliers, but consumers were smitten, and they flocked to Korvettes. The company's popularity, in turn, won over some manufacturers as suppliers, drawn as they were to the prospect of high-volume sales. Other suppliers were willing to produce knockoffs of popular branded products to sell under the Kor-Val private label (Barmash 1981: 11, 63).

Korvettes' pugnacity—and its success—in the red-hot consumer market of the 1950s and 1960s inevitably drew imitators and competitors, and these decades witnessed a dramatic influx of discounters. Indeed, in 1962 alone, over twenty retail chains launched discount operations, a development that *Fortune* magazine covered in a series of articles under the headline "The Distribution Upheaval" (Petrovic and Hamilton 2006: 112; Hyman 2012: chap. 5).[22] Some of these newly launched discounters, such as Walmart (about which I will have more to say later), were entirely new operations. Many, however, were spin-offs of existing operations as department stores sought to extend their markets. Examples include Dayton's of Minnesota, which launched Target in 1962, but other, less successful examples are Jefferson Ward (a spinoff of Montgomery Ward) and Treasure Island (J. C. Penney) (Lock 2022: 152).

Other entrants came from the other direction, as previous five-and-dimes expanded their operations and moved to the suburbs. Variety store retailers such as Woolworths and Ben Franklin, it will be recalled, sold a range of general merchandise such as hardware, toys, and light home furnishings at low prices. Many of these companies had moved slightly upmarket in the 1920s to sell a wider range of somewhat higher-priced everyday goods. But in the 1960s, many of them turned to the more lucrative discount format, moving out of downtown areas and into the suburban malls that were popping up across the country. Examples include Woolworths's Woolco (founded in

---

22. See Michael Lisicky, "From Kmart to Walmart: The Discount Store Class of 1962," *Forbes*, April 25, 2021, https://www.forbes.com/sites/michaellisicky/2021/04/25/from-kmart-to-walmartthe-discount-store-class-of-1962/?sh=f726d37346cb.

1962 in Columbus, Ohio); Meijer (a supermarket chain, headquartered in Grand Rapids, Michigan), and Shopko (launched in Green Bay, Wisconsin) (drugs, cosmetics, and housewares). CVS (short for Consumer Value Store), which would go on to become the largest retail pharmacy in the country, was founded in 1963, specializing initially in health and beauty aids but adding pharmacies soon after.

The most successful of the large discounters in its time was Kmart, which grew after its 1962 launch to become by far the dominant discounter through the 1970s (Lock 2022; Hyman 2012: 132). Kmart had its origins in a five-and-dime (S. S. Kresge), founded in Detroit in 1899 by Sebastian Sperling Kresge, who began a career in retail working as a traveling salesman (one of his early clients was Frank Woolworth). By 1962, S. S. Kresge had already grown to become the country's third-largest variety store chain.[23] But the company's fortunes soared after it launched its discounting arm, Kmart, which opened its first eighteen stores in that year and grew rapidly to eight hundred by a decade later. Like other discounters, Kmart made a fortune selling name-brand merchandise at a heavy discount, though it would also later move into some private-label brands by contracting with suppliers willing to replicate products of well-known nationally advertised brands that could be sold under the K label. Building on its tremendous size and scale and adopting innovations such as centralized cashier stations, Kresge became the country's second-largest retailer by 1977 (trailing only Sears), with the lion's share of its business coming from Kmart operations (Kresge itself was phased out in 1994).

Thus, as established department stores angled for the attention of middle-class consumers with the allure of credit, large discount stores such as Walmart, Target, and Kmart entered the retail market with a high-volume, low-cost model catering to lower-income Americans. These big discounters built their stores on the outskirts of cities in or near the new shopping centers that were cropping up (with their own ample parking!), in a direct challenge to the established retailers (Endsley 1967). Indeed, discounters were often kept out of the country's suburban malls at the behest of the dominant "anchor" department stores (Barmash 1981: 184). Discount merchandising nonetheless grew explosively in the 1960s, and by the beginning of the 1970s it had become the largest segment of the retailing market, commanding 20 percent of sales of general merchandise (compared to 14 percent for department stores) (Vance and Scott 1994: 58)

23. See Lisicky, "From Kmart to Walmart."

Patterning themselves after the big supermarkets such as A&P and lower-cost health and beauty stores such as Walgreens that had come to dominate their markets by offering goods at lower prices, these newcomers did a phenomenal business. A big part of their success, as Hyman notes, was due to innovations such as open racks that allowed customers to shop more independently, handling merchandise directly and without having to rely on store employees (2012: chap. 5). These measures—alongside resolute opposition to union organization that set them apart from more established department stores—allowed the country's new discounters to radically slash labor costs. Their success was immediately apparent: by 1965 discounters had already surpassed department stores in total sales volume (Adams 2006: 214).

Conclusion

In the United States, the postwar growth model relied heavily on consumption-driven growth, and it rested on a tenuous three-way balance of power—between large oligopolistic manufacturers, organized workers, and large incumbent retailers. The kinds of countervailing dynamics that Galbraith envisioned, alongside enhanced antitrust enforcement, supported a temporary truce among the three in a period in which rapid growth allowed all to thrive.

However, the foundations of organized labor's rights were narrowly defined and fragile from the start. Favorable macroeconomic conditions had facilitated increasing unionization, but prior legislation had planted the seeds for management to reassert its power. Taft-Hartley had strengthened employer rights in industrial conflicts and given its blessing to right-to-work laws that provided manufacturers with a ready nonunion exit option, producing a fractured regulatory landscape that limited organized labor's foothold to specific regions and sectors.

The entry of disruptive discounters, encouraged by favorable court decisions upholding their right to cut prices, would trigger an upheaval in distribution that would unsettle the postwar consensus that prevailed in the golden era of postwar growth. America's biggest (and most unionized) manufacturers resisted the unwinding of fair trade, but the courts had tilted the playing field toward low-cost retailers, and the rapid advance of the largest of these would transform the American retail landscape and indeed the American political economy as a whole.

8

Discount Nation

The entry of a large number of discounters in the 1960s fueled intense competition in the consumer goods market until the first oil crisis of 1973 put an end to the postwar boom. The 1970s marked a critical turning point in the evolution of discount retailing, as inflation and declining purchasing power triggered a massive shakeout in the industry. The discount sector became increasingly concentrated just as American manufacturers found themselves plagued with problems of surplus capacity. This combination of trends shifted the balance of power decisively away from unionized manufacturers and toward a few dominant and anti-union low-cost retailers.

As consumer spending fell, competition among the many discounters that had entered the market became brutal. The list of casualties is long and includes many of the new entrants described in the previous chapter (Petrovic and Hamilton 2006: 113). Korvettes was among the first of the major players to go, succumbing in 1980. J. C. Penney shut down its Treasure Island discount arm in 1981; Woolworths's Woolco followed just one year later; and Montgomery Ward's Jefferson Ward hung on until 1985. Kresge's Kmart emerged from the scrum and remained the undisputed industry leader through the 1970s and into the 1980s (in 1977, it was the second-largest retailer behind Sears). But it, too, began to wobble in the face of intense competition, including the steady advance of Walmart, which grew slowly, focusing initially exclusively on the South and targeting small cities (with populations under ten thousand) that were otherwise underserved by large retailers.[1]

Based on a methodical expansion strategy, Walmart steadily climbed from the forty-eighth position among the fifty largest retailers to the seventeenth in just four years (1979–83). Kmart, which presided over a much more sprawling nationwide empire that resulted in higher transportation costs, sought to shore up sales by diversifying into home improvement (purchasing Builders Square in 1984), books (buying Walden Books in the same year), and drugs (Payless in 1985) (Lock 2022: 211–17). If anything, though, these moves contributed to its struggles, as it found itself caught between strategies based on offering rock-bottom prices on one hand and catering to a somewhat more discriminating department-store clientele on the other (Lock 2022: 229). Kmart, moreover, was slower than competitors (Walmart in particular) in adopting computer-based technologies for inventory control and logistics. While Target was carving out a niche offering slightly higher-quality discount merchandise in a (marginally) less barren environment, Walmart was setting a torrid pace in terms of low pricing. Advertisements for the company's grand opening (on July 2, 1962, in Rogers, Arkansas) had featured General Electric mixers at 51 percent below the manufacturer's recommended price, Polaroid cameras at a 26 percent price reduction, and Sunbeam irons at a 34 percent reduction—all supposedly backed by manufacturers' guarantees but in fact often acquired through intermediaries (Vance and Scott 1994: 44–45).

As the discount sector underwent consolidation and concentration in the context of slumping consumer demand, the balance of power shifted from manufacturers to the retailers on whom they relied to move their products (Petrovic and Hamilton 2006: 110–11). Whereas in the past, discounters were scrounging around (often through back channels) to secure supplies at the lowest possible price, now manufacturers—saddled with high fixed costs—were relieved to have surplus goods taken off their hands by large discount firms, at whatever price. This is the beginning of what many observers call a monumental shift from a "push system"—in which manufacturers push goods out to retailers in anticipation of demand and where production dictates how much product will be pushed onto the market—to a "pull system" in which retailers track current demand and pull the goods in the sense of

---

1. Walmart was originally called Wal-Mart but changed its name in 2018 to remove the hyphen. For ease of exposition I will refer to it as Walmart throughout.

dictating when and how much suppliers produce (Lichtenstein 2006: 11–12; Bonacich 2006; Watson 2011: 3; Petrovic and Hamilton 2006).[2] In such a context, large retailers enjoy outsized power, power that allows them to extract sweet deals from suppliers desperate to unload their goods.

No company was better at exploiting the shifting balance of power than Walmart, which grew rapidly in the 1980s and 1990s. By 1989 it had climbed to fifth place in *Fortune*'s Service 500 list, and in 1991 the company embarked on another huge expansion. It opened thirty-six new stores on a single day (January 30, 1991) and proceeded to launch operations in six new states and to open three massive new distribution centers (up to sixteen total) that increased the company's distribution capacity by nearly 25 percent (Vance and Scott 1994: 157–58). So-called supercenters—large-format operations that offer the usual vast selection of merchandise alongside new full-service supermarkets—were now a central element in the business plan. In 1990 there had been nine Walmart Supercenters in the United States, but by 2000 the number had risen to 888 (Fishman 2011: 3). In 2004, Walmart was opening supercenters at a rate of four per week, in 2005 at a rate of five per week (Fishman 2011: 10). By 2011, over half of Americans lived within five miles of a Walmart outlet, and fully 90 percent of Americans lived within fifteen miles (Fishman 2011: 5, 213).

Walmart's Rise: How the South Came to Love the Chain

The retail shakeout of the 1970s had resulted in a far more concentrated discount sector, with Kmart, Target, and Walmart emerging from the fray as the undisputed leaders.[3] Over the next two decades, however, it was Walmart that grew to dominate the others (Kmart filed for Chapter 11 bankruptcy in 2002 and folded entirely in 2017 after a merger in 2005 with Sears failed to reverse either's fortunes) (Lock 2022: 241–42). Walmart had risen from fifth to first in *Fortune*'s Service 500 list, and when *Fortune* issued a combined list (one that included both service and manufacturing firms) in 1996, Walmart was already in fourth place (behind the much older industrial heavy hitters

---

2. Bonacich provides a particularly clear definition of the difference (2006: 169–70). The push system was "dominated by large consumer goods manufacturers. It involved long production runs to gain efficiencies of scale and minimize unit costs. It led to inventory surpluses which were pushed out to retailers." In the pull system, by contrast, retailers monitor consumer behavior, and, based on this information, suppliers "are required to meet short lead times and to make more frequent deliveries of smaller lots," i.e., lean retailing.

3. See Kwon et al. 2023 on the rise in concentration in the retail sector beginning in the 1970s.

General Motors, Ford, and Exxon). By 2002 it had climbed further to the top of the list, and it has commanded that position (with just three exceptions, in 2006, 2009, and 2012) ever since.[4]

The company's meteoric rise has been extensively documented by others (Vance and Scott 1994; Abernathy et al. 1999: chaps. 3 and 4; Lichtenstein 2006 and 2009), and that history need not be rehearsed at length here. For present purposes, the important point is that Walmart's success is at once deeply paradoxical and paradigmatic for understanding the trajectory of retail development in the United States. It is paradoxical because Walmart originated and grew to dominance in the American South—which, as we saw, was the epicenter of resistance to chain stores for much of the twentieth century. It is paradigmatic because the strategies the company's founder Sam Walton deployed to achieve this success both hark back to those pioneered by the likes of Montgomery Ward and presage those on which Amazon's Jeff Bezos would later build his own rival retailing empire.

In explaining Walmart's success, economists typically point to key managerial and technological innovations that allowed the company to outgrow and outcompete its rivals (Basker 2007; Carden 2012). Basker argues that technology and scale were at the heart of Walmart's advantages in logistics, supply chain management, and inventory control. Carden sees the company as an agent of "creative destruction," using managerial and organizational innovations to realize new levels of efficiency to achieve economies of scale and scope (Carden 2012: 11). For his part, Sam Walton viewed his practices and policies as part of the inevitable march of history toward efficiency in the retail market: "What happened was absolutely a necessary and inevitable evolution in retailing, as inevitable as the replacement of the buggy by the car and the disappearance of the buggy whip makers. The small stores were just destined to disappear, at least in the numbers that once existed, because the whole thing is driven by customers, who are free to choose where they shop" (Howard 2015: 7).

Volumes have been written that breathlessly recount the technological and managerial innovations that account for the company's success. Many are not unique to Walmart but characteristic of all discounters and indeed most chain retailers generally, including centralized checkout, cash-and-carry, no credit. Others are features that Walmart has perfected. This goes especially for the areas of logistics and inventory control, where Walmart was an early adopter of Universal Product Codes (UPC) and real-time tracking, practices

---

4. In those years ExxonMobil took the top spot because of high oil prices.

that allow the company to monitor in detail what products are selling at what locations and in combination with what other products, and to automatically replenish stock accordingly (Hoopes 2006: 91). Unlike other retailers, Walmart also controlled its own distribution network, including fully automated distribution centers and a fleet of trucks driven by independent contractors. Control over logistics was key to keeping costs low because, combined with computerized inventory control, it allowed the company to keep the merchandise moving to where it was needed (Abernathy et al. 1999: chap. 4). Vance and Scott report that in the 1980s, Walmart's distribution costs were just 1.3 percent of sales, compared to Kmart's 3.5 percent and Sears's 5 percent (1994: 92).[5]

Technology and managerial skills may have played a role, but as previous chapters have documented, the course of American retailing has always been deeply shaped by politics. Walmart's successes can be traced to the same elements that have run through the entire history of American retailing (and this book): a legal regime uniquely congenial to strategies organized around price-cutting, and a fragmented political landscape that allowed aggressive regulatory arbitrage in the face of countervailing political winds.

Walmart's success is partly premised on specific features of the regional political economy of the South. Bethany Moreton's study of the company provides insight into how Sam Walton won over rural southerners who historically had been chain retailers' fiercest foes, or, as she puts it, how he turned "the populist heritage [of the South] into positive enthusiasm for a corporate giant" (Moreton 2010: 23). A part of the challenge was to overcome deep-seated suspicions of "foreign" (read: northern) operatives and distant robber barons. Walton addressed this challenge through "the conscious crafting of a populist corporate image from Ozarks culture," emphasizing his own southern roots and cultivating an image of Christian humility and thrift (2010: 37). In a manner strongly reminiscent of the strategies that Montgomery Ward had used to win over rural customers a century before (see chapter 3), Walmart channeled rural white populists' sentiments by portraying himself as a homegrown alternative to distant retail interests, and as consumers' staunchest ally in restraining prices. Newspaper announcements of Walmart openings often featured short biographies of Sam Walton, highlighting his humble origins and southern roots (*Daily Standard* [Sikeston,

---

5. See O'Sullivan (2019: 20–29) on the policies and practices Walmart deploys to achieve advantage.

Missouri], March 4, 1968: 13; *Miller County Autogram-Sentinel* [Tuscumbia, Missouri], February 24, 1972: 5).

Walmart was indeed received with open arms in the South, which includes some of the country's poorest regions and where residents had to travel for hours to buy many consumer goods. Consumers were excited by the low prices and the range of products that new Walmart stores offered. In Sikeston, Missouri, the mayor and the head of the Chamber of Commerce turned out for Walmart's grand opening, and the local newspaper carried coverage under the headline "Cost of Living Goes Down in Sikeston and Southeast Missouri" (*Daily Standard*, March 4, 1968: 13). Describing Walmart's arrival in Livingston, Alabama, Kiviat writes that "with its unrivaled selection, [Walmart was] a wonderland," and its "everyday low prices" were a godsend in a county in which 40 percent of the population fell below the poverty line (Kiviat 2006: 3–4). The store's opening was met with a big public celebration, with "Livingston High School cheerleaders ril[ing] up the crowd as a local radio station broadcast live" (Kiviat 2006: 9; for another example of the kind of hoopla Walmart openings inspired, see *Sequoyah County Times* [Sallisaw, Oklahoma], July 20, 1972: 10).

State and local leaders were thrilled with the jobs and tax revenues the company brought with it. Miss Kansas participated in the ribbon-cutting for a new outlet in Junction City, as did the governor, who praised the company for boosting local employment and declared "this is the type of firm that Kansas needs" (*Junction City Union*, May 9, 1972). When the Livingston location mentioned above was replaced by a twenty-four-hour supercenter in Demopolis, a half-hour away, the company's arrival again met with enthusiasm, both for the expected boost in employment (350 jobs) and the bump in the community's tax base (Kiviat 2006: 44). State Senator Bobby Singleton gushed: "This is so important for west Alabama, not only to Demopolis, but to the entire region. This is something most cities want but can't get. Thank you Walmart" (Kiviat 2006: 46).

Beyond the economic impact, Walton's emphasis on piety, frugality, and traditional family values (the Walmart "family") also appealed to the new Christian right that was gaining prominence in the South at this time (Moreton 2010: chaps. 8 and 9).[6] Store openings often featured religious and nationalist elements, beginning with an invocation and the national anthem and sometimes ending with a choral rendition of a religious hymn

---

6. Ralph Reed, the head of the Christian Coalition in the 1990s, once remarked that "if you want to reach [the Christian population] on Saturday, you do it in Walmart" (Moreton 2010: 90).

(for an example, see Kiviat 2006: 45, 49). Walton also tapped into a rich vein of southern populism that was not just hostile to outside influence but also skeptical of a strong central government. From the start, the company was antiregulation, anti–big government, anti–New Deal liberalism, and anti-union. At the company's annual shareholder meeting in 1991, the prominent conservative radio personality Paul Harvey praised Walmart for creating something "better than communism, socialism, and capitalism. We have created enlightened consumerism" (Moreton 2010: 248).

THE WALMART BUSINESS MODEL

As important as cultural resonance may have been, the Walmart business model also rested on the key material advantages on offer in the South, the most important of which was the ability to draw on a plentiful supply of low-wage labor. Retail has never been a high-wage sector, and it has always lagged far behind manufacturing in unionization rates. Nonetheless, in the American North and Midwest, unions had made inroads with some large retail chains, including A&P, which, as noted in chapter 6, had signed collective agreements in 1938 and 1939 to secure organized labor's political support in defeating the national chain store tax. Beyond A&P, however, unions had also made significant headway in organizing downtown department stores, which relied on skilled salespeople with experience and knowledge of the departments in which they worked (Adams 2006: 215). Large Midwest-based mail order firms such as Sears and Montgomery Ward were hostile toward organized labor and were mostly successful in heading off unionization drives. But they, too, were often forced to offer generous benefits and competitive wages because of the threat of unionization in the regions in which they operated.

The discounters that had entered the market in the 1950s and 1960s were a different story, far more ferociously anti-union because of the thin margins and high turnover on which their business model rested. Some of the smallest ones (e.g., Crazy Eddie's, a short-lived consumer electronics chain) relied almost entirely on illegal employment (sublegal wages paid under the counter) (Stoller 2019: 382–83). The largest, however, developed elaborate union-avoidance schemes. For example, Kmart had a security department dedicated to tracking union organizing efforts across all its stores (Adams 2006: 225).

Walmart's union avoidance strategies fit comfortably within this broader pattern, and in fact the company's earliest expansions went even further than most in exploiting loopholes in the Fair Labor Standards Act, which exempted retail establishments with less than $1 million in total sales from minimum wage requirements. To take advantage of the loophole, Walton launched three different companies in three different cities in Arkansas, each with majority ownership in a trust administered by his wife and with Walton himself serving as chairman of the board for all of them (Adams 2006: 218).[7] But Walton had the additional advantage in launching and expanding first in the South, which, as we saw earlier, had taken a hard turn against unions after the Taft-Hartley bill of 1947 and where virtually all states had passed right-to-work laws that discouraged unionization.

Walton wrapped his hard-core anti-unionism in a folksy labor culture based on an open-door policy in which workers with complaints were meant to approach their managers directly. He cast unions as foreign influences that threatened what he called the Walmart family: "We resent outsiders coming in and saying things which aren't true and trying to change the company that has meant so much to all of us" (Wartzman 2022). But in the face of actual unionization drives, the company quickly took off the gloves, dedicating enormous resources to shutting down potential membership drives with the usual toolbox of strategies available to American employers—holding captive meetings with employees to emphasize the dire consequences of unionization, stonewalling in negotiations, and firing strikers and union organizers (Wartzman 2022; Reich and Bearman 2020).

Salaried supervisors were instructed to notify headquarters "whenever there was the slightest hint of an organizer coming around" (Wartzman 2022). For example, when OUR Walmart (Organization United for Respect at Walmart) formed (with financial and other support from organized labor) in the early 2010s, the company sprang into action, hiring an intelligence-gathering service from the defense contractor Lockheed Martin to report to headquarters any and all organizing activities across the company's vast network of retail outlets and warehouses (Berfield 2015). The lack of a union presence allows the company to violate labor laws with impunity. For this, the company is notorious. A study by Human Rights Watch uncovered myriad complaints and lawsuits against the company for a variety of violations, including requiring employees to work off the clock (Human Rights Watch 2007; Lichtenstein 2010: 143–44; Reich and Bearman 2020).

Beyond the advantages it drew from state laws that actively discourage unionization, the company has benefited from various direct and indirect

7. The courts would later rule this a clear case of tax avoidance in 1967.

public supports, including free riding on public infrastructure. As other observers have noted, the company's low wages and paltry benefits are subsidized by the government indirectly. A 2020 report by the nonpartisan Government Accountability Office based on data from eleven states found that Walmart was consistently among the top four companies whose employees depend on food stamps (SNAP benefits) and Medicaid (Derysh 2020).[8] In Georgia, for instance, parents who worked at Walmart accounted for over ten thousand of the kids covered by the state's insurance program for poor children (Fishman 2011: 240). One reason for the heavy reliance on state aid is that the company employs large numbers of part-time workers who are frequently denied access to company benefits. Walmart employees working fewer than twenty-four hours per week had already lost their health insurance coverage in 2011, and after the Affordable Care Act passed in 2014, the company further tweaked eligibility criteria to deny coverage to employees working fewer than thirty hours/week (Tabuchi 2014).[9] In such strategies, Walmart is by no means alone: in 2013, well over half of America's large retail chains (62 percent) did not provide health care benefits to their part-time employees (Tabuchi 2014).

The company also relies heavily on other public supports. These include the usual tax breaks and subsidies the company has extracted from states and municipalities eager to encourage local investment as Walmart expanded its network of stores and distribution centers (Strasser 2006: 54). Even in Livingston, Alabama, the impoverished community referenced earlier, the city council unanimously approved the company's request for $1.5 million worth of municipal bonds to cover construction (Kiviat 2006: 9). Other public support comes in the form of national public infrastructure, especially the highways that link it to its suppliers and customers. The company benefited disproportionately from trucking deregulation in the 1980s, which allowed it to employ nonunion independent drivers—key links in the company's vaunted distribution system. Prior to the 1980s, trucking had been both heavily regulated and heavily unionized (Hamilton 2014). But as Shane Hamilton has shown, what was once a narrow loophole in trucking regulation grew to a full-scale movement to deregulate the industry, setting in motion a downward spiral in wages and working conditions among the country's long-haul truckers toward what one former trucker describes as an industry composed of "sweatshops on wheels" (Belzer 2000).

8. For full report, see "Millions of Full-Time Workers Rely on Federal Health Care and Food Assistance Programs," GAO, October 2020, https://www.gao.gov/assets/720/710299.pdf.

9. Currently, Walmart defines full-time employment as thirty-four or more hours per week and offers health coverage only for those working thirty-plus hours per week.

WALMART AND ITS SUPPLIERS

Lean retailing of the sort practiced by Walmart rests on two pillars—maintaining extremely low labor costs and dominating and squeezing suppliers. The anti-union activities described above help Walmart maintain low labor costs. But the other part of the story has to do with Walmart's domination of suppliers and its ability to shift costs and risks onto the producers who rely on Walmart to bring their goods to market. Lynn recounts how Walmart brought even the country's most dominant producers to heel through relentless pressure to supply it with goods at prices and on terms that the retailer itself handed down (2006: 32–33). For example, the mastery of logistics for which Walmart receives accolades from business writers is only partly a function of Walmart's precocious introduction of the use of UPC codes on a company-wide basis. The technology reinforced the company's dominance over its suppliers because Walmart quickly offloaded the responsibility (and costs) of the shift to bar codes to the producers, who were forced to implement the technology and to gather and share information on the movement of their products for Walmart (Lichtenstein 2010: 57; Lynn 2006: 34; Petrovic and Hamilton 2006: 132).

The resulting massive database over which Walmart presides not only gives the company tremendous insight into the movement of goods through its network to improve the efficiency of its operations; it also yields tremendous informational advantages for the company (Abernathy et al. 1999: chap. 4; Watson 2011: 75). In an earlier iteration, Sears had collected information on customers and purchases to identify its best customers for special treatment (Emmet and Jeuck 1950: 90). A&P improved on Sears's crude methods but similarly gathered information on its sales to learn what products were most favored in different regions (for example, consumers in Philadelphia and New England had different preferences when it came to the color and saltiness of their butter [Levinson 2011: 105]). Walmart now enjoys access to data providing insight into what is selling where and when, and on a monumental scale. Translating this into the ability to squeeze suppliers is central to the business model: economists have found that for suppliers who have Walmart as a primary customer, profits fall as sales rise (Fishman 2011: 162–63).

Producers that had once done battle with retailers over their price lists now approached large retailers such as Walmart in supplicant mode, often establishing sales offices near Walmart's Arkansas headquarters. Procter & Gamble, which as we saw in earlier chapters was a staunch advocate of fair trade, was one of the first to set up a sales office in northwest Arkansas.[10] Fishman writes that by 2011 more than seven hundred companies had established offices in and around the Bentonville headquarters (2011: 63). Walmart was already P&G's biggest customer in the 1990s (Lichtenstein 2006: 13), and by 2005, Walmart's share of P&G's sales matched that of the company's next nine distributors combined (Fishman 2011: 12). P&G was by no means alone in its reliance on distribution through Walmart: in 2004, Walmart sales accounted for 28 percent of all of Dial soap sales, 25 percent of Clorox's, and 16 percent of General Mills's (Kumar and Steenkamp 2007: 156).

The greater the dependence of American manufacturers on Walmart as a share of shipments and the more attractive access to its vast customer base became to overall sales, the greater their willingness to accommodate Walmart's demands with respect to cost control and pricing (Petrovich and Hamilton 2006: 119, 131). The asymmetry in power is acute since Walmart has plenty of alternative suppliers, and the company aggressively pushes the products of rivals if they can offer their goods at a better price. In the late 1990s the company also took advantage of US trade agreements to extend its use of global sourcing as a lever "to put further downward pressure on the cost of the goods it sells" (O'Sullivan 2019: 22).

The so-called China shock—that is, the entry of China into the World Trade Organization in 2001—is widely thought to have decimated American manufacturing (Autor et al. 2016). But the China shock was in reality substantially a Walmart shock because this single company, by 2003, accounted for 10 percent of all American imports from China (Moreton 2009: 343n21). Scott (2015) gives 11.2 percent as a "conservative estimate" of Walmart's share of total imports from China (among the hundred top importers) for the entire period between 2001 and 2013. And in 2018, Walmart was still "by far" the largest importer of goods coming into the United States by ocean container, though other mass retailers such as Target, Home Depot, and Lowe's were not far behind (O'Sullivan 2019: 22).[11]

---

10. P&G opened an office there in the 1980s, and a 2003 article reported an influx of "hundreds of name-brand suppliers" setting up offices near Walmart headquarters, "sending top representatives to the Bentonville, Ark., area to be near the retail titan and, they hope, get a bigger chunk of sales from the nation's largest vendor of DVDs, books, groceries, toys and a host of other products." See "Bentonville, Ark., has become new address for US retailers," September 22, 2003, *Daily Record* [Maryland], https://thedailyrecord.com/2003/09/22/bentonville-ark-has-become -new-address-for-us-retailers/.

11. In 2018 Walmart imported 940,410 twenty-foot equivalent units (TEUs); Target imported 631,621; Home Depot (417,100); and Lowe's (307,625) (O'Sullivan 2019: 22n74).

While Walmart's initial strategy had been premised on selling branded goods at low prices, in the 1990s the company introduced its own private-label goods (often partnering with East Asian producers). These products were mostly lower-cost alternatives to brands that the company used as "a stick and a benchmark" to push its suppliers to lower their costs (Watson 2011: 57).[12] For example, in 1993, Walmart introduced its Great Value detergent, which competed head on with, and was often displayed next to, P&G's more expensive Tide brand (Hays 2005). Companies that are particularly dependent on Walmart find themselves under relentless pressure to lower prices. The president of Lovable Company (once a major manufacturer of intimate apparel) put it this way: "They have such awesome purchasing power that they write their own ticket. If they don't like your prices, they'll go vertical and do it themselves—or they'll find someone that will meet their terms" (Fishman 2011: 97). An internal Bain & Company study of Walmart's impact on its suppliers found that, as Walmart "consumes a greater chunk of a company's sales, it simultaneously offers a smaller slice of profitability. Companies doing 10 percent or less of their business with Wal-Mart had operating profit margins of 12.7 percent. Companies that became . . . captive suppliers to Wal-Mart—selling more than 25 percent of their goods to Wal-Mart—see their profit margin cut almost in half, to 7.3 percent" (Fishman 2011: 162–63).

Robinson-Patman in the Postwar Period

Of course, the problem of powerful buyers is precisely what the Robinson-Patman Act, as discussed in chapter 6, was meant to address. That law, originally directed at A&P, sought to restrain the power of large purchasers to solicit and accept (or demand and extort) favorable terms and prices from suppliers seeking their business, winning concessions that were denied to their smaller competitors. As we saw, Robinson-Patman had triggered a drop in A&P's share value and profits, and some evidence suggests that the law cast a pall on aggressive pricing moves by businesses generally, as cautious firms avoided bold maneuvers lest they draw the attention of regulators (Rowe 1962: 549).

However, Robinson-Patman was also notoriously vague and ambiguous and thus difficult to enforce. The Department of Justice brought forward

---

12. Watson distinguishes this use of private-label products from that of other large-format discounters such as Carrefour and Tesco, which offer such goods at different price points and not just to pressure suppliers (2011: 62–63; 128).

almost no Robinson-Patman cases (Edwards 1959: 67), but in the 1950s and early 1960s, the Federal Trade Commission (FTC) pursued a relatively hard line (Posner 1970: 370). The number of Robinson-Patman cases the agency brought rose from 66 in the early 1950s to 227 later in the decade (1955–59). Cases peaked in the 1960–64 period at 545, before dropping back in the late 1960s, on the eve of the discount shakeout and just as Walmart was gathering steam (Posner 1970: 370n9). Even when it did bring cases, moreover, the FTC sometimes encountered resistance in the courts, which were more open to arguments in defense of price differences.

One early indication of the tension between the FTC and the courts on this matter was visible in a 1951 Supreme Court ruling on an FTC case against Standard Oil. In this case, the FTC had challenged Standard Oil's right to sell gasoline to four large jobber customers for a lower per-gallon price than it sold to smaller individual service stations in the area. Standard Oil responded to the complaint by referring to the provision in Robinson-Patman that allowed sellers to grant discounts to meet competition, arguing that the concession had been necessary to retain the jobbers as customers in the face of competition from other companies. In its decision, the court ruled in favor of Standard Oil, making clear that the "meeting competition" defense was an "absolute and not a conditional barrier to Robinson-Patman Act convictions" (Cohen 1965: 716).

A part of the enforcement problem was in the way the law itself was framed (Edwards 1959: 63). Though the law was meant to rein in powerful buyers, most of its provisions were in fact aimed at restraining the actions of sellers (their suppliers)—a somewhat convoluted construction that Congress thought "would help sellers resist special price demands by large buyers" (Barrett et al. 1954: 246). However, Cohen contended that, logically, lawmakers had it backward. He argued that the emphasis should be on the buyer (retailer) who extracts concessions, not on sellers who have no incentive to lower their prices but for pressure from buyers or in the face of competition (the latter, again, being a permissible defense under Robinson-Patman) (Cohen 1965: 719). Edwards made the same point much more bluntly, arguing that attacking price discrimination "primarily by action against the weak sellers who succumbed to the pressure [of powerful buyers] . . . bears some resemblance to an effort to stamp out mugging by making it an offense to permit oneself to be mugged" (1959: 63, 516). Moreover, cases were decided and settled too late to prevent a downward price spiral, because by the time a suit could be mounted against overaggressive retailers, the competitive pressure on *other* retailers had already taken hold (Cohen 1965: 738–39).

Only one section of the law (Section 2(f)) targeted buyers directly by making it illegal for any buyer "knowingly to induce or receive a discrimination in price which is prohibited" by the law (Cohen 1965: 719). But the first big test of this provision, in the 1953 *Automatic Canteen Co. v. FTC*, resulted in a defeat for the FTC (Edwards 1959: 72, 501–11; Rowe 1962: 541–42; Cohen 1965: 731). Automatic Canteen Co. was the dominant player in the vending-machine candy market (Barrett et al. 1954). The company was charged with violating the Robinson-Patman Act by "knowingly inducing and receiving price discriminations in the purchase of confectionary products," securing prices that were up to 33 percent lower than those paid by competitors (Barrett et al. 1954: 247). The dispute came to center "around the question of who (the FTC or the buyer) must introduce evidence as to the buyer's knowledge of the relative size of the cost savings and the price differentials" (Barrett 1954: 247). In its decision, the court rejected the FTC's prima facie case against the company and placed the burden of proof on the FTC instead (Edwards 1959: 79, 81, 488).[13]

Moreover, the evidentiary burden on the FTC under the law as it was interpreted was "a forbidding one" (Edwards 1959: 511) because the commission had to prove that the discrimination had the capacity to injure competition, that the seller's behavior could not be justified under the cost defense, and that the buyer knowingly induced concessions that could not be justified by cost (Edwards 1959: 511–12, 63). Edwards's 1959 study concluded that because of the many hurdles the FTC would have to clear to proceed directly against buyers "the existing interpretation of the law has no doubt given comfort to the aggressive buyer" (1959: 515). Small wonder, then, that his research also found that in the wake of this key case "further enforcement of Section 2(f) appears to have come to a practical standstill" (1959: 72).

A further problem with the enforcement of Robinson-Patman was that even in the case of successful litigation (typically pursued under one of the other sections of the law), the penalties assessed on the violators were frequently too modest to deter offenders.[14] Most FTC cases were settled with a cease and desist order, and the FTC did issue a large number of these (of

---

13. Edwards reports that the court's logic was that the commission was better placed than the victims to determine whether the cost defense was viable because of the FTC's "broad power of investigation and subpoena" (1959: 506).

14. On the low penalties, see *Price Discrimination, the Robinson-Patman Act and Related Matters: Hearings Before the House Select Committee on Small Business*, 84th Cong., 1st sess. (1955: 374), and *Small Business and the Robinson-Patman Act: Hearings Before the Special Subcommittee on Small Business and the Robinson-Patman Act of the House Select Committee on Small Business*, 91st Cong., 1st sess. (1969).

430 Robinson-Patman cases decided by the end of 1957, fully 72 percent resulted in a cease and desist order) (Edwards 1959: 66). But firms charged with violations often just accepted the FTC's orders because there was no real follow-up or compliance checks (Edwards 1959: 88; Cox et al. 1969: 166). "In effect, the seller is informed that what he had already done is illegal, and that he should not do it again" (Cohen 1965: 720). Because the FTC had to go after violators one at a time (and often at great expense), the law had no real deterrent effect. In fact, it arguably gave competitors a boost because "those [firms] chosen for [FTC] proceedings will inevitably be handicapped so long as their competitors continue to engage in conduct they can no longer emulate" (Edwards 1959: 89).

Private cases—rare before World War II but more prevalent afterward—also largely failed to address the power of buyers (Barber 1961; Tomlin 1964). It had seemed possible that private enforcement would both facilitate the identification of violations and, with that, exert a deterrent effect. In the event, however, very few private suits attempting to claim damages actually prevailed. Out of a total of 111 private suits, only six were successful (Barber 1961: 191–92). Moreover, the damages recovered were often rather small, even for those cases in which the plaintiffs won. Injured parties could in principle claim treble damages, but actual awards were rare in the extreme (Cohen 1965: 720). The damages for the six successful cases ranged from a low of $3,030 to a high of $180,000 (Barber 1961: 192), which was pocket change for the country's biggest retailers. Contemporary observers concluded that statutory authorization for private recovery under Robinson-Patman was "desirable but ineffective" (Tomlin 1964: 168).

From the perspective of those contemplating a suit, efforts to invoke Robinson-Patman were a high-risk, low-reward proposition. The prospects for success were dim, not least because of the high evidentiary bar set by the court. The plaintiff had to prove that the defendant had violated the act and that this had resulted in injury to himself. Furthermore, the plaintiff had to determine the amount of resulting damages. All of these factors were difficult to address because the necessary evidence was almost impossible to secure (Tomlin 1964: 177–78; Barber 1961: 195–98). Against these dim prospects for success, potential plaintiffs had to contemplate the high costs of pursuing the litigation, particularly against the biggest distributors. This included court costs (one survey found that in four of ten cases, the cost exceeded $100,000 [Tomlin 1964: 178]). But it also included the potentially high risk of alienating a key distributor, thus inviting retaliation. As Barber put it, "The realities of litigation: cost, time and headaches in a setting of unequal power" presented a daunting picture for potential plaintiffs (1961: 203).

It should therefore not come as a surprise that the first two studies of the enforcement of the Robinson-Patman Act (by Edwards 1959 and Rowe 1962) revealed a picture sometimes at odds with its authors' intentions. Both studies note the dearth of cases brought under Section 2(f) that target buyers directly. Rowe assembled statistics on FTC enforcement of Robinson-Patman for the first twenty-five years of the law's history (from 1936–61), including a breakdown by the statutory provision invoked in each complaint (1962: 536–39). This exercise revealed the "conspicuous . . . sparseness of cases against buyers under Section 2(f). Only 3.6 percent of all complaints and 4.3 percent of all orders have been addressed to buyers' extractions of discriminatory prices" (1962: 536–37). By contrast, a majority (56 percent) of FTC complaints (and 63 percent of orders) concerned sections 2(c) (on brokerage) and 2(d) (promotions) (Rowe 1962: 537–38). Rowe and Edwards both attribute this imbalance to the fact that complaints under 2(c) and 2(d) did not require proof of competitive injury and neither allowed for a defense to justify the challenged price discrimination. By contrast, and as noted, 2(f) charges must both overcome cost defense justifications of the price differential and show that the buyer was aware that the transaction was illegal (Rowe 1962: 538; Edwards 1959: 71, 104).

A second finding from both Edwards's and Rowe's studies was that the FTC proceedings often went after smaller firms or buying groups of small merchants (e.g., automotive parts distributors) rather than the country's largest companies (Edwards 1959: 627–28; Rowe 1962: 542). As noted in chapter 6, brokerage provisions were directed at (and successful against) A&P, but they also hobbled voluntary chains and cooperative associations such as Red and White and IGA. The result was "a substantial impairment of the strength of the voluntary group" (Edwards 1959: 122, 124, 126). As soon as they were denied the opportunity to collect brokerage fees for connecting suppliers with their members, the functions of these cooperative associations were taken over by private organizations that then acquired the trademarks and brands these groups had cultivated collectively (Edwards 1959: 128–29).

Thus, the provisions in Robinson-Patman concerning brokerage arrangements had clearly hurt A&P, but they also "appear to have reduced the size and effectiveness of voluntary groups, with the amount of the damage depending on the previous division of emphasis between group buying and other activities" (Edwards 1959: 130). In so doing the law "curbed not only the practices of the powerful but also the practices of others designed to furnish protection against the powerful" (Edwards 1959: 626; see also 46, 66, 627). Rowe's overall assessment was more pointed: "The act's chartless enforcement . . . largely missed the 'big buyer' . . . and often boomeranged on the smaller competitor, the act's intended beneficiary . . ." (551). "Out of the 1,040 Robinson-Patman complaints by the FTC in twenty-five years of enforcement, only 28 percent smote corporations noticed by a listing in *Moody's Industrials* for 1960, and only 13 percent charged concerns ranked by *Fortune*'s 1961 directory of the 500 largest industrial or the 50 largest merchandising corporations in the United States" (1962: 542).

This record of enforcement, Rowe suggests, "indicates a more successful adaptation by larger firms to the legal intricacies of Robinson-Patman. . . . The predominant FTC enforcement against commercial pygmies may thus demonstrate that the giants have learned better how to live with the act" (1962: 543). In testimony before a congressional subcommittee on small business, the legal scholar Richard Posner explained that "larger or vertically integrated firms are often able to arrange their affairs so as to avoid being subject to the act" (*Small Business and the Robinson-Patman Act* 1969: 147). In general, large corporations with legal departments were successful in finding ways around the law. As Rowe archly commented, "Often, given the time and the talents of counsel, the law, like love, could find a way" (1962: 550).

Looking back on the enforcement record of the 1960s in a 1979 post-mortem panel on Robinson-Patman, the assistant director of the FTC's Bureau of Competition conceded that although the agency had brought a large number of cases in the early 1960s, they were difficult to win "even in the best of times" (Hamill 1979: 1686–87). Why? Because "almost every phrase, or series of words in the Robinson-Patman Act is an invitation to litigation" (Hamill 1979: 1688). He noted that the agency's most recent loss, in a case against A&P for a 2(f) violation that had dragged on for nearly a decade (*A&P v. Borden*), had proved to be "a hard lesson" for the FTC because it "reflects the conservative attitude of the Supreme Court on Robinson-Patman issues, generally" (Hamill 1979: 1690).[15]

The Rise of the Chicago School in Antitrust Jurisprudence

In fact, the FTC had already long since eased up on Robinson-Patman complaints. As early as 1964, the Bureau of National Affairs's *Antitrust & Trade Regulation Report* noted that the FTC had declined to pursue cease and desist orders in key cases. The report's authors clearly welcomed this development,

---

15. See also the remarks by A&P lawyer Denis McInerney and the response by the FTC's James C. Hamill (Panel Discussion 1979).

calling it a "significant departure from past practice" and hailing it as an indication that the agency "seem[ed] to be taking tentative steps toward Robinson-Patman enforcement policy of pragmatic discretion, rather than dogmatic reaction" (BNA 1964: 1). The FTC increasingly invoked "public interest" considerations into its rulings, refusing to issue cease and desist orders in some cases (Cohen 1965: 736). Calvani's figures record a "radical decrease in the number of Robinson-Patman investigations initiated by the commission" between 1967 and 1973 (Calvani 1979: 1697), and the number of complaints began dropping off even earlier, in 1965, a development he attributes to "increasing judicial hostility toward the Robinson-Patman Act" (1708) and to increased attention on the part of FTC staff to the costs of litigation (1693). The number of Robinson-Patman cases the FTC brought fell from a high of 545 (1960–64) to just 102 (1965–69) and then declined to a trickle (Posner 1970: 370n9; Calvani 1979: 1698–99; Foster 2022; Foster in progress).[16]

By the late 1960s, a range of economists and legal scholars—some but not all attached to what we now know as the Chicago school of law and economics—had become vocally skeptical about the wisdom of Robinson-Patman and indeed the entire postwar antitrust regime. Robinson-Patman came in for sharp criticism by the Task Force on Productivity and Competition appointed by President Richard Nixon in 1968—a group that included key leaders of the Chicago school, Posner and George Stigler. Both testified to a congressional subcommittee on small business and the Robinson-Patman Act that if it were up to them the law would be repealed. Posner, for his part, criticized the FTC for wasteful, drawn-out cases that cost the taxpayers dearly and often resulted in expensive losses (*Small Business and the Robinson-Patman Act* 1969: 156).[17] Stigler, a leading light in the Chicago school, was most dismissive, asserting that "if all the prominent economists in favor of the Robinson-Patman Act were put in a Volkswagen, there would still be room for a portly chauffeur" (*Small Business and the Robinson-Patman Act* 1969: 146).

16. While it does not affect the interpretation of the general trend (toward declining enforcement), the higher numbers in the earlier period were likely bundles of closely related matters, when a single enforcement campaign generated several respondents (thanks to William Kovacic for pointing this out to me).

17. Other legal scholars and economists who were not connected to the Chicago school sometimes shared the view that the FTC was wasting resources on trivial cases and failing to go after abuses by large corporate monopolies and oligopolies. The FTC's work was subject to a scathing critique on these grounds by a group of law students associated with consumer advocate Ralph Nader ("Nader's Raiders") (Cox et al. 1969: 165–66).

Enforcement of the Robinson-Patman Act was dealt another blow during the Ford administration, when the Department of Justice issued a report heavily critical of the law (DOJ 1977). In a sustained broadside (peculiar in its timing, given that enforcement had already declined to a trickle), the report asserted that the law distorted markets, created price rigidities, and supported inefficiencies in distribution—all of which operated to the detriment of consumers and society at large.[18] In sharp contrast to the studies by Edwards and Rowe discussed previously, the report claimed that the evidentiary burdens to establish price discrimination were light and that the penalties imposed on violators were harsh. The report's overall conclusion was that "the greater the business community's compliance with Robinson-Patman, whether as a result of voluntary action or vigorous public or private enforcement, the greater the act's deleterious impact upon competition" (1977: 250). Though the report fell short of recommending repeal, virtually all of the "remedies" it proposed involved a weakening of the law's strictures (1979: 260–69).

The fading enforcement of Robinson-Patman reflected a deeper reorientation that had begun in the 1960s and culminated in a full embrace of the Chicago school orthodoxy in the 1980s. The legal revolution it inspired, and the backdrop against which American discount chains in general, and Walmart in particular, grew to scale brought a sharp decline in *all* forms of antitrust enforcement against dominant market actors. As is well known, Robert Bork played a starring role in elevating Chicago school thinking in the area of antitrust, though other more moderate economists and legal scholars had smoothed the path by lending legitimacy to the rightward shift.[19]

18. As Peinert and Van Dyck (2022) note, the report contains precious little actual evidence of its claims about the impact of Robinson-Patman, and its authors acknowledge that they cannot really prove that the law increased prices to consumers (Peinert and Van Dyck 2022 provide a survey of the several inconclusive studies of this). Moreover, the arguments in the report about the burdens the law imposes on firms rely heavily on counterfactuals about "opportunity costs"— i.e., "the costs to an entrepreneur of having to take the second-best alternative because his first choice is blocked by Robinson-Patman" (DOJ 1977: 38). The report also argues that concerns about possible predatory pricing are overblown, again based less on empirics than on "logic and inference," as, for example, in the testimony of the University of Virginia economist Kenneth Elzinga, who insisted "on logical grounds that predatory pricing would be a very rare occurrence as a monopolizing device; it simply doesn't wash from a standpoint of logic" and who argued that empirical verification of this claim is impossible "unless some brilliant economist devises a test that heretofore has not been observed" (1977: 39).

19. William Kovacic (2007) cites Phillip Areeda and Donald Turner—neither of whom were associated with the Chicago school—as critical actors in this transition (see Areeda and Turner 1975 on predatory pricing). Unlike Bork, who saw virtually all government intervention in pricing as distortionary, Harvard-based Areeda and Turner acknowledged the potential for predatory pricing to result in harms while also, however, advocating for dramatically raising the bar for

Bork's influential book, *The Antitrust Paradox* (published in 1978), essentially turned the Supreme Court's previous antitrust jurisprudence upside down. He claimed (based, as Sanjukta Paul [2020a] has pointed out, on a dubious reading of the history of the Sherman Act) that the intent of Congress with this law was to promote consumer welfare.

The term "consumer welfare" was itself ambiguous and generated a great deal of confusion (Hovenkamp 2019: 65; Orbach 2013: 2253, 2255, 2272–74). Bork himself meant it as a shorthand for total economic output or allocative efficiency, though, as Khan points out, "courts and antitrust authorities [subsequently] largely measured it through effects on consumer prices" (2017: 720).[20] These ideas had steadily gained influence in legal circles throughout the late 1960s and 1970s.[21] In 1981 Reagan elevated them to government policy with his appointments of Borkian acolyte William F. Baxter to head the DOJ's Antitrust Division and fellow Chicago schooler James Miller III as FTC chair. Henceforth, antitrust policy and enforcement would fully embrace the Chicago school formula: the core criterion against which anticompetitive actions would be judged was whether they explicitly harmed consumer welfare, defined largely in terms of price.

This reorientation played not just to the interests of many large producers (who were increasingly free to impose vertical restraints on weaker actors), but also and a fortiori to the interests of large discount retailers who could now take full advantage of the power asymmetries noted above to deliver low prices to consumers. In this changed legal environment, predatory

---

demonstrating such harms. On Kovacic's account of what he calls the "Chicago/Harvard Double Helix," Areeda and Turner lent legitimacy (and ultimately greater durability) to the shift that we often attribute to the Chicago school, precisely because they were less incendiary and strident in tone than Bork, even though their own writing, like Bork's, advocated greater forbearance toward dominant actors (Kovacic 2007: 70). Kovacic also emphasizes the impact of Areeda and Turner's work on Stephen Breyer, their one-time Harvard colleague, who as associate justice on the Supreme Court also played a role in "mainstreaming" an overall more permissive approach to American antitrust jurisprudence (2007: 8, 47).

20. Early court decisions that invoked the consumer welfare standard (e.g., *Reiter v. Sonotone* 1979) likely played a role in entrenching the centrality of prices. Frank Easterbrook, who served in the solicitor general's office under Bork and who took *The Antitrust Paradox* as his guide, emphasized that "however you slice the legislative history, the dominant theme is the protection of consumers from overcharges" (Orbach 2013: 2274).

21. Chicago school orthodoxy was heavily promoted throughout the judiciary, including through short (two- to three-week) courses sponsored by the Manne Economic Institute designed to familiarize federal judges with the kind of market-oriented cost-benefit analysis that underpins the law and economics approach to jurisprudence (Ash et al. 2020). Research by Ash et al. showed that judges who had participated in these programs did indeed subsequently rely on the language and cost-benefit logic of economics in their written opinions (Ash et al. 2020: 3).

pricing (i.e., aggressive price-cutting designed to eliminate competitors) was recoded as welfare-enhancing and therefore "almost categorically pro-competitive" (Arslan 2022: 6). The depths of Baxter's commitment to low prices could be seen in his department's adamant opposition to all efforts by Congress in the 1980s to offer relief to domestic manufacturers experiencing intense competition, especially from Japan (on this episode see Arslan 2022: 10–13). Congressional appeals to grant antitrust law exemptions to beleaguered American firms were brushed back; in Senate hearings in 1990, Baxter testified that "he would rather 'grant them [failing companies] a license to import heroin'" (Arslan 2022: 10).

Many policymakers—on both the left and right—worried about a growing US trade deficit and claimed that Japanese competitors were engaged in collusive practices that put American firms at an unfair disadvantage. However, the DOJ and the Supreme Court held firm on behalf of low prices. In an important case in 1986, *Matsushita Electric Industrial Corporation v. Zenith Radio Corporation*, Zenith sought to sue Japanese competitors for underwriting predatory prices in the American market by setting high prices for their goods in Japan (Arslan 2022: 13; Khan 2017: 727–28). The DOJ's brief to the court reflected the new antitrust view, arguing that this was all just a matter of "vigorous price competition" (Arslan 2022: 13).

The Supreme Court sided with the DOJ, ruling against Zenith with the argument that its claims of predatory pricing were "speculative." The language of the court's decision reflected a full-throated embrace of the Borkian view, as articulated in *The Antitrust Paradox*, in which Bork had maintained that "the real danger for the law is less that predation will be missed than that normal competitive behavior will be wrongly classified as predatory and suppressed" (Khan 2017: 728). In a formulation that harks back to Galbraith's views on countervailing power, Justice Lewis Powell (writing for the 5–4 majority in the case) put it this way: "Cutting prices in order to increase business often is the very essence of competition. Thus mistaken inferences in cases such as this one are especially costly, because they chill the very conduct the antitrust laws are designed to protect" (Khan 2017: 728)

A subsequent Supreme Court case, *Brooke Group Ltd. v. Brown & Williamson Tobacco* (1993) rendered laws against predatory pricing practically impossible to enforce.[22] In this case, Brown & Williamson was accused of

---

22. I thank Erik Peinert for emphasizing the importance of this case to me; see also Peinert and Van Dyck (2022).

predatory pricing via extreme volume rebates on its generic cigarettes. A suit brought by a competitor (and recent entrant into the generic cigarette market, Liggett) alleged that, with below-cost pricing, Brown & Williamson sought to force Liggett to raise the list prices on its own generics in order to maintain profits on its (B&W's) branded cigarette products (Khan 2017: 729).[23] The court's ruling raised the bar considerably for establishing the case for predatory pricing, with the plaintiff responsible not just for proving that it had suffered injury due to the pricing practices of the defendant but also for establishing that the prices are below the defendant firm's cost and that the defendant could reasonably expect to recoup the losses (Peinert and Van Dyck 2022).[24]

A decade later, the bipartisan Antitrust Modernization Commission (AMC), created by an act of Congress in 2002 during the George W. Bush administration, gave its blessing to these developments in a 2007 report (AMC 2007). The report begins with a blanket endorsement of the new "consumer welfare" standard and the shift toward a law and economics logic in antitrust theory and practice. The commission was clearly happy to report that "substantial economic learning now undergirds and informs antitrust analysis" (AMC 2007: 4). "Economic learning has provided the foundation for updated antitrust analysis in part by revealing the potential procompetitive benefits of some business conduct previously assumed to be anticompetitive" (AMC 2007: 5).

The commission evinced no worries about possible abuses by dominant actors: "Although it is possible to disagree with the decisions in particular cases, in general the courts have appropriately recognized that vigorous competition, the aggressive pursuit of business objectives, and the realization of efficiencies not available to competitors are generally not improper, even for a 'dominant' firm and even where competitors might be disadvantaged" (2007: 12). In contrast to the 1977 DOJ report, the AMC report had no trouble recommending that Congress "repeal the Robinson-Patman Act in its entirety" (2007: 20). Claiming that the act had limited "the extent of discounting generally and therefore . . . likely caused consumers to pay higher prices than they otherwise would," the commission concluded that the act

---

23. See Brooke Group Ltd. v. Brown & Williamson Tobacco Corp., 509 U.S. 209 (1993), https://supreme.justia.com/cases/federal/us/509/209/.

24. A later case, *Volvo Trucks North America v. Reeder-Simco GMC, Inc.* (2006) narrowed the scope of Robinson-Patman even further. See Volvo Trucks North America, Inc. v. Reeder-Simco GMC, Inc., 546 U.S. 164 (2006), https://supreme.justia.com/cases/federal/us/546/164/.

"is fundamentally inconsistent with the antitrust laws and harms consumer welfare" (2007: 311, 312).[25]

As antitrust theory and practice had come under the growing influence of Chicago school thinking, low-cost American retailers were free to extract the steep discounts on supplies that allowed them to pursue their signature cut-throat pricing strategies (Khan 2017: 722–30 on forbearance toward preda-tory pricing after 1980). In short, FTC enforcement of buyer power, never strong to begin with, had declined starting in the late 1960s and petered out entirely just as large discounters such as Kmart and Walmart were taking off (Calvani 1979: 1697–99). As Brian Callaci and Sandeep Vaheesan (2022) put it: "Walmart rose to power in part by ignoring the Robinson-Patman Act (a relatively safe business practice since the 1980s), engaging in conduct ranging from demanding discounts, forcing suppliers to guarantee its mar-gins, and even inspecting suppliers' books to check their margins."[26]

The dynamics between discount retailers and producers have knock-on effects that extend beyond the prices that discounters are able to extract from their suppliers. Wilmers (2018), for example, has found that powerful buyers such as Walmart wield "substantial power over working conditions among their suppliers" (2018: 213). Based on panel data on publicly traded companies, he shows that dependence on large buyers resulted in reduced wages for the suppliers' own workforces. His research shows that the shifting balance of power between large retailers and the firms that supply them has contributed significantly to wage stagnation in the United States since the late 1970s (Wilmers 2018). Although the exact mechanisms behind these findings have not yet been fully teased out, Naidu et al. suggest that they may be due to the fact that "large retailers require their suppliers to pay workers below some firm-imposed cap to reduce competition for workers among the suppliers [thus] enabling suppliers to pass on labor cost savings to the retailer" (Naidu et al. 2018: 597). They argue that if this is the case, large retailers such as Walmart are engaged in a form of anticompetitive behavior that is in effect "the mirror image of resale price maintenance"

---

25. Although the authors acknowledged that they could not really determine the impact of the law on consumer prices, the report nonetheless concluded that "anecdotal evidence and informed judgement based on economic theory suggests that the additional costs to consumers of seventy years of forgone discounts are likely substantial" (2007: 322).

26. Moreover, and as Levinson (2023) points out, Robinson-Patman lost its grip as Walmart and other discounters began to rely more heavily on securing supplies from low-cost producers abroad since suppliers in other countries are under no obligation to sell their goods to all American customers at the same price.

since "supplier wage suppression results in an effective cartel among suppliers, who are able to pay their workers below the marginal product, and pass on some of the savings to the buyer" (Naidu 2018: 597).

The American antitrust regime, however, is currently ill-equipped (and, more importantly, until recently has been disinclined) to recognize such behavior as anticompetitive. And the problem extends beyond the ascendance of Chicago school thinking. Since the inflationary 1970s, the price of goods had been on the minds of not just conservatives but also liberals (Short 2022). As Khan notes, in the 1970s even putatively progressive consumer advocates such as Ralph Nader "came to support an antitrust regime centered on lower prices" that accorded with the Chicago school view—albeit arriving at this position from a diametrically opposed vantage (one that, unlike Bork, advocated more rather than less government regulation in the consumer goods market).

Indeed, a bipartisan concern with prices had also resulted in the last vestiges of fair trade being swept away in 1975, as consumer-oriented liberals joined with market-oriented conservatives to repeal the Miller-Tydings and McGuire acts that had protected state fair trade laws, thus restoring the ban on RPM nationwide (Bean 1996: 84). The Consumer Goods Pricing Act—sponsored by Barbara Jordan, an influential progressive Democratic congresswoman from Texas, and signed into law by Republican President Gerald Ford—passed with an overwhelming majority (380–11). In his signing statement, Ford commended Congress for bipartisan support for the bill and argued that state fair trade laws had been a response to the "unique economic conditions" of the Depression that had long since passed. Now, he said, "the best way we can protect the consumer is to identify and eliminate costly, inefficient, and obsolete laws and regulations."[27]

Yet by the 1980s and 1990s, the DOJ and the courts—by this time, as we have seen, fully in thrall to Chicago school thinking—had begun to take an increasingly benign view of vertical restraints imposed by dominant firms on other actors in the distribution chain, replacing *per se* rules against such arrangements and applying instead the much more forbearing rule-of-reason analysis. This reorientation was reflected in a series of landmark decisions—*Sylvania* (1977), *Monsanto* (1984), and *Sharp* (1988)—in which the Supreme Court successively relaxed restrictions on resale price

---

27. See Gerald R. Ford, "Statement on the Consumer Goods Pricing Act of 1975," American Presidency Project, https://www.presidency.ucsb.edu/documents/statement-the-consumer-goods-pricing-act-1975.

maintenance arrangements.[28] These developments then culminated in a landmark decision in 2007 that overturned the decades-old rule enshrined in the 1911 *Dr. Miles* decision (discussed in chapter 4) that had banned resale price maintenance. In its 2007 *Leegin* decision the court replaced the previous *per se* prohibition on resale price maintenance with the more permissive rule-of-reason analysis with respect to vertical price restraints (on *Leegin*, see Brunell 2007; Khan and Vaheesan 2017).

Such decisions were based on the Chicago school logic that manufacturers, acting rationally, would seek to keep distribution costs as low as possible (or be punished in the market) so that any increase in the gap between the wholesale and the retail price must mean that the retailer is delivering some benefit (for example, some service or information about the product) that justifies the increase. Thus, as industrial concentration increased in the United States (thanks not least to the Chicago school's lenient approach toward mergers and acquisitions), conservatives and progressives had essentially traded places in the battles that had raged over resale price maintenance in the 1920s. In the changed context since the 1980s, resale price maintenance had taken on a wholly new meaning. For early-twentieth-century progressives like Brandeis, price maintenance had been about protecting small producers (and, secondarily, small retailers) from domination by large corporations in the interest of innovation and competition; by the 1990s and 2000s it was embraced by the right for the way it allowed powerful actors to achieve operating efficiencies in the interest of "weeding out" weaker firms (Easterbrook 2007: 3).[29] With the *Leegin* decision, fair trade had completed its migration from a cause

28. As Kovacic and Shapiro summarize (2000: 53): "The pivotal event was the Supreme Court's decision in *Continental T. V. Inc. v. GTE Sylvania Inc.* (433 U.S. 36 [1977]), which held that all nonprice vertical restrictions—like the location clauses challenged in this case—warrant rule of reason analysis. The court prominently cited Chicago school commentary and emphasized that the analysis of economic effects provided the proper basis for evaluating conduct under the antitrust laws. Minimum retail price maintenance agreements remained illegal *per se*, but later decisions toughened evidentiary tests for proving the existence of such arrangements, as in *Monsanto Co. v. Spray-Rite Service Corp.* (465 U.S. 752 [1984]) and *Business Electronics Corp. v. Sharp Electronics Corp.* (485 U.S. 717 [1988])." Both the *Monsanto* and *Sharp* decisions increased the room for producers to impose unilateral restraints of various sorts.

29. As the Chicago school's Easterbrook put it in a keynote article titled "Chicago on Vertical Restrictions," "What is good for small dealers and worthy men, in Justice Peckham's phrase, is usually bad for everyone else. Competition is a gale of creative destruction (this is Joseph Schumpeter's memorable line), and it is by weeding out the weakest firms that the economy as a whole receives the greatest boost" (Easterbrook 2007: 3)

championed by the progressive left to that of the libertarian right (Phillips Sawyer 2018: 315–18; Sandel 1996: 246–49).[30]

Even as Chicago school conservatives were recoding vertical price restraints as presumptively efficient rather than probably abusive, liberals had worried that the revival of resale price maintenance would simply benefit large manufacturers at the expense of (especially low-income) consumers. In a dissenting opinion on the *Leegin* case, the court's liberal justices—Stephen Breyer, joined by Ruth Bader Ginsburg, David Souter, and John Paul Stevens—argued that the *per se* ban on resale price maintenance imposed under *Dr. Miles* should have been maintained in part because Congress had clearly expressed its preference for such a rule in the 1975 Consumer Goods Pricing Act. As Sandel put it, "For progressives of old, the chains had been the villains . . . [but] for modern liberals, the discounters had become the heroes" (1996: 248).

This is the context in which left-leaning economists such as Jason Furman (chairman of the Council of Economic Advisers and chief economist in the Obama administration) could code Walmart as "a progressive success story," celebrating the way in which its price reductions have benefited American workers or at least, as he admits, those "outside of the retail sector."[31] Indeed, as Carden (2012: 9; 2013: 409) notes, a large share of American families shop at Walmart, and poorer families shop there more. A study by Basker (2007: 187) found that 53 percent of Americans with incomes of less than $20,000 shop "regularly" at Walmart (alongside 33 percent of those with incomes above $50,000) (Carden 2012: 9). A Pew Research Center survey recorded widespread public acceptance of large discount retailers, a striking turnaround compared to the 1930s and 1940s. Only 19 percent of those polled thought Walmart was bad for their community (68 percent thought it good), and only a slightly higher number (24 percent) thought it was bad

30. It is perhaps worth mentioning that in comparative perspective the United States is something of an outlier on this. RPM is now illegal under EU rules, and as Brunell points out, "The vast majority of advanced industrial countries generally ban minimum resale price maintenance and treat it more harshly than nonprice vertical restraints" (Brunell 2007: 521). Even Canada, which "bars nonprice vertical restraints only when likely to substantially lessen competition, treats resale price maintenance as a criminal offense" (Brunell 2007: 522).

31. See Jason Furman, "Walmart: A Progressive Success Story," November 28, 2005, https://www.mackinac.org/archives/2006/walmart.pdf; also his comments at an event ("Debating Walmart's Impact on American's Workers") held at the Center for American Progress, November 16, 2005, https://www.americanprogress.org/events/debating-wal-marts-impact-on-americas-workers/.

for the country (Pew Research Center 2005).[32] This is also the context, to circle back to chapter 1, in which economists who are otherwise critical of growing concentration in the American economy would praise Walmart as an example of "efficient concentration" (Philippon 2019: 31).

By the 2000s (and arguably much earlier), the reality was that Walmart had worked its way not just into the core of the American retail market but into the center of the American political economy as a whole. By 2005, the company's chief marketing officer was pleased to report that 93 percent of all American households had at least one Walmart shopper (Fishman 2011: 288–89).[33] Walmart had also become a hugely important source of employment. Fishman notes that "for two-thirds of Americans, Walmart is the single largest employer in the state" and that "more than 70 percent of all new retailing jobs in the United States in the . . . seven years [between 2004 and 2011] came just from the growth of Walmart" (2011: 15, 107).

Conclusion

At first blush it seems puzzling why the South—once the bastion of anti-chain store populism—came to be home to the country's most successful retail chain. Chapters 5 and 7 unspool the puzzle, showing how, even as they fought the chains, southern states also supported policies (notably in the conflicts over Miller-Tydings) that exerted downward pressure on the price of goods manufactured in the industrial North. Gavin Wright emphasizes the persistence into the postwar period of the South as "a low-wage region in a high-wage country" (Wright 1987: 170). There, employers had

---

32. Moreover, even if Walmart is not universally loved, it is nearly universally frequented. A study of shoppers in Oklahoma categorized 29 percent of respondents as "Walmart missionaries" (who report that they love the store and shop there on average over seven times per month, spending more than $400). Fifteen percent of shoppers are "conflicted" (disliking the store because of its negative impact on wages, jobs, and the community), though they continue to shop there (this group constitutes "by a wide margin" Walmart's second-most frequent shoppers, visiting 5.6 times per month and spending almost as much as the retailer's biggest fans). "Enthusiasts" (another category) who have a positive view of the store actually go to Walmart less often and spend less than the "conflicted." But even Walmart "rejectors" reported that they shop there an average of nine times per year, spending on average $450 (Fishman 2011: 220). These results are based on a survey conducted by Foote Cone & Belding and published in the *Oklahoma Journal Record* (see Heidi R. Centrella, "National Researchers Study Wal-Mart's Impact on OK Consumers," March 10, 2004). Leo J. Shapiro & Associates, a market research firm based in Chicago, did much of the research and provided Fishman with the company's original report.

33. Ehrenreich cites a Walmart manager who suggested that the company's customers shop there three times a week (2001: 156).

long relied on low labor costs, and state governments even worried that major investments in education risked prompting out-migration (Wright 1987: 170). The distinctive features of the political economy of the American South—a vast nonunionized labor market filled with low-skill, low-wage workers—made it an ideal location for the kind of lean retailing model that thrives on thin margins and high turnover. Sam Walton himself embodied a combination of Montgomery Ward's folksy charm ("I'm one of you") and Richard Warren Sears's ruthless business instincts to drive a model that could take root in this fertile soil.

From its southern base, Walmart could then expand, thanks to the congenial legal and political environment of the American political economy that had supported the explosion of discount retailing in the United States in the 1960s. The low prices and the savings the company was passing on to consumers were gained not just through Walton's legendary thrift and managerial genius, but through a significant externalization of the costs: onto labor, in the form of low wages and paltry (or no) benefits; onto the taxpayers, who underwrite low labor costs through public programs and infrastructure and location incentives; and onto suppliers, who are pressed to lower prices, often at the expense of their own profits and workers' wages (Lichtenstein 2006: 30). The company's strategies thus took full advantage of America's uniquely permissive political economic landscape, one that provides ample opportunity for companies to avoid collective bargaining, to play jurisdictions against one another, and to exploit the ascendance of Chicago school theories that valorized aggressive cutthroat pricing as welfare enhancing.

By the 2000s at the latest, discount retailers, led by Walmart, had reshaped the entire American retail landscape—promoting deregulation, hastening the decline of American manufacturing, and driving the growth of low-wage, low skill employment—all the while cultivating a large and loyal consumer base. Some, though not all, of these developments found strong parallels across the Atlantic, as European countries developed their own vibrant consumer and retailing practices in the postwar and contemporary periods. These are the comparisons to which I now return.

9

Comparative Perspectives on Contemporary American Lean Retailing

Previous chapters have chronicled the long march to dominance in the United States of a particular model of retailing that elevates consumers' preferences for low prices above all other interests. I have argued that this outcome—taken for granted by most Americans today—was not the inevitable result of neutral market forces but has instead been powerfully shaped by law and politics. To underscore the point, this chapter circles back to Europe, focusing now on developments in the postwar period. It assesses the relative resilience of Europe's alternative model of retail capitalism in the face of the growing influence of American cultural norms and consumption patterns (De Grazia 2005).

The Great Depression and World War II inspired significant institutional changes in the United States, including organized labor's full incorporation and the introduction of key social protections. What these events did not do, however, was fundamentally alter the overall trajectory toward a growth model organized around consumers and consumption. After a brief flirtation with a more state-led corporatist model of economic steering in the 1930s, the United States quickly reverted to the more familiar consumerist orientation, one that focuses primarily "on rights and interests on the demand side of the market—in particular, on the consumer economic interest, understood primarily as an interest in competitive prices" (Whitman 2007: 340).

Meanwhile, most Western European countries settled back into their previous producerist orders in the immediate postwar period. The emphasis in the late 1940s and 1950s was on rebuilding industry, a project that often involved either state-sponsored industrial policy or the institutionalization of tripartite corporatist bargaining (Shonfield 1965). In line with Whitman's characterization, Europe's producerist order reenforced and emphasized "rights and interests on the supply side of the market," focusing on the concerns of organized producer groups (unions, industry and trade associations, and in some cases small shopkeepers) (Whitman 2007: 340).

With the partial exception of Britain (where finance played a central role), much of Europe would pursue growth strategies premised on manufacturing exports, often emphasizing industrial over consumer goods (Baccaro and Pontusson 2016). Particularly in Europe's coordinated market economies, the focus was on promoting a strong export sector rather than delivering low consumer prices. But this would change in the 1960s, as full employment and rising wages enhanced attention to issues of consumption and consumer protection by generating a boom in consumer purchasing (Logemann 2008, 2012b; Trumbull 2006a; 2012b).

This chapter analyzes how retailing unfolded in Europe in this new context. It identifies important parallels to developments in the United States, in particular the end of resale price maintenance (RPM) in the 1960s and 1970s, a decline in union membership, and the emergence of discount retailers of various sorts virtually everywhere. But it also highlights continuing differences and the ways in which the kind of big-box discount retailers that are so ubiquitous in the United States have (so far) typically been more hemmed in in Europe. Constraints imposed by countervailing producer-group interests, an overall less fragmented regulatory landscape, and an antitrust regime more skeptical toward dominant actors have offered disruptive retailers fewer opportunities for regulatory arbitrage—and, for now at least, forestalled a full Walmartization of European retail.

Postwar Growth Regimes in Europe and the United States

The literature on postwar growth regimes is vast, so a full account is not necessary here (for a recent overview, see Hall 2020; Hassel and Palier 2021; Baccaro and Pontusson 2016). Simplifying greatly, most European governments institutionalized a strong role for organized producer groups in the postwar order. In large part as a consequence of differences (discussed above) in the rules governing competition policy in the late nineteenth and early twentieth centuries, most of these countries brought with them from the prewar period well-organized employer, trade, and labor organizations (chapter 2; Thelen 2020). These groups were incorporated into the postwar order, either assisting in state-led industrial policy or participating directly in tripartite corporatist arrangements for guiding national economic policymaking.

On the labor side, Europe's postwar governments recognized unions as legitimate representatives of the interests of the working class, broadly defined. In sharp contrast to the United States, organized labor was often empowered to negotiate wages and working conditions that would apply to entire sectors or even the entire labor market. The precise mechanisms varied cross-nationally: in some cases, this involved industry- or national-level collective bargaining, in other cases statutory bargaining extensions (SBEs) through which the government would apply the terms of union contracts to workers who otherwise would have been uncovered (on the latter, see Günther and Höpner 2023). Scandinavia occupies one end of the spectrum in this regard; there, highly centralized unions and employer associations worked out national standards for wages and working hours. In Germany, broad multisectoral bargaining under the leadership of the metalworkers union (IG Metall) and its employer counterpart (Gesamtmetall) set the parameters for the economy as a whole. Even in more liberal Britain, where unions were far less centralized, organized labor was well incorporated into the immediate postwar order, first through the unions' close connections to the Labour government that assumed power in 1945, then extended by subsequent conservative governments through institutionalized tripartite consultation in national economic planning in the 1960s.

On the producer side, the trade associations that had formed across Europe (thanks to the permissive stance toward horizontal coordination discussed in previous chapters) reemerged to represent the political and economic interests of specific sectors. The process was relatively unproblematic in the countries that were allied with the United States during the war, but it was also true for defeated Germany. While Americans presided over the dismantling of that country's most notorious cartels, its first postwar competition law (the 1957 Law Against Restraints on Competition) continued to allow for considerable coordination, especially among small- and medium-sized enterprises. Despite then-chancellor Ludwig Erhard's express preference for policies to promote consumption, industrial interests fought fiercely to retain strong trade associations and other institutions that they saw as critical to reviving German industry's strength in high-quality industrial goods for export (Freyer 2006: 263–69; Gerber 1998: chap. 8).

As noted previously, consumption in Europe (especially consumption of household conveniences such as washing machines) had lagged behind the United States throughout the interwar period and into the postwar period of reconstruction. But this changed dramatically in the 1960s as postwar growth ushered in a golden era of sustained economic prosperity. Full employment and rising wages generated a surge in consumer purchasing. It was in this context, as Trumbull notes, that early postwar goals of rebuilding industry gave way to "new priorities that focused on the goal of consumer welfare" (2006: 159).

Other scholars have documented key cross-Atlantic differences that emerged in this period, including in consumer credit (Logemann 2008, 2011; Trumbull 2012a, 2014); in consumer protection (Trumbull 2006a, 2012b); in how issues of worth and valuation figure into consumption (Beckert 2011; 2016; Beckert and Musselin 2013); and in the balance between public and private consumption (Logemann 2012b). In what follows I will focus instead on three other realms that have influenced the shape of the retail landscape in Europe and the United States: the competition (antitrust) policies that affect the opportunities for large discount retailers to dominate suppliers to drive ever-lower prices; the labor regimes that influence the capacity of retailers to achieve competitive advantage through union avoidance and labor sweating; and the rules that define the spatial and temporal parameters of shopping. Developments in some areas (in particular, resale price maintenance and labor relations) point to parallels and partial convergence between the United States and Europe. But developments in other areas (rules governing the behavior of dominant economic actors, and the spatial and temporal parameters of retail) indicate continuing differences.

Competition Policy and Antitrust

Everywhere, resale price maintenance arrangements were casualties at some point in the 1950s through the 1970s, though the timing and the dynamics of their demise varied. In the United States, where collective defense of RPM through horizontal coordination (among competitors or potential competitors in a market) had been illegal throughout the twentieth century, and where efforts on the part of individual firms to defend prices were costly and often ineffective, RPM eroded as a result of regulatory arbitrage and outright rule-breaking even where state-level fair trade laws remained on the books. In Europe, by contrast, where RPM was imbricated in the denser associational landscape described above, de facto price maintenance often outlived the laws that made it lawful.

As discussed in chapter 5, RPM was strongest and persisted longest in Europe's coordinated market economies. Throughout the interwar period and indeed well into the post–World War II years, RPM arrangements, including horizontal price agreements among manufacturers or distributors, were allowable, although government agencies were authorized to investigate the impact of such agreements and empowered to take action against those that were seen as clashing with the public interest.

In Scandinavia, RPM was ultimately ruled illegal in the mid-1950s, but, as noted earlier, the bans imposed in Denmark and Sweden at that time did not prohibit manufacturers from recommending prices, and they also left ample room for coordinated action by trade associations to encourage firms to adhere to the recommendations. The distinction that policymakers drew was not between collectively and individually enforced RPM, but rather between binding and recommended resale prices (with only the former considered unlawful) (Kjølby 1966: 159). The primary concern was to ensure that new competitors could enter the market and that firms that wished to deviate from suggested prices were free to do so. Thus, manufacturers often continued to recommend prices, and even where they did not, trade associations sometimes developed their own lists of suggested prices and distributed these to their members (Trolle 1966: 140).

These forms of coordination allowed RPM arrangements to endure informally in Scandinavia even after the legal protections on these practices were removed. Retailers and distributors who complied with recommended prices gave a range of reasons for doing so. For some, it was worries about possible disruption in receiving supplies from producers; for others, it was loyalty to fellow retailers. Still others complied out of concerns about the reaction of competitors, since price reductions could set off a competitive spiral of price-cutting (Kjølby 1966: 167). Reporting on the results of one of the few available studies of adherence to recommended prices (in the late 1950s and early 1960s), Kjølby's figures indicate that compliance in Denmark was 85 percent, Sweden 90 percent, and Norway 95 percent for over half the items included in the study (1966: 166).[1]

The persistence of de facto price maintenance after its de jure elimination was annoying to critics of the practice. Writing in 1966, the assistant head of

---

1. Studies of compliance are scant, but the limited available evidence also suggests that there was wide variation across different product lines (Kjølby 1966: 165).

the Monopolies Control Authority for Denmark, H. Kjølby, noted that the effectiveness of his country's 1955 prohibition on resale price maintenance had been compromised "by the widespread observance of recommended prices" (177). His resigned conclusion was that competition cannot be created by new laws "if the enterprises are not interested in competing with one another," and he bemoaned that in "a fair number of commodity fields" the ban on RPM in Denmark appeared "to have had hardly any effect so far" (1966: 175, 176).

In Germany, RPM was on shakier ground by the 1960s though it remained legal even longer than in these other countries. The 1957 competition law mentioned above left RPM untouched after intense lobbying by the Trademark Protection Association, and the practice remained "a prominent feature of the German consumer goods market throughout the 1950s and '60s" (Logemann 2012: 49). While RPM contracts remained legal, companies were required to register their prices with the newly founded competition authority (Bundeskartellamt), which was empowered to intervene against "abusive" practices (Teupe 2016: 258). Yet intense competition in the consumer goods market rendered RPM increasingly difficult to sustain (see Teupe 2016 for a full analysis). Discounters in key retail sectors (e.g., electronics) moved in with strategies not unlike (and sometimes based on) those of their American counterparts. For some product lines, well-organized producer groups fought back collectively to deny discounters access to their goods (e.g., manufacturers of televisions organized into a so-called television cartel) (Teupe 2016: 264–82). But such arrangements repeatedly collapsed in the face of collective action problems as competition heated up.

The German government finally banned RPM in 1974 (books excepted) in the second reform of the anticartel law (*2. Kartellgesetznovelle*) (Epple 2014: 175–86). But as in Scandinavia, informal, coordinated compliance in some sectors continued after the legal ban. Manufacturers were still free to post recommended prices, and although the share of goods with such prices printed on the products themselves (thus visible to consumers) fell from 30 percent to 14 percent of total retail stock in the two years immediately following the law, price lists distributed to retailers (not visible to consumers) rose from 22 percent to 37 percent in the same period. The reliance of small shops (annual sales of under 250,000 deutsche marks) on recommended retailer price lists grew strongly (up from 22 percent to 42 percent of inventory) (Trumbull 2006a: 152–53). The Bundeskartellamt looked into the situation in 1975 but concluded that "protection of brands and distribution, not protection of the consumer, is . . . still the predominant criterion for interpreting the [new competition law]" (Trumbull 2006a: 153). The German parliament concurred, viewing recommended prices as conveying useful information to consumers as to product quality (Trumbull 2006a: 153).

Even in America's Anglo-Saxon (and common-law) cousin, Britain, RPM fell away gradually and ultimately only with a significant push from the government. As noted in chapter 5, RPM had been widely practiced in the interwar period and indeed into the postwar period before collective defense of prices was rendered illegal with the 1956 Restrictive Practices Act. Mercer's figures indicate that the share of consumer expenditure on price-maintained goods before 1956 was between 44 and 55 percent, but even after 1956, RPM remained "extensive" at between 30–40 percent of consumer expenditures (Mercer 1998: 3, 4). One reason for this was that in Britain—in contrast to the United States—courts were inclined to uphold the rights of individual firms to set prices through the 1950s (Mercer 1998: 24). The Conservative government of Alec Douglas-Home (1963–64) finally moved to ban all forms of RPM (with the Resale Prices Act of 1964) because policymakers had come to the conclusion that "market forces alone would not bring about its demise: the practice was firmly entrenched and required tough, unequivocal legislation" (Mercer 1998: 4).[2]

The demise of RPM opened the door for discount retailing everywhere, although in some branches discounters relied less on reducing prices on branded goods than on selling alternative cheaper private-label products. In Germany, hard-discount grocery chains—in particular Aldi and Lidl—have thrived since the 1960s and 1970s with a business model that rests on high-volume sales of a limited range of mostly low-quality, almost all private-label products at low prices, and offering virtually no service. Sweden, for its part, is famous for its high-volume, low-cost clothing chain H&M as well as the low-cost furniture retailer IKEA. Less visible to foreign observers, the tiny town of Ullared in Sweden (population 560) is the home of a gigantic superstore (Gekås) offering over one hundred thousand different products. The United Kingdom has huge supermarkets (Tesco and Sainsbury), and thanks to Walmart's previous acquisition of the British grocery chain ASDA, it also has a number of supercenters that offer both groceries and a wide range of other merchandise. In short, Europe is by no means devoid of large retailers and discounters, and indeed in many cases this reflects the entry of American companies or the adoption of practices pioneered in America.

---

2. This ushered in a period of intense concentration in retail (as multiples grew at the expense of small merchants) and a decisive shift in the balance of power, as producers in many areas (Mercer singles out groceries and electrical goods in particular) "have taken on the role of subcontractors to large retailers" (Mercer 1998: 23).

Even as resale price maintenance arrangements faded, however, European competition policy remained distinct and in fact has recently pulled away from the American model on some key dimensions (see Foster and Thelen 2023 and 2024 for a more comprehensive discussion). The United States to this day has never seriously wavered from its traditional strict prohibition against almost all forms of horizontal coordination (i.e., among competitors or potential competitors in a market).[3] European competition regimes charted a different course in the postwar period. Even as they implemented stronger rules against cartels and outright price-fixing, postwar Europe's coordinated market economies maintained their more flexible and forbearing position on other forms of interfirm coordination among nondominant actors. Greater leniency was applied above all to small- and medium-sized enterprises engaged in forms of coordination such as joint standard-setting or research and development that were seen as supporting innovation or improving efficiency. In Germany, this outcome reflected the preferences of the country's producer groups (both trade associations and unions) and the influence of the trade associations in the negotiations behind the 1957 competition law. A later 1965 revision of the law in fact opened more avenues for certain forms of coordination among small- and medium-sized firms even as it strengthened antitrust enforcement against dominant players and instituted greater scrutiny of proposed mergers (Teupe 2016: 256).[4]

But the story was largely the same in virtually all coordinated market economies. Similar to Brandeis's arguments of the 1920s, competition authorities viewed some forms of coordination among small- and medium-sized firms not as anticompetitive but as competition-enhancing for the way they allowed smaller players to survive and compete more effectively against larger companies. Importantly, greater forbearance toward such "healthy" forms of horizontal coordination among nondominant actors was coupled with increasingly stringent rules against abuse of dominance by powerful ones.[5] Coordinated market economies thus combined their long-standing

3. The only exception is the short-lived experimentation with cooperative associationalism in the 1920s in a few sectors (see Berk 2009), and, of course, the brief ill-fated NIRA.

4. The law also enlisted consumers in monitoring what it called "unfair" practices, including misleading advertising and "unfair terms of sale." While framed as protection for consumers, the legal action blocked such activities but without any compensation for consumers (Trumbull 2006a: 63–64)

5. In Germany, for example, the formal end to RPM did create an important opening for discount chains to grow, but policymakers were also sufficiently concerned about the possibility of powerful retailers abusing their market power to demand excessive concessions from their suppliers that they created a new division within the competition authority (in 1980) devoted

leniency toward certain forms of cooperation among nondominant firms with stricter constraints on dominant actors, the latter reflecting the influence of the so-called ordoliberal school of economic thought that prevailed in Germany in the postwar period. Ordoliberals were resolutely antiplanning, but they were also concerned about how private economic power could be wielded by dominant actors in ways that could distort or even destroy competition (Foster 2022: 1667).[6]

This ordoliberal competition paradigm would in turn provide much of the inspiration for the European Union's competition law (Foster 2022: 1667–70).[7] Indeed, over time, the EU gravitated toward an evermore skeptical stance toward powerful firms' behavior. Enforcement against anticompetitive strategies increased sharply starting in the 2000s: "Since receiving the power to enforce EU abuse of dominance rules in 2004, national competition authorities have finalized more than 500 abuse of dominance decisions—or one-third of all decisions . . ." (Foster and Kohl 2023: 24). Moreover, and in stark contrast to trends that had been unfolding in the United States since the 1970s, the European Commission came to understand "abuse of dominance" to include not just practices that harmed consumers but also those that had a negative impact on the competitive structure of whole industries. This stance also informs the national-level regulations that complement EU-level antitrust laws. For example, in 2001, Walmart lost an antitrust case brought by Germany's Bundeskartellamt for predatory pricing as harmful to independents and to competition in the long run (Andrews 2000; Mitchell 2003).[8]

As Foster notes, the United States and Europe have presented mirror images of antimonopoly enforcement since the 1970s (2022: 1658–59). Figure 9.1 charts the number of successful antimonopoly cases on both sides of the Atlantic between 1970 and 2019. It shows that enforcement against dominant actors plummeted in the late 1970s in the United States with the ascendance of the Chicago school, just as enforcement in Europe was picking up speed.

---

to monitoring monopsony power (*Nachfragemacht*) with a particular focus on grocery chains (Kurzlechner 2008: 188).

6. This emphasis, as Foster notes, likely reflected at least in part the concerns about the dominance of American manufacturers in the immediate postwar period.

7. On differences between the competition regimes in the European Union and United States, see Foster (2022) and Foster (2024); also Foster and Kohl (2023) and Foster and Thelen (2023 and 2024).

8. A study of private antitrust enforcement in Germany between 2005 and 2007 by Peyer (2010) showed that a large majority of cases brought under German law (57.6 percent) involved claims of abuse of dominance (2010: 57).

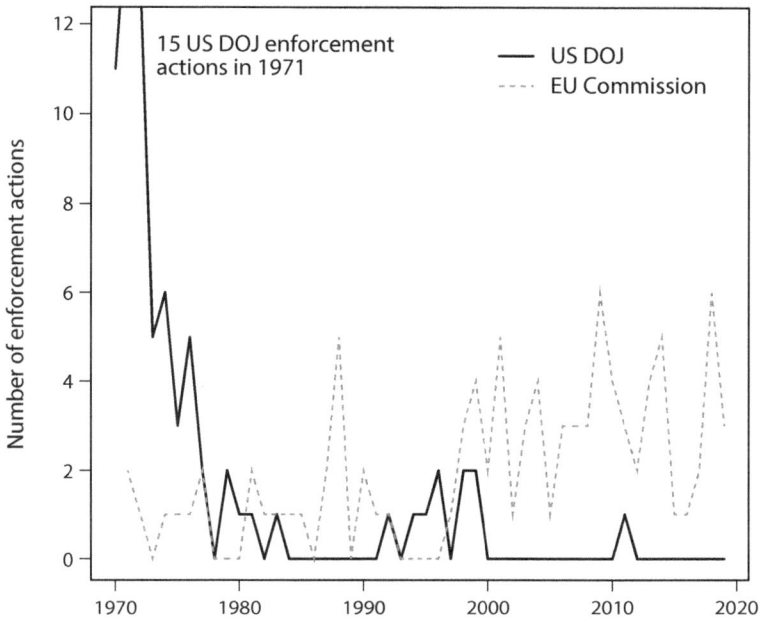

FIGURE 9.1. Number of monopoly/dominance prosecutions or prohibitions. *Sources:* US Department of Justice, European Commission. *Note:* This figure records the number of successful antimonopoly/dominance enforcement actions by the US DOJ and the European Commission from 1970–2019. The US DOJ figures are the number of criminal or civil monopoly cases won at the district court level under Section 2 of the Sherman Act. The EU figure is the number of prohibition or commitment decisions made under Article 102 (formerly Article 86 or Article 82). For more detail, see Foster and Thelen (2024: Online Appendix, Part 1); also Foster (in progress).

In other words, as American antitrust was turning to extreme forbearance toward dominant actors (and vertical restraints of all varieties), European antitrust jurisprudence was moving in the opposite direction, assuming a more aggressive approach (see Foster 2022; Foster and Thelen 2024). European law regulates more strictly a host of exclusionary practices that alongside predatory pricing include margin squeezes, exclusive dealing, exclusive purchasing, exclusionary discounts, tying, refusals to deal, discrimination, and other exploitative abuses (Carree, Günster, and Schinkel 2010; Foster 2022; Graf et al. 2023). Nearly half of the abuse of dominance decisions handed down by the European Union between 2009 and 2019 required dominant players to facilitate access for competitors to some essential resource; nearly a quarter (21 percent) stopped a dominant company from using its power in one market to gain advantage in another one in ways that limited competition or consumer choice; and 15 percent addressed predatory behavior that was seen as interfering with the competitive process (Foster 2022: 1670). Importantly in the digital era, European competition law increasingly includes extensive obligations for dominant companies to facilitate access to essential facilities, to provide interoperability information, and to license intellectual property.

In sum, in the United States, the courts' emphasis on a particular version of consumer welfare elevated price considerations and provided a boon to large low-cost retailers such as Walmart and later Amazon. By contrast, the European approach to competition policy, in its stance on both vertical and horizonal restraints, reflects a longer-standing concern for preserving market competition. So while price maintenance arrangements are now history in Europe, measures directed against cartels and price-fixing were either accompanied or followed by rules that provide greater cover for nondominant firms to coordinate some of their activities in order to compete more effectively against larger players, alongside other complementary rules that take a much more aggressive approach to abuse of dominance and predatory pricing.

Labor Regimes and Employment Relations in Retail

The power of dominant companies is not just limited by the legal framework, but also by the strength of countervailing social and economic interest groups. Given the importance of low labor costs to the strategies of large discounters, arguably the most important of these countervailing forces in the retail sector is that exercised by organized labor. This is an area in which Europe has moved closer to the United States, though there are still significant differences in the legal and institutional resources available to unions to challenge the power of large firms. In Europe as in the United States, retail employees are among the worst paid and most precarious on the labor market. Yet as Carré and Tilly (2017) have pointed out, even bad jobs are better in some countries than in others, and the United States does not fare well in such comparisons.

Unionization and collective-bargaining coverage rates in retailing—well below the national average in all countries—are lower in the United States than in its peer democracies. According to the Bureau of Labor Statistics, as of 2022 only 4.2 percent of American workers in the wholesale and retail trade sector were members of a union, and because of the rules governing union recognition and certification noted in chapter 7, collective bargaining coverage is only slightly higher, at 4.8 percent of workers (Bureau of Labor Statistics 2024, table 3). In Europe, union membership in retail is also low, at 12 percent in the United Kingdom (DBEIS 2022; Payne et al. 2022: 6), but it rises to between 30 and 48 percent in Scandinavia, at 32 percent in Denmark and 48 percent in Sweden (Ilsøe et al. 2017: 894; LO 2022: 9). However, because of differences in the structure of bargaining and the character of union rights in Europe, collective bargaining coverage is often significantly higher than in the United States: 28 percent in Germany (HDE 2024), 29 percent in the UK (DBEIS 2022), and nearly 60 percent in the Scandinavian countries.[9]

In Sweden, continued comparatively high union coverage and sectoral agreements have provided a partial shield against labor exploitation despite declining membership and increasing competition with the entry of foreign discount chains since the 2000s (O'Brady 2018: 336–38; Kjellberg and Nergaard 2022). Sweden's retail union (Handels) has often been able to force foreign discounters to sign on to sectoral agreements, preventing "low-road competitors . . . from making union avoidance a precondition of competitiveness" (O'Brady 2018: 338). Germany's hard-discount grocer Lidl, for example, is notorious for such strategies in its home country, but the chain is reportedly "'rather good' at complying with the terms of the Swedish retail agreement" (O'Brady 2018: 338). When Lidl entered the Swedish market, it assumed a generally cooperative approach, including joining the employers' association and engaging in collective bargaining with the union (O'Brady 2021: 1099).

Collective agreements for the retail sector in Sweden, as in other Scandinavian countries, provide extensive protections with respect to working hours, such as one month's notice of changes to employees' schedules, limits on working time reductions, and employees' right to refuse work on weekends. And national-level basic agreements and work environment agreements, along with data protection laws, provide safeguards against

9. The figure for Denmark is 57 percent according to Ilsøe (2017: 894). The latest published figure for Sweden (from 2007) was 73 percent (Kjellberg 2009: 2), but union economists suggest it is currently likely lower, somewhere between 50 and 60 percent (I thank LO's Fredrik Söderqvist for this estimate). We know that as of 2015, only 45 percent of *firms* in the retail sector were covered by collective agreements negotiated with the union (Kjellberg 2020; 2022). But retailing has many small shops, and unionization rates are the highest in the large companies. One of the three largest retailers in Sweden is Coop, which, along with other labor movement consumer co-ops discussed in previous chapters, has a collective agreement with its own employer association (Fremia, previously KFO).

worker monitoring and surveillance (Payne et al. 2022: 15–16 on Norway). The Swedish retail union has agreements that impose restrictions on the use of fixed-term contracts, including a 2012 agreement that stipulates that general fixed-term (*allmän vistid*) jobs must be converted to permanent contracts after twelve months. While the constraints on the use of various nonstandard employment arrangements are far stricter than in the United States, the use of part-time and fixed-term jobs, and the increased use of *hyvling* ("planing," in which employers reduce working hours for individual workers), remain problems for the retail union despite the contractual protections (Kjellberg 2023: 29; Kjellberg and Nergaard 2022).

Retail unions are significantly weaker in the UK, and collective bargaining coverage far less extensive, though unions there have succeeded in organizing some of the country's biggest retailers. In contrast to the United States, unions in the UK often conclude company-level agreements that cover all stores within a chain (Payne et al. 2022: 6). Thus, for example, the country's big-four supermarkets—Tesco, Sainsbury's, Morrisons, and even Walmart knockoff ASDA (which together account for over 65 percent of the food retail market)—all have agreements with organized labor (for the first three, with the Union of Shop, Distributive, and Allied Workers or USDAW; and with GMB for the last[10]) (Davey 2024). As in Sweden, however, the entry of foreign-owned nonunion discounters such as Lidl and Aldi have exposed them to more intense competition (Mintel 2021). Also similar to Sweden, Lidl in particular has resisted unionization, though in 2016 the UK's Central Arbitration Committee (an independent body endowed with statutory powers to revolve labor disputes) sided with the GMB in its bid to negotiate for warehouse workers in Bridgend (BBC 2016).

The largest union in the retail sector, USDAW, has a particularly strong presence at sector-leading Tesco, where it has achieved an average union density of 50 percent. The Tesco-USDAW agreement is in fact the largest private-sector agreement in the UK (Payne et al. 2022: 7, 9). The partnership between Tesco and USDAW operates on the basis of employee forums at the store, regional, and national levels, and it is credited with helping to improve work conditions, provide training and career opportunities, and increase salaries and bonuses for staff. The agreement has been criticized as resting on the union's moderation and compliancy (Geppert et al. 2014;

---

10. GMB is a general union organizing a range of sectors. GMB originally stood for General Municipal Boilermakers, and, since the name stuck, the initials GMB are now used as the official name of the union.

Wood 2016), though there are clearly still elements of contestation—as evidenced, for example, in the recent court battle over Tesco's fire-and-rehire (at lower benefits) policy (Butler 2022). In general, and as Alex Wood's ethnographic study of paired US and UK retailers showed, workers in the UK enjoy overall more protections as a result of a stronger union presence (including union policing of disciplinary and grievance procedures at the firm) and greater statutory rights and protections than their American counterparts (Wood 2020: 20–21).

As perhaps already evident, labor relations in the German retail sector have deteriorated significantly with the rise of the hard-discount grocers, especially after 2000, when the employers' association for the retail sector abandoned the use of statutory bargaining extensions (Günther 2021: 150–54; Günther and Höpner 2023: 95).[11] In 2006, Walmart famously crashed out of the German retail market just nine years after it had arrived, having foundered on a number obstacles, including contentious relations with the country's retail union, ver.di.[12] Perhaps ironically (but similar in many ways to trends in the United States), some of Germany's discounters offer compensation at a rate that exceeds collectively bargained or statutory minimum rates as part of their union avoidance strategy (O'Brady 2021: 1097). Also similar to the United States, anecdotal evidence of labor violations and union-busting strategies abound. For example, Lidl has been accused of abusive employment practices and of creating a "climate of fear" at its stores in Germany, some of these recorded in a catalog of complaints assembled by ver.di (Paterson 2004). Similarly, Aldi has been engaged in union-busting strategies, most recently to prevent the establishment of a second works council at Aldi-Süd (LabourNet Germany 2022).

Relations with organized labor are overall less contentious, and labor conditions less onerous, in other areas of German retail. In a study of retail warehouses in Germany (with comparisons to France), Gautie et al. (2020) documented a general convergence on many of the features of warehouse work that are characteristic of liberal market economies like the United States (e.g., automation and neo-Taylorist work arrangements). But the authors also found that the influence of worker representatives (statutory works councils in the German case) resulted in a "less intense" version of

11. Wortmann has suggested that these hard discounters are complementary to the German growth regime because the success of Germany's export-oriented high-quality manufacturing sector increasingly relies on the existence of a low-wage service sector to keep labor costs in check (Wortmann 2020: 19; Hassel 2014: 75; Günther and Höpner 2023: 91).

12. See Trumbull and Gay (2019) and Christophersen (2007) for full analysis.

these practices (Gautie et al. 2020: 774, 791). While works councils were unable to steer the technological choices of these increasingly automated warehouses, they were able to block employers' use of digital technologies to surveil and discipline workers (Gautie 2020: 786–89). Labor law and union rights allowed employee representatives to impose some safeguards, thus contributing to "somewhat less intense forms of neo-Taylorism" (2020: 790–91). In particular, stronger privacy protections have prevented employers from following the lead of large American retailers in using data on employees in performance management (Gautie 2020: 790).

A shared trend in the retail sector that spans all countries is a shift toward increasing reliance on part-time, fixed-term, or other atypical employment contracts. Based on figures from the Bureau of Labor Statistics and Eurostat, the share of part-time workers employed in the wholesale and retail sectors ranges from 27 percent in the United States to 30.5 percent and 34.3 percent in Sweden and Denmark, respectively, to 33.3 percent in Germany and 36.7 percent in the UK (2019 figures).[13] Everywhere, this has led to a deterioration in wages, working conditions, and benefits.

However, here it is useful to bear in mind that the baseline benefits for part-time employees are far lower for American workers compared to their European counterparts (Thelen 2019). Not only do part-time workers enjoy greater job protections than even their full-time counterparts in the United States' system of at-will employment (Thelen 2019: 13, figure 5),[14] but part-time work in Europe also comes attached to an overall more generous package of protections and benefits. The best known difference pertains to health insurance, which in the United States has traditionally been provided by employers. While the Affordable Care Act now requires firms to offer health insurance to employees who work at least thirty hours per week, the requirement does not extend to part-time workers. Figures from the Bureau of Labor Statistics (2023) suggest that as of March 2023 only about a quarter of part-time workers were offered employer-sponsored health care plans. Beyond these well-known differences, part-time workers in Europe are entitled (on a prorated basis) to many of the same benefits that full-time

---

13. The figures here are the most recent (2019) figures on retail specifically—from the Bureau of Labor Statistics (for the United States) and from Eurostat (for the European countries). Because they are not measured in precisely the same way they are not perfectly comparable, but they do give a broad general sense of the share of part-time work in the sector across these countries. (The OECD does not report sector-level figures for part-time work.)

14. Under the American system of at-will employment, employers can fire an employee at any time and for almost any reason.

workers enjoy, including sick pay, parental leave, vacation time, and in some cases the right to training.

All of these are benefits that part-time workers in the United States rarely enjoy (indeed, full-time workers are often not entitled to several of them). Take one of the most fundamental such benefits: paid sick leave. The United States is the only advanced industrial democracy in which workers have no federally guaranteed entitlement to paid days off when they are too sick to come to work.[15] Surveys conducted by the Bureau of Labor Statistics show that a mere 30 percent of workers in the lowest income decile enjoy any paid sick leave at all, and only about 40 percent of those in the lowest quartile have access to paid sick leave (Thelen 2019: 14, figure 6b). The picture is the same for paid vacation and paid holidays. Workers in Europe are entitled to between twenty and thirty paid vacation or holidays per year, prorated for part-time workers. The United States, by contrast, is the only rich industrial country that provides *no* federally guaranteed paid vacation time.[16]

Employment in retail specifically often involves highly irregular hours and changing schedules. Here, too, Europe offers greater protections and predictability for part-time workers and for workers with certain kinds of atypical employment arrangements (e.g., temporary agency and contract workers). According to the EU Directive on Transparent and Predictable Working Conditions that went into effect in 2022, employers "must specify which days and times [employees] can be obliged to work" and can then "only schedule them on these days, otherwise employees are not obliged to work." Furthermore, employers must inform workers of their upcoming schedules with at least four days' notice, and employees who have been with a firm for at least twenty-six weeks can "submit a written, substantiated request . . . for a more predictable working relationship."[17] Among the protections enjoyed by many European (but not American) workers are

15. State-level governments can mandate sick leave, but only seventeen of the country's fifty states contain provisions that mandate paid time off for medical reasons. See "Paid Sick Leave Laws by State for 2024," Paycor, last updated December 2023, https://www.paycor.com/resource-center/articles/paid-sick-leave-laws-by-state/.

16. Again, states can pass laws requiring this, but only Maine and Nevada require paid vacation (and not for all employees). See "Vacation Time Laws for Employees: 50-State Survey," Justia, https://www.justia.com/employment/employment-laws-50-state-surveys/vacation-time-laws-for-employees-50-state-survey/.

17. If the employer cancels a worker's scheduled hours within the four days, the employee is still entitled to those wages. See "EU Directive on Transparent and Predictable Working Conditions," PWC, July 20, 2022, https://www.pwc.nl/en/insights-and-publications/services-and-industries/people-and-organisation/eu-directive-on-transparent-and-predictable-working-conditions.html.

provisions that require employers to pay supplements for "unsocial" work hours (evenings, nights, and weekends).[18]

Compare this to the situation of their American counterparts. Carré and Tilly (2017) note that even full-time retail workers in the United States are not guaranteed full-time hours, citing a survey of California retail workers that showed that only one-third were promised a set minimum number of hours, that nearly half had schedules that varied week by week, and that one-quarter had to be on standby to work on the same day (2017 and 2018). A survey of low-skill service workers in the Washington, DC, area similarly revealed that over 40 percent of workers received less than one week notice of their upcoming work schedules (nearly 30 percent less than three days) (Schwartz et al. 2015). Moreover, further changes after the initial posting left over 50 percent of these workers with less than one to two days' notice (25 percent with less than twenty-four hours) (Thelen 2019: 11, figures 4a and 4b). And despite tighter labor markets since the pandemic (and the broad—albeit mostly performative—outpouring of appreciation for the essential workers who kept pharmacies and retail shops running through the crisis), nothing in the empirical record suggests that work conditions have improved for American retail workers. On the contrary, ongoing research by Daniel Schneider and colleagues documents continued instability in working hours and scheduling for low-wage retail workers (Zundl et al. 2022: 1–3).

A key loophole in European regulations that retail employers have been quick to exploit is that they rarely specify a minimum threshold for working hours (Ilsøe et al. 2017). Thus, despite regulations establishing limits on the maximum length of the workday and regulations regarding scheduling, the lack of a collectively bargained or statutorily established minimum number of hours has left employers free to hire some workers with low weekly working hours. Thus, "mini-jobs" in Germany, so-called zero-hour or flex-contracts in the UK, and various forms of marginal part-time work in Scandinavia are a source of erosion in labor standards and one that is especially pronounced in retail (Ilsøe and Larsen 2021; Rasmussen et al. 2019).[19] The

18. Ilsøe and colleagues find that in retail (and other low-wage services) such supplements often result in the hourly wages of part-time and irregular workers being higher than the collectively bargained minimum, though the lack of a minimum threshold for worker hours means that their overall yearly earnings are low (Ilsøe et al. 2017: 889, 899).

19. In the UK, payments for unsocial hours have declined as some retailers have increased their use of flexi-contracts, in which workers can be guaranteed as few as 7.5 hours per week (Payne 2022: 7, 12). In Germany, according to the German retail employers' association HDE, mini-jobbers make up over a quarter (26 percent) of all retail employees as of 2017 (part-time workers account for 36 percent, and full-time just 38 percent). See HDE, "Retail in Germany:

difference to the United States is that European retailers have far fewer ways to achieve the flexibility they think they need, and they are also forced to offer not just more benefits but also more generous pay due to the existence of a stronger social net and thus an overall higher reservation wage.

The point of this exercise is not to minimize the plight of low-wage retail workers in Europe; it is simply to highlight the ways in which the unique features of the American political economy have afforded discount retailers extraordinary latitude to achieve low costs through labor-sweating strategies. In Europe, it is not impossible but it is more difficult to gain competitive advantage by free riding on public benefits or by denying workers core benefits and protections. Some of the constraints on European retailers—for example, concerning unsocial working hours—are also related to the regulations governing shopping hours, a topic to which I now turn.

The Spatial and Temporal Bounds of Retailing

Some of the most striking differences between Europe and the United States concern the spatial and temporal bounds of retailing. In terms of the geography of shopping, urban studies scholars point to the ways in which most American cities enforce a much sharper separation of commercial and residential areas than European cities, which more often allow for a mixing of these functions (Hirt 2012, 2014; Cullingworth 1993). Economic historians and sociologists, for their part, have emphasized a second, even more pronounced difference, namely the continued vibrancy of central shopping districts in most European cities compared to the hollowing out of downtown retailing and the growth of suburban malls and big-box discount centers on the outskirts of American towns and cities (Logemann 2012b: chaps. 5 and 6; Jackson 1985: 257–61).[20] Such differences in the spatial configuration of retailing are related as well to important cross-Atlantic differences in the temporal parameters of shopping, in particular greater restrictions on retail opening hours across most of Europe.

An American strolling through the streets of European cities is likely to be struck not just by the greater density of housing but also by the way in which many residential streets feature a jumble of other functions—for

Collective Bargaining and [*sic*] Competetiveness," http://erc-online.eu/wp-content/uploads/2019/06/2018-09-18-Roma_HDE_17-18_09.pdf.

20. On the surprising origins of the American shopping mall, which emerged out of the perversion of a concept developed by a Viennese socialist, Victor Gruen, who fled the Nazis in 1938, see Johnson 2016; Welsh 2022; Gruen Shopping Towns USA.

example, apartment buildings that include one or more small professional offices, or shops and restaurants scattered among residential units of different sizes. As Beatley (2000: 41) summarizes, European cities "exhibit a much higher level of mixing and integration of functions" than their American counterparts. The difference is not hard and fast, but in general, the United States relies much more on detailed and often rigid specification of permissible land-uses (Hirt 2012 and 2014; Nivola 1999).[21]

A key explanation for this difference concerns the balance between state planning authority (stronger in Europe) and individual property rights (heavily prioritized in American-style zoning) (Sir Peter Hall 2002: 205; Cullingworth 1993: 218–21; Hirt 2012: 376; Hirt 2014: chap. 1). Planning and zoning are not really distinct (zoning can be a tool in planning), and the two can serve the same functions—namely, to "segregate land uses thought to be incompatible" (Sir Peter Hall and Tewdwr-Jones 2020: 294). In fact, as Rodgers and Hirt have documented, urban planning, including the delineation of different zones (e.g., to separate noxious industry or other public hazards and nuisances from residential areas), was imported to the United States from Europe during the Progressive Era (Rodgers 1998: 184–86; Hirt 2014: chap. 6). But, as Rodgers points out, "like every policy import, once extracted from its original economic and political setting, zoning proved an enormously malleable device, open to a multitude of purposes and possessors" (1998: 184). Whereas planning in Europe allows for greater government discretion (to take the "public interest" into consideration), zoning in the United States evolved in such a way that it tends to limit administrative discretion and prioritize individual property rights (Rodgers 1998: 186; Hirt 2014: 156–57).

As a vast literature has documented, American zoning historically was (and still is) used to effectively exclude ethnic and racial minorities (Cohen 2003: chap. 5; Rothstein 2012; Thurston 2012). Of relevance in the present context, many of the same motives flowed into the strict separation of residential and commercial districts in the United States. The first comprehensive zoning code in the United States—adopted in 1916 in New York—separated residential and industrial districts, "but it also included a particularly American component: the business zone" (Hirt 2012: 377; Jacobs 1961). In the United

---

21. Older cities of the Northeast tend to exhibit a denser and more mixed-function pattern than the suburbs and cities of the South and West that grew after the widespread diffusion of the American version of zoning (Weir 2022). Hirt's analysis of zoning districts across twenty-five major American cities showed that while there are some mixed-use districts, they typically make up a small proportion of the overall city. Moreover, in all the cities she studied, the residential category generally prohibits nonresidential, including commercial, uses (Hirt 2014: 52–57).

States, the concept of nuisance was broadly construed and was deployed as a justification for keeping commerce out of residential areas (Cullingworth 1993: chap. 2). The argument was that shops would bring traffic and noise, as well as draw in "strangers" (shoppers) and "outsiders" (lower-class retail workers) and invite loitering and idleness (Hirt 2014: 157–61; 172).

The separation of commercial and residential areas is linked to an even more striking difference in the geography of retailing in Europe and the United States—namely, the ubiquity in the latter of huge shopping malls and big-box discount centers on the outskirts of town. The outward trend had started in the 1920s, when major chains such as Sears began opening retail outlets on the periphery of cities to take advantage of lower land prices and growing car ownership (Hanchett 1989; Emmet and Jeuck 1950: chap. 21; Jackson 1985: 257–61). President Franklin D. Roosevelt's promotion of home ownership (for white middle-class families) in the 1930s and 1940s fueled the growth of the suburbs, which accelerated the hollowing out of central retailing districts. As Cohen notes, the white middle-class homeowners who flocked to the suburbs in this period "increasingly viewed returning to urban downtowns to shop as inconvenient, and . . . retailers came to realize that suburban residents with their young families, new homes, and vast consumer appetites, offered a lucrative frontier ripe for conquer" (Cohen 2003: 257).

Moreover, and as Jan Logemann in particular has emphasized (2012b: chap. 5), other important differences in government policy in Europe and the United States played a profoundly important role in either preserving or further undermining central shopping districts. Postwar European governments invested heavily in public transportation with an eye toward maintaining a vibrant city center, and indeed they were often inspired by a desire to avoid the kind of sprawl that was developing in the United States (Logemann 2012b: chap. 5). Meanwhile, US government policy went in a radically different direction, doubling down on "automobile usage and thus individualized modes of transportation" (Logemann 2012b: 166). The Interstate Highway Act of 1956 further encouraged car ownership and in so doing "ripped the heart" out of many cities (phrase is adapted from Cullingworth 1993: 157).

Even as the new suburban shopping centers were reconfiguring the geography of shopping, the discount retailers discussed in chapters 7 and 8 played a starring role in redefining the *temporal* parameters of shopping in ways that also set the United States apart from its peers. Indeed, the spatial configuration of retailing operated in tandem with changes in the temporal dimension, because a trip to the shopping mall or discount supercenter on the outskirts of town is only feasible where shopping hours extend well beyond the usual workweek (Logemann 2012b: chap. 6). Conversely, where shopping hours are limited, consumers are incentivized to rely more heavily on nearby neighborhood stores, particularly for everyday items. However, the driving force for the widespread deregulation of shopping hours in the United States was not the large established department stores that anchored the country's new suburban malls but instead the discounters that moved in alongside them.

Although most European countries have relaxed their limits on shopping hours over the past few decades, shopping hours remain much more restricted.[22] Most European countries have shorter shopping hours and impose more restrictions on Sunday shopping than in the United States, where retail hours are largely unregulated (prior to the COVID-19 pandemic, Walmart offered 24/7 shopping—and Walmart was by no means the first or only retailer to stay open all night) (Fishman 2011: 10, 230).[23] Far from being a simple reflection of cultural differences, this outcome was the result of intense regulatory arbitrage and outright rule-breaking, unimpeded by countervailing forces such as organized labor.

With the notable exception of Scandinavia, where union strength rather than state legislation places limits on retail hours, most Western European countries impose statutory restrictions on the hours that retailing establishments can remain open, and in many cases, they impose an almost complete ban on Sunday selling.[24] Again, a few examples from the experience of other countries can illustrate the extent to which disruptive retailers in the United States exploited regulatory and legal gaps to expand the temporal bounds of consumption in ways that their European counterparts have not been allowed to match.

22. Even in France, which Trumbull (2012b: chap. 4) sees as closest to the US model of retailing along many dimensions, Sunday shopping has remained limited, despite liberalization. The most recent law, passed in 2015, allows stores to open on twelve Sundays per year (up from five), contingent on mayoral approval, even as it attaches conditions designed to accommodate unions—namely, the provision that workers cannot be forced to work on Sunday and are entitled to receive double their usual compensation if they do agree to work voluntarily (Rose and Picy 2015). Exceptions to Sunday closing laws are generally limited to tourist areas or shopping weekends around Christmas.

23. Several grocery chains in the United States also offered 24/7 shopping before the pandemic, and some have resumed these hours. On Walmart, see WSFA 12 News Staff, "Walmart: No Plans to Make Stores 24/7 Again," August 12, 2022, https://www.wtvy.com/2022/08/12/walmart-no-plans-make-stores-247-again/.

24. For an overview, see European Commission 2017. Retail hours were deregulated in Sweden in 1996, though labor laws and collective bargaining place limits on working hours.

In Germany, the introduction of limits on shopping hours was historically tied up with the regulation of working times (George 1996; Spiekermann 2004; Rühling 2004). Store opening hours were unregulated until 1891, when concerns about labor unrest prompted the government to pass a worker protection law (*Arbeiterschutzgesetz*) that restricted opening hours on Sundays to five hours in a move that small independent merchants opposed as an encroachment on their right to conduct their business without state interference (Spiekermann 2004: 29–30). Shopping and working hours continued to be restricted in the Weimar Republic through a national law passed in 1919 that introduced an eight-hour workday and also called for stores to be closed between 7 p.m. and 7 a.m. (and with Sundays designated as a day of rest for most workers).

The post-WWII boom in consumption during the "economic miracle" introduced new tensions into the question of shopping hours, and in 1953–54, three prominent chain stores (C&A Brenninkmeyer, Salamander, and Woolworths) launched what became known as the shop-closing war (*Ladenschluß-Krieg*) by remaining open on Saturday afternoons (*Süddeutsche Zeitung*, February 22, 1954). Unions responded by organizing protests that swelled to several thousand people, resulting in the passage of the *Ladenschlußgesetz* or Shop Closing Act of 1956, which passed "with the support of unions, retailers' associations, and conservative Catholics" (De Grazia 1998: 80; Rühling 2004: 166; Trumbull 2006a: 57).[25] The law prohibited general retailing on Sundays (bakeries and florists excepted) and established closing hours (6:30 p.m. on weekdays and 4 p.m. on Saturdays—revised two years later to 2 p.m.) (Spiekermann 2004: 38). The coalition of small retailers, churches, and unions defended this regime until 1989, when pressures from liberals and younger consumers succeeded in securing an extension of Thursday shopping hours until 8 p.m. (so-called long Thursday). A similar coalition (including also working women) forced a further liberalization of shopping hours in 1996 (to typically 8 p.m. evenings, Monday through Saturday) though restrictions on Sunday shopping remain in place.

25. Labor unions anchored the pro-regulation camp with the argument that limits on shopping hours prevent employers from demanding excessive overtime. Small retailers were no friends of state interventions of this sort, and certainly not allied with labor on most issues, but they found themselves aligned with labor on this issue. They were having trouble recruiting help in a period of intense labor shortages, and standardizing working hours mitigated competition on this front. For the various positions see Rühling 47–49; *Süddeutsche Zeitung*, June 24, 1953: 2; *Süddeutsche Zeitung*, May 8, 1953: 6 (Ressort Bayern); *Süddeutsche Zeitung*, October 25, 1956; *Süddeutsche Zeitung*, December 3, 1954; *Süddeutsche Zeitung*, March 12, 1957; Disch 1965: 625.

In the UK, the hot button issue has been Sunday shopping, which has been regulated since the mid-nineteenth century. For much of the postwar period, the Shops Act of 1950 (supported by the same coalition of small trades, unions, and religious groups as in Germany) restricted what types of goods could be sold on Sundays and also limited shopping hours generally to 8 p.m. (Burke and Shackleton 1992: 303). Between 1950 and 1985 repeated attempts to liberalize shopping hours went nowhere (thirteen private member bills were defeated by large majorities) (Jaffer and Kay 1986: 171). In 1985 Prime Minister (and grocer's daughter) Margaret Thatcher made the removal of statutory restrictions on shopping hours part of the conservative platform, but the Shops Bill that her government introduced failed in dramatic fashion. Seventy-two Conservative backbenchers defected, emboldened by opposition from both retail unions and large department stores such as Marks and Spencer, Sainsbury's, and John Lewis (Burke and Shackleton 1992: 306).

British unions subsequently softened their position (partly, again, in deference to the growing number of women in their ranks), which facilitated a compromise under the 1994 Sunday Trading Act that allowed a partial liberalization (Maher 1995). Under this law, shops can open on Sundays, but large stores are limited to a maximum of six hours. This law remains in effect as of 2024, having survived an attempt by David Cameron's Conservative government to abolish all statutory restrictions, which again failed due to Tory backbench defections. A 2020 survey shows that a strong majority (58 percent) of British citizens support the existing restrictions (Otte 2020).

Shopping hours were traditionally restricted in the United States as well, though, in this case, conflicts over extending retail hours were fought in state legislatures and in the courts. Restrictions on shopping hours were part of a broader suite of so-called blue laws in the United States that restricted activity on Sundays. Religiously motivated and imported from England, these laws prohibited all sorts of activities, not just selling but also various forms of entertainment, though in the 1920s and 1930s the growing use of cars to access forms of entertainment such as baseball games and movies had already eroded their grip somewhat (Endsley 1967: 22). Most of the formal prohibitions had been relaxed or abolished by the 1950s (Teupe 2019: 398), but even where Sunday shopping was no longer expressly prohibited, it was not common— that is, until discount houses entered the picture like "a bolt of lightning" (Endlsey 1967: 22).[26]

26. Discounters were not the only retailers who challenged Sunday shopping laws. Teupe (2019), for example, points to the role of Jewish businessmen seeking to stay open on Sundays to make up for closings on the Jewish Sabbath. But Endsley (1967) makes clear that it was the influence of large national discount chains that provoked widespread deregulation.

The shopping-hours wars that unfolded in the late 1950s and early 1960s began as upstart discounters moved in alongside the country's expanding malls, challenging department stores on both price and convenience (Cohen 2004: 272; Endsley 1967). While department stores typically stayed open only one or two evenings a week, most of the new discounters remained open for business six nights a week (Endsley 1967: 80), and they brazenly flaunted long-standing norms by selling on Sundays. They were opposed in this by the country's large prestige department stores (supported by the National Retail Merchants Association) because the latter were more heavily staffed and therefore bore higher labor costs (Howard 2015: 182; Endsley 1967: 176). Thus, large department stores such as Macy's, Marshall Field's, Sears, Wards, and J. C. Penney all worked alongside allies—above all, small merchants but also churches and citizen groups that were worried about traffic—in opposing Sunday retailing (Buntz 1968: 9; Cohen 2004: 271).

Seeking either to reactivate dormant blue laws or, in many cases, to pass new legislation against Sunday selling, these groups initially enjoyed considerable success. While only nine states had Sunday retail prohibitions on the books before the 1950s, the figure rose to twenty-seven states by 1953, and at the height of the blue laws, forty-nine states had legislation (all but Alaska) (Teupe 2019: 389). These laws took a wide variety of forms. Some banned all commercial transactions beyond those that "involved some kind of . . . necessity" (Teupe 2019: 389). Others regulated the specific type of store that could remain open, carving out exceptions of the sort that we saw in some European countries to permit the sale of certain goods. Some imposed restrictions only on stores above a certain size, along the lines of the 1994 Sunday Trading Act in the UK.

Despite the flurry of legislation, however, the Sunday shopping wars were by no means over. Discounters intent on disrupting retail trading activated their legal teams to challenge these laws in court. E. B. Weiss, the vice president of merchandising for a prominent advertising agency and a critic of Sunday blue laws, declared in 1962 that "our giant discount chains are determined to fight the Sunday issue through to a successful conclusion and they are making the necessary legal investments" (1962: 38). Their lawyers found much to work with in the ambiguity of state laws, whose meaning was blurred further by the rapid changes in the types of retail operations they were meant to govern. Some states tried to restrict Sunday sales only to essential goods or to only those merchandisers who traded in particular product lines. But that was almost impossible to interpret and enforce, given the strong trend toward large stores selling a wide variety of different lines of merchandise. Other states attempted to set limits on Sunday retailing that would only apply to stores above a certain size. But these laws virtually invited lawsuits charging discriminatory treatment under Article 14 of the US Constitution.

The overall result was ongoing contestation in the courts. Efforts to enforce state laws were met with a variety of different legal strategies, including those claiming violation of equal protection rights or due process; unconstitutional vagueness (e.g., revolving around the definition of "necessity"); or discriminatory enforcement (Dilloff 1980 provides an overview of the challenges to the laws across different states; see also Robbins 2022). Of the laws passed in the first wave of legislation (to 1953), supreme courts in eight states declared such laws illegal (Endsley 1967). In at least one case, in Nebraska, the court ruled in favor of discounters with the argument that it was obvious that "the real purpose of Sunday closing laws is not to protect religious worship or provide family unity," but instead "to enlist the power of the state to protect narrow commercial interests, influenced by the fierce competition between the discount store and the downtown merchants" (Buntz 1968: 9). In the face of widespread legal confusion and contestation, state legislatures sometimes washed their hands of the matter by delegating the whole issue to localities to regulate for themselves, which of course inspired competition among towns and cities in a downward deregulatory spiral (Dilloff 1980: 685).

Moreover, even where shop closing laws were not struck down by the courts, enforcement emerged as a huge problem. Local police did not appreciate having the issue foisted onto them: Who, after all, were they meant to arrest? Shoppers? Managers? (Endsley 1967). Rules governing opening hours were so unenforced and so widely ignored that many retailers were not even aware of their existence. Writing in 1967, Endsley reports that almost one-third of retailers surveyed in those states that had restrictions did not know about the law (33.5 percent of the stores that were open on Sundays and 24 percent of stores that were closed were unaware that there were rules regulating Sunday trading) (1967: 156). This stands in sharp contrast to discount store managers in these states, *all of whom* (in Endsley's survey) were well aware of the existence of such laws (Endsley 1967: 155). They were simply ignoring them, partly based on the belief (or, in fact, the observation) that their competitors in the discount business were also not complying.

Retailers who were knowingly operating in violation of the law often simply paid the fines, viewing them as an "acceptable cost of doing business" (Teupe 2019: 394; Dilloff 1980: 695–96). As Endsley notes, "In many areas, retailers find it profitable to stay open on Sunday when such openings are against the law, as the fine imposed is considered insignificant to the revenues obtained by being open" (Endsley 1967: 42). Weiss reports that "giant retailers can afford to risk fines—and remain open on Sundays," noting that one such discounter, Bargain City, had paid $40,000 in fines for violating Virginia's Sunday shopping laws for over two years running. This worked out to about $320 per Sunday opening, "a cost that could quite easily be absorbed if volume is large enough" (1962: 39). But anyway, he writes, the cost was usually far lower: "In most states, fines run from $1.00 to $10.00 for each Sunday opening" (1962: 39). The state of New York recorded 19,914 violations of shopping hours in 1962, a figure exceeded only by traffic violations (Teupe 2019: 394). Weak penalties and spotty enforcement of existing blue laws "meant discounters could essentially keep any hours they desired" (Howard 2015: 182). Sometimes fines increased, but resourceful lawyers still found legal loopholes, and violators exploited loose enforcement because, as in the battles over fair trade, uneven enforcement could be leveraged to fight back in court with the countercharge of discrimination.

Some states (e.g., Pennsylvania, Massachusetts, and New Jersey) faced challenges to the constitutionality of their blue laws on grounds of the First Amendment (religious freedom) and Fourteenth Amendment (due process) (Endsley 1967: 40–41).[27] Such challenges made their way to the Supreme Court, which in 1961 upheld states' rights to enact blue laws. But while the decision upheld the constitutionality of the state laws, it did not resolve the underlying issues and indeed went no further than to confirm that the states were well within their power to regulate Sunday selling—and good luck figuring out how to do that.

In Europe, rule-breaking of the sort that was rampant in the United States typically met with opposition from small merchants, religious groups and also unions. In the United States, such conflicts were channeled through the courts, and when they were litigated, retailers often prevailed with arguments resting on the usual claims of property rights or discrimination.[28] And

---

27. First Amendment challenges (charging that blue laws were a violation of the separation of church and state) were not only brought by merchants (on such cases, see Dilloff 1980: 683; Teupe 2019). Perhaps the most important early case, in 1961 (*McGowan v. Maryland*), involved an employee (Margaret McGowan) who worked for a discount chain store. In this case the claim was that the original (Christian) justification for the blue laws—to encourage church attendance—represented state action favoring a particular religion (Laband and Heinbuch 1987: 40). To this, the court's majority responded that, despite the original religious motivations for the laws, the state now had a secular interest in maintaining a day of rest and recreation.

28. By contrast, in Europe, efforts to liberalize shopping hours through appeal to the courts have not succeeded. In 1993, the European Court of Justice ruled that national laws that restrict

(Here is a list of laws that have been proposed. Would you read down that list and for each one tell me whether you would be for or against such a law?) A law against retail stores being open on Sundays (except for delicatessens, drugstores).

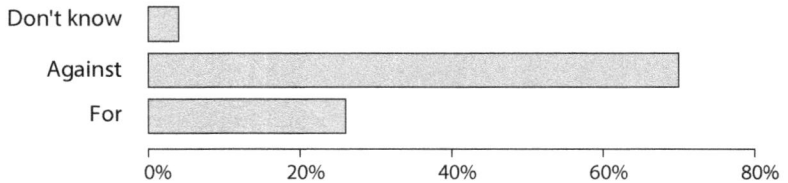

FIGURE 9.2. Support for regulations on retail opening hours, 1977.
Source: Roper Organization, Roper Reports no. 1977–01, Business/Politics/Consumerism, Question 84, USROPER.77-1.R20G. (Cornell University, Roper Center for Public Opinion Research, 1976).

as litigation dragged on, stores stayed open and Americans grew accustomed to these hours and wanted to keep them. Thus, for example, a Roper poll from 1977 revealed that a large majority of Americans opposed laws that would prevent retailers from staying open on Sundays. Asked whether they would favor a law against retail stores being open on Sundays (with exceptions for delicatessens and drugstores), a large majority responded that they would oppose such legislation (figure 9.2).

Over time, the growing popularity of Sunday shopping and continued rampant rule-breaking produced institutional tensions that the courts found uncomfortable and ultimately unsustainable. In a key case in 1976, the New York Court of Appeals disparaged state blue laws as a "crazy quilt," a collection of exceptions whose unenforceability encouraged an "erosive disrespect for the law" (Teupe 2019: 392, 394). State after state abandoned their Sunday selling laws either officially or unofficially. Whereas in 1953 forty-nine state had blue laws, by the mid-1960s these numbers had dwindled

---

or prohibit certain selling arrangements lie outside the scope of the EU's "foundational freedoms" and therefore are fully legal so long as such provisions "apply to all relevant traders operating within the national territory and so long as they affect in the same manner, in law and in fact, the marketing of domestic products and of those from other Member States" (Keck and Mithouard; see https://eur-lex.europa.eu/resource.html?uri=cellar:33d39041-a6c3-45e3-aalc-36f81759419b .0002.06/DOC_2&format=PDF). The case was brought—nota bene—by a French discounter that had run afoul of France's laws against predatory (below-cost) pricing. The court's ruling upheld France's right to set such laws, but the ruling also applies to a broader range of "selling modalities," including national laws regulating shopping hours. I thank Martin Höpner for drawing my attention to this case.

significantly. By 1967 twenty-four states now either had no legislation or only loose enforcement, and only sixteen states were bothering to uphold their laws (Endsley 1967: 34–35). The last statewide prohibition on Sunday commerce, in North Dakota, was repealed in 1991, and remaining restrictions on Sunday morning opening hours were lifted in 2019 (Stone 2018). The sole remaining place where retail is still prohibited on Sundays is Bergen County, New Jersey (Stone 2018; MacKinnon 2015).

In sum, and as so often in the efforts to regulate retail, the fragmented regulatory landscape of the American political economy resulted in a war of attrition and culminated in a deregulatory race to the bottom.

Pockets of Resistance

Finally—and although it would require another book to fully unpack the point—some sectors in Europe have successfully resisted the encroachment of the discount chains almost entirely. This applies above all to pharmacies. In most European countries, purchasing common remedies such as acetaminophen (used, for example, in Tylenol) requires a trip to a pharmacy and interaction with a pharmacist. In the United States, by contrast, chain retailers such as CVS and Walmart offer a wide range of over-the-counter drugs (including, often, their own private-label brands). Beyond this, though, these chains have incorporated their own pharmacies and absorbed a large share of the prescription market itself; during the pandemic, they also administered vaccination shots on site.[29]

America's independent pharmacists, it will be recalled from chapters 5 and 7, were at the heart of the resistance to chain stores from the 1930s through the 1950s in the battles over fair trade and over chain store taxation. It is a measure of how thoroughly they were defeated to note that the three largest pharmacies in the United States today are among the country's largest chains: Walgreens, CVS Health, and Walmart. Vertical and horizontal mergers have resulted in a sector dominated by large chain pharmacies and have also allowed the entry of most major regional supermarket chains into the market as well. A 2021 study showed that among the approximately sixty thousand retail pharmacies in the United States, two-thirds are retail chains, supermarkets, or mass retailers. And while one-third of all retail pharmacies are independent, these account for a mere 6 percent of total sales. The

---

29. CVS pharmacists were even authorized to write prescriptions for some drugs under some circumstances—Paxlovid, for instance, for customers over sixty-five.

big chain pharmacies generate 40 percent of retail prescription revenues alongside shares for supermarkets and mass retailers (of 9 percent and 7 percent, respectively), with mail order pharmacies making up the remaining 37 percent of retail pharmacy sales (Seely and Singh 2021).[30]

The UK and Switzerland stand out in Europe for the larger presence of chain pharmacies, particularly after the purchase of the UK Boots chain in 2014 by Walgreens. The picture is different in many other European countries, however, where as late as 2004 only licensed pharmacists could establish pharmacies. In many cases, individual pharmacists could not "own or be responsible for more than one pharmacy," a regulation that essentially blocked the entry of the kind of large managed pharmacy chains that proliferated in the UK and United States (Taylor et al. 2004; Pisek 2017). So while these sorts of companies have made inroads in the UK, they account for only 10.4 percent of all pharmacies across the countries that are still in the European Union.

Pisek attributes the slow integration of the pharmaceutical sector to "varied conditions for the operation of pharmacies in the Member states and the problems of health financing in some of the countries" (Pisek 2017). Some countries—for example, the Netherlands, Norway, and Sweden—have deregulated pharmacy ownership over the last decade. Others, such as Austria, continue to allow only single-branch pharmacies, and pharmacy chains are also not allowed in France and Spain. Germany (along with Denmark and Italy) now allows small groups of up to four pharmacies. Beyond this, many countries have seen the growth of virtual chains that allow small pharmacists to combine forces in purchasing, management, and loyalty programs as a way to achieve scale and scope efficiencies while remaining independent.[31]

Conclusion

In her 2005 book, Victoria De Grazia argued that America's "irresistible" market empire was reshaping Europe, "spreading consumer-oriented capitalism" as "alternative strategies fell before it." Some of what is documented in the previous pages confirms her predictions with respect to discount

---

30. Sales figures are from 2017.
31. PR Newswire, "Over Half of Europe's Pharmacies are Grouped into Wholly Owned or Affiliated to Chains - Says New Report," December 7, 2015, https://www.prnewswire.com/news -releases/over-half-of-europes-pharmacies-are-grouped-into-wholly-owned-or-affiliated-to -chains---says-new-report-300188788.html.

retailing. In contrast to accounts (e.g., Watson 2011) that view lean retailing as uniquely American, and operating on a logic that sets it apart from other countries, all of the rich democracies now have prominent discounters competing for consumer dollars.

In Europe, discounters are particularly prominent in the grocery sector. The UK's Tesco, France's mega-retailer Carrefour, and Germany's hard-discount grocery chains Aldi and Lidl have all enjoyed tremendous success.[32] Much as De Grazia might have predicted, many of Europe's discounters drew specifically on the American model (e.g., Carrefour's founders were inspired to launch Europe's first hypermarket in 1963 after attending business seminars in the United States), though in reality there has been intense borrowing in both directions.[33] Such borrowing and exchange is nothing new, for as Jan Logemann (2019) has argued, Europeans and European émigrés were central players in the transatlantic flow of ideas and innovations from the 1930s to the 1960s that shaped advertising and consumer culture in the United States.

While signs of convergence are unmistakable, this chapter also suggests that the European embrace of the American model has been a reluctant and so far partial one. The question, however, is whether the differences noted here can hold up in a context in which retail has increasingly moved online. Take first the regulations discussed above that preserve central retail districts and limit shopping hours. The growth of online retailing has long since breached this Maginot line because there are now literally no limits as to when and where consumers can shop. Some of the pockets of resistance noted above—for example, pharmacies in many countries—remain. But one suspects that their days may be numbered.

When it comes to labor, however, it is a somewhat more mixed story. The shift from brick-and-mortar retailing to e-commerce has been associated with increased fissurization of work, which we know erodes collective

32. Gunnar Trumbull (2012b) explains the success of mass retailers in France by pointing to important parallels to the United States, in particular: (a) a majoritarian electoral system that (à la Rogowski and Kaiser [2002]) creates "a median-voter bias that favored broad consumer interests" and thwarts the formation of the kinds of cross-class and cross-party coalitions (e.g., between Social Democrats/labor and religious parties) that placed bounds on mass retailers elsewhere; and (b) a postwar production regime organized around Fordist mass production strategies that were naturally aligned with mass distribution (2012: 121–22).

33. Walmart borrowed from Carrefour the model of hybrid supermarket and discount stores (starting in 1998) (Kumar and Steenkamp 2007: 81). And fans of Trader Joe's in the United States are often surprised to learn that this is owned by Aldi.

bargaining coverage and weakens unions (Weil 2014). Yet a stronger social net and greater labor protections (including new EU regulations pertaining to gig work) do set some limits on European retailers in ways that interfere with some of the most exploitative practices that make shopping so quick and convenient for American consumers.

That leaves antitrust and the capacity and will of antitrust regulators to preserve competition in a field that has so far proved especially vulnerable to the advance of large low-cost retailers. The EU's more aggressive approach to dominant actors seems especially important, and the Digital Markets Act of 2022 represents a significant effort to regulate the behavior of dominant online platforms. Amazon is among the firms designated as key gatekeepers in the new law, and as such, it will be subject to regulations that are designed to protect competition in the market (e.g., imposing rules about nondiscriminatory treatment of services and products; introducing requirements to share information and data with their dependent third-party merchants; and allowing these merchants to conclude contracts with other firms and platforms) (Foster 2022; Foster and Thelen 2024; Cioffi, Kenney, and Zysman 2022; Kelly 2019).

The next chapter considers in more detail the strategies of this latest, most disruptive actor on the retail scene.

PART V

The Amazon Economy

10

The Amazon Economy

On August 17, 2021, the *New York Times* reported that Amazon had "eclipsed Walmart to become the world's largest retail seller outside China" (Weise and Corkery 2021). Walmart's huge lead (Amazon was founded only in 1994) had so far allowed it to hold on to the top position within the American retail market, in large part because of the introduction of full-service supermarkets.[1] However, that is expected to change by the time this book appears (Kulp 2022). Although Amazon's growth was accelerated by the pandemic, business observers are not surprised. As a *Forbes* article laconically observed: "It had to happen" (Loeb 2022).

Amazon's rise to dominance in the retail sector is well enough known that a lengthy recounting of the history is not necessary (see Stone 2013; Gaster 2020; Kenney et al. 2021). Officially launched on July 16, 1995, from Seattle, Washington, Amazon began as an online bookseller. Founder Jeff Bezos already had big plans for expansion but settled on a start in books, an easily shipped, nonperishable commodity that lent itself to online sales. Importantly, individual titles are standardized and uniform—that is, identical to one another—so that Amazon's lower prices would be immediately visible to customers. By 1998 the self-described "Earth's biggest bookstore" had

---

1. Walmart went from selling essentially no groceries in 1990 to commanding 16 percent of the national grocery market by 2011, alongside 21 percent of the market in toys, 23 percent of health and beauty products, and 27 percent of household goods (Fishman 2011: 150, 233–34). And since 2011, Walmart has built on its lead in groceries and is now reported to account for 30 percent of the grocery market (Peinert and van Dyck 2022).

expanded its horizons, adding CDs and later electronics, toys, and tools to its product catalog. Today, consumers can purchase almost anything they want at what is now dubbed "the everything store" (Stone 2013).

Fueled by an early IPO in 1997 in the heady days of the dot-com boom, the company focused relentlessly on rapid expansion, incurring massive losses through the first seven years of its operation, posting its first (and modest) profit in 2003. The company had survived the dot-com bust in part by introducing a new feature in 2000, Amazon Marketplace, which offered other businesses and merchants the opportunity to list their products alongside those in the company's own catalog, with Amazon claiming a commission on each sale.[2] A few years later, in 2007, it would offer these third-party (3P) sellers the opportunity (again, for a fee) to have Amazon store and deliver their goods though a new service, Fulfillment by Amazon (FBA). The company got a further boost that same year, when it essentially captured the e-reader market with the introduction of the Kindle (Stone 2013: chap. 8).[3] Along the way, Amazon also acquired other companies, including Zappos (online shoe sales), Quidsi (household essentials), and the Whole Foods grocery chain.

Two of the company's most successful innovations were the introduction of one-click buying and Amazon Prime. Amazon's "buy now with 1-Click" button—for which the company was awarded a patent in 1999—allows shoppers to avoid having to enter shipping and credit card information or even placing items in a virtual shopping cart for checkout. All you have to do is press a single button to activate preloaded payment and shipping information, and the product is on its way. Suddenly shopping on Amazon was almost frictionless (Stone 2013: 77). The company followed up in 2005, launching Amazon Prime. For a $79 annual membership fee, Amazon users could enjoy unlimited two-day shipping at no extra cost and one-day shipping for $3.99. Because Amazon at the time was charging $9.48 per shipment, Prime members needed to place fewer than ten orders in a year for the membership to pay off (Del Ray 2019).[4]

2. Although it is sometimes difficult to distinguish the two on the Amazon site itself, first-party sellers are vendors who sell to Amazon, which in turn sells to consumers. Third-party sellers do not sell *to* Amazon; they sell directly to customers but *through* the platform (Weigel 2023: 3).

3. Although my focus here is on Amazon's retail operations, it is worth noting that the company subsequently launched a cloud computing service (Amazon Web Services) and a video streaming service, among other initiatives beyond retailing.

4. In the meantime, Prime membership costs $139 but includes also additional perks such as access to video streaming through Prime Video.

By making shopping extremely easy, the idea was that customers would take advantage of the convenience to buy more frequently (not just higher-priced or difficult-to-find consumer durables, but also lower-priced every-day nondurables) and ultimately spend more money on the site. Although the company incurred years of massive losses when Amazon Prime was first introduced, as Prime membership grew, the gambit proved highly success-ful and lucrative. Vijay Ravindran (at the time, director of the Amazon's ordering division) remembered Bezos arguing that Amazon Prime would change the shopper's psychology so that he or she was not entirely focused on lower prices but also on the convenience and near-immediate satisfaction of purchasing on the site: "I think that completely changed the mentality. It was brilliant. It made Amazon the default" (quoted in Del Ray 2019). Two-day shipping also transformed shopping, completely resetting consumers' expectations about how quickly they could reasonably expect to receive the goods they ordered. It has since become the industry standard in the United States for all the big retailers.

Whole New Ball Game or Back to the Future?

Clearly, the battles over market share in retail are now taking place on the internet, and e-commerce is a realm that Amazon pioneered and now domi-nates. The contrast to Walmart's brick-and-mortar presence has caused busi-ness analysts to speak of a wholly different model of retailing.[5] But how different is Amazon, really, from what has come before? Here the longer-term historical perspective in this book can help us sort out what elements of the Amazon model are truly distinctive.

Some superficial (albeit important) differences between the Amazon and Walmart models are immediately obvious. Because of the space con-straints of brick-and-mortar retail, Walmart had always relied on offering a vast, though finite, range of popular branded products. As the size of its supercenters and hypermarkets grew, the selection increased, but ulti-mately still within constraints set by the space itself. Amazon, by contrast, grew on the strength of a completely different approach, by mastering retailing "on the long tail"—that is, offering a virtually limitless selection that includes not just popular items but also niche products that may appeal

---

5. Weise and Corkery (2021) quote Juozas Kaziukenas of the research company Marketplace Pulse as saying: "Walmart has been around for so long, and now Amazon comes around with a different model and replaces them as No. 1."

only to a few customers.[6] From its earliest days as a bookseller, Amazon distinguished itself from then-dominant competitors such as Barnes & Noble by offering customers the chance to acquire even the most obscure titles (Stone 2013: 26).

These differences had knock-on effects for how Amazon competed with other low-cost retailers. Many prominent hard discounters (e.g., Aldi and Lidl) rely almost exclusively (90 percent plus) on selling a limited number of private-brand items at ultralow cost. Other big retailers (e.g., Sainsbury and Tesco) that had traditionally specialized in higher quality private-label goods now offer these alongside other lower priced alternatives—essentially catering to consumers across a range of price points (Kumar and Steenkamp 2007). Walmart (as we saw in chapter 8) traditionally operated on a quite different model, focusing almost exclusively on selling branded goods at unbeatable prices. And while the company now carries a range of private-label products, as Watson (2011: 57–58) notes, these are primarily used to exert pressure on the suppliers of the branded goods. As the company's CEO from 2010–14, Bill Simon, put it, "We are a house of brands. We prefer to sell national brands because that's how we can differentiate ourselves in price better. When we sell Oreos and our competitors sell Oreos, and our Oreos are cheaper than their Oreos, the customer knows that we have a better price. When we sell cream-filled chocolate sandwich cookies and they sell cream-filled sandwich cookies, and you're not sure whether the quality is the same, it's very hard to differentiate yourself" (Roberts and Berg 2012: 24).

Amazon's format allows it to play the entire field—competing head to head with the country's biggest discounters while also catering to customers with very different price points. And whereas a product already has to be popular to get a spot on the shelf at Walmart, Amazon is able to offer a far wider range of goods. When it introduced Marketplace, Amazon essentially moved the goalposts by inviting third-party sellers to advertise and distribute their goods directly on the Amazon site, in competition with other Amazon sellers and indeed often Amazon itself (Gaster 2020: chap. 5). With unlimited shelf space, the company can focus both on volume sales of the most popular products and brands while also offering niche items. It is not limited to selling new products, but it can also offer used goods as well, displayed right alongside the new. Combining discounting with long-tail

6. On the long tail, see Anderson (2004). Writing in 2020, Robin Gaster notes that Amazon carries 350 million different items, which is more than twenty times the number sold even through Walmart's e-commerce operation (2020: 3).

retailing, these moves are what allowed Amazon to become the go-to site on which consumers can find almost anything they might want to buy.

There was also a sharp contrast between the growth strategies that Walmart and Amazon pursued. As we saw in chapter 8, Sam Walton grew his company in slow, methodical fashion—focusing first on a limited number of regional markets in close proximity to the Bentonville headquarters and then expanding by clustering several outlets in each new location before launching in more distant markets. This contrasts with Amazon's growth model, in which Bezos embarked immediately on an aggressive "get big fast" strategy to achieve scale and scope economies through relentless expansion into an ever-wider range of goods (Stone 2013; 2021: 6–7). Amazon's initial explosive growth was based on a business strategy that involved "a willingness to sustain losses and invest aggressively at the expense of profits," a strategy made possible by generous infusions of capital from deep-pocketed investors willing to bet on the company's long-term prospects even as it absorbed losses year after year (Khan 2017: 746–47; Rahman and Thelen 2019).[7]

Yet this is a model we have seen before, in particular in the strategy of Richard Warren Sears, who, over a century ago, similarly overtook the more methodical Montgomery Ward by expanding at a furious pace. The images that Amazon biographer Brad Stone (2013: 38–39) paints of the early Amazon years (with Bezos and friends in his garage frantically wrapping books that they then drove to the post office) bear a strong resemblance to those recounted in Emmet and Jeuck's (1950: 64–65) history of Sears in its early years, when orders on heavily discounted items piled up and employees worked frenetically to keep pace. (The parallels between Montgomery Ward, who won over rural consumers in the nineteenth century through personal outreach, and Sam Walton, who won over the South with homey charm, are also unmistakable.)

Other features of Amazon's business model are also very familiar. The PR teams of both Walmart and Amazon boast about their meritorious cultures of frugality (e.g., Sam Walton drove a beater his whole life, and Jeff Bezos famously continues to outfit his offices with door-desks and to charge his employees for parking and snacks) (Stone 2013: 70). Yet the reality is that these companies' low-cost strategies are underwritten by high turnover alongside predatory pricing designed to vanquish competitors (Gaster 2020:

---

7. Financialization played a key role here. Investors underwrote years of profitless growth for Amazon at the same time that private equity firms were purchasing brick-and-mortar retailers and sending them into bankruptcy (with thanks to an anonymous reviewer for emphasizing this point).

chap. 6). Bezos has been explicit about pursuing a famous flywheel approach to the company's growth, in which increasing the number of sellers and the range of goods available on the platform draws in more customers, earning the company commissions that it can then plow back into operations to lower prices and reduce delivery times even further, which in turn draws in more customers and sellers, in a never-ending cycle of expansion (Stone 2021: 8). In many ways this is but the latest version of the age-old strategy of other discounters such as Walmart, which also used high-volume sales to lower prices, squeeze suppliers, draw in more consumers, and enhance its power to secure even greater concessions from suppliers that it then passed on to consumers.

The low-price strategy includes the aggressive use of loss leaders—another long-standing staple of discount retailers, as the history recounted in previous chapters shows (see also O'Sullivan 2019).[8] Low, low prices (and often predatory pricing) and thin margins are as central to the Amazon model as they were to the low-cost retailers of yesteryear. Early on, Amazon took a page from the 1910 playbook of Macy's, challenging book publishers by selling well below cost in order to build its customer base and by offering e-books at cut-rate prices to support sales of its Kindle (on this case see Stone 2013: chap. 8; Khan 2017: 756–58). When Kindle launched in 2007, Amazon "stunned" the book industry by announcing that it would offer all *New York Times* bestsellers and new releases for $9.99 (well below the wholesale price, typically around $15.00, and far below the usual list prices of around $30 for hardcover books) (Gaster 2020: 23; Stone 2013: 251, 255–57). "Infuriated" publishers were largely helpless as Amazon engaged in what many considered predatory pricing, "allow[ing] customers to check out prices in brick-and-mortar stores and then get a discount if they bought from Amazon" (Neary 2012).

Amazon similarly deployed predatory pricing to break into the lucrative baby product market. Observing the success of Quidsi, an independent online retailer that ran a highly successful unit, Diapers.com, that sold baby products for home delivery, Amazon initially approached the company's founders with the offer to purchase the firm. Spurned by Quidsi's owners, Amazon unleashed pricing bots to track (and undercut, often by as much as 30 percent) the prices offered on Diapers.com. The relentless pressure on

---

8. There is a legal distinction (albeit hard to enforce) between loss leading (which is legal) and predatory pricing (which is not) that turns on the question of whether the below-cost pricing is selective or pervasive and intended to generate monopoly power (Khan 2017: 759).

Quidsi ultimately forced its founders to the negotiating table, where Bezos acquired the company in 2010 (Oremus 2013). This was a move to which the Federal Trade Commission—by this time fully committed to Chicago school thinking—offered its blessing (Stoller 2019: 444).[9] Amazon had done the same thing to Zappos, exposing the company to relentless price pressure (especially on shipping charges) before purchasing the firm.

Another similarity lies in the sophisticated data collection and logistics that figure prominently in Walmart's and Amazon's strategies for analyzing consumer behavior and for reducing distribution costs (therefore prices) to enhance sales (Gaster 2020: chap. 4; Petrovic and Hamilton 2006). Large retailers have long collected and sought to leverage detailed information about what products customers are buying. As early as the 1910s, Sears's accounting department kept records on the purchasing behavior of between four million and six million customers to identify its most loyal customers and best-selling products (Emmet and Jeuck 1950: 90, 462–63). This kind of data collection also figured prominently in A&P's strategy in the 1930s and 1940s, as well as in Walmart's adoption of UPC bar codes in the 1980s (Petrovic and Hamilton 2006: 116–18). Today, Amazon has perfected the practice of collecting and leveraging highly detailed information about the shopping habits of individuals to enhance sales. Amazon can now serve up ads to customers who shopped but did not purchase, and it can even prepopulate orders for items a customer once viewed or purchased and may wish to reorder. Shiller (2020) shows that Amazon's personalization of prices based on detailed web-browsing histories could increase profits by 13 percent relative to the case where it only had access to basic demographic information (Shiller 2020: 868–69).

Vast troves of data also power sophisticated logistics systems that are designed to eliminate waste and inefficiencies throughout both companies' operations. As noted in chapter 8, Walmart was famous for revolutionizing retailing logistics. These lessons were not lost on Jeff Bezos, who poached Walmart's Jimmy Wright and put him in charge of building out Amazon's own logistics infrastructure (Stone 2013: 72–73). When Amazon outgrew the system that Wright had created, he was replaced by Jeff Wilke who, as chief operations officer, presided over the development of an even more

---

9. The FTC reviewed the deal under Section 7 of the Clayton Act, the provision that governs mergers, as well as Section 5 of the Federal Trade Commission Act, which targets general unfair practices. The commission concluded that "no further action is warranted . . . at this time" and closed the investigation. See "Letter from Donald S. Clark, Sec'y, FTC, to Peter C. Thomas," Simpson Thacher & Bartlett LLP, March 23, 2011, http://perma.cc/7E5A-LYMB.

extensive and efficient system. By expediting throughflow and reducing shipping times, these innovations contributed mightily to the success of Amazon Prime. Just as Otto Doering was credited with masterminding Sears's state-of-the art logistics system a century ago (a vast network of pneumatic tubes for rapidly sending communications and customer orders across departments within the company), Jeff Wilke and then Dave Clark have done the same for Amazon, producing the company's highly efficient distribution centers (Stone 2013: 163–67).

Extensive information about consumer behavior and control over logistics are not just important for reducing inefficiencies within the firm's own operations, however. They also serve the key purpose of enhancing its bargaining power over suppliers and third-party sellers on the platform (Petrovic and Hamilton 2006). In that sense, control over data and logistics have become increasingly important as part of the broader strategy—again by no means unique to Amazon—of underwriting low prices to consumers by extracting concessions from the suppliers and vendors that rely on the platform. Amazon's approach to publishers in the context of the Kindle launch provides a case in point (Stone 2013: 242–46). Smaller publishers had originally embraced Amazon, seeing the company as a welcome alternative outlet for their titles, a way to work around big chains such as Barnes & Noble and Borders that had exploited their market power to negotiate favorable terms. But once these publishers had become dependent on the platform, Amazon often extracted its own concessions against the threat to remove their titles from the company's all-important recommendation algorithm. Stone (2013: 243) describes a project within Amazon, internally dubbed the "gazelle" project (in reference to wounded gazelles pursued by cheetahs), in which managers were tasked with identifying the most vulnerable publishers (i.e., those that relied most heavily on Amazon to reach consumers) and to use this information to secure better terms for the platform.

Amazon's grip is especially strong when it comes to the myriad third-party merchants that sell on the site. Small-business entrepreneurs have virtually no chance of making it onto the shelves of big brick-and-mortar retailers such as Walmart, which mostly offer products that already have achieved broad popularity and name recognition. By contrast, Amazon's Marketplace offers smaller firms (independent merchants, small manufacturers, and inventors) the opportunity to reach a vast customer base with innovative niche products. Moira Weigel (2023), who has conducted the most in-depth study of Amazon's third-party sellers, notes that the number of such sellers is almost impossible to know exactly. However, "respected industry analysts" suggest that more than six million sellers were active on Amazon in 2021, with an additional two thousand new sellers joining the platform every day (2023: 4). By expanding the range of goods on the platform, third-party sellers have fueled the Amazon flywheel, and they now make up a substantial share of Amazon's overall business. In 2020 Bezos reported that third-party sales accounted for more than 60 percent of all the goods purchased on the Amazon site (Weigel 2022). Because Amazon claims approximately 34 percent on each transaction (up from 19 percent in 2014), the fees they pay are a huge source of revenue for the company (Weigel 2022; Weigel 2023: 4).[10]

Amazon is foundationally committed to matching the lowest prices available at any outlet, and its automated bots constantly scan for lower prices on its own platform and elsewhere (Gaster 2020: 103). This means that third-party sellers are exposed to intense price competition, both with each other and with Amazon's own retail operations. Kenney et al. (2021: 16) report that until 2019 Amazon required its vendors to sign contracts containing price parity agreements that forbade them from selling their product more cheaply elsewhere (Kelly 2019). Although it can no longer dictate prices to its third-party sellers on the site, Amazon does encourage reductions by making available its "Marketplace Web Services" that inform these vendors of movement of the prices of their competitors (Gaster 2020: 139). Some reports suggest that the company told some of its largest third-party sellers that they "can't list new products until they match prices offered by Amazon's retail competitors"—this, in order to "protect the customer experience" (Long 2021). Strategies such as these essentially take Walmart's price-cutting practices a step further. While Walmart uses its monopsony power to squeeze the margins of suppliers, Amazon mobilizes competition (including via automation) to exert constant, intense downward pressure on prices (Gaster 2020: 142). Moreover, in the late 2010s, Amazon began recruiting "hundreds of thousands" of new third-party sellers from outside the United States, with Chinese sellers most dominant (Weigel 2023: 21–22). By 2020 approximately 40 percent of Amazon's third-party businesses were based in China, against 54 percent in the United States (Weigel 2023: 5).

Sellers on Amazon compete not just for sales but for advertising and space on the site. Just as Walmart rewarded pliant suppliers with prime shelf space and advertising, Amazon now requires major concessions from third-party

10. Third-party sellers, as noted, can also participate in Fulfillment by Amazon for an additional fee. Gaster cites estimates that 60 percent of Marketplace sales are fulfilled by Amazon, and adding these fees means that Amazon's share of the sale can rise to as much as 45 percent (2020: 108).

sellers to secure a coveted spot in the "buy box" on the Amazon website. While the decision about product placement in the buy box depends on a variety of metrics, Amazon requires that sellers meet "performance-based requirements," including quick, reliable delivery, to be eligible. This has enhanced the appeal of using Fulfillment by Amazon for sellers since it improves their product's visibility and increases the likelihood of "winning the buy box" (Morrison 2021). And as sellers are paying more (e.g., FBA fees) in the hopes of generating more sales, Amazon's recent push into digital advertising has led to soaring costs for advertising on the platform, making it that much harder for sellers to compete for clicks (Morrison 2021; Palmer 2021b).

Furthermore, Amazon, like Walmart, is not hesitant to cannibalize suppliers or third-party sellers by offering cheaper, private-brand alternatives to items that prove especially popular. Merchants who rely on Amazon have charged that the company launches its own private-label knockoffs for products that show strong sales (Mattioli 2020). In one case, Amazon was accused of directly copying the design of a top-selling camera bag and selling it under the Amazon Basics brand (Palmer 2021a). A report of the House Judiciary Committee in 2020 found that "Amazon's market power is at its height in its dealings with third-party sellers," allowing them, among other things, to replicate products that its sales data demonstrate to be particularly popular and then to engage in "self-preferencing" by placing their own brand higher than the competitor in the search results (Nadler and Cicilline 2020: 16; Weigel 2023: 32; Stone 2021: 377).

Bezos defends Amazon's business model by claiming to be an ally of the small businesses it hosts—making it possible for them to reach the platform's vast consumer base and thus compete with big-box retailers such as Walmart. It is certainly true that Amazon Marketplace has contributed to the flourishing of new businesses that, in a Walmart world, would never have gotten off the ground. But the company has power and extracts steep rents, exercising control over dependent downstream actors without bearing the risk of business failure in the cutthroat environment that Amazon itself cultivates. Many of the third-party sellers with whom Weigel spoke captured the ambiguity of their relationships with Amazon, characterizing it as "their best available deal" (Weigel 2023: 36).

Weigel draws the analogy to what Tressie McMillan Cottom calls "predatory inclusion" (Weigel 2023: 35). Previously excluded actors (e.g., small innovative producers, stay-at-home-moms-turned-entrepreneurs) can participate in the market for the first time but on terms that Amazon controls and that can be predatory. Many fail, but others succeed and reap the benefits of their access to Amazon's large customer base. However, third-party sellers are entirely dependent on Amazon and therefore vulnerable to the platform's policies and terms (Khan 2017). As Kenney et al. note, "The most important clause in these contracts is that the platform has the right to unilaterally change the contract at its discretion. . . . The terms and conditions are, in effect, private regulatory systems that exercise power" (2021: 5). One of the conditions of selling on the platform requires that third-party merchants agree to Amazon's Business Services Agreement, which shields Amazon from class action suits by requiring that any disputes that arise are subject to arbitration (Gaster 2020: 116; on this general phenomenon see Staszak 2023). Small wonder, then, that few merchants opt to pursue disputes.[11] Much like the disputes over Robinson-Patman reported in chapter 8, taking on Amazon is a high-risk, low-reward proposition since even a victory is likely to get the plaintiff booted off the site.

Political Playbooks

Beyond key aspects of the basic business model, the political playbooks of today's mass retailers also replicate and reproduce strategies pioneered by their predecessors: engaging in regulatory arbitrage as they "move fast and break things"; exploiting possibilities offered by the regulatory fragmentation of competing city and state jurisdictions; actively repurposing public infrastructure for private ends; avoiding unionization and often dodging employment laws; and weaponizing consumers to achieve their political ends.

As we have seen, regulatory arbitrage runs through the history of American retailing. Large retailers in the 1920s did not wait for the government to regulate consumer credit before they found ways to allow customers to purchase "on time" in ways that ultimately produced the credit cards that became ubiquitous by the 1970s (chap. 4; Hyman 2011: chaps. 4 and 5; Hyman 2012: chap. 4; Mandell 1990). Discounters in the 1960s flagrantly ignored fair trade laws and shopping hour regulations, aggravating manufacturers and regulators but ingratiating themselves with consumers and ensconcing themselves in the market.[12]

---

11. A House of Representatives staff report found that only 163 of the company's millions of merchants initiated arbitration between 2014–19 (Gaster 2020: 116).

12. Amazon would later contribute materially to further encroachments on Sunday working hours, exerting pressure on UPS and FedEx to deliver on Sundays and national holidays (which they ultimately began doing, in 2019) (Stone 2021: 242).

Like their mass-retailing predecessors, Walmart and Amazon have aggressively exploited the regulatory fragmentation of the American political economy to advance their own goals. Bezos chose a base in Seattle, a tech hub in a state with a smaller population than, for example, California, to take advantage of Supreme Court rulings that at the time exempted mail order companies from having to collect sales taxes on goods shipped to other states. For nearly two decades, Amazon benefited from the fact that its products cost consumers 5–10 percent less than competitors who had a physical presence in the receiving state.[13] When individual states began passing laws to extend their sales tax requirements to include Amazon, the company deployed an army of lawyers working with a color-coded map of the United States to issue instructions to executives and managers and to arrange operations to work around the rules (Stone 2013: 287–91).[14] As Kenney et al. note: "Amazon served the high-sales tax California market from low-sales tax Nevada and, similarly, the high-sales tax East Coast markets from low-sales tax Virginia" (2021: 17). The Supreme Court finally stepped in to close the loophole in 2012, but by this time Amazon had already established a vast and loyal consumer base—including millions of Amazon Prime members—across the country.[15]

Like almost every other large company contemplating an investment in the United States, America's big retailers have taken advantage of competition across states and localities by promising to create jobs and spur economic growth. As Strasser (2006: 54) points out, Walmart's expansion—the construction of new warehouses and supercenters across the country—was heavily subsidized by state and local governments that were often only too happy to help, offering enticements such as tax-exempt bond financing, property tax breaks, state corporate income tax credits, and/or government financed infrastructure such as roads and water lines. Amazon adopted the same strategy, "pitting politicians from neighboring municipalities against each other in a prisoner's dilemma" as it grew (Grabar 2016). An analysis by

13. The original court case ruling dates back to 1967 (*National Bellas Hess, Inc. v. Department of Revenue of the State of Illinois*). In the case, the Supreme Court ruled that Illinois could not require a Missouri-based mail order company to collect taxes on goods shipped and sold into the state since it did not maintain any offices, warehouses, or employees in the state. This court ruling was upheld in 1992 in the case of *Quill v. North Dakota* (Fassler 2018).

14. See Institution on Taxation and Economic Policy, "A Visual History of Sales Tax Collection at Amazon.com," December 23, 2020, https://itep.org/a-visual-history-of-sales-tax-collection-at-amazon-com/.

15. And once the issue was settled, Amazon moved quickly to open fulfillment centers and offices in the more populous areas that it had avoided for tax reasons—a move that was enormously important in facilitating two-day (and later one-day and same-day) shipping (Stone 2021: 11).

the nonprofit Institute for Local Self-Reliance estimates that more than half of the company's warehouse facilities were subsidized by taxpayers, for example, through exemptions from property or corporate income taxes (Grabar 2016). Amazon's search for a location for its second headquarters took these forms of venue arbitrage to new levels. The company engaged cities across North America in a public bidding war that attracted 238 proposals filled with various concessions such as tax breaks, subsidies, and access to mass transit lines (Garfield 2018). Good Jobs First, which tracks subsidies to companies, calculates that Amazon had secured over $6.7 billion in state and local awards over more than 340 investment projects as of 2024.[16]

Like Walmart, Amazon relies on public infrastructure in other ways as well. Similar to Sears a century ago, Amazon from the start relied heavily on the US postal system (Gaster 2020: 78–79). For over two decades, Amazon was shipping most of its goods in this way and at a special volume discount rate.[17] In the meantime, the company has built out its own delivery services, including a fleet of trucks and airplanes alongside an army of independent truckers and gig workers whom it can hire on a short-term basis through its Amazon Relay (for truckers) and Amazon Flex (for local delivery drivers) apps (Gaster 2020: 71–74; Stone 2021: 238–39). Although the US Postal Service now delivers a small share of Amazon packages, the company still relies on it for some last-mile deliveries to more remote, low density areas that the company views as too expensive to handle itself (Gaster 2020: 70–71, 78–79; O'Donovan and Bogage 2023; Premack 2020).

Today's retail giants also continue to benefit from the United States' comparatively congenial antitrust regime. Previous chapters documented how key court decisions allowed large retailers to scale up quickly. More recently, Walmart and Amazon have benefited from the ascendance of Chicago school legal theories and their emphasis on consumer welfare and price. As just one example among many, to expand its market share in books Amazon was able to approach, and extract concessions from, individual publishers one at a time, while the publishers themselves were prevented from mounting a collective response because of rules against collusion (Gaster 2020: 16). When five major publishers sought to defend themselves by concluding a deal with

---

16. Good Jobs First, "Amazon Tracker: Discover How Much the Public Is Subsidizing One of the Largest Retailers," last updated February 6, 2024, https://goodjobsfirst.org/amazon-tracker/.

17. Gaster (2020: 78) reports that in 2017 Amazon was shipping 60 percent of its goods through the USPS, 25 percent through UPS, and 15 percent through its own services. Such discounts were why Donald Trump's postmaster general, Louis DeJoy—himself a founder and CEO of a competing freight company—was critical of USPS operations.

Amazon rival Apple that would allow them to retain control over the price of their books, they were the ones hit with an antitrust lawsuit, for colluding to raise prices on e-books (Khan 2017: 758). By contrast, a Department of Justice investigation into allegations that Amazon was engaging in predatory pricing turned up no "persuasive evidence" of this (Khan 2017: 758).

The labor strategies of both Walmart and Amazon also fit comfortably within a longer tradition among low-cost retailers to underwrite low prices with low labor costs. Frank Woolworth's aphorism from 1892 appears to still guide American retailers to this day: "We must have cheap help or we cannot sell cheap goods" (Strasser 2006: 31). Sam Walton embraced the same principle, emphasizing that payroll was "one of the most important parts of overhead" and that success in retailing turned crucially on keeping overhead costs low (Lichtenstein 2010: 117). While Amazon famously raised hourly pay for its full-time warehouse workers to $15 per hour, well above the industry average, it also employs large numbers of part-time and temporary workers on less favorable terms. Amazon often also claims credit for the benefits it offers, which for full-time workers include health insurance, sick pay, and forty hours (= one week) annual vacation time in an employee's first year—a package worth boasting about in the United States, perhaps, but paltry compared to Europe.[18]

Moreover, conditions of work at Amazon warehouses are harsh, and protections are few. In 2002 the company reportedly used a system that assigned points to employees for various infractions (Stone 2013: 190; Gaster 2020: 257–58). Arriving late to work "cost" an employee half a point; failing to appear for work at all on a given day would result in three points; and even calling in sick got a worker one point. Any employee who accumulated six points in a year would be let go (Stone 2013: 190). Workers are heavily monitored during the day, and in the past they were reportedly allowed just eighteen minutes of time off-task per shift—to use the restroom, for example (Gaster 2020: 267)—though the schedule has since been relaxed to provide a half hour for lunch and two fifteen-minute breaks during a ten-hour shift. Amazon employment contracts include provisions for mandatory overtime that commit workers to stay on as needed for an additional 1.5 to 2 hours (in some cases after an already long ten-hour shift). The company particularly relies on overtime in peak periods—for example, around the holidays. Workers can be notified of additional hours "as late as the end of the shift the day before" (Gaster 2020: 259–60).

18. Amazon, "Paid Time Off for US Amazon Employees," https://www.amazon.jobs/en/landing_pages/pto-overview-us. Vacation time increases to two weeks (eighty hours) for workers in their second year with the company, though given the pace and physical demands of the work, the average employee does not make it that far (see Greenhouse [2022], who reports that the average Amazon employee stays but eight months).

As already hinted, Amazon's automated warehouses contain elaborate surveillance systems that allow the company to track workers' movements and to penalize employees who fail to keep up. The company's advanced automation warehouse systems set a relentless pace for employees (Delfanti 2021). The system also monitors trade union activities as part of Amazon's elaborate union avoidance strategies. As Brishen Rogers has detailed (2023), both Walmart and Amazon deploy sophisticated surveillance technologies to nip potential unionization drives in the bud. Against this backdrop, the recent (2022) success of the Amazon Labor Union to organize workers at the Staten Island warehouse is notable, even if, so far, it's an exception.

Moreover, and as with the discount retailers that preceded them, Amazon and Walmart are notorious for labor violations. Walmart, as we saw, has been the subject of numerous investigations of the National Labor Relations Board for requiring its "associates" to work overtime hours off the clock. Amazon, for its part, regularly runs afoul of labor safety regulations laid down by the Occupational Safety and Health Administration (OSHA). Most recently, in December 2022, OSHA issued Amazon fourteen citations for failing to record and report worker injuries and illnesses. As part of the same investigation, OSHA found that Amazon workers in at least three warehouses suffered from a higher risk of back injuries and other musculoskeletal disorders as a result of the physical intensity and long hours required to complete their assigned tasks (OSHA 2023). The company consistently reports a higher rate of serious injury incidences compared to other non-Amazon warehouses (Greene and Alcantara 2021).

Finally, Amazon follows a long line of others in actively weaponizing its consumers in an effort to influence its regulatory environment (Culpepper and Thelen 2020). At the turn of the last century, large mail-order retailers mobilized rural consumers to secure the passage of parcel post. In the 1930s and 1940s A&P mobilized a national legislative campaign and state referenda to thwart chain store taxes. Walmart helped to fund a California referendum in 2004 that succeeded in overturning a state law that would have required large firms to pay a greater share of the health insurance costs of their employees (Lichtenstein 2006: 7).

Amazon employs similar strategies today.[19] Along with other tech giants, Amazon has mobilized its users in a concerted effort to discourage lawmakers from passing stricter antitrust legislation. Their methods are reminiscent

---

19. In fact, according to a *Washington Post* review of Stone's 2013 book, Bezos apparently required its top managers and board members to read Levinson's 2011 book on A&P to understand how a big retailer can deal with public attacks (reported in Levinson 2021).

of the well-worn strategies of previous retailers: organizing petition drives and otherwise "spreading the message that the [proposed] bills could mean the end of services popular with tens of millions of Americans."[20] Amazon has also encouraged its third-party merchants and business owners who rely on the platform to send emails directly to senators to declare their opposition to antitrust legislation.[21] It set up a website called Support Small Sellers to encourage small businesses to raise their concerns directly with members of Congress, emphasizing that regulatory proposals could "jeopardize Amazon's ability to operate a marketplace for sellers" and "hurt hundreds of millions of consumers."[22]

Courting Consumers

Like other large retailers that came before, Amazon's strategies have all been designed to serve a single goal, and it is one that runs like a red thread through the entire history of American retailing—to cultivate a large and loyal consumer base by delivering goods as fast and as cheaply as possible. Sears and Montgomery Ward relentlessly pursued customer satisfaction (or your money back!). Beyond its vast catalog, Sears also emphasized rapid delivery, reorganizing operations so that orders could be processed within forty-eight hours (Emmet and Jeuck 1950: 133–34). Walmart is also legendary for its focus on offering consumers "everyday low prices" and the ease of one-stop shopping.

Bezos embraced the same script of putting consumers first, famously insisting on leaving one chair symbolically empty in meetings with vendors—for the customer (Stone 2013: 338). The entire Amazon business model is organized around an obsession with the consumer experience. Beyond its selection,

20. Birnbaum 2022; see also Connected Commerce Council, "Millions of Small Businesses Are at Risk," https://connectedcouncil.org/smb-risk/. Amazon does not always win, of course. For example, the company initially prevailed in a 2018 battle over a bill passed (and then rescinded) by the Seattle City Council that would have taxed large businesses based on the number of employees. The City Council backed down in the face of a threatened referendum (Samuels 2018). Two years later, however, Amazon lost the fight when the Seattle City Council passed a "JumpStart Seattle" tax that imposes additional taxes on the city's largest employers and highest-income citizens (Palmer 2020b).

21. See "US Sellers: Write to Your Senators and Urge Them to Oppose S. 2992, the American Innovation and Choice Online Act," a post by Dharmesh M. Mehta on an Amazon message board, https://sellercentral.amazon.com/seller-forums/discussions/t/2886de2d5262731f46b49b2e724d4296.

22. In the meantime, this website (https://supportsmallsellers.us/) has been discontinued. See also Levinson 2021.

low costs, and easy one-click shopping, Amazon has relentlessly innovated to reduce delivery times (what was once two-day shipping became next-day delivery and, in some areas, same-day delivery). It has also streamlined processes for returning items—e.g., through drop-off at any UPS or Whole Foods store—with no repackaging required and no questions asked. In some cases, you don't even have to return the product to get your refund. As one top executive put it: "It's like a religion about the customer" (Gaster 2020: 5).[23]

The strategy has earned the company accolades from industry experts and also proved popular with consumers.[24] The most recent *Fortune* survey (of nearly four thousand corporate executives, directors, and analysts) in 2023 placed Amazon in second place, tied with Microsoft and behind perennial leader Apple, for "world's most admired" company.[25] Amazon and Walmart occupy the top two positions in the annual report on the most valuable retail brands by the leading brand valuation consultancy Brand Finance; Amazon receives top marks for providing "outstanding value to its shoppers . . . and [delivering] a slick shopping experience [that is] irresistible for many consumers, even those who question Amazon's values and broader corporate reputation."[26] Bezos was honored as *Time* magazine's person of the year in 1999, and since 2019 his portrait hangs among other luminaries in the Smithsonian National Portrait Gallery (Stone 2021: 1).

Amazon's success with consumers, and especially American consumers, is well known. The company has been especially successful in the area in which it got its start, books: in 2020 Amazon was selling more than 80 percent of all e-books and over half of all printed books sold in the United States (Gaster 2020: 10). An NPR/Marist poll found that 69 percent of Americans say they have purchased an item online, and, among online shoppers, almost all (92 percent) bought something through Amazon. A 2019 survey of over two thousand American consumers reported that 89 percent of buyers were

---

23. During the pandemic, Walmart and Amazon followed anti-price-gouging rules to the letter, both to please consumers and to appease regulators (with thanks to Melike Arslan for this point).

24. Walmart, too, has always pursued an aggressive image-enhancement PR presence, responding immediately to any and all critical stories that appear in newspaper outlets, even those with a small circulation. The company also actively exploited the publicity it received for the effective and efficient logistics system it mobilized to deliver supplies to victims of Hurricane Katrina (Fishman 2011: 231).

25. See "World's Most Admired Companies," *Forbes*, https://fortune.com/ranking/worlds-most-admired-companies/.

26. See Brand Finance, "Retail 100 2024: The Annual Report on the Most Valuable and Strongest Retail Brands," https://brandirectory.com/rankings/retail and https://brandirectory.com/rankings/retail/table.

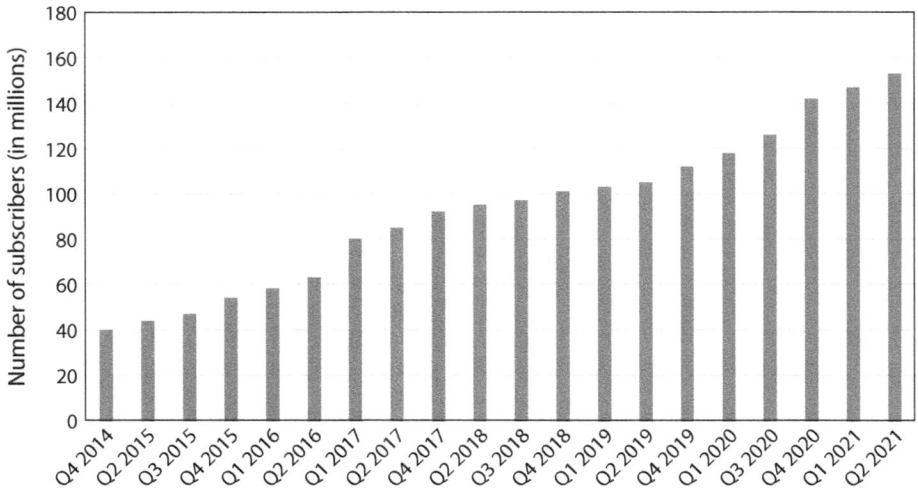

FIGURE 10.1. Number of Amazon Prime members in the United States, 2014–21. *Source:* Statista 2023.

more likely to purchase products from Amazon than through other sites. Most Amazon shoppers (82 percent) cited price as the leading reason why they shop on the platform, alongside free and fast shipping (79.8 percent).[27]

Amazon Prime has been especially successful. Prime membership has grown steadily since its 2005 launch to nearly 200 million globally (over 150 million in the United States alone) (see figure 10.1).[28] Nearly two-thirds (64 percent) of online shoppers in the United States are Amazon Prime members.[29] And the program has had exactly the results that Bezos

27. See Maryam Mohsin, "10 Amazon Statistics You Need to Know," Oberlo, August 21, 2023, https://www.oberlo.com/blog/amazon-statistics. In January 2020, the results indicated that the number one reason for using Amazon was still the company's "fast, free delivery" (79.8 percent of internet users), while "best pricing" had dropped to just under 50 percent. See "Reasons for Internet Users in the United States to Shop on Amazon as of January 2020," Statista 2024, https://www.statista.com/statistics/670499/us-amazon-usage-reason/.

28. See Statista, "Number of Amazon Prime Members in the United States from 1st Quarter 2016 to 1st Quarter 2023," https://www.statista.com/statistics/1223385/amazon-prime-subscribers-in-the-united-states/. For global figures, see Marketplace Pulse, "Amazon Subscription Services Sales," https://www.marketplacepulse.com/stats/amazon-subscription-services-sales.

29. See "NPR/Marist Poll: Amazon Is a Colossus in a Nation of Shoppers," NPR, https://www.npr.org/about-npr/617470695/npr-marist-poll-amazon-is-a-colossus-in-a-nation-of-shoppers; also https://techjury.net/blog/amazon-statistics/; Statista, "Share of Amazon Customers in the United States Who Are Amazon Prime Members from 2018 to 2023," https://www.statista.com/statistics/234253/share-of-amazon-prime-subscribers-in-the-united-states/.

anticipated: a February 2019 survey showed that 20 percent of Amazon Prime members said they shopped on the site a few times a week, 7 percent said almost daily (Mohsin 2023).

Moreover, American consumers don't just use Amazon, they seem to love it. According to a 2020 survey of the "Most Loved Brands in America" by Morning Consult, Amazon ranked fourth (behind the USPS, Google, and UPS). Amazon Prime also (separately) made the top-ten list (at no. 7).[30] (By contrast, the most loved brands in Germany are mostly car manu-facturers, though dm-drogerie markt—a large retailer selling cosmetics, health care products, and everyday household wares—also made it into the top five.[31]) If you ask American consumers point-blank whether they think it is a good thing that "more online shopping through Amazon and other online retailers [. . .] has reduced the number of department stores and shopping malls," a slim majority (52 percent) express "mixed" feel-ings, and about equal numbers of respondents see these trends as "good" and "bad" for the country (NBC News/*Wall Street Journal* Poll 2017). And larger majorities think it is a shame that small merchants and downtown retail districts have declined. But these sentiments seem not to translate well into actual shopping habits. As figure 10.2 shows, well before the pandemic, consumers had already abandoned locally owned shops and department stores in favor of big-box and online shopping, with the latter overtaking the former in 2013.

A prepandemic YouGov Poll in 2018 showed that fully 76 percent of Americans had a favorable opinion of Amazon, against just 16 percent who viewed the company unfavorably.[32] A Harris Poll conducted in collaboration with Harvard's Center for American Political Studies fielded in June 2021, during the COVID crisis, asked a similar question, and the results showed that Amazon commanded a favorability rating of 72 percent (unfavorable

30. See Morning Consult, "Most Loved Brands 2020," https://morningconsult.com/most-loved-brands-2020/. These results are based on interviews conducted online with a national sample of over six thousand adults. The index is based on four metrics: favorability (percentage of consumers with a favorable opinion of the brand); trust score (percentage of consumers who trust the brand to do the right thing); community impact score (percentage of consumers who say the brand has a positive impact on their local community); and net promoter score (for which consumers are asked to rate brands on a scale from 1–10 based on how likely they would be to promote a given brand).

31. NetBase, "Top Loved German Brands: 2019," https://www.rankingthebrands.com/The-Brand-Rankings.aspx?rankingID=424&year=1324.

32. Seven percent answered "don't know." See "The Economist/YouGov Poll," April 2018, https://docs.cdn.yougov.com/3g689cgf7m/econTabReport.pdf.

In which one or two of the following ways have you already done or plan to do most of your holiday shopping?

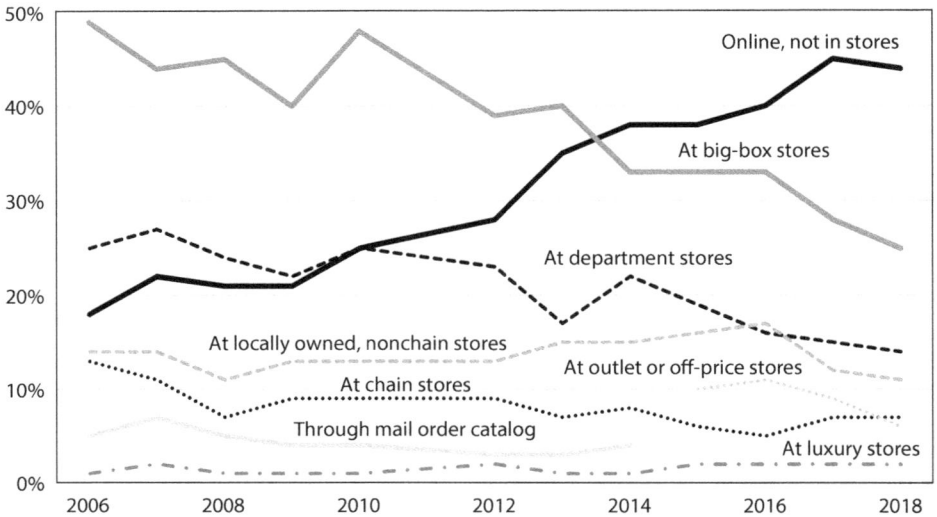

FIGURE 10.2. Preferred holiday shopping venues, 2006–18.
Source: CNBC Polls, various years, Public Opinion Strategies/Hart Research Associates (Cornell University: Roper Center for Public Opinion Research).

19 percent), coming in second only to the US military.[33] Amazon's favorability ratings subsequently declined, partly perhaps in response to revelations about the hazardous working conditions in its warehouses.[34] But again, you would never know it from Americans' shopping behavior: orders and profits have continued to soar (Palmer 2020a; Weise 2021; Rapp 2021). Both before and after the pandemic, the reality is that many Americans view Amazon in much the same way that rural consumers in the Midwest in the late nineteenth century viewed Sears—as a godsend. For some it is the low prices, for others the variety of goods on offer, for still others (full disclosure: this includes me) for the time it saves them.[35]

33. The results are based on a survey of just over two thousand registered voters. "Harvard CAPS/Harris Poll," June 15–17, 2021, https://drive.google.com/file/d/1OgPzcB75uxXiFmTjUUb-ITIr7BFdFFhw/view.

34. Amazon's favorability rating in the 2022 YouGov brand ratings dropped to 69 percent, though the number of respondents who had an "unfavorable" view of the company also dropped, to 10 percent. Nearly 20 percent declared themselves neutral (YouGov Brand Rating October 2022). On warehouse conditions, see, among others, Harris 2020.

35. Do I think that one of the largest and most powerful companies in the world could accomplish all these things without resorting to predatory pricing, labor sweating, and margin squeezing of their third-party sellers? Yes. And, as elaborated in chapters 9 and 11, I think European regulators

Cultivating consumers is not just a winning business strategy; it also pays political dividends. As Pepper Culpepper and I have argued, assembling a large and loyal (in some ways also captive and dependent) consumer base can yield a potent form of business power because it generates direct relationships between the firm and its users that "politicians and regulators are reluctant to antagonize" (2020: 295). Or, as Weigel puts it, "it is hard to get constituents excited about cracking down on a company that most of them like and use regularly" (2021).

Thus, there are ways in which Amazon has been transformative: the company has clearly upended not just where, but how, we shop. Yet this should not obscure the fact that it has succeeded with business strategies and a political playbook that are long-standing and well known in the context of the evolution of American retailing as a whole.

---

are on the right track in their approach to dealing with large retail platforms such as Amazon (as are many of the proposals that came out of the House Judiciary Committee's 2020 report, especially relating to Amazon's relationship with its third-party sellers). But beyond changes to antitrust legislation, and as elaborated in more detail in chapter 11, American labor law is clearly overdue for a radical overhaul (Block and Sachs n.d.).

11

Conclusion

THE HIGH COST OF LOW PRICES

Contrary to Sam Walton's assertion that the rise of mega-retailers like his own Walmart was the natural consequence of neutral market forces and the inevitable triumph of efficiency, we have seen how politics has shaped the retail landscape we live in today.[1] The preceding chapters have shone a light on the role of America's large retailers in actively cultivating a deeply consumerist political economy, one whose origins reach further back into history than most previous accounts suggest. Already since the turn of the previous century, large-scale, low-cost retailers in the United States have faced weaker countervailing forces and enjoyed a far more permissive regulatory landscape than their counterparts in Europe. Comparative analysis allows us to identify the features of the American political economy that provided these firms with an extraordinarily hospitable context in which to grow and thrive.

Two such features stand out. First, the United States' distinctive antitrust regime actively favored large retailers, both through its secondary (indirect) and its primary (direct) effects. In terms of the former, American antitrust in the late nineteenth and early twentieth centuries had an important impact on *other groups*—disarticulating forms of associationalism that in Europe survived and served either as alternatives (cooperatives) or as countervailing

---

1. I thank Emily Zackin for the subtitle of this chapter.

274

forces (trade associations, encompassing labor unions) to the rise of big low-cost private retailers. As for the latter, the direct effects of American antitrust jurisprudence operated in a variety of ways over time—from the early prohibition on resale price maintenance in the 1910s, through crucial cases in the 1950s that hobbled efforts to limit aggressive price-cutting, up to the current prevailing explicitly proconsumer orientation of antitrust law.

Second, America's mass retailers benefited enormously from a fragmented regulatory landscape that divided authority across different branches and levels of government. The system of checks and balances and the patchwork of national and subnational regulatory regimes that characterize the American political economy lay out a terrain that is far from politically neutral. This decentralized political system does not, as the folk wisdom would have it, disperse power (see Miller 2023). Instead, it operates as a powerful filter that favors already privileged actors who have the resources and the capacity to maneuver across venues, even as it exacerbates the collective action problems that confront larger but more dispersed interests with fewer resources (Hacker et al. 2015: 199–202). In retailing, as we saw, this fractured regulatory landscape often played to the strengths of large corporate retailers organized on a national level while inhibiting a swift and coordinated public policy response to the challenges they posed.

The payoffs to viewing the American political economy in comparative perspective and through a fresh lens that focuses on retailing and distribution rather than the more familiar focus on production are several. For starters, this analysis brings entirely *new actors* to the fore. Political economists have long heaped attention on manufacturing and, as a consequence, we know a great deal about the role of industry and industrial interests in the evolution of American capitalism. Yet, clearly, America's premier retailers—from Richard Warren Sears to Sam Walton and Jeff Bezos—have profoundly influenced the trajectory of American capitalism. The country's mass-retailing pioneers played a key role in turning citizens into consumers beginning well over a century ago, and their successors have continued to advance a relentless campaign organized around consumer convenience and low prices.

Although specific identifiable actors vigorously promoted these outcomes, they did not achieve them alone. Large retailers prevailed through the alliances they forged over time, by enlisting the support of rural consumers in the early years of mail order retail; partnering with the government and building an alliance with consumer groups to combat inflationary pressures in the 1910s and 1920s; and courting consumers to oppose manufacturer efforts to control prices in the 1950s and 1960s. These coalitions were challenged, as we saw, by a shifting group of economic interests at various junctures—small merchants, brand manufacturers, and workers. But as they grew, large low-cost retailers drew in a social coalition of groups that came to rely on them in various ways and that could then be mobilized and weaponized to head off subsequent regulatory efforts.

This study of the politics of distribution has also drawn attention to *arenas* that have not received the attention they are due in the literature on the comparative political economy of rich democracies. In particular, my analysis has highlighted the importance of the courts as a venue in which some of the most consequential battles in retailing—particularly over prices—were fought.[2] Aggressive retailers not only contested the laws that politicians promulgated, they also actively challenged the interpretation of these laws as well as their on-the-ground enforcement. While legal scholars and students of American political development have long appreciated the central role played by the judiciary in shaping the evolution of American capitalism (Skowronek 1982; Bensel 2000; Whitman 2007; Forbath 1991; Hattam 1993; Winkler 2019), scholars of comparative political economy have overlooked the courts almost entirely. Yet, as we have seen, at key junctures American courts tipped the balance of power—between large and small retailers, between producers and distributors, and between owners and workers—in ways that have had deep and enduring consequences.

Antitrust jurisprudence in particular played an outsized role in the evolution of American capitalism and, in retrospect, it is hard to see how we could have missed this.[3] Hall and Soskice's seminal *Varieties of Capitalism* placed issues of coordination at the center of their theory of divergent models of political-economic development. The distinction they draw between liberal and coordinated economies turns entirely on the question of whether firms have the capacity to coordinate among themselves in the market (2001: chap. 1). Generations of comparative political economists have taken for granted that such capacity is a function of the way in which producer groups (firms and workers alike) are organized.

However, as we have seen, such organization (or the lack of it) is itself an outcome that was profoundly influenced by legislation and court decisions that either sanctioned or condemned the kinds of horizontal associationalism that emerged in the turbulent markets of the late nineteenth

2. On the importance of the courts within the American political economy generally, see Rahman and Thelen (2022).

3. Recent work, notably by Foster (2022) and Foster and Kohl (forthcoming) is providing a welcome corrective.

century and that continues to serve as contested terrain in antitrust theory and jurisprudence (Khan 2016; Paul 2020a; Vaheesan and Pasquale 2018; Vaheesan 2020). In fact, bringing antitrust to the fore in the area of retail and distribution not only helps us understand the historically evolved differences between liberal and coordinated market economies (à la Hall and Soskice). It also makes sense of how the distinctive features of the American antitrust regime generated a consumerist orientation (à la Whitman) that also stands out among its common-law peers.

Finally, focusing on the evolution of *discount* retailing (alongside the better-known story of the role of credit within the postwar American political economy) gives us a different angle on the crisis of American manufacturing and rising inequality since the 1970s. Full employment and general prosperity in the so-called golden era of postwar American capitalism from the 1950s to the early 1970s gave rise to a (fragile and ultimately short-lived) truce between organized labor and capital. American industry was hegemonic in world markets, and America's manufacturing unions were relatively strong. Collective bargaining allowed American workers (especially but not exclusively in industry) to share the fruits of increasing productivity and efficiency and to take part in the period's prosperity in the form of rising wages and expanding benefits.

Yet as a rich literature has documented, the breakdown of the postwar consensus beginning in the 1970s brought a steep decline in unionization, a deterioration in benefits, and rising inequality (see Hall 2020). The way that story is typically told, American industry declined in the face of intensified competition from lower-cost producers abroad, with union strength collapsing as manufacturing firms launched an extended assault on organized labor to reduce labor costs (Goldfield 1989). Such accounts are not wrong, but they are radically incomplete, for they assign no particular role to American retailers—as if they were just serving as a kind of a passive transmission belt, simply offering consumers a choice, with consumers going for the lower prices.

The account advanced here, by contrast, shows that low-cost, high-convenience retailers played a much more active role in accelerating the decline of American manufacturing and undermining the American postwar growth model generally (Lichtenstein 2006). The factors highlighted in these pages—an extraordinarily congenial legal regime combined with a fragmented regulatory landscape—promoted a *particular model* of retailing to dominance, a model of ultra-lean retailing based on narrow margins and dominated by players (Walmart and now Amazon) that enjoy enormous power over both workers and suppliers (Watson 2011). The business model that these companies have perfected is premised on cutting their own labor costs to the bone. But it is also premised on forcing the manufacturers who supply them to accept ever-narrower margins and therefore to cut their own costs (O'Sullivan 2019). These are pressures that American producers passed on to workers—first by moving to the nonunion South and later through extensive outsourcing and subcontracting.

These pressures increased dramatically as large retailers such as Walmart seized on changing trade relations and turned increasingly to low-wage producers abroad to supply them (Hamilton et al. 2011). Amazon's Marketplace now relies heavily on these same trade flows, in this case through commissions collected on sales by a growing number of third-party sellers based in China and India. Moreover, the impact of lean retailing also resonates more broadly (Abernathy et al. 1999). A kind of contagion took hold in the United States as these leading retailers began to set the terms for the myriad adjacent industries that serve them (e.g., trucking, logistics, warehousing), as well as those for all their competitors who now need to match the torrid pace they have set.

A BITTER EQUILIBRIUM

Once you are in this cycle of low margins and low wages, you also begin to have a population of low-income workers who rely on discount retailers such as Walmart to help them make ends meet (Desmond 2023; Ehrenreich 2001). As elaborated at length elsewhere (Thelen 2019), the United States stands out in comparison to peer democracies for the large number of workers who are precariously employed in jobs characterized by low wages, few (often no) benefits, and unstable working hours. The latest OECD figures from 2021, for example, show that the size of the low-pay sector in the United States (as a percentage of the total workforce) stands at 22.7 percent, far above the OECD average of 13.6 percent (OECD 2022).[4] The country's in-work poverty rates are even more jarring: as of 2019 (the most recent comparative figures), 14.8 percent of working Americans were living in households with incomes below 60 percent of median disposable household income, as against an OECD average of 9.3 percent (Hick and Marx unpublished estimate).[5]

---

4. The OECD definition is the share of workers earning less than two-thirds of median earnings.

5. The most recent published figures are older, from 2017, but the overall picture is the same (see Hick and Marx 2023: 496, figure 34.1).

Tighter labor markets since 2022 have reduced unemployment, but they have not reversed the fortunes of most low-skill retail workers. In 2023, the median Walmart worker was taking home just $27,326 (Waldman 2024), barely above the official poverty level for a family of three ($24,860) but well below that for a family of four ($30,000).

In such a context, large discount retailers have paradoxically become part of the infrastructure of the lives of many citizens, and not only for the low prices they offer. Higher-income consumers with flexible work schedules have the time and the luxury to shop around in small specialty stores. But the situation is quite different for low-income groups that work long hours (in some cases, two jobs), have little or no paid time off or vacation days, and cannot afford the high cost of day care for their small children. For people like this—and that is a large share of Americans—the best option may be to go to a big-box store, put your children in the cart, and buy everything you need in one go—and at almost any time of day or night. In many of America's more remote rural areas—where main-street shopping has long been hollowed out—the only thing worse than having a Walmart in the area is not having a Walmart nearby.[6]

Indeed, dependence on large discount chains runs deeper still, pervading other realms in ways that are completely taken for granted by most Americans but that are highly anomalous in comparative perspective. When the COVID-19 pandemic hit, European countries mobilized their extensive health care infrastructure to administer vaccines. In the United States, by contrast, the government turned to large retail chains to perform these functions. Americans lined up (virtually and physically) at chains such as CVS, Walgreens, and Walmart to get their shots (CDC 2023; Redman 2021; Rosenthal 2023; Grabenstein 2022). Walmart played a central role in administering vaccines in rural communities that are woefully underserved by the American health care system, and in reaching low-income groups that lack the paid time off that would be needed to visit a clinic during regular business hours.

The point here, of course, is not to celebrate these big discounters; quite the contrary. It is instead to point out that the United States is in a deep equilibrium, one that is sustained not just by the popularity of these big retailers (though that too) but also by the infrastructural role they have come to play in the lives of many Americans.

---

6. Walmart caters to Americans of modest means in other ways as well. For example, the company welcomes RV (recreational vehicle) travelers (often lower- or lower-middle-class travelers) to park overnight for free in its vast parking lots.

Paths Forward

Finding a way out of such a deep equilibrium is not easy, but, again, a comparative perspective offers insight into possible paths forward. As we have seen, Europe has not been immune to the spread of lean retailing practices, but it continues to have somewhat stronger guardrails to protect against some of the worst effects. Based on the analysis in chapter 9, we can identify two promising reform pathways to steer outcomes in retailing in more socially sustainable directions. The first runs through antitrust reform and the second runs through labor law reform. I discuss each, briefly, in turn.

In the United States, a new generation of neo-Brandeisians has been appointed to positions of power in both the Federal Trade Commission and the Department of Justice in the last few years. Committed to reforming American antitrust policy and practice, and drawing inspiration from the ideas promoted by Louis Brandeis in the 1920s, they argue that competition law should "protect market structures that [distribute] individual opportunity and prosperity" and ensure that "excessive concentrations of private power" do not undermine economic freedom and democracy (Khan 2018: 132; Dayen 2023). These developments have opened up new space for a debate long stifled by the hegemony of the neoliberal Chicago school paradigm (for an extended analysis, see Foster and Thelen 2023, 2024). In retail specifically, the Chicago school's emphasis on consumer welfare has made it difficult to go after large low-cost retailers who, by definition, are offering consumers low prices. Indeed, current FTC chair Lina Khan rose to prominence with a powerful critique of how Chicago school thinking had actively facilitated the rise of Amazon despite clear signs that the company was abusing its dominant position in the market (Khan 2016).

The FTC is now taking a much harder line on dominant tech platforms generally, including closer scrutiny of Amazon's business practices. Khan initially took aim at the company for its promotion of Prime membership,[7] and, as this book goes to press, she is also suing the company for a range of abusive and discriminatory practices relating to its treatment of third-party sellers (FTC 2023). In the United States, closer scrutiny of the strategies of dominant actors signals an important reorientation away from recent policy and practice, where large players are often celebrated for the efficiency gains

---

7. The FTC has recently brought a case against Amazon that charges that consumers are tricked into signing up for the service and then confront obstacles when they attempt to end their membership.

they achieve. Such gains are often assumed to be passed on to consumers despite evidence that Europe's overall less concentrated markets have actually delivered lower and even declining consumer markups since the 1990s (Cavalleri et al. 2019; Gutiérrez and Philippon 2023; Vaheesan 2020; Grullon, Larkin, Michaely 2019; Barkai 2020; Hovenkamp and Shapiro 2018). The new orientation is a welcome shift and one that, as outlined in chapter 9, could bring the United States closer to the EU's approach, with a competition regime that is organized less around consumers and more around ensuring a competitive market (Foster and Thelen 2023, 2024).

Cracking down on dominant actors is clearly critical, not least because there is growing evidence that market concentration does not just produce deleterious effects in product markets. The negative impact of concentration also operates through labor market monopsony power that depresses wages in local labor markets (Benmelech et al. 2018; Naidu et al. 2018; Azar et al. 2022; Posner 2021; Yeh et al. 2022; on retail specifically, see Bonanno and Lopez 2012; Chava et al. 2022; Neumark et al. 2008; Peralta and Kim 2019; Wiltshire 2023). The problem is pervasive, but it is especially acute in rural areas, where one or two employers often dominate the market for specific occupations (Willingham and Ajilore 2019).[8] Based on their analysis of such monopsony effects, Naidu et al. (2018) make a strong case for antitrust authorities to expand their enforcement horizons to consider the impact of mergers and increasing concentration on both product markets and labor markets.

Closer antitrust scrutiny of dominant actors is thus one important aspect. But comparing Europe to the United States also highlights the central importance of the other part of Brandeis's antimonopoly agenda—namely, bolstering the power of nondominant actors to allow them to engage in collective self-help in the market, endowing them with what Sanjukta Paul terms "countervailing coordination rights" to confront dominant actors (Paul 2020a; Vaheesan 2020: 28). As the previous chapters have documented, one of the key differences to emerge from the United States' and Europe's different competition regimes is the survival in the latter of better-organized producer groups that are more capable of countervailing the power of dominant firms.

In previous work, I have shown that in Europe, disruptive market entrants with winner-take-all ambitions are likely to encounter stronger headwinds from government regulators, labor unions, and organized

---

8. And the problem is further exacerbated by employers' use of nonpoaching agreements and noncompete clauses in employment contracts, both of which limit the ability of workers to move across jobs.

business interests (Thelen 2018; Rahman and Thelen 2019). In Europe, trade groups and employer associations have a strong interest in inhibiting the advance of would-be monopolists, particularly those perceived to be seeking competitive advantage through illegitimate (or illegal) market strategies.[9] As defenders of a level playing field, such groups are often important in heading off what they see as unfair, destructive competition in otherwise well-functioning (because well-regulated) markets.

As we have seen, American antitrust policy historically has not been as forbearing toward the kinds of horizontal coordination that are more common in Europe's coordinated market economies. But empowering weaker actors and actively facilitating their efforts at collective self-help in the market can serve as a crucial complement to stricter regulatory oversight of the dominant players (Paul 2020a makes this point especially powerfully). Indeed, the analysis in the preceding chapters makes clear that regulatory efforts only work if complemented by strong countervailing social forces that can enforce and monitor compliance. In the context of contemporary American retailing (to invoke an example from Vaheesan 2020: 29), strengthening small-business interests would involve forbearance toward coordination among Amazon's third-party sellers, allowing them to negotiate collectively to enhance their power vis-à-vis the platform on which they all so existentially depend.

Perhaps the most important reforms, however, would focus on strengthening the democratic forces within firms and industries by empowering workers and unions (Anderson 2017). In recent years, a growing chorus of scholars—both economists and legal scholars—has pointed to fundamental weaknesses in American labor law (Block and Sachs n.d.; Callaci 1999, 2021; Callaci and Vaheesan 2022; Weil 2014; Steinbaum 2019). The ground rules governing collective bargaining have always put American unions at a distinct disadvantage relative to their European counterparts (for a full analysis, see chap. 9; Thelen 2019).

Across the Atlantic, the number of workers who are covered by collective contracts is often several times higher than in the United States, and even in some countries with comparable levels of union membership. This is because in most European countries organized labor's rights are grounded in legal frameworks that recognize that the power asymmetries that inhere in employment relationships can only be redressed through

---

9. For instance, Uber's conquest of Europe was far more difficult and less successful because of the opposition mounted by organizations of incumbent transportation providers (Thelen 2018).

coordinated action and *collective* representation of workers' interests (Dukes 2011: 4–5). The distinctly individualist and voluntarist foundations of American labor law, by contrast, stand in the way of the more encompassing bargaining arrangements that are more common in Europe (Rogers 2019). Only in the United States are unions required to fight, one workplace at a time, for the right to represent workers through demonstration of majority support in adversarial elections in which employers possess powerful tools to resist unionization.

The impact of the long-standing weaknesses in American labor law has been amplified by recent trends toward "fissurization"—through which leading companies increasingly eschew direct employment in favor of subcontracting and outsourcing (Weil 2014). In the American context, Chicago school forbearance toward vertical contracting has allowed large corporations to exercise almost complete control of their subcontractors and franchisees, while fissurization absolves them of accountability for the labor practices of these subordinates (Callaci 2021a; also Steinbaum 2019). And while this problem is by no means restricted to the United States, in Europe its impact is mitigated where more encompassing industry-wide bargaining provides some shelter for workers in smaller firms and where stronger labor laws offer more foundational protections for workers even in poorly organized sectors.

A related but analytically distinct problem is firms' increasing use of independent contractors as an alternative to direct employment or subcontracting to smaller firms. This is a problem on both sides of the Atlantic, because even in Europe, independent contractors (because technically self-employed) fall outside the purview of union bargaining. The classic case is ride-sharing apps, where companies like Uber exert extreme control over the pay and working conditions of their putatively self-employed drivers. But we see this phenomenon in retail as well, for example, in the increasing use by Walmart of independent truckers to transport goods. In the United States, independent contractors are not just denied the opportunity to bargain collectively; efforts at coordinated self-defense are often met with antitrust charges of price-fixing (Paul 2016: 1032–33; Paul 2019: 66; Steinbaum 2019).

Here again, Europe has not been immune to the problems generated by the growth of gig work. However, more generous social policies raise the reservation wage for work generally and thus also raise the bar for these types of employment. Moreover, European law has also moved toward recognizing the rights of pseudo-self-employed workers to defend themselves collectively in the market. In 2014, the European Court of Justice extended collective bargaining rights to workers who are formally self-employed but in fact dependent on a shared employer (so-called false, or fake, self-employed) (Šmejkal 2015; Ankersmit 2015). Following these decisions, the European Commission adopted new guidelines that further clarify that European competition rules against price-fixing do not apply to independent contractors who seek to organize as long as they are "in a situation comparable to workers" and are in a "weak negotiating position" (European Commission 2022).

Antitrust and labor law are but two areas that call out for reform. Any number of further measures—for example, limiting jurisdictional competition over private investment or linking public investment to stronger labor protections—could also be mentioned. My objective here is not to provide an exhaustive list of reform remedies. It is, rather, to underscore the myriad ways in which law and policy continue to shape how markets operate and influence the outcomes they generate. If policy and political choice are what brought America to the deep equilibrium we have today, then policy and political will can also help us find our way to better outcomes.

Finally, viewing the American political economy through the lens of retail casts consumers in a rather unflattering light. In principle, consumers have a lot of power in the United States, but that power is rarely wielded on behalf of workers. On the contrary, when there is no organized countervailing power—for example, advocating on behalf of workers—American consumers are often drawn into an alliance with low-cost retailers and therefore into complicity in the strategies they deploy. Sometimes this is explicit, as in the cases detailed above in which large retailers have succeeded in mobilizing consumers to take their side in legislative battles with politicians and regulators. But often it is far more subtle, as in the uncomfortable disconnect between the values most citizens hold (e.g., in support of decent and dignified work) and their actual shopping behavior.

Everything I have seen suggests that it is unrealistic to pin our hopes for change on collective self-restraint by consumers, because, as I have demonstrated, the core problem is not just pervasive, it is structural. It has to do with the way in which the institutions of our political economy have rewarded business models that are organized around regulatory arbitrage and reducing labor costs to a bare minimum. When this translates into the lower prices that consumers crave and that the American antitrust regime sanctifies, that is a powerful force and one that in the United States faces very few countervailing forces. The political theorist Jane Mansbridge has made the case that the role of government is to exercise "legitimate coercion" to solve pressing and socially important collective action problems (Mansbridge 2018). Because individually it is often hard to do the right thing, we sometimes need to be forced, together, to do that thing. It seems to me that unwinding the current bitter equilibrium of American retail capitalism will require a heavy dose of legitimate coercion, especially on behalf of the vulnerable workers whose interests are too easily obscured by the seductions of the Amazon economy.

BIBLIOGRAPHY

Abernathy, Frederick, John Dunlop, Janice Hammond, and David Weil. 1999. *A Stitch in Time: Lean Retailing and the Transformation of Manufacturing. Lessons from the Apparel and Textile Industries*. New York: Oxford University Press.

Adams, Thomas Jessen. 2006. "Making the New Shop Floor." In *Wal-Mart: The Face of Twenty-First-Century Capitalism*, edited by Nelson Lichtenstein. New York: New Press.

Aléx, Peder. 1999. "Swedish Consumer Cooperation as an Educational Endeavor." In *Consumers against Capitalism? Consumer Cooperation in Europe, North America, and Japan, 1849–1990*, edited by Ellen Furlough and Carl Strikwerda. New York: Rowman and Littlefield.

Allender, Mary. 1993. "Why Did Manufacturers Want Fair Trade?" *Essays in Economic and Business History* 11 (1993): 218–30.

Anderson, Chris. 2004. "The Long Tail." *Wired*, October 1. https://www.wired.com/2004/10/tail/.

Anderson, Elisabeth. 2008. "Experts, Ideas, and Policy Change: The Russell Sage Foundation and Small Loan Reform, 1909–1941." *Theory and Society* 37, no. 3 (January): 271–310.

Anderson, Elizabeth. 2017. *Private Government: How Employers Rule Our Lives (and Why We Don't Talk About It)*. Princeton, NJ: Princeton University Press.

Andrews, Edmund L. 2000. "International Business: Germany Says Wal-Mart Must Raise Prices." *New York Times*, September 9.

Andrias, Kate. 2019. "An American Approach to Social Democracy: The Forgotten Promise of the Fair Labor Standards Act." *Yale Law Journal* 128, no. 3: 616–709.

Ankersmit, Laurens. 2015. "Albany Revisited: The Court Directs NCA to Carry a More Social Tune." European Law Blog, March 3. https://europeanlawblog.eu/2015/03/03/albany-revisited-the-court-directs-nca-to-carry-a-more-social-tune/.

Ansell, Ben. 2014. "The Political Economy of Ownership: Housing Markets and the Welfare State." *American Political Science Review* 108, no. 2 (May): 383–402.

Antitrust Modernization Commission. 2007. *Report and Recommendations*. https://govinfo.library.unt.edu/amc/report_recommendation/amc_final_report.pdf

Areeda, Phillip, and Donald F. Turner. 1975. "Predatory Pricing and Related Practices under Section 2 of the Sherman Act." *Harvard Law Review* 68, no. 4 (February): 697–733.

Autor, David, David Dorn, and Gordon Hanson. 2016. "The China Shock: Learning from Labor Market Adjustment to Large Changes in Trade." NBER Working Paper 21906. https://www.nber.org/system/files/working_papers/w21906/w21906.pdf.

Azar, José, Ioana Marinescu, and Marshall Steinbaum. 2022. "Labor Market Concentration." *Journal of Human Resources* 57, issue S (April): 167–99.

Baccaro, Lucio, and Sinisa Hadziabdic. 2022. "Operationalizing Growth Models." MPIfG Discussion Paper 22/6. Max Planck Institute for the Study of Societies.

Baccaro, Lucio, and Jonas Pontusson. 2016. "Rethinking Comparative Political Economy: The Growth Model Perspective." *Politics and Society* 44, no. 2: 175–207.

Baily, Martin Neil, and Robert M. Solow. 2001. "International Productivity Comparisons Built from the Firm Level." *Journal of Economic Perspectives* 15, no. 3 (Summer): 151–72.

Banken, Ralf. 2021. "Vom Warenhaus zum Online-Versand. Die Entwicklung des Einzelhandels im 20. Jahrhundert." In *Konsum im 19. und 20. Jahrhundert*, edited by Christian Kleinschmidt and Jan Logemann, 483–514. Berlin: Walter de Gruyte.

Banken, Ralf, Christian Kleinschmidt, and Jan Logemann. 2021. "Absatz und Reklame: Die Anfänge von modernem Einzelhandel und die Werbung bis zum Ersten Weltkrieg." In *Konsum im 19. und 20. Jahrhundert*, edited by Christian Kleinschmidt and Jan Logemann, 191–210. Berlin: Walter de Gruyter.

Barber, Richard J. 1961. "Private Enforcement of the Antitrust Laws: The Robinson-Patman Experience." *George Washington Law Review* 30, no. 2 (December): 181–230.

Barmash, Isadore. 1981. *More than They Bargained for: The Rise and Fall of Korvettes*. New York: Lebhar-Friedman Books/Chain Store Publishing Corp.

Barrett, Edward W. 1954. "The Automatic Canteen Co. Case and Buyer's Liability under the Robinson-Patman Act." *Journal of Marketing* 18, no. 3 (January): 246–54.

Barron, Hal S. 1997. *Mixed Harvest: The Second Great Transformation in the Rural North, 1987–1930*. Chapel Hill: University of North Carolina Press.

Basker, Emek. 2007. "The Causes and Consequences of Wal-Mart's Growth." *Journal of Economic Perspectives* 21, no. 3 (Summer): 177–98.

BBC. 2016. "Lidl Stores under Fire over Trade Union Stance," September 19. https://www.bbc.com/news/uk-wales-south-east-wales-37410609.

Bean, Jonathan J. 1996. *Beyond the Broker State: Federal Policies toward Small Business 1936–1961*. Chapel Hill: University of North Carolina Press.

Beatley, Timothy. 2000. *Green Urbanism: Learning from European Cities*. Washington, D.C.: Island Press.

Beckert, Jens. 2011. "The Transcending Power of Goods: Imaginative Value in the Economy." In *The Worth of Goods: Valuation and Pricing in the Economy*, edited by Jens Becker and Patrick Aspers, 106–28. Oxford: Oxford University Press.

———. 2016. *Imagined Futures: Fictional Expectations and Capitalist Dynamics*. Cambridge, MA: Harvard University Press.

Beckert Jens, and Christine Musselin, eds. 2013. *Constructing Quality: The Classification of Goods in Markets*. Oxford: Oxford University Press.

Belschner, Reimar, and Beate L. Matthes. 2013. "Eine kurze Geschichte des Konsumevereins und der GEG in Mannheim." In *Konsumgenossenschaft und GEG in Mannheim*. Mannheim: Rhein-Neckar Industriekultur e.V. 2013.

Belzer, Michael H. 2000. *Sweatshops on Wheels: Winners and Losers in Trucking Deregulation*. New York: Oxford University Press.

Benmelech, Efraim, Nittai Bergman, and Hyunseob Kim. 2018. *Strong Employers and Weak Employees: How Does Employer Concentration Affect Wages?* National Bureau of Economic Research, working paper. DOI 10.3386/w24307.

Bensel, Richard. 2000. *The Political Economy of American Industrialization, 1877–1900*. New York: Cambridge University Press.

Berfield, Susan. 2015. "How Walmart Keeps an Eye on Its Massive Workforce." *Bloomberg*, November 24. https://www.bloomberg.com/features/2015-walmart-union-surveillance/.

Berger, Raoul. 1935. "Usury in Installment Sales." Abstracted from *Law and Contemporary Problems* 148 (April).

Berger, Suzanne. 1977. "D'une bourtique à l'autre: Changes in the Organization of the Traditional Middle Classes from the Fourth to Fifth Republics." *Comparative Politics* 10, no. 1: 121–36.

Berghoff, Hartmut. 2001. "Enticement and Deprivation: The Regulation of Consumption in Prewar Nazi Germany." In *The Politics of Consumption*, edited by Martin Daunton and Matthew Hilton. New York: Berg Publishing.

———. 2009. "Träume und Alpträume. Konsumpolitik im Nationalsozialistischen Deutschland." In *Die Konsumgesellschaft in Deutschland 1890–1990: Ein Handbuch*, edited by Heinz Gerhard Haupt and Claudius Torp.Frankfurt a.M. u. New York: Campus Verlag.

———. 2012. "Consumption Politics and Politicized Consumption: Monarchy, Republic, and Dictatorship in Germany, 1900–1939." In *Decoding Modern Consumer Societies*, edited by Berghoff and Uwe Spiekermann, 125–48. New York: Palgrave.

———. 2021. "Front und Heimatfront: Konsum in den Weltkriegen des 20. Jahrhunderts." In *Konsum im 19. Und 20. Jahrhundert*, edited by Christian Kleinschmidt and Jan Logemann, 537–62. Berlin: Walter de Gruyter.

Berghoff, Hartmut, ed. 1999. *Konsumpolitik. Die Regulierung des privaten Verbrauchs im 20. Jahrhundert*. Göttingen: Vandenhoeck and Ruprecht.

Berghoff, Hartmut, and Ingo Köhler. 2019. *Family Businesses in Germany and the United States since Industrialization: A Long-Term Historical Study*. Munich: Stiftung Familienunternehmen.

Berghoff, Hartmut, and Uwe Spiekermann. 2012. "Taking Stock and Forging Ahead: The Past and Future of Consumption History." In *Decoding Modern Consumer Societies*, edited by Berghoff and Spiekermann. New York: Palgrave.

Berghoff, Hartmut, Jan Logemann, and Felix Römer, eds. 2016. *The Consumer on the Home Front: World War II Civilian Consumption in Comparative Perspective*. Oxford: Oxford University Press.

Berk, Gerald. 1994. *Alternative Tracks: The Constitution of American Industrial Order, 1865–1917*. Baltimore, MD: Johns Hopkins University Press.

———. 1996. "Communities of Competitors: Open Price Associations and the American State, 1911–1929." *Social Science History* 20, no. 3 (Fall): 375–400.

———. 2009. *Louis D. Brandeis and the Making of Regulated Competition, 1900–1932*. New York: Cambridge University Press.

Birnbaum, Emily. 2022. "Amazon and Google Deploy Their Armies to Thwart Antitrust Bills." *Politico*, January 4. https://www.politico.com/news/2022/01/04/amazon-google-thwart-antitrust-bills-526460.

Bittman, Simon. 2021. "Turning Wages into Capital Differentiation on the Market for Unsecured Loans in the United States, 1900–1945." *European Journal of Sociology* 62, no. 2 (August): 213–48.

Blackhawk, Maggie, Daniel Carpenter, Tobias Resch, and Benjamin Schneer. 2020. "Replication Data for: Congressional Representation by Petition: Assessing the Voices of the Voteless in a Comprehensive New Database, 1789–1949 [dataset]." Harvard Dataverse, doi.org/10.7910/DVN/JMOXQI.

———. 2021. "Congressional Representation by Petition: Assessing the Voices of the Voteless in a Comprehensive New Database, 1789–1949." *Legislative Studies Quarterly* 46, no. 3 (August): 817–49.

Block, Sharon, and Benjamin Sachs. n.d. *Clean Slate for Worker Power: Building a Just Economy and Democracy*. Report of the Labor and Worklife Program, Harvard Law School. https://lwp.law.harvard.edu/sites/projects.iq.harvard.edu/files/lwp/files/full_report_clean_slate_for_worker_power.pdf.

Bludau, Kuno. 1968. *Nationalsozialismus und Genossenschaften. Schriftenreihe des Forschungsinstituts der Friedrich-Ebert-Stiftung*. Hannover: Verlag für Literatur und Zeitgeschehen.

BNA. 1964. *Antitrust and Trade Regulation Report*, report no. 173. November 3. Washington DC: US Bureau of National Affairs.

Boarnet, Marlon, and Randall Crane. 1999. "The Impact of Big Box Grocers on Southern California: Jobs, Wages, and Municipal Finances." Orange County Business Council. https://citeseerx.ist.psu .edu/document?repid=rep1&type=pdf&doi=ae949b59cb2ae2a867c05f716a947dabcd59e2fa.

Bolin, Richard G. 1971. "United States v. Topco Associates, Inc.: Illegal Combination and/or Pro-competitive Arrangement?" *Indiana Law Journal* 47, no. 1 (Fall): 157–68.

Bonacich, Edna, and Khaleelah Hardie. 2006. "Wal-Mart and the Logistics Revolution." In *Wal-Mart: The Face of Twenty-First-Century Capitalism*, edited by Nelson Lichtenstein. New York: The New Press.

Bonanno, Alessandro, and Rigoberto A. Lopez. 2012. "Wal-Mart's Monopsony Power in Metro and Non-Metro Labor Markets." *Regional Science and Urban Economics* 42, no. 4: 569–79. doi.org/10.1016/j.regsciurbeco.2012.02.003.

Bonow, Mauritz. 1938. "The Consumer Cooperative Movement in Sweden." *Annals of the American Academy of Political and Social Science* 197 (May): 171–84.

Bösche, Burchard, and Jan-Frederik Korf. *Zentralverband deutscher Konsumgenossenschaften* e.V. 2003. http://klaus.lhorn.de/GW/BERICHT/ZDK.pdf

Bowman, Ward S. 1955. "The Prerequisites and Effects of Resale Price Maintenance." *University of Chicago Law Review* 22, no. 4 (Summer): 825–73.

Brady, Robert A. 1943. *Business as a System of Power*. New York: Columbia University Press.

Brand, Donald R. 1988. *Corporatism and the Rule of Law*. Ithaca, NY: Cornell University Press.

Brandeis, Louis. 1913. "Competition That Kills." *Harper's Weekly*, November 15. https://louisville .edu/law/library/special-collections/the-louis-d.-brandeis-collection/business-a-profession -chapter-15.

Brody, David. 1980. *Workers in Industrial America: Essays on the Twentieth Century Struggle*. Oxford: Oxford University Press.

Bronnenberg, Bart J., and Paul B. Ellickson. 2015. "Adolescence and the Path to Maturity in Global Retail." *Journal of Economic Perspectives* 29, no. 4 (Fall): 113–34.

Brown, H. Claire. 2019. "The Wild Story of How America Almost Banned Chain Grocery Stores." *The Counter*, April 23. https://thecounter.org/ap-food-retail-small-business-grocery-chain -store-ban/.

Brown, Harold. 1969. *Franchising: Trap for the Trusting*. Boston: Little, Brown.

Brown, Stephen. 1990. "Innovation and Evolution in UK Retailing: The Retail Warehouse." *European Journal of Marketing* 24, no. 9 (September): 39–54.

Bruenig, Matt. 2018. "Small Businesses Are Overrated." *Jacobin*, January 16. https://jacobin.com /2018/01/small-businesses-workers-wages.

Brunell, Richard. 2007. "Overruling Dr. Miles: The Supreme Trade Commission in Action." *Antitrust Bulletin* 52, nos. 3 and 4 (Fall/Winter): 475–529.

Buntz, James R. 1968. "Brandeis and Sunday Opening: A Case Study." MBA thesis, Creighton University. https://researchworks.creighton.edu/esploro/outputs/graduate/Brandeis-and-Sunday -Opening-A-Case/991005932425402656/filesAndLinks?institution=01CRU_INST&skip UsageReporting=true&recordUsage=false&index=0.

Bureau of Labor Statistics. 2019. "Persons at Work in Nonagricultural Industries by Class of Worker and Usual Full- or Part-Time Status." In "Current Population Survey, 2019 Annual Averages." https://www.bls.gov/cps/aa2019/cpsaat21.htm.

Bureau of Labor Statistics. 2023. "Percentage of Private Industry Workers with Access to Employer-Provided Benefits by Work Status." March 2023, https://www.bls.gov/charts /employee-benefits/percent-access-benefits-by-work-status.htm#.

Bureau of Labor Statistics. 2024. "News Release USDL-24-0096." January 23. Washington, DC: US Department of Labor. https://www.bls.gov/news.release/pdf/union2.pdf.

Burke, Terry, and J. R. Shackleton. 1992. "The Sunday Trading Battle in England and Wales." *Journal of Interdisciplinary Economics* 4, no. 4 (July): 301–15. doi.org/10.1177/02601079X9200400402.

Burt, Steve. 1995. "Understanding the Arrival of Limited Line Discount Stores in Britain." *European Management Journal* 13, no. 1 (March): 110–19. doi.org/10.1016/0263-2373(94)00063-D.

Bush, Egbert T. 1906. "A Rural View of Rural Free Delivery." *North American Review* 182, no. 592 (March): 381–90.

Butler, Sarah. 2022. "Union Wins Right to Challenge Tesco Fire and Rehire Policy at Supreme Court." *Guardian*, December 22. https://www.theguardian.com/business/2022/dec/22/usdaw-union-right-to-challenge-tesco-fire-and-rehire-supreme-court.

Calder, Lendol. 1999. *Financing the American Dream: A Cultural History of Consumer Credit*. Princeton, NJ: Princeton University Press.

Callaci, Brian. 1999. "The Historical and Legal Creation of a Fissurized Workplace: The Case of Franchising." PhD diss., UMass Amherst, October.

———. 2021a. "Control without Responsibility: The Legal Creation of Franchising, 1960–1980." *Enterprise and Society* 22, no. 1 (March): 156–82. doi.org/10.1017/eso.2019.58.

———. 2021b. "What Do Franchisees Do? Vertical Restraints as Workplace Fissuring and Labor Discipline Devices." *Journal of Law and Political Economy* 1, no. 3: 397–444. doi.org/10.5070/LP61353764.

Callaci, Brian, and Sandeep Vaheesan. 2022. "How an Old US Antitrust Law Could Foster a Fairer Retail Sector." *Harvard Business Review*, February 9. https://hbr.org/2022/02/how-an-old-u-s-antitrust-law-could-foster-a-fairer-retail-sector.

Calvani, Terry. 1979. "Effect of Current Developments on the Future of the Robinson-Patman Act." *Antitrust Law Journal* 48, no. 4 (August): 1692–1710.

Capper-Kelly Fair Trade Bill: Hearing Before the Senate Committee on Interstate Commerce, 72nd Cong. 191–203 (1932) (statement of Rep. Eugene Cox).

———. 207–17 (1932) (statement of Chester A. Gray, Washington Representative of the American Farm Bureau Federation).

Carden, Art. 2013. "Retail Innovations in American Economic History: The Rise of Mass-Market Merchandisers." In *Routledge Handbook of Major Events in Economic History*, edited by Randall E. Parker and Robert Whaples, chap. 33. New York: Routledge.

Cardiff-Hicks, Brianna, Francine Lafontaine, and Kathryn Shaw. 2015. "Do Large Modern Retailers Pay Premium Wages?" *ILR Review* 68, no. 3: 633–65. doi.org/10.1177/0019793915570877.

Carpenter, Daniel P. 2000. "State Building through Reputation Building: Coalitions of Esteem and Program Innovation in the National Postal System, 1883–1913." *Studies in American Political Development* 14, no. 2 (October): 121–55. doi.org/10.1017/S0898588X00003382.

Carpenter, Daniel P. 2001a. *The Forging of Bureaucratic Autonomy: Reputations, Networks, and Policy Innovation in Executive Agencies, 1862–1928*. Princeton, NJ: Princeton University Press.

———. 2001b. "The Political Foundations of Bureaucratic Autonomy: A Response to Kernell." *Studies in American Political Development* 15, no. 1 (Spring): 113–22.

———. 2021. *Democracy by Petition: Popular Politics in Transformation, 1790–1870*. Cambridge, MA: Harvard University Press.

Carré, Françoise, and Chris Tilly. 2017. *Where Bad Jobs Are Better*. New York: Russell Sage Foundation.

———. 2018. "A Global Look at What Makes US Retail Jobs So Bad." *Perspectives on Work* 22 (2018): 30–34.

Carruthers, Bruce. 2022. *The Economy of Promises: Trust, Power and Credit in America*. Princeton, NJ: Princeton University Press.

Carruthers, Bruce, Timothy Guinnane, and Yoonseok Lee. 2012. "Bringing 'Honest Capital' to Poor Borrowers: The Passage of the US Uniform Small Loan Law." *Journal of Interdisciplinary History* 42, no. 3 (Winter): 393–418.

Cassidy, Thomas Francis. 1896. *Contracts in Restraint of Trade*. Thesis for bachelor of law degree, Cornell University School of Law.

Caughey, Devin. 2018. *The Unsolid South*. Princeton, NJ: Princeton University Press.

Cavalleri, Maria, Alice Eliet, Peter McAdam, Filippos Petroulakis, Ana Soares, and Isabel Vansteenkiste. 2019. "Concentration, Market Power, and Dynamism in the Euro Area." European Central Bank Discussion Papers, working paper, March. https://www.ecb.europa.eu/pub/pdf/scpwps/ecb.wp2253~cf7b9d7539.en.pdf.

CDC (Center for Disease Control). 2023. "The Federal Retail Pharmacy Program for COVID-19 Vaccination," August 18. https://archive.cdc.gov/#/details?q=retail%20pharmacy%20program&start=0&rows=10&url=https://www.cdc.gov/vaccines/covid-19/retail-pharmacy-program/index.html.

Centre for European Policy Studies. 2023. "Lending to Households in Europe 1995–2021: ECRI Statistical Package 2022." Harvard Dataverse. doi: 10.7910/DVN/NZBQX5.

Chandler, Alfred D. 1962. *Strategy and Structure: Chapters in the History of the Industrial Enterprise*. Cambridge, MA: MIT Press.

———. 1990. *Scale and Scope: The Dynamics of Industrial Capitalism*. Cambridge, MA: Belknap Press.

Chang, Eric, Mark Andreas Kayser, Drew A. Linzer, and Ronald Rogowski. 2011. *Electoral Systems and the Balance of Consumer-Producer Power*. New York: Cambridge University Press.

Chava, Sudheer, Alexander Oettl, Manpreet Singh, and Linghang Zeng. 2022. "Creative Destruction? Impact of E-Commerce on the Retail Sector." NBER working paper 30077. https://www.nber.org/system/files/working_papers/w30077/w30077.pdf

Christiansen, Niels Finn. 1999. "Between Farmers and Workers: Consumer Cooperation in Denmark, 1850–1940." In *Consumers against Capitalism? Consumer Cooperation in Europe, North America, and Japan, 1849–1990*, edited by Ellen Furlough and Carl Strikwerda. New York: Rowman and Littlefield.

Christophersen, Susan. 2007. "Barriers to US Style Lean Retailing: The Case of Wal-Mart's Failure in Germany." *Journal of Economic Geography* 7, no. 4 (February): 451–69.

Cioffi, J. W., M. F. Kenney, and J. Zysman. 2022. "Platform Power and Regulatory Politics: Polanyi for the Twenty-First Century." *New Political Economy* 27, no. 5: 1–17.

Cohen, Edward E. 1965. "Meeting Competition under the Robinson-Patman Act: Effective Enforcement through Flexible Interpretation." *University of Pennsylvania Law Review* 113, no. 5 (March): 715–40.

Cohen, Lizabeth. 1998. "The New Deal State and the Making of Citizen Consumers." In *Getting and Spending: European and American Consumer Societies in the Twentieth Century*, edited by Susan Strasser, Charles McGovern, and Mattias Judt. New York: Cambridge University Press.

———. 2004. *A Consumers' Republic: The Politics of Mass Consumption in Postwar America*. New York: Vintage.

Cole, George Douglas Howard. 1944. *A Century of Co-operation*. Allen and Unwin for the Co-operative Union.

Coles, Tim. 1999. "Competition, Contested Retail Space and the Rise of the Department Store in Imperial Germany." *International Review of Retail, Distribution and Consumer Research* 9, no. 2: 275–89.

Cooke, Amanda, and Avi Freidman. 2001. "Ahead of Their Time: The Sears Catalogue Prefabricated Houses." *Journal of Design History* 14, no. 1: 53–70.

Covarrubias, Matias, Germán Gutiérrez, and Thomas Philippon. "From Good To Bad Concentration? US Industries over the Past 30 Years." *NBER Macroeconomics Annual* 34.

Cox, Edward F., Robert C. Fellmeth, and John E. Schulz. 1969. *"The Nader Report" on the Federal Trade Commission*. New York: Richard W. Baron.

Cox, Reavis. 1948. *The Economics of Installment Buying*. New York: Ronald Press.

Craig, David R., and Werner K. Gabler. 1940. "The Competitive Struggle for Market Control." *Annals of the American Academy of Political and Social Science* 209 (May): 84–107.

Cross, Gary. 2000. *An All-Consuming Century: Why Commercialism Won in Modern America*. New York: Columbia University Press.

Crossick, Geoffrey. 1984. "The Petite Bourgeoisie in Nineteenth-Century Britain: The Urban and Liberal Case." In *Shopkeepers and Master Artisans in Nineteenth-Century Europe*, edited by Geoffrey Crossick and Heinz-Gerhard Haupt. London: Routledge.

Cullingworth, J. Barry. 1993. *The Political Culture of Planning: American Land Use Planning in Comparative Perspective*. New York: Routledge.

Culpepper, Pepper, and Katheen Thelen. 2020. "Are We All Amazon Primed? Consumers and the Politics of Platform Power" *Comparative Political Studies* 53, no. 2 (February): 288–318.

Curry, A. H., et al. 1966. *Partners for Profit: A Study of Franchising*. New York: American Marketing Association.

Davey, James. 2024. "As Tesco and Sainsbury's Seize the Moment, UK Grocery Laggards Face Uphill Task." Reuters, March 11. https://www.reuters.com/business/retail-consumer/tesco-sainsburys-seize-moment-uk-grocery-laggards-face-uphill-task-2024-03-11/.

Davis, Gerald F., and Aseem Sinha. 2021. "Varieties of Uberization: How Technology and Institutions Change the Organization(s) of Late Capitalism." *Organization Theory* 2, no. 1: 1–17.

Dayen, David. 2023. "A Pitched Battle on Corporate Power." *American Prospect*, January 25. https://prospect.org/economy/2023-01-25-pitched-battle-corporate-power/.

DBEIS (Department for Business, Energy, and Industrial Strategy). 2022. "Trade Union Membership Statistics 2021: Tables." https://assets.publishing.service.gov.uk/government/uploads/system/uploads/attachment_data/file/1078005/Trade_Union_Membership_Statistics_Tables_May_2022.ods.

De Grazia, Victoria. 1998. "Changing Consumption Regimes in Europe 1930–1970." In *Getting and Spending: European and American Consumer Societies in the Twentieth Century*, edited by Susan Strasser, Charles McGovern, and Matthias Judt, 59–84. New York: Cambridge University Press.

———. 2005. *Irresistible Empire: America's Advance through Twentieth-Century Europe*. Cambridge, MA: Belknap Press.

Delfanti, Alessandro. 2021. *The Warehouse Workers and Robots at Amazon*. London: Pluto Press.

Del Ray, Jason. 2019. "The Making of Amazon Prime, the Internet's Most Successful and Devastating Membership Program." *Vox*, May 3. https://www.vox.com/recode/2019/5/3/18511544/amazon-prime-oral-history-jeff-bezos-one-day-shipping.

Department of Justice (DOJ). 1977. *Report on the Robinson-Patman Act*. Washington, DC.

Derysh, Igor. 2020. "Government Study Shows Taxpayers Are Subsidizing 'Starvation Wages' at McDonald's, Walmart." *Salon*, December 12. https://www.salon.com/2020/12/12/government-study-shows-taxpayers-are-subsidizing-starvation-wages-at-mcdonalds-walmart/.

Desmond, Matthew. 2023. *Poverty, By America*. New York: Penguin Random House.

Deutsch, Tracey. 2010. *Building a Housewife's Paradise*. Chapel Hill: University of North Carolina Press.

Dicke, Thomas S. 1992. *Franchising in America: The Development of a Business Method, 1840–1980*. Chapel Hill: University of North Carolina Press.

Dilloff, Neil J. 1980. "Never on Sunday: The Blue Laws Controversy." *Maryland Law Review* 39, no. 4: 679–714.

Disch, Wolfgang Karl Anton. 1965. "Überholtes Ladenschlußgesetz." *Wirtschaftsdienst* 45, no. 12.

Du Bois, W.E.B. 1907. *Economic Co-operation among Negro Americans: Report of Social Study Made by Atlanta University, under the Patronage of the Carnegie Institution of Washington, D.C.* Atlanta, GA: Atlanta University Press.

Duke Law Journal [no author listed]. 1961. "The Parke, Davis Case: Refusal to Deal and the Sherman Act." *Duke Law Journal* 1961, no. 1 (Winter): 120–32.

Dukes, Ruth. 2011. "Hugo Sinzheimer and the Constitutional Function of Labour Law." In The Idea of Labour Law, edited by Guy Davidov and Brian Langille. Oxford: Oxford University Press, 2011. Chapter available online: https://papers.ssrn.com/sol3/papers.cfm?abstract_id=3676349.

Dunlavy, Colleen. 2024. *Small, Medium, Large: How Government Made the US into a Manufacturing Powerhouse*. New York: Polity Books.

Durkin, Thomas A. 2000. "Credit Cards: Use and Consumer Attitudes, 1970–2000." *Federal Reserve Bulletin* (September).

Easterbrook, Frank H. 2007. "Chicago on Vertical Restrictions." *Competition Law International* 3 (February). https://chicagounbound.uchicago.edu/cgi/viewcontent.cgi?article=8027&context=journal_articles.

Edwards, Corwin D. 1959. *The Price Discrimination Law*. Washington, DC: The Brookings Institution.

Ehrenreich, Barbara. 2001. *Nickel and Dimed: On (Not) Getting By in America*. New York: Henry Holt and Co.

Ekberg, Espen. 2017. "Against the Tide: Understanding the Commercial Success of Nordic Consumer Co-operatives, 1950–2010." In *A Global History of Consumer Co-operation Since 1850*, edited by Mary Hilson, Silke Neunsinger, and Greg Patmore, 698–727. Boston: Brill.

Emmet, Boris, and John E. Jeuck. 1950. *Catalogues and Counters: A History of Sears, Roebuck and Company*. Chicago: University of Chicago Press.

Endsley, Fred R. 1967. "Current Status of Sunday Closing Laws in the United States and Their Marketing Implications in Selected Metropolitan Areas." PhD diss., LSU Historical Dissertations and Theses.

Epple, Matthias. 2014. *Die Wurzeln der Vertikalen Preisbindung in Deutschland: Eine Rechtshistorische Analyse*. Baden-Baden: Nomos Verlagsgesellschaft.

Ergen, Timur, and Sebastian Kohl. 2021. "Is More *Mittelstand* the Answer? Firm Size and the Crisis of Democratic Capitalism." *Analyse & Kritik* 43, no. 1: 41–70.

Ershkowitz, Herbert. 1999. *John Wanamaker: Philadelphia Merchant*. Conshohocken, PA: Combined Publishing.

Esping-Andersen, Gøsta. 1985. *Politics against Markets*. Princeton, NJ: Princeton University Press.

European Commission. 2017. *Operational Restrictions in the Retail Sector*. Brussels: European Commission.

———. 2022. *Communication from the Commission: Guidelines of the Application of Union Competition Law to Collective Agreements regarding the Working Conditions of Solo Self-Employed Persons* 22/C 374/02. Brussels. https://eur-lex.europa.eu/legal-content/EN/TXT/?uri=CELEX%3A52022XC0930%2802%29.

Evans, Charles E. 1936. "Anti-Price Discrimination Act of 1936." *Virginia Law Review* 23, no. 2 (December): 140–77.

Fabia, Sina. 2021. "Individualisierung, Pluralisierung und Massenkonsum." In *Konsum im 19. Und 20. Jahrhundert*, edited by Christian Kleinschmidt and Jan Logemann, 337–62. Berlin: Walter de Gruyter.

Fairbairn, Brett. 1994. "History from the Ecological Perspective: Gaia Theory and the Problem of Cooperatives in Turn-of-the-Century Germany." *American Historical Review* 99, no. 4 (October): 1203–39.

———. 1999. "The Rise and Fall of Consumer Cooperation in Germany." In *Consumers against Capitalism? Consumer Cooperation in Europe, North America, and Japan, 1849–1990*, edited by Ellen Furlough and Carl Strikwerda. New York: Rowman and Littlefield.

Fassler, Joe. 2018. "Sales Tax Avoidance Is in Amazon's DNA. This Supreme Court Case Could Change That." *The Counter*, April 17. https://thecounter.org/amazon-a-whole-foods-south-dakota-wayfair-supreme-court-sales-tax/.

Feil, Christoph. 2013. In *Konsumgenossenschaft und GEG in Mannheim. Mannheim: Rhein-Neckar Industriekultur e.V. 2013.* https://www.rhein-neckar-industriekultur.de/sites/default/files/KONSUM-Buch_Teaser.pdf.

Feldenkirchen, Wilfried. 1992. "Competition Policy in Germany." *Business and Economic History* 21: 257–69.

Fernie, John, and Frances Pierrel. 1996. "Own Branding in French and UK Grocery Markets." *Journal of Product and Brand Management* 5, no. 3 (June): 48–59.

Fishkin, Joseph, and William Forbath. 2022. *The Anti-Oligarchy Constitution Reconstructing the Economic Foundations of American Democracy.* Cambridge, MA: Harvard University Press.

Fishman, Charles. 2011. *The Wal-Mart Effect.* New York: Penguin.

Forbath, William. 1991. *Law and the Shaping of the American Labor Movement.* Cambridge, MA: Harvard University Press.

Fortune. 1937. "The Fortune Quarterly Survey: VII." January.

Foster, Chase. In progress. *Trust on Trial: Competition, Coordination Rights, and the Legal Order* (book manuscript).

———. 2019. "The Politics of Delegation: Constitutional Structure, Bureaucratic Discretion, and the Development of Competition Policy in the United States and the European Union, 1890–2017." PhD diss., Harvard.

———. 2022. "Varieties of Neoliberalism: Courts, Competition Paradigms and the Atlantic Divide in Antitrust." *Socio-Economic Review* 20, no. 4 (October): 1653–78.

———. 2024. "Legalism without Adversarialism? Bureaucratic Legalism and the Politics of Regulatory Implementation in the European Union." *Regulation and Governance* 18, no. 1 (January): 53–72.

Foster, Chase, and Kathleen Thelen. 2023. "Brandeis in Brussels? Bureaucratic Discretion, Social Learning, and the Development of Regulated Competition in the European Union." Regulation and Governance (December 9). https://onlinelibrary.wiley.com/doi/epdf/10.1111/rego.12570.

———. 2024. "Coordination Rights, Competition Law and Varieties of Capitalism." Online first, *Comparative Political Studies* (July 18).

Freyer, Tony. 1992. *Regulating Big Business: Antitrust in Great Britain and America.* New York: Cambridge University Press.

———. 2006. *Antitrust and Global Capitalism, 1930–2004.* Cambridge: Cambridge University Press.

Froelich, Walter. 1939. "European Experiments in Protecting Small Competitors." *Harvard Business Review.*

FTC (Federal Trade Commission). 1945. *Report of the Federal Trade Commission on Resale Price Maintenance.* Washington, DC: US GPO.

———. 2023. "FTC Sues Amazon for Illegally Maintaining Monopoly Power." September 26. https://www.ftc.gov/news-events/news/press-releases/2023/09/ftc-sues-amazon-illegally-maintaining-monopoly-power.

Fulcher, James. 1991. *Labour Movements, Employers, and the State.* Oxford: Clarendon Press.

Fulda, Carl H. 1951. "Food Distribution in the United States: The Struggle between Independents and Chains." *University of Pennsylvania Law Review* 99, no. 8 (June): 1051–62.

———. 1954. "Resale Price Maintenance." *University of Chicago Law Review* 21, no. 2 (Winter): 175–211.

Fuller, Wayne E. 1959. "The South and the Rural Free Delivery of Mail." *Journal of Southern History* 25, no. 4 (November): 499–521.

———. 1964. *RFD: The Changing Face of Rural America.* Bloomington: Indiana University Press.

———. 1972. *The American Mail: Enlarger of the Common Life*. Chicago: University of Chicago Press.

Furlough, Ellen, and Carl Strikwerda. 1999. "Economics, Consumer Culture and Gender: An Introduction to the Politics of Consumer Cooperation." In *Consumers against Capitalism? Consumer Cooperation in Europe, North America, and Japan, 1849–1990*, edited by Ellen Furlough and Carl Strikwerda. New York: Rowman and Littlefield.

Galambos, Louis. 1966. *Competition and Cooperation: The Emergence of a National Trade Association*. Baltimore, MD: Johns Hopkins Press, 1966.

Galbraith, John Kenneth. 1952. *American Capitalism: The Concept of Countervailing Power*. Boston: Houghton Mifflin, 1952.

Garfield, Leanna. 2018. "Amazon Has Announced the Top Contenders in Its $5 Billion Bidding War for HQ2." *Business Insider*, January 18. https://www.businessinsider.com/amazon-headquarters-city-proposals-hq2-2017-10#newark-new-jersey-7-billion-in-tax-incentives-4.

Gaster, Robin. 2020. *Behemoth, Amazon Rising: Power and Seduction in the Age of Amazon*. UK: Incumetrics Press.

Gautie, Jerome, Karen Jaehrling, and Coralie Perez. 2020. "Neo-Taylorism in the Digital Age: Workplace Transformations in French and German Retail Warehouses." *Relations Industrielles/Industrial Relations* 75, no. 4 (Fall): 774–95.

Gaventa, John. 1980. *Power and Powerlessness: Quiescence and Rebellion in an Appalachian Valley*. Urbana: University of Illinois Press.

George, Torsten. 1996. "Historische Entwicklung der Ladenöffnungszeiten." In *Das Ladenschlussgesetz auf dem Prüfstand*. Deutscher Universitätsverlag, Wiesbaden, 1996.

Geppert, M., Williams, K., Wortmann, M., Czarzasty, J., Kağnicioğlu, D., Köhler, H.-D., Royle, T., Rückert, Y., and Uçkan, B. 2014. "Industrial relations in European hypermarkets: Home and host country influences." *European Journal of Industrial Relations* 20, no. 3: 255–71.

Gerber, David J. 1985. "Antitrust Law and Economic Analysis: The Swedish Approach." *Hastings International and Comparative Law Review* 8, no. 1: 1–39.

———. 1998. *Law and Competition in Twentieth-Century Europe: Protecting Prometheus*. New York: Oxford University Press.

Gerstle, Gary. 2016. *Liberty and Coercion: The Paradox of American Government from the Founding to the Present*. Princeton, NJ: Princeton University Press.

Glickman, Lawrence B. 1997. *A Living Wage: American Workers and the Making of Consumer Society*. Ithaca, NY: Cornell University Press.

———. 2009. *Buying Power: A History of Consumer Activism in America*. Chicago: University of Chicago Press.

Goldberg, Charles L. 1928. "Co-Operative Marketing and Restraint of Trade." *Marquette Law Review* 12, no. 4 (June): 270–92.

Goldfield, Michael. 1989. *The Decline of Organized Labor in the United States*. Chicago: University of Chicago Press.

Goodwyn, Lawrence. 1976. *The Populist Moment in America*. New York: Oxford University Press.

Gourevitch, Alexander. 2015. *From Slavery to the Cooperative Commonwealth*. New York: Cambridge University Press.

Grabar, Henry. 2016. "How Did Amazon Conquer American Retail? $760 Million in Public Money Didn't Hurt." *Slate*, December 1. https://slate.com/business/2016/12/how-did-amazon-conquer-american-retail.html.

Grabenstein, John. 2022. "Essential Services: Quantifying the Contributions of America's Pharmacists in COVID-19 Clinical Interventions." *Journal of the American Pharmacists Association* 62, no. 6 (November–December): 1929–45.

Graf, Thomas, Henry Mostyn, and Leonor Vulpe Albari. 2023. "Dominance and Monopolies: European Union." *Lexology*, September 28. https://thelawreviews.co.uk/title/the-dominance-and-monopolies-review/european-union.

Greene, Jay and Chris Alcantara. 2021. "Amazon Warehouse Workers Suffer Serious Injuries at Higher Rates than Other Firms." *Washington Post*, June 1. https://www.washingtonpost.com/technology/2021/06/01/amazon-osha-injury-rate/.

Greenhouse, Steven. 2022. "Amazon Chews through the Average Worker in 8 Months. They Need a Union." *Guardian*, February 4.

Grether, Ewald T. 1934. "Resale Price Maintenance in Great Britain." *Quarterly Journal of Economics* 48, no. 4 (August): 620–44.

———. 1939. *Price Control under Fair Trade Legislation.* New York: Oxford University Press.

Grewal, David Singh, and Jedediah Purdy. 2014. "Introduction: Law and Neoliberalism" *Law and Contemporary Problems* 77, no. 4: 1–23.

Guinnane, Timothy W. 2012. "State Support for the German Cooperative Movement, 1860–1914" *Central European History* 45 (2012): 208–32.

Günther, Wolfgang. 2021. *Staatliche Stützung der Tarifpolitik.* Wiesbaden: Springer Verlag VS.

Günther, Wolfgang, and Martin Höpner. 2023. "Why Does Germany Abstain from Statutory Bargaining Extensions? Explaining the Exceptional German Erosion of Collective Wage Bargaining." *Economic and Industrial Democracy* 44, no. 1: 88–108.

Guth, James L. 1982. "Farmer Monopolies, Cooperatives, and the Intent of Congress: Origins of the Capper-Volstead Act." *Agricultural History* 56, no. 1 (January): 67–82.

Gutiérrez, Germán, and Thomas Philippon. 2023. "How European Markets Became Free." *Journal of the European Economic Association* 21, no. 1 (February): 251–92.

Hacker, Jacob, Paul Pierson, and Kathleen Thelen. 2015. "Drift and Conversion: Hidden Faces of Institutional Change." In *Advances in Comparative Historical Analysis*, edited by James Mahoney and Kathleen Thelen, 180–210. New York: Cambridge University Press.

Hacker, Jacob, Alexander Hertel-Fernandez, Paul Pierson, and Kathleen Thelen, eds. 2022. *The American Political Economy: Politics, Markets, and Power.* New York: Cambridge University Press.

Hähnel, Paul Lukas. 2021. "Verbraucherpolitik im Kaiserreich." In *Konsum im 19. Und 20. Jahrhundert*, edited by Christian Kleinschmidt and Jan Logemann, 211–34. Berlin: Walter de Gruyter.

Håkansson, Per. 2000. "Swedish Retail History and Its Effects on Distributor Own Branding." PhD diss., Stockholm School of Economics.

Hall, Peter A. 2020. "The Electoral Politics of Growth Regimes." *Perspectives on Politics* 18, no. 1 (March): 185–99.

Hall, Peter A., and David Soskice. 2001. *Varieties of Capitalism.* Oxford: Oxford University Press.

Hall, Sir Peter. 2002. *Urban and Regional Planning.* London: Routledge.

Hall, Sir Peter, and Mark Tewdwr-Jones. 2020. *Urban and Regional Planning.* 6th edition. London: Routledge.

Hallsworth, A., and J. Bell. 2003. "Retail Change and the United Kingdom Co-operative Movement—New Opportunity Beckoning?" *International Review of Retail, Distribution and Consumer Research* 13, no. 3: 301–15. doi.org/10.1080/0959396032000101363.

Hamann, A. 2006. *The European Black Book on Lidl.* Berlin: Ver.di.

Hamill, James C. 1979. "FTC Approach to the Robinson-Patman Act in the Wake of the A&P Decision." *Antitrust Law Journal* 48, no. 4: 1686–91.

Hamilton, Gary, Benjamin Senauer, and Misha Petrovic, eds. 2011. *The Market Makers: How Retailers Are Reshaping the Global Economy.* Oxford: Oxford University Press.

Hamilton, Richard. 1975. *Restraining Myths.* New York: Halsted Press, 1985.

Hamilton, Shane. 2014. *Trucking Country: The Road to America's Wal-Mart Economy.* Princeton, NJ: Princeton University Press.

Hanna, John. 1930. "Cooperative Associations and the Public." *Michigan Law Review* 29, no. 2: 148–90.

———. 1948. "Antitrust Immunities of Cooperative Associations." *Law and Contemporary Problems* 13 (Summer): 488–508.

Harris, John. 2020. "How Amazon Became a Pandemic Giant—and Why That Could Be a Threat to Us All." *Guardian*, November 18. https://www.theguardian.com/technology/2020/nov/18/how-amazon-became-a-pandemic-giant-and-why-that-could-be-a-threat-to-us-all.

Harris, William D., and Paul D. Larson. n.d. "The Evolution of the Manufacturer's Drummer." Unpublished manuscript, University of Oklahoma.

Harvard Law Review [no author listed]. 1933. "Developments in the Law: Unfair Competition: 1932." *Harvard Law Review* 46, no. 7 (May): 1171–1202.

———. 1937. "Resale Price Maintenance: The Miller-Tydings Enabling Act." *Harvard Law Review* 51, no. 2: 336–45.

———. 1955. "Notes: The Operation of Fair-Trade Programs." *Harvard Law Review* 69, no. 2: 316–73.

Hassel, Anke. 2014. "The Paradox of Liberalization—Understanding Dualism and the Recovery of the German Political Economy." *British Journal of Industrial Relations* 52, no. 1: 57–81.

Hassel, Anke, and Bruno Palier. 2021. *Growth and Welfare in Advanced Capitalist Economies: How Have Growth Regimes Evolved?* Oxford: Oxford University Press.

Hattam, Victoria. 1993. *Labor Visions and State Power*. Princeton, NJ: Princeton University Press.

Hawley, Ellis W. 1995. *The New Deal and the Problem of Monopoly*. New York: Fordham University Press.

Haydu, Jeffrey. 2014. "Consumer Citizenship and Cross-Class Activism: The Case of the National Consumers' League, 1899–1918." *Sociological Forum* 29, no. 3: 628–49.

Hays, Constance. 2005. "What's Behind the Procter Deal? Wal-Mart." *New York Times*, January 29.

HDE (Handelsverband Deutschland). 2024. *Tarifbindung*. Berlin: HDE. https://einzelhandel.de/tarifbindung#EdTB.

Hellerstein, Louis A. 1942. "Federal Regulation of Consumer Credit." *Rocky Mountain Law Review* 14, no. 3: 178–92.

Herman, Edward S. 1959. "A Statistical Note on Fair Trade." *Antitrust Bulletin* 4: 583–92.

Hersch, Philip L. 1994. "The Effects of Resale Price Maintenance on Shareholder Wealth: The Consequences of Schwegmann." *Journal of Industrial Economics* 42, no. 2 (June): 205–16.

Hick, Rod, and Ive Marx. 2023. "Poor Workers in Advanced Democracies: On the Nature of In-work Poverty and Its Relationship to Labour Market Policies." In *Handbook of Labour Market Policy in Advanced Democracies*, edited by Daniel Clegg and Niccolo Durazzi, 495–505. UK: Edward Elgar Publishing.

Hild, Matthew. 1997. "Organizing across the Color Line: The Knights of Labor and Black Recruitment Efforts in Small-Town Georgia." *Georgia Historical Quarterly* 81, no. 2 (Summer): 287–310.

Hilson, Mary. 2017. "Consumer Co-operation in the Nordic Countries, c. 1860–1939." In *A Global History of Consumer Co-operation since 1850*, edited by Mary Hilson, Silke Neunsinger, and Greg Patmore, 121–44. Boston: Brill.

———. 2017. "Rochdale and Beyond: Consumer Co-operation in Britain before 1945." In *A Global History of Consumer Co-operation since 1850*, edited by Mary Hilson, Silke Neunsinger, and Greg Patmore, 59–77. Boston: Brill.

Hilson, Mary, Silke Neunsinger, and Greg Patmore, eds. 2017. *A Global History of Consumer Co-operation since 1850*. Boston: Brill.

Hirt, Sonia. 2012. "Mixed Use by Default: How the Europeans (Don't) Zone." *Journal of Planning Literatures* 27, no. 4: 375–93.

———. 2014. *Zoned in the USA: The Origins and Implications of American Land-Use Regulation*. Ithaca, NY: Cornell University Press.

Hollander, S. C. "United States of America." In *Resale Price Maintenance*, edited by B. S. Yamey. Chicago: Aldine Publishing Company.

Hoopes, James. 2006. "Growth through Knowledge: Wal-Mart, High Technology and the Ever Less Visible Hand of the Manager." In *Wal-Mart: The Face of Twenty-First-Century Capitalism*, edited by Nelson Lichtenstein. New York: The New Press.

Hosgood, Christopher. 1989. "The 'Pigmies of Commerce' and the Working-Class Community: Small Shopkeepers in England. 1870–1914." *Journal of Social History* 22, no. 3: 439–60.

———. 1992. "A 'Brave and Daring Folk'? Shopkeepers and Trade Associational Life in Victorian and Edwardian England." *Journal of Social History* 26, no. 2: 285–308.

Hovenkamp, Herbert. 2019. "Is Antitrust's Consumer Welfare Principle Imperiled?" *Journal of Corporation Law* 45, no. 1: 65–94.

Howard, Vicki. 2015. *From Main Street to Mall: The Rise and Fall of the American Department Store*. Philadelphia: University of Pennsylvania Press.

Howell, Chris. 2005. *Trade Unions and the State: The Construction of Industrial Relations Institutions in Britain, 1890–2000*. Princeton, NJ: Princeton University Press.

Hower, Ralph M. 1946. *History of Macy's of New York, 1858–1919*. Cambridge, MA: Harvard University Press.

Human Rights Watch. 2007. "Discounting Rights: Wal-Mart's Violation of US Workers' Right to Freedom of Association." Human Rights Watch, April 30. https://www.hrw.org/reports/2007/us0507/5.htm.

Humbach, John A. 1966. "Fair Trade: The Ideal and the Reality." *Ohio State Law Journal* 27: 144–75.

Hyman, Louis. 2011. *Debtor Nation: The History of America in Red Ink*. Princeton, NJ: Princeton University Press.

———. 2012. *Borrow: The American Way of Debt*. New York: Vintage.

———. 2012. "The Politics of Consumer Debt: US State Policy and the Rise of Investment in Consumer Credit, 1920–2008." *Annals of the American Academy of Political and Social Science* 644 (November): 40–49.

Ilsøe, A., and T. P. Larsen, eds. 2021. *Non-standard Work in the Nordics: Troubled Waters under the Still Surface*. Report from *The Future of Work: Opportunities and Challenges for the Nordic Models*. Nordic Council of Ministers. https://norden.diva-portal.org/smash/get/diva2:1525814/FULLTEXT01.pdf.

Ilsøe, Anna, Trine Pernille Larsen, and Jonas Felbo-Koldig. 2017. "Living Hours under Pressure: Flexibility Loopholes in the Danish IR-Model." *Employee Relations* 39, no. 6: 888–902.

Ingram Paul, and Rao Hayagreeva. 2004. "The Enactment and Repeal of Anti-Chain-Store Legislation in America." *American Journal of Sociology* 110, no. 2 (September): 446–87.

Isaacs, Nathan. 1928. "The Legal Status of Agricultural Cooperation." *Columbia Law Review* 28, no. 3 (March): 394–95.

Jackson, Gregory. 2001. "The Origins of Nonliberal Corporate Governance in Germany and Japan." In *The Origins of Nonliberal Capitalism: Germany and Japan in Comparison*, edited by Wolfgang Streeck and Kozo Yamamura. Ithaca, NY: Cornell University Press.

Jackson, Kenneth. 1985. *Crabgrass Frontier*. Oxford: Oxford University Press.

Jacobs, Jane. 1961. *The Death and Life of the Great American Cities*. New York: Random House.

Jacobs, Meg. 2005. *Pocketbook Politics: Economic Citizenship in Twentieth Century America*. Princeton, NJ: Princeton University Press.

Jacobson, Lisa. 2004. *Raising Consumers: Children and the American Mass Market in the Early Twentieth Century*. New York: Columbia University Press.

Jacoby, Sanford. 1986. "Employee Attitude Testing at Sears, Roebuck and Company, 1938–1960." *Business History Review* 60, no. 4 (Winter): 602–32.

Jaffer, S. M., and J. A. Kay. 1986. "The Regulation of Shop Opening Hours in the United Kingdom." In *Law and Economics and the Economics of Legal Regulation*, edited by J.-M. G. von der Schulenburg and G. Skogh, 169–83. Springer Netherlands. doi.org/10.1007/978-94-009-4442-8_9.

Jefferys, James. 1954. *Retail Trading in Britain 1850–1950*. Cambridge: Cambridge University Press.

J.H.E., Jr. 1941. "Cooperative Marketing Associations and the Restraint of Trade." *Virginia Law Review* 27, no. 5 (March): 674–86.

John, Richard R. 1995. *Spreading the News: The American Postal System from Franklin to Morse*. Cambridge, MA: Harvard University Press.

Jonsson, Pernilla. 2017. "From Commercial Trickery to Social Responsibility: Marketing in the Swedish Cooperative Movement in the Early Twentieth Century." In *A Global History of Consumer Co-operation Since 1850*, edited by Mary Hilson, Silke Neunsinger, and Greg Patmore, 642–67. Boston: Brill.

Josephson, Matthew. 1934. *The Robber Barons*. New York: Harcourt.

Kanter, Carl I., and Stanford G. Rosenblum. 1955. "The Operation of Fair-Trade Programs." *Harvard Law Review* 69, no. 2: 316–52.

Kay, J. A., C. N. Morris, S. M. Jaffer, and S. A. Meadowcroft. 1984. *The Regulation of Retail Trading Hours*. Institute for Fiscal Studies. https://ifs.org.uk/comms/r13.pdf.

Kelly, M. 2019. "Amazon Silently Ends Controversial Pricing Agreements with Sellers." *The Verge*, March 11. https://www.theverge.com/2019/3/11/18260700/amazon-anti-competitive-pricing-agreements-3rd-party-sellers-end.

Kenney, Martin, Dafna Bearson, and John Zysman. 2021. "The Platform Economy Matures: Measuring Pervasiveness and Exploring Power." *Socio-Economic Review* 19, no. 4 (October): 1451–83.

Kessler, William C. 1936. "German Cartel Regulation under the Decree of 1923." *Quarterly Journal of Economics* 50, no. 4 (August): 680–93.

Khan, Lina. 2016. "Amazon's Antitrust Paradox." *Yale Law Journal* 126, no. 3: 710–805.

Khan, Lina, and Sandeep Vaheesan. 2017. "Market Power and Inequality: The Antitrust Counter-revolution and Its Discontents." *Harvard Law and Policy Review* 11: 235–94.

Kiehling, Hartmut. 1996. "Die wirtschaftliche Situation des deutschen Einzelhandels in den Jahren 1920 bis 1923." *Zeitschrift für Unternehmensgeschichte* 41, no. 1: 1–27.

Kiviat, Barbara. 2006. "The Town That Wal-Mart Left: How Livingston, Alabama Fought for—and Lost—Its Most Important Store." Unpublished master's thesis, Columbia University Graduate School of Journalism, New York.

Kjellberg, Anders. 2009. "Facklig Organisationsgrad och Kollektivavtalens Täckningsgrad i vissa Branscher i Privat Sektor 2007." In *Avtalsrörelsen och Lönebildningen 2008*, edited by I. G. Kuylenstierna, & A-M. Egerö, vol. 8, 30–34. Medlingsinstitutet.

———. 2020. *Den Svenska Modellen i en Oviss Tid—Fack, Arbetsgivare och Kollektivavtal på en Föränderlig Arbetsmarknad*. Stockholm: Arena Idé. https://arenaide.se/wp-content/uploads/sites/2/2020/06/arena-ide-svenska-modellen-i-en-oviss-tid-v3.pdf.

———. 2022. *Kollektivavtalens Täckningsgrad samt Organisationsgraden hos Arbetsgivarförbund och Fackförbund*. Studies in Social Policy, Industrial Relations, Working Life and Mobility Research Reports, Department of Sociology, Lund University.

———. 2023. *The Nordic Model of Industrial Relations: Comparing Denmark, Finland, Norway and Sweden*. Lund University.

Kjellberg, Anders, and Nergaard, K. 2022. "Union Density in Norway and Sweden: Stability versus Decline." *Nordic Journal of Working Life Studies* 12, no. S8.

Kjølby, H. 1966. "Denmark." In *Resale Price Maintenance*, edited by B. S. Yamey. Chicago: Aldine Publishing Company.

Knake, Sebastian. 2021. "Die Geschichte des Konsumentenkredits in internationaler Perspektive." In *Konsum im 19. und 20. Jahrhundert*, edited by Christian Kleinschmidt and Jan Logemann, 391–431. Berlin: De Gruyter.

Knupfer, Anne Meis. 2013. *Food Co-ops in America: Communities, Consumption, and Economic Democracy*. Ithaca, NY: Cornell University Press.

Kocka, Jürgen. 1997. *Europäische Konsumgeschichte: Zur Gesellschafts- und Kulturgeschichte des Konsums, 18. Bis 20. Jahrhundert.* Frankfurt: Campus.

Koenen, Anne. 2002. "Fear of Shopping in Germany: The Americanization of Consumption in Early Mail-Order Business." In Amerikanische *Populärkultur in Deutschland,* edited by Katya Kanzler and Heike Paul. Leipzig: Leipziger Universitätsverlag.

Korf, Jan-Frederik. 2008. *Von der Konsumgenossenschaftsbewegung zum Gemeinschaftswerk der Deutschen Arbeiterfront.* Hamburg: Heinrich-Kaufmann Stiftung.

Kovacic, William. E. 2007. "The Intellectual DNA of Modern US Competition Law for Dominant Firm Conduct: The Chicago/Harvard Double Helix." *Columbia Business Law Review* 1, no. 1: 2–80.

Kovacic, William E., and Carl Shapiro. 2000. "Antitrust Policy: A Century of Economic and Legal Thinking." *Journal of Economic Perspectives* 14, no. 1 (Winter): 43–60.

Kreps, Theodore J. 1940. "Review of Grether's Price Control under Fair Trade Legislation." *Columbia Law Review* 40, no. 6: 1110–15.

Kretschmer, Sebastian. 2006. "Der Institutionelle Wandel der EDEKA-Gruppe." Institut für Genossenschaftswesen (Münster), Band 66. Aachen: Shaker Verlag.

Kühnert, Jürgen. 2009. *Die Geschichte der Buchpreisbindung in Deutschland: Von ihren Anfängen bis ins Jahr 1945.* Harrassowitz Verlag.

Kumar, Nirmalya and Jan-Benedict Steenkamp. 2007. *Private Label Strategy.* Boston: Harvard Business School Press.

Kulp, Patrick. 2022. "Amazon Will Overtake Walmart as the Biggest US Retailer by 2024, Report Says." *Adweek,* June 1. https://www.adweek.com/commerce/amazon-will-overtake-walmart-as-the-biggest-u-s-retailer-by-2024-report-says/.

Kursh, Harry. 1969. *Franchise Boom.* Englewood Cliffs, NJ: Prentice-Hall Publishers.

Kurzer, Ulrich. 1997a. "Die Konsumgenossenschaften in Deutschland bis zum Ende der Weimarer Republik—eine Skizze ihrer Entwicklung." In *Nationalsozialismus und Konsumgenossenschaften: Gleichschaltung, Sanierung, und Teilliquidation zwischen 1933 und 1936,* edited by Ulrich Kurzer. Studien und Materialien zum Rechtsextremismus. Herbolzheim: Centaurus Verlag & Media. doi.org/10.1007/978-3-86226-854-2_2.

———. 1997b. *Nationalsozialismus und Konsumgenossenschaften.* Centaurus Verlag.

Kurzlechner, Werner. 2008. *Fusionen-Kartelle-Skandale: Das Bundeskartellamt als Wettbewerbshüter und Verbraucheranwalt.* München: Redline Wirtschaft FinanzBuch Verlag.

Kwon, Spencer, Yueran Ma, and Kaspar Zimmermann. 2023. "100 Years of Rising Corporate Concentration." SAFE working paper no. 359. February 7. dx.doi.org/10.2139/ssrn.3936799.

Laband, David N., and Deborah Hendry Heinbuch. 1987. *Blue Laws: The History, Economics, and Politics of Sunday-Closing Laws.* Lexington MA: D. C. Health and Company.

LabourNet Germany, "'Klima der Angst': Streit um Betriebsrat bei Aldi Süd in NRW." LabourNet Germany, July 1.

Lamoreaux, Naomi R. 1985. *The Great Merger Movement in American Business, 1895–1904.* Cambridge: Cambridge University Press.

Lapidus, John. 2013. "Why Such a Permissive Attitude Towards Monopolistic Associations? Social Democracy up to the First Swedish Law on Cartels in 1925." *Scandinavian Journal of History* 38, no. 1 (February): 65–88.

Larson, Trine P., Anna Ilsøe, and Emma S. Bach. 2022. "Innovative Union Service and Nonstandard Workers in Denmark." Employment Relations Research Centre. Department of Sociology, University of Copenhagen.

Latham, Frank. 1972. *1872–1972, A Century of Serving Customers: The Story of Montgomery Ward.* Montgomery Ward.

Leach, William. 1993. *Land of Desire: Merchants, Power, and the Rise of a New American Culture.* New York: Vintage.

Lebergott, Stanley. 1976. *The American Economy: Income, Wealth, and Want*. Princeton, NJ: Princeton University Press.

Lebhar, Godfrey M. 1959. *Chain Stores In America: 1859–1959*. New York: Chain Store Publishing Corporation.

Leikin, Steven. 1999. "The Citizen Producer: The Rise and Fall of Working-Class Cooperatives in the United States." In *Consumers against Capitalism? Consumer Cooperation in Europe, North America, and Japan, 1849–1990*, edited by Ellen Furlough and Carl Strikwerda. New York: Rowman and Littlefield.

Leopold, Louis. 1917. "Der Verband Deutscher Waren- und Kaufhäuser." *Zeitschrift für die gesamte Staatswissenschaft* 73, no. 1/2: 1–44.

Letwin, William L.1954. "The English Common Law Concerning Monopolies." *University of Chicago Law Review* 21, no. 3 (Spring): 355–85.

Levinson, Marc. 2011. *The Great A&P and the Struggle for Small Business in America*. New York: Hill and Wang.

———. 2021. "How Did Amazon Grow So Fast? By Thinking Outside the Shopping Box." *Washington Post*, May 7.

———. 2023. "The FTC May Crack Down on Price Discrimination. Will It Matter?" *Washington Post*, May 23. https://www.washingtonpost.com/made-by-history/2023/05/23/federal-trade-commission-price-discrimination/.

Lewis, Joshua, and Edson Severnini. 2017. "Short- and Long-Run Impacts of Rural Electrification: Evidence from the Historical Rollout of the US Power Grid." *IZA DP*, no. 11243.

Lichtenstein, Nelson. 2006. "Wal-Mart: A Template for Twenty-First-Century Capitalism." In *Wal-Mart: The Face of Twenty-First-Century Capitalism*, edited by Nelson Lichtenstein. New York: The New Press.

———. 2009. *The Retail Revolution*. New York: Henry Hold and Company.

Lindblom, C. E. 1977. *Politics and Markets*. New York: Basic Books.

Little, Becky. 2021. "Why the Roaring Twenties Left Many Americans Poorer." History Channel, March 26. https://www.history.com/news/roaring-twenties-labor-great-depression.

LO (Sweden) Landsorganisationen i Sverige. 2022. *Facklig anslutning år 2022*. Stockholm: LO. https://www.lo.se/home/lo/res.nsf/vRes/lo_fakta_1366027478784_facklig_anslutning_2022_pdf/$File/Facklig_anslutning_2022.pdf.

Lock, Christopher. 2022. *Blue Light Special: The History and Memories of Kresge's & Kmart*. Florida: CenterLine Publishing.

Loeb, Walter. 2022. "Why Amazon Is Winning the Consumer Battle over Walmart." *Forbes*, May 2. https://www.forbes.com/sites/walterloeb/2022/05/02/why-amazon-is-winning-the-consumer-battle-over-walmart/?sh=593b41e318b6.

Logemann, Jan. 2008. "Different Paths to Mass Consumption: Consumer Credit in the United State and West Germany during the 1950s and 60s." *Journal of Social History* 41, no. 3: 525–59.

———. 2011. "Americanization through Credit? Consumer Credit in Germany, 1860s–1960s." *Business History Review* 85, no. 3: 529–50.

———. 2012a. *The Development of Consumer Credit in Global Perspective: Business, Regulation, and Culture*. New York: Palgrave Macmillan.

———. 2012b. *Trams or Tailfins? Public and Private Prosperity in Postwar West Germany and the United States*. Chicago: University of Chicago Press.

———. 2019. *Engineered to Sell: European Émigrés and the Making of Consumer Capitalism*. Chicago: University of Chicago Press.

———. 2021. "Dynamiken der Massenkonsumgesellschaft im 20. Jahrhundert, 1918–2008." In *Konsum im 19. und 20. Jahrhundert*, edited by Christian Kleinschmidt and Jan Logemann, 297–335. Berlin: Walter de Gruyter.

Long, Katherine Ann. 2021. "Amazon Push for Lower Prices Could Be Bad for Shoppers Everywhere." *Seattle Times*, November 13. https://www.seattletimes.com/business/amazon/amazon-pushes-for-lower-prices-that-could-be-bad-for-shoppers-everywhere/.

Luchsinger, L. Louise, and Patrick M. Dunne. 1978. "Fair Trade Laws. How Fair?" *Journal of Marketing* 42, no. 1 (January): 50–53.

Lukes, S. 2005. *Power: A Radical View*. 2nd edition. Basingstoke, UK: Palgrave Macmillan.

Lynn, Barry C. 2006. "Breaking the Chain: The Antitrust Case against Wal-Mart." *Harper's*, July.

MacGregor, D. H. 1932. "Review of Price Cutting and Price Maintenance by E.R.A. Seligman and R. A. Love." *Economic Journal* 42, no. 3: 454–58.

MacIntyre, Everette. 1960. "The Role of the Robinson-Patman Act in the Antitrust Scheme of Things-The Perspective of Congress." Section of Antitrust Law, vol. 17, proceedings at the annual meeting. Washington, D.C., August 28–31: 325–42.

MacKinnon, J. B. 2015. "America's Last Ban on Sunday Shopping." *New Yorker*, February 7. https://www.newyorker.com/business/currency/americas-last-ban-on-sunday-shopping.

Macleod, David I. 2009. "Food Prices, Politics, and Policy in the Progressive Era." *Journal of the Gilded Age and Progressive Era* 8, no. 3 (July): 365–406.

Maher, Imelda. 1995. "The New Sunday: Reregulating Sunday Trading Legislation." *Modern Law Review* 58, no. 1: 72–86.

Mandell, Lewis. 1990. *The Credit Card Industry: A History*. Boston: Twayne Publishers.

Manning, Robert D. 2000. *Credit Card Nation: The Consequences of America's Addiction to Credit*. New York: Basic Books.

Martens, Holger. 2015. "Das Genossenschaftsgesetz von 1889 und der Gründungsboom in Hamburg." In *125 Jahre Genossenschaftsgesetz. 100 Jahre Erster Weltkrieg*, edited by Heinrich-Kaufmann Stiftung. https://www.kaufmann-stiftung.de/documents/TB9.pdf.

Martin, Cathie Jo, and Duane Swank. 2012. *The Political Construction of Business Interests*. New York: Cambridge University Press.

Mattioli, Dana. 2020. "Amazon Scooped up Data From Its Own Sellers to Launch Competing Products." *Wall Street Journal*, April 23. https://www.wsj.com/articles/amazon-scooped-up-data-from-its-own-sellers-to-launch-competing-products-11587650015.

Maurer Law [no author]. 1952. "Cooperatives and the Antitrust Laws." *Indiana Law Journal* 27, no. 3 (Spring): Article 5. Digital Repository Maurer Law. https://www.repository.law.indiana.edu/ilj/vol27/iss3/5.

McCraw, Thomas K. 1984. *Prophets of Regulation*. Cambridge, MA: Harvard University Press.

McCurdy, Charles W. 1978. "American Law and the Marketing Structure of the Large Corporation, 1875–1890." *Journal of Economic History* 38, no. 3 (September): 631–49.

McFall, Liz. 2016. "What's in a Name? Provident, the People's Bank and the Regulation of Brand Identity." In *The Routledge Companion to Banking Regulation and Reform*, edited by Ismail Ertürk and Daniela Gabor, 55–73. New York: Routledge.

McGovern, Charles F. 2006. *Sold American: Consumption and Citizenship, 1890–1945*. Chapel Hill: University of North Carolina Press.

———. 1998. "Consumption and Citizenship in the United States, 1900–1940." In *Getting and Spending: European and American Consumer Societies in the Twentieth Century*, edited by Susan Strasser, Charles McGovern, and Mattias Judt. New York: Cambridge.

McInerney, Denis. 1979. "The A&P Case and Its Implications." *Antitrust Law Journal* 48, no. 4: 1676–85.

McKibben, Michael. 1985. "The Resale Price Maintenance Compromise: A Presumption of Illegality." *Vanderbilt Law Review* 38, no. 1 (January).

McQuaid, Kim. 1976. "An American Owenite: Edward A. Filene and the Parameters of Industrial Reform, 1980–1937." *American Journal of Economics and Sociology* 35, no. 1 (January): 77–94.

Mehrotra, Ajay K. 2022. "Experts, Democracy, and the Historical Irony of US Tax Policy." *Modern American History* 5, no. 3 (November): 239–62.

Mercer, Helen. 1995. *Constructing a Competitive Order: The Hidden History of British Antitrust Policies*. New York: Cambridge University Press.

———. 1998. "The Abolition of Resale Price Maintenance in Britain in 1964: A Turning Point for British Manufacturers?" Working paper in economic history no. 39/98, LSE. http://eprints.lse.ac.uk/22406/1/39_98.pdf

———. 2017. "The Making of the Modern Retail Market: Economic Theory, Business Interests and Economic Policy in the Passage of the 1964 Resale Prices Act." *Business History* 59, no. 5: 778–801.

Miller, Lisa. 2023. "Checks and Balances, Veto Exceptionalism, and Constitutional Folk Wisdom: Class and Race Power in American Politics." *Political Research Quarterly* 76, no. 4: 1604–18.

Minimum Resale Prices: Hearings Before a Subcommittee of the House Committee on Interstate and Foreign Commerce, 82nd Cong. 9–12 (1952) (statement of John W. Dargavel, Executive Secretary of the National Association of Retail Druggists).

Mintel. 2021. *Supermarkets-UK-2021*. Mintel Group Ltd.

Mitchell, Stacy. 2003. "German High Court Convicts Wal-Mart of Predatory Pricing." Institute for Local Self-Reliance, February. https://ilsr.org/german-high-court-convicts-walmart-predatory-pricing/.

Mohsin, Maryam. 2023. "10 Amazon Statistics You Need to Know." Oberlo, August 21. https://www.oberlo.com/blog/amazon-statistics.

Moore, Ted. 2017. "Chained Stores: Utah's First Referendum and the Battle Over Local Autonomy." *Utah Historical Quarterly* 85, no. 2 (Spring): 145–61.

Moreton, Bethany. 2006. "It Came from Bentonville: The Agrarian Origins of Wal-Mart Culture." In *Wal-Mart: The Face of Twenty-First-Century Capitalism*, edited by Nelson Lichtenstein. New York: The New Press.

———. 2009. *To Serve God and Wal-Mart: The Making of Christian Free Enterprise*. Cambridge, MA: Harvard University Press.

Morrison, Sara. 2021. "Amazon's Strategy to Squeeze Marketplace Sellers and Maximize Its Own Profits Is Evolving." *Vox*, December 1. https://www.vox.com/recode/22810795/amazon-marketplace-prime-report.

Naidu, Suresh, Eric A. Posner, and Glen Weyl. 2018. "Antitrust Remedies for Labor Market Power." *Harvard Law Review* 132, no. 2 (December): 536–601.

NBC News/*Wall Street Journal* Poll. 2017. Ithaca, NY: Cornell University, Roper Center for Public Opinion Research Web. https://www.wsj.com/public/resources/documents/17312NBCWSJ2017SocialTrendsPoll09062017Release.pdf.

Neary, Lynn. 2012. "Publishers and Booksellers See a 'Predatory' Amazon." NPR, January 23. https://www.npr.org/2012/01/23/145468105/publishers-and-booksellers-see-a-predatory-amazon.

Nembhard, Jessica Gordon. 2017. "African American Consumer Co-operation: History and Global Connections." In *A Global History of Consumer Co-operation since 1850*, edited by Mary Hilson, Silke Neunsinger, and Greg Patmore, 176–200. Boston: Brill.

Neumark, David, Junfu Zhang, and Stephen Ciccarella. 2008. "The Effects of Wal-Mart on Local Labor Markets." *Journal of Urban Economics* 63, no. 2: 405–30. doi.org/10.1016/j.jue.2007.07.004.

Neunsinger, Silke, and Greg Patmore. 2017. "Conclusion: Consumer Co-operatives Past, Present and Future." In *A Global History of Consumer Co-operation since 1850*, edited by Mary Hilson, Silke Neunsinger, and Greg Patmore, 727–51. Boston: Brill.

Niemi, Albert W., Jr. 1980. *US Economic History*. 2nd edition. Chicago: Rand McNally Publishing Co.

Nivola, Peitro S. 1999. *Laws of the Landscape: How Policies Shape Cities in Europe and America.* Washington, DC: The Brookings Institution.

Nonn, Christoph. 1999. "Von Konsumentenprotest zum Konsens: Lebensmittelverbraucher und Agrarpolitik in Deutschland 1900–1955." In *Konsumpolitik: Die Regulierung des privaten Verbrauchs im 20. Jahrhundert,* edited by Hartmut Berghoff, 23–36. Gottingen: Vandenhoeck und Ruprecht.

Nörr, Knut Wolfgang. 1995. "Law and Market Organization: The Historical Experience of Germany from 1900 to the Law against Restraints of Competition (1957)." *Journal of Institutional and Theoretical Economics* 151, no. 1 (March): 5–20.

Nugent, Rolf, and Leon Henderson. 1934. "Installment Selling and the Consumer: A Brief for Regulation." *Annals of the American Academy of Political and Social Science* 173, no. 1 (May): 93–103.

O'Brady, Sean. 2018. "Rethinking Precariousness and Its Evolution: A Four-Country Study of Work in Food Retail." *European Journal of Industrial Relations* 25, no. 5 (December).

———. 2021. "Fighting Precarious Work with Institutional Power: Union Inclusion and Its Limits across Spheres of Action." *British Journal of Industrial Relations* 59, no. 4: 1084–1179.

O'Donovan, Caroline, and Jacob Bogage. 2023. "A Rural Post Office Was Told to Prioritize Amazon Packages. Chaos Ensued." *Washington Post,* November 28.

Orbach, Barak. 2013. "How Antitrust Lost Its Goal." *Fordham Law Review* 81, no. 5: 2253–78.

Oremus, Will. 2013. "The Time Jeff Bezos Went Thermonuclear on Diapers.com." *Slate,* October 10. https://slate.com/technology/2013/10/amazon-book-how-jeff-bezos-went-thermonuclear-on-diapers-com.html.

OSHA (Occupational Safety and Health Administration). 2023. "Federal Safety Inspections at Three Amazon Warehouse Facilities Find Company Exposed Workers to Ergonomic, Struck-by Hazards." January 18. https://www.osha.gov/news/newsreleases/national/01182023.

O'Sullivan, Mary. 2019. "Economic Fetishes of 'Modern' Retail Capitalism." Political Economy Working Paper Series, no. 2/2019. University of Geneva. http://archive-ouverte.unige.ch/unige: 129348.

Otte, Jedidajah. 2020. "England Could Suspend Sunday Trading Laws in Push to Boost Economy." *Guardian,* June 6. https://www.theguardian.com/world/2020/jun/06/england-could-suspend-sunday-trading-laws-in-push-to-boost-economy.

Palamountain, Joseph. 1955. *The Politics of Distribution.* Cambridge, MA: Harvard University Press.

Palmer, Annie. 2020a. "How Amazon Managed the Coronavirus Crisis and Came Out Stronger." CNBC, September 29. https://www.cnbc.com/2020/09/29/how-amazon-managed-the-coronavirus-crisis-and-came-out-stronger.html.

———. 2020b. "Seattle Passes Payroll Tax Targeting Amazon and Other Big Businesses." CNBC, July 7. https://www.cnbc.com/2020/07/07/seattle-passes-payroll-tax-targeting-amazon-and-other-big-businesses.html.

———. 2021a. "Amazon Accused of Copying Camera Gear Maker's Top-Selling Item." CNBC, March 4. https://www.cnbc.com/2021/03/04/amazon-accused-of-copying-camera-gearmaker-peak-designs-top-selling-item-.html.

———. 2021b. "Amazon Is Piling Ads into Search Results and Top Consumer Brands Are Paying up for Prominent Placement." CNBC, September 19. https://www.cnbc.com/2021/09/19/amazon-piles-ads-into-search-results-as-big-brands-pay-for-placement.html.

Panel Discussion. 1979. Panel Discussion [of Robinson-Patman in the Wake of A&P Decision]. *Antitrust Law Journal* 48, no. 4: 1711–18.

Parcel Post: Hearing Before the House Committee on the Post Office and Post Roads, 61st Cong. 163–76 (1910) (statement of E. W. Bloomingdale).

———. 61st Cong. 178–86 (1910) (statement of W. P. Bogardus).

————. 61st Cong. 323–43 (1910) (statement of James Cowles, Secretary-Treasury of the Postal Progress League).

————. 61st Cong. 247–61 (1910) (statement of George Green, Secretary of the Illinois Retail Merchants' Association).

————. 61st Cong. 274–86 (1910) (statement of George Maxwell).

————. 61st Cong. 187–218 (1910) (statement of S. R. Miles).

————. 61st Cong. 299–306 (1910) (statement of Willard Richardson, National Association of Retail Druggists).

————. 61st Cong. 82–119 (1910) (statement of A. C. Shuford, Secretary of the Farmers' Union).

————. 61st Cong. 25–54 (1910) (statement of John Stahl, Legislative Agent of the Farmers' National Congress).

————. 61st Cong. 233–47 (1910) (statement of Charles Underhill, Retail Hardware Merchants of Massachusetts).

Parcel Post: Hearing Before the House Committee on the Post Office and Post Roads, 62nd Cong. 698–702 (1911) (statement of Allen Clark).

————. 62nd Cong. 589–613 (1911) (statement of M. L. Corey, Secretary of the National Retail Hardware Association).

————. 62nd Cong. 780–85 (1911) (statement of Mrs. Charles Craigie, President of the Brooklyn Public Library Association).

————. 62nd Cong. 814–22 (1911) (statement of W. T. Creasy, Master State Grange of Pennsylvania).

————. 62nd Cong. 756–59 (1911) (statement of Florence Etheridge).

————. 62nd Cong. 404–42 (1911) (statement of John Green, Secretary of the National Association of Retail Grocers).

————. 62nd Cong. 753–55 (1911) (statement of William Gude, Society of American Florists and Ornamental Horticulturists).

————. 62nd Cong. 851–75 (1911) (statement of George Hampton, Secretary of the Farmers' National Committee on Postal Reform and the Postal Express Federation).

————. 62nd Cong. 79–80 (1911) (statement of Rep. Francis B. Harrison).

————. 62nd Cong. 365–71 (1911) (statement of Edward Moon).

————. 62nd Cong. 541–88 (1911) (statement of E. B. Moon, Secretary of the American League of Associations).

————. 62nd Cong. 3–9 (1911) (statement of Rep. William Sulzer).

Parcel Post: Hearings Before the Subcommittee on Parcel Post of the Senate Committee on Post Offices and Post Roads, 62nd Cong. 1238–1252 (1912) (statement of Senator Obadiah Gardner).

————. 62nd Cong. 1161–200 (1912) (statement of O. B. George, Adams and Southern Express Cos.).

————. 62nd Cong. 1214–32 (1912) (statement of William Johnson, United States Express Co.).

Parliamentary Debates, Commons, 5th series, vol. 319, 1205–64 (1937). https://api.parliament.uk /historic-hansard/commons/1937/jan/29/shops-retail-trading-safeguards-bill.

Paster, Thomas. 2015. "Bringing Power Back. A Review of the Literature on the Role of Business in Welfare State Politics." MPIfG discussion paper 15/3, Max-Planck-Institut für Gesellschaftsforschung.

Paterson, Tony. 2004. "Workers 'Grossly Abused' by German Supermarket Giant." December 11. https://www.independent.co.uk/news/world/europe/workers-grossly-abused-by-german -supermarket-giant-683349.html.

Patmore, Greg. 2017. "Fighting Monopoly and Enhancing Democracy." In *A Global History of Consumer Co-operation since 1850*, edited by Mary Hilson, Silke Neunsinger, and Greg Patmore, 507–26. Boston: Brill.

Paul, Sanjukta. 2016. "The Enduring Ambiguities of Antitrust Liability for Worker Collective Action." *Loyola University Chicago Law Journal* 47: 969–1048.

———. 2019. "Fissuring and the Firm Exception," *Law and Contemporary Problems* 82, no. 3: 65–88.

———. 2020a. "Antitrust As Allocator of Coordination Rights." *UCLA Law Review* 67, no. 2: 2020.

———. 2020b. "Coordination beyond the Corporation with Sanjukta Paul." Interview by Scott Ferguson, Maximillian Seijo, and William Saas. *Monthly Review*. https://mronline.org/2020/05/18/coordination-beyond-the-corporation-with-sanjukta-paul/.

———. 2024. Forthcoming. *Solidarity in the Shadow of Antitrust*. New York: Cambridge University Press.

Payne, Jonathan, Caroline Lloyd, and Secki P. Jose. 2023. "They Tell Us after They've Decided Things: A Cross-country Analysis of Unions and Digitalization in Retail." *Industrial Relations* 54: 3–19.

Peinert, Erik. 2020. "Monopoly Politics: Price Competition and Learning in the Evolution of Policy Regimes." PhD diss., Brown University. https://repository.library.brown.edu/studio/item/bdr:26tvrfdt/.

———. 2023. "Monopoly Politics: Price Competition, Learning, and the Evolution of Policy Regimes." *World Politics* 75, no. 3: 566–607.

Peinert, Erik, and Katherine Van Dyck. 2022. "The Needless Desertion of Robinson-Patman." *ProMarket*, October. https://www.promarket.org/2022/10/10/the-needless-desertion-of-robinson-patman/?mc_cid=eeb84540a0&mc_eid=da50b484da.

Peel, Roy V. 1937. "Consumers' Coöperation in the Scandinavian Countries." *Annals of the American Academy of Political and Social Science* 191 (May): 165–76.

Pelletier, Harold. 1969. "Review of Brown's Franchising: Trap for the Trusting." *Southwestern Law Journal* 23, no. 3: 602–8.

Peralta, Denis, and Man-Keun Kim. 2019. "Big-Box Retailers, Retail Employment, and Wages in the US." *Review of Urban and Regional Development Studies* 31, no. 1–2: 102–17. doi.org/10.1111/rurd.12092.

Petrovic, Misha, and Gary G. Hamilton. 2006. "Making Global Markets: Wal-Mart and Its Suppliers." In *Wal-Mart: The Face of Twenty-First-Century Capitalism*, edited by Nelson Lichtenstein. New York: The New Press.

Pew Research Center. 2005. "Wal-Mart a Good Place to Shop But Some Critics Too." https://www.pewresearch.org/politics/2005/12/15/wal-mart-a-good-place-to-shop-but-some-critics-too/.

Peyer, Sebastian. 2010. "Myths and Untold Stores: Private Antitrust Enforcement in Germany." ESRC Center for Competition Policy, working paper 10–12.

Phillips Sawyer, Laura. 2015. "The US Experiment with Fair Trade Laws: State Police Powers, Federal Antitrust, and the Politics of 'Fairness,' 1890–1938." Working paper 16–060.

———. 2018. *American Fair Trade: Proprietary Capitalism, Corporatism, and the "New Competition," 1890–1940*. New York: Cambridge University Press.

Philippon, Thomas. 2019. *The Great Reversal: How America Gave Up on Free Markets*. Cambridge, MA: Belknap Press.

Pisek, Jaroslav. 2017. "How Strong Are the Pharmacy Chains within the EU?" International Scientific Congress, November 9. http://ocs.ef.jcu.cz/index.php/inproforum/INP2017/paper/viewFile/943/595.

Pitofsky, Robert, and Kenneth W. Dam. 1968. "Is the Colgate Doctrine Dead?" *Antitrust Law Journal* 37, no. 4 (August): 772–88.

Plummer, Wilbur. 1927. "Social and Economic Consequences of Buying on the Instalment plan." *Annals of the American Academy of Political and Social Science* 129 (January): 1–57.

———. 1930. *National Retail Credit Survey*. Washington, DC: US Government Printing Office.

Pollman, Elizabeth, and Jordan M. Barry. 2017. "Regulatory Entrepreneurship." *Southern California Law Review* 90: 383–448.

Pope, Daniel. 1983. *The Making of Modern Advertising*. New York: Basic Books.

Posner, Eric. 2021. *How Antitrust Failed Workers.* New York: Oxford University Press.

Posner, Richard. A. 1970. "A Statistical Study of Antitrust Enforcement." *Journal of Law and Economics* 13, no. 2: 365–420.

Postel, Charles. 2007. *The Populist Vision.* Oxford: Oxford University Press.

Power, Garrett. 1989. "The Advent of Zoning." *Planning Perspectives* 4 (1989): 1–13.

Prasad, Monica. 2012. *The Land of Too Much: American Abundance and the Paradox of Poverty.* Cambridge, MA: Harvard University Press.

Premack, Rachel. 2020. "The Postal Service Is Subsidizing Jeff Bezos' Quest to Turn Amazon into a Delivery Machine . . ." *Business Insider*, May 6. https://www.businessinsider.com/amazon -usps-rural-packages-deliveries-2020-5.

Price Discrimination: Hearings Before a Subcommittee of the Committee of the Judiciary, United States Senate. 74th Cong., 44–49 (1936) (statement of Charles F. Adams).

———. 61–75 (1936) (statement of Charles Wesley Dunn).

———. 52–54 (1936) (statement of Carl Jungbluth).

———. 41–44 (1936) (statement of Irving Klein).

———. 113–24 (1936) (statement of Benjamin C. Marsh).

———. 90–92 (1936) (statement of Virginia Huntley Morrison).

———. 124–27 (1936) (statement of Louis Rose).

———. 29–32 (1936) (statement of Wheeler Sammons).

———. 93–94 (1936) (statement of George H. Thompson).

Price Regulation for Trade-Marked Articles: Hearings Before the Committee on Interstate and Foreign Commerce of the House of Representatives, 69th Cong. 13–39 (1926) (statement of W.H.C. Clarke, American Fair Trade League).

———. 69th Cong. 3–13 (1926) (statement of Rep. Clyde Kelly).

———. 74th Cong., 1st sess. 29–127 (1936).

———. 84th Cong., 1st sess. 372–75 (1955).

Priest, George L. 2014. "Bork's Strategy and the Influence of the Chicago School on Modern Antitrust Law." *Journal of Law and Economics* 57: S3 (August): S1–S17.

Purvis, Martin. 1992. "Co-operative retailing in Britain." In *The Evolution of Retail Systems, c. 1800–1914*, edited by John Benson and Gareth Shaw, 107–34. London: Leicester University Press.

Rahman, K. Sabeel, and Kathleen Thelen. 2019. "The Rise of the Platform Business Model and the Transformation of Twenty-First Century Capitalism." *Politics and Society* 47, no. 2 (June): 177–204.

———. 2022. "The Role of the Law in the American Political Economy." In *American Political Economy*, edited by Jacob S. Hacker, Alexander Hertel-Fernandez, Paul Pierson, and Kathleen Thelen. New York: Cambridge University Press, 2022.

Rapp, Nicolas. 2021. "Just How Massive Amazon Has Grown during the Pandemic, in 8 Charts." *Fortune*, October 18. https://fortune.com/2021/10/18/amazon-massive-growth-covid -pandemic-8-charts/.

Rasmussen, S., J. Nätti, T. P. Larsen, A. Ilsøe, and A. H. Garde. 2019. "Nonstandard Employment in the Nordics—Toward Precarious Work?" *Nordic Journal of Working Life Studies* 9, no. S6. doi.org/10.18291/njwls.v9iS6.114689.

Reagin, Nancy. 1998. "Comparing Apples and Oranges: Housewives and the Politics of Consumption in Interwar Germany." In *Getting and Spending: European and American Consumer Societies in the Twentieth Century*, edited by Susan Strasser, Charles McGovern, and Matthias Judt, 241–62. New York: Cambridge University Press.

Redman, Russel. 2021. "Walmart, CVS, Walgreens Participate in COVID-19 Vaccine PSAs." *Supermarket News*, March 18. https://www.supermarketnews.com/issues-trends/walmart -cvs-walgreens-participate-covid-19-vaccine-psas.

Rees, J. Morgan. 1922. "Trusts in British Industry 1914–21: A Study of Recent Developments in Business Organization." *Journal of the Royal Statistical Society* 86, no. 2 (March): 251–54.

Regulation of Prices: Hearings Before the Committee on Interstate and Foreign Commerce of the House of Representatives, 64th Cong. 79–90 (1917) (statement of J. M. Barnes, Head of Credit at Marshall Field & Co.).

———. 64th Cong. 114–59 (1917) (statement of Percy S. Straus, Vice President of R. H. Macy & Co.).

———. 64th Cong. 4–78 (1917) (statement of Edmond E. Wise).

———. 64th Cong. 283–87 (1917) (statement of Mary Wood, of the New York State Federation of Women's Clubs).

Reich, Adam, and Peter Bearman. 2020. *Working for Respect: Community and Conflict at Walmart*. New York: Columbia University Press.

Richter, Klaus. 2007. *Die Wirkungsgeschichte des deutschen Kartellrechts vor 1914*. Tübingen: Mohr Siebeck.

Robbins, Ira P. "The Obsolescence of Blue Laws in the 21st Century." *Stanford Law and Policy Review* 33: 289–334.

Roberts, Bryan, and Natalie Berg. 2012. *Walmart: Key Insights and Practical Lessons from the World's Largest Retailer*. London: Kogan Page.

Robinson, Glen O. 1994. "Explaining Vertical Agreements: The Colgate Puzzle and Antitrust Method." *Virginia Law Review* 80, no. 3 (April): 577–623.

Rodgers, Daniel T. 1998. *Atlantic Crossings: Social Politics in a Progressive Age*. Cambridge, MA: Harvard University Press.

Rogers, Brishen. 2019. *Testimony before the House Education and Labor Committee Hearing on the Future of Work*. https://rooseveltinstitute.org/publications/testimony-before-the-house-education-and-labor-committee-hearing-on-the-future-of-work/.

———. 2023. *Data and Democracy at Work: Advanced Information Technologies, Labor Law and the New Working Class*. Cambridge, MA: MIT Press.

Rogowski, Ronald, and Mark Andreas Kayser. 2002. "Majoritarian Elector Systems and Consumer Power: Price-Level Evidence from the OECD Countries." *American Journal of Political Science* 46, no. 3: 526–39.

Rose, Michel, and Emile Picy. 2015. "France Passes Law to Open Up Sunday Shopping." Reuters, February 14. https://www.reuters.com/article/us-france-sunday-idUSKBN0LI0U520150214/.

Rose, Stanley D. 1949. "Resale Price Maintenance." *Vanderbilt Law Review* 3, no. 24. December.

Rosen, Jeffrey. 2010. "Why Brandeis Matters." Review of Urofsky's Biography. *New Republic*, June 29.

Rosenberg, Stephen D. 2021. *Time for Things: Labor, Leisure, and the Rise of Mass Consumption*. Cambridge, MA: Harvard University Press.

Rosenthal, Marie. 2023. "New Report: Pharmacists Providing Vaccinations More Often than Physicians." *Pharmacy Practice News*, February 13. https://www.pharmacypracticenews.com/Covid-19/Article/02-23/New-Report-Pharmacists-Providing-Vaccinations-More-Often-Than-Physicians/69473.

Ross, Martha, and Nichole Bateman. 2019. "Meet the Low-Wage Workforce." Metropolitan Policy Program at Brookings. https://www.brookings.edu/research/meet-the-low-wage-workforce/.

Rothstein, Richard. 2017. *The Color of Law*. New York: Norton and Co.

Rowe, Frederick M. 1962. *Price Discrimination under the Robinson-Patman Act*. Boston: Little, Brown and Company.

———. 1980. "Political Objectives and Economic Effects of the Robinson-Patman Act: A Conspicuous US Antitrust Failure." *Zeitschrift für die gesamte Staatswissenschaft* 136, no. 3: 499–509.

Roy, William G. 1997. *Socializing Capital: The Rise of the Large Industrial Corporation in America*. Princeton NJ: Princeton University Press.

Rühling, Michael. 2004. *Das Ladenschlussgesetz vom 28. November 1956: Vorgeschichte, Entstehung des Gesetzes und weitere Entwicklung.* Frankfurt am Main: Peter Lang.

Ryan, Andrea, Gunnar Trumbull, and Peter Tufano. 2011. "A Brief Postwar History of US Consumer Finance." *Business History Review* 85, no. 3 (Autumn): 461–98.

Ryant, Carl G. 1973. "The South and the Movement against Chain Stores." *Journal of Southern History* 39, no. 2 (May): 207–22.

Saker, Victoria A. 1992. "Creating an Agricultural Trust: Law and Cooperation in California, 1898–1922." *Law and History Review* 10, no. 1 (Spring): 93–129.

Samuels, Alana. 2018. "How Amazon Helped Kill a Seattle Tax on Business." *The Atlantic*, June 13. https://www.theatlantic.com/technology/archive/2018/06/how-amazon-helped-kill-a-seattle-tax-on-business/562736/.

Sandel, Michael J. 1996. *Democracy's Discontent: America in Search of a Public Philosophy.* Cambridge, MA: Belknap Press.

Sanders, Elizabeth. 1986. "Industrial Concentration, Sectional Competition, and Antitrust Politics in America, 1880–1980." *Studies in American Political Development* 1 (Spring): 142–214.

———. 1999. *Roots of Reform: Farmers, Workers, and the American State, 1877–1917.* Chicago: University of Chicago Press.

Schneiberg, Marc. 2011. "Toward an Organizationally Diverse American Capitalism? Cooperative, Mutual, and Local, State-Owned Enterprise." *Seattle University Law Review* 34: 1409–34.

———. 2013. "Movements as Political Conditions for Diffusion: Anti-Corporate Movements and the Spread of Cooperative Forms in American Capitalism." *Organization Studies* 34, no. 5–6: 653–82.

Schneiberg, Marc, Marissa King, and Thomas Smith. 2008. "Social Movements and Organizational Form: Cooperative Alternatives to Corporations in the American Insurance, Dairy, and Grain Industries." *American Sociological Review* 73, no. 4: 635–67.

Schor, Juliet B. 1992. *The Overworked American: The Unexpected Decline of Leisure.* New York: Basic Books.

Schragger, Richard C. 2005. "The Anti-Chain Store Movement, Socialist Ideology, and the Remnants of the Progressive Constitution, 1920–1940." *Iowa Law Review* 90, no. 3: 1011–94.

———. 2016. *City Power: Urban Governance in a Global Age.* Oxford: Oxford University Press.

Schweikert, Robert. n.d. *Die Sparkassen der Konsumgenossenschaften.* Hamburg: Verlag Deutscher Konsumvereine.

Schweitzer, Arthur. 1946. "Big Business and Private Property under the Nazis." *Journal of Business of the University of Chicago* 19, no. 2 (April): 99–126.

Scott, Robert E. 2015. "A Conservative Estimate of 'The Wal-Mart Effect,'" Economic Policy Institute, December 9. https://www.epi.org/publication/the-wal-mart-effect/.

Scroop, Daniel. 2007. "'Where Does the Local Have an End and the Nonlocal a Beginning?' The Anti-Chain Store Movement, Localism, and National Identity." In *Consuming Visions: New Essays on the Politics of Consumption in Modern America*, edited by Daniel Scroop. Newcastle: Cambridge Scholars Publishing.

———. 2008. "The Anti-Chain Store Movement and the Politics of Consumption." *American Quarterly* 60, no. 4: 925–49.

Sears Catalogue. 1908. Northfield, IL: DBI Books, Inc.

"Sears' Sales Set a High in Month." 1959. *New York Times*, October 7.

Secchi, Corrado. 2017. "Affluence and Decline: Consumer Cooperatives in Postwar Britain." In *A Global History of Consumer Co-operation since 1850*, edited by Mary Hilson, Silke Neunsinger, and Greg Patmore, 527–49. Boston: Brill.

Seely, Elizabeth, and Surya Singh. 2021. "Competition, Consolidation, and Evolution in the Pharmacy Market." Commonwealth Fund, August 12. https://www.commonwealthfund .org/publications/issue-briefs/2021/aug/competition-consolidation-evolution-pharmacy -market.

Seligman, Edwin. 1927. *The Economics of Installment Selling: A Study in Consumers' Credit*. New York: Harper and Brothers.

Seligman E.R.A., and R. A. Love. 1932. *Price Cutting and Price Maintenance*. New York: Harper and Brothers.

Senate Report. 1956. *Report of the Select Committee on Small Business on a Study of Fair Trade, Based on a Survey of Manufacturers and Retailers*. US Senate. US Congressional Serial Set (1956): I-28. Washington, DC: US Government Printing Office.

Shamir, Ronen. 1995. *Managing Legal Uncertainty: Elite Lawyers in the New Deal*. Durham, NC: Duke University Press.

Shaw, Gareth, Andrew Alexander, John Benson, and Deborah Hodson. 2000. "The Evolving Culture of Retailers Regulation and the Failure of the 'Balfour Bill' in Interwar Britain." *Environment and Planning A* 32: 1977–89.

Shiller, Benjamin Reed. 2020. "Approximating Purchase Propensities and Reservation Prices from Broad Consumer Tracking." *International Economic Review* 61, no. 2: 847–70.

Shonfield, Andrew. 1965. *Modern Capitalism: The Changing Balance of Public and Private Power*. Oxford: Oxford University Press.

Short, Nicholas. 2022. "Antitrust Reform in Political Perspective: A Constructive Critique for the Neo-Brandeisians." Unpublished manuscript, Harvard University. https://nick-short.com/wp -content/uploads/2022/08/antitrust-reform-in-political-perspective.pdf.

Sklar, Kathryn Kish. 1995. *Florence Kelley and the Nation's Work: The Rise of Women's Political Culture, 1830–1900*. New Haven, CT: Yale University Press.

———. 1998. "The Consumers' White Label Campaign of the National Consumers' League 1898–1918." In *Getting and Spending: European and American Consumer Societies in the Twentieth Century*, edited by Susan Strasser, Charles McGovern, and Mattias Judt. NY: Cambridge.

Sklar, Martin J. 1988. *The Corporate Reconstruction of American Capitalism, 1890–1916*. New York: Cambridge University Press.

Skowronek, Stephen. 1982. *Building a New American State: The Expansion of National Administrative Capacities, 1877–1920*. New York: Cambridge University Press.

Small Business and the Robinson-Patman Act: Hearings Before the Special Subcommittee on Small Business and the Robinson-Patman Act of the House Select Committee on Small Business, 91st Cong., 1st sess. 145–93 (1969).

Šmejkal, Vaclav. 2015. "Competition Law and the Social Market Economy Goal of the EU." *International Comparative Jurisprudence* 1, no. 1: 33–43.

SoRelle, Mallory E. 2020. *Democracy Declined: The Failed Politics of Consumer Financial Protection*. Chicago: University of Chicago Press.

———. 2023. "Privatizing Financial Protection: Regulatory Feedback in the Credit Welfare State." *American Political Science Review* 117, no. 3: 985–1003.

Sparks, Cory Lewis. 2000. "Locally Owned and Operated: Opposition to Chain Stores, 1925–1940." PhD diss., Louisiana State University.

Spellman, Susan. 2016. *Cornering the Market: Independent Grocers and Innovation in Small Business*. Oxford: Oxford University Press.

Spicer, Jason. 2022. *Co-operative Enterprise in Comparative Perspective: Exceptionally Un-American?* Oxford: Oxford University Press.

Spiekermann, Uwe. 1994. *Warenhaussteuer in Deutschland: Mittelstandsbewegung, Kaptalismus, und Rechtsstaat im späten Kaiserreich*. Frankfurt/Main: Peter Lang.

———. 2004. "Freier Konsum und Soziale Verantwortung: Zur Geschichte des Ladenschlusses." *Deutschland im 19. und 20. Jahrhundert. Zeitschrift für Unternehmensgeschichte* 49, no. 1: 26–44.

Spillman, Lyn 2012. *Solidarity in Strategy*. Chicago: University of Chicago Press.

Stechow, Henning von. 2002. *Das Gesetz zur Bekämpfung des unlauteren Wettbewerbs von 27. Mai 1896*. Berlin: Duncker and Humblot.

Steinbaum, Marshall. 2018. "A Missing Link: The Role of Antitrust Law in Rectifying Employer Power in Our High-Profit, Low-Wage Economy." Roosevelt Institute, April. https://roose veltinstitute.org/publications/missing-link-antitrust-law-rectifying-employer-power-high -profit-low-wage-economy/.

———. 2019. "Antitrust, the Gig Economy and Labor Market Power." *Law and Contemporary Problems* 82, no. 3: 45–64.

Stenovec, Timothy. 2014. "The Time Amazon Stabbed a German Knife Maker in the Back." *Huffington Post*, June 16. https://www.huffpost.com/entry/amazon-hachette-knife-wusthof_n _5492582.

Stoller, Matt. 2019. *Goliath: The 100-Year War between Monopoly Power and Democracy*. New York: Simon and Schuster.

Stone, Brad. 2013. *The Everything Store: Jeff Bezos and the Age of Amazon*. New York: Little, Brown and Company.

———. 2021. *Amazon Unbound: Jeff Bezos and the Invention of a Global Empire*. New York: Simon and Schuster.

Stone, Lyman. 2018. "Why We Need 'Blue Laws,' the Religious Tradition That Sanctifies Life Outside of Work." *Vox*, October 2. https://www.vox.com/the-big-idea/2018/10/2/17925828 /what-were-blue-laws-labor-unions.

Storrs, Landon. 2000. *Civilizing Capitalism: The National Consumers' League, Women's Activism, and Labor Standards in the New Deal Era*. Chapel Hill: University of North Carolina Press.

Strasser, Susan. 1989. *Satisfaction Guaranteed: The Making of the American Mass Market*. New York: Pantheon Books.

———. 2006. "Woolworth to Wal-Mart: Mass Merchandising and the Changing Culture of Consumption." In *Wal-Mart: The Face of Twenty-First-Century Capitalism*, edited by Nelson Lichtenstein. New York: The New Press.

Strasser, Susan, Charles McGovern, and Matthias Judt, eds. 1998. *Getting and Spending: European and American Consumer Societies in the Twentieth Century*. New York: Cambridge University Press.

Streeck, Wolfgang. 1991. "On the Institutional Conditions of Diversified Quality Production." In *Beyond Keynesianism: The Socio-Economics of Production and Full Employment*, edited by Egon Matzner and Wolfgang Streeck, 21–61. Aldershot: Edward Elgar.

Swenson, Peter. 2002. *Capitalists against Markets*. New York: Oxford University Press.

Tabuchi, Hiroko. 2014. "Walmart to End Health Coverage for 30,000 Part-Time Workers." *New York Times*, October 7. https://www.healthcare-now.org/blog/wal-mart-to-end-health -insurance-for-part-time-employees/.

Tagiuri, Giacomo. 2021. "Regulating Market Entry: EU Law and the Protection of Small Independent Shops." Paper presented at SASE Conference, virtual, July 5.

Tedlow, Richard S. 1976. "The National Association of Manufacturers and Public Relations during the New Deal." *Business History Review* 50, no. 1 (Spring): 25–45.

———. 1981. "From Competitor to Consumer: The Changing Focus of Federal Regulation of Advertising, 1914–1938." *Business History Review* 55, no. 1 (Spring): 35–58.

Teupe, Sebastian. 2016. *Die Schaffung eines Marktes: Preispolitik, Wettbewerb, und Fernsehgeräte in der BRD und den USA, 1945–1985*. Berlin: De Gruyter Oldenbourg.

———. 2019. "Breaking the Rules: Schumpeterian Entrepreneurship and Legal Institutional Change in the Case of 'Blue Laws,' 1950s–1980s." *Management and Organizational History* 14, no. 4: 382–407.

Thelen, David P. 1972. *The New Citizenship: Origins of Progressivism in Wisconsin, 1885–1900.* Columbia: University of Missouri Press.

Thelen, Kathleen. 2004. *How Institutions Evolve: The Political Economy of Skills in Germany, Britain, the United States and Japan.* New York: Cambridge University Press.

———. 2018. "Regulating Uber: The Politics of the Platform Economy in Europe and the United States." *Perspectives on Politics* 16, no. 4 (December).

———. 2019. "The American Precariat: US Capitalism in Comparative Perspective." *Perspectives on Politics* 17, no. 1 (March).

———. 2020. "Employer Organization and the Law: American Exceptionalism in Comparative Perspective." *Law and Contemporary Problems* 83, no. 2: 23–48.

Thelen, Kathleen, and Christa van Wijnbergen. 2003. "The Paradox of Globalization: Labor Relations in Germany and Beyond." *Comparative Political Studies* 36, no. 8 (October): 859–80.

Theriault, Sean M. 2003. "Patronage, the Pendleton Act, and the Power of the People." *Journal of Politics* 65, no. 1: 50–68.

Thurston, Chloe N. 2018. *At the Boundaries of Homeownership: Credit, Discrimination, and the American State.* New York: Cambridge University Press.

To Amend the Clayton Act: Hearing Before the House Committee on the Judiciary, 74th Cong., 1st sess., 124–28 (1935) (statement of G.A. Boger).

———. 147–64 (1935) (statement of William H. Eden).

———.164–66 (1935) (statement of Robert C. Hibben).

———. 118–124 (1935) (statement of Karl C. King).

———. 173–93 (1935) (statement of B. D. Silliman).

———. 114–18 (1935) (statement of Gerard M. Ungaro).

———. 89–90 (1935) (statement of Robert E. Wood).

———. 236–38 (1935) (letter submitted by National Association of Manufacturers Economist Noel Sargent).

To Amend the Clayton Act: Hearing Before a Subcommittee on the House Committee on the Judiciary, 74th Cong., 2nd sess. 429–46 (1936) (statement of Charles Wesley Dunn).

Tobriner, Matthew O. 1928. "The Constitutionality of Cooperative Marketing Statutes." *California Law Review* 17, no. 1 (November): 19–34.

Tomlin, W. Dalton. 1964. "Private Recovery under the Robinson-Patman Act: An Analysis and a Suggestion." *Texas Law Review* 43, no. 2 (December): 168–93.

Tornau, Joachim. 2016. "Einzelhandel schert aus." *Mitbestimmung* 4 (August): 2016.

Trolle, Ulf af. "Sweden." In *Resale Price Maintenance*, edited by B. S. Yamey. Chicago: Aldine Publishing Company.

Trumbull, Gunnar. 2006a. *Consumer Capitalism: Politics, Product Markets, and Firm Strategy in France and Germany.* Ithaca, NY: Cornell University Press.

———. 2006b. "National Varieties of Consumerism." *Jahrbuch für Wirtschaftsgeschichte* 42, no. 1: 77–93.

———. 2012a. "Banking on Consumer Credit: Explaining Patterns of Household Borrowing in the United States and France." In *The Development of Consumer Credit in Global Perspective: Business, Regulation, and Culture*, edited by Jan Logemann. New York: Palgrave Macmillan.

———. 2012b. *Strength in Numbers: The Political Power of Weak Interests.* Cambridge, MA: Harvard University Press.

———. 2014. *Consumer Lending in France and America: Credit and Welfare.* New York: Cambridge University Press.

Twyman, Robert W. 1954. *History of Marshall Field and Co., 1852–1906*. Philadelphia: University of Pennsylvania Press.

US Department of Agriculture (USDA). 2002. *Antitrust Status of Farmer Cooperatives: The Story of the Capper-Volstead Act*. Washington, DC: Rural Business Cooperative Service.

Vaheesan, Sandeep. 2020. "Privileging Consolidation and Proscribing Cooperation: The Perversity of Contemporary Antitrust Law." *Journal of Law and Political Economy* 1, no. 1.

Vaheesan, Sandeep, and Frank Pasquale. 2018. "The Politics of Professionalism: Reappraising Occupational Licensure and Competition Policy." *Annual Review of Law and Social Science* 14: 309–27.

Vance, Sandra, and Roy Scott. 1994. *Wal-Mart: A History of Sam Walton's Retail Phenomenon*. New York: Twayne Publishers.

Vose, Clement. 1957. "The National Consumers' League and the Brandeis Brief." *Midwest Journal of Political Science* 1, no. 3–4 (November): 267–90.

Waldman, Adelle. 2024. "Not Just Wages: Retailers Are Mistreating Workers in a More Insidious Way." *New York Times*, February 19.

Wartzman, Rick. 2022. "A Brief History of the Attempts to Unionize Walmart." LitHub https://lithub.com/a-brief-history-of-the-attempts-to-unionize-walmart/.

Watson, Bartholomew Clark. 2011. "Nation of Retailers: The Comparative Political Economy of Retail Trade." PhD diss., University of California, Berkeley.

Weber Waller, Spencer. 2004. "The Antitrust Legacy of Thurman Arnold." *St. Johns' Law Review* 78: 569–613.

Webster, Anthony. 2012. "Building the Wholesale: The Development of the English CWS and British Co-operative Business, 1863–1890." *Business History* 54, no. 6 (October): 883–904.

Webster, Anthony, John F. Wilson, and Rachael Vorberg-Rugh. 2017. "Going Global: The Rise of the CWS as an International Commercial and Political Actor, 1863–1850." In *A Global History of Consumer Co-operation since 1850*, edited by Mary Hilson, Silke Neunsinger, and Greg Patmore, 559–83. Boston: Brill.

Weigel, Moira. 2022. "What You Don't Know about Amazon." *New York Times*, April 21. https://www.nytimes.com/2022/04/21/opinion/amazon-product-liability.html.

———. 2023. *Amazon's Trickle-Down Monopoly: Third Party Sellers and the Transformation of Small Businesses*. Data and Society Research Institute. https://datasociety.net/library/amazons-trickle-down-monopoly/.

Weil, David. 2014. *The Fissured Workplace*. Cambridge, MA: Harvard University Press.

Weil, Gordon L. 1977. *Sears, Roebuck, USA: The Great American Catalog Store and How it Grew*. New York: Stein and Day.

Wein, Josef. 1968. *Die Verbandsbildung im Einzelhandel*. Berlin: Duncker and Humblot.

Weise, Karen. 2021. "Amazon's Profit Soars 220 Percent as Pandemic Drives Shopping Online." *New York Times*. April 29. https://www.nytimes.com/2021/04/29/technology/amazons-profits-triple.html.

Weise, Karen, and Michael Corkery, 2021. "People Now Spend More at Amazon than at Walmart." *New York Times*, August 17.

Weiss, E. B. 1962. *Never on Sunday?* New York: Doyle Dane Bernbach, Inc.

Weston, Glen E. 1963. "Fair Trade, Alias 'Quality Stabilization': Status, Problems and Prospects." Section of Antitrust Law, vol. 22. Proceedings at the Spring Meeting. Washington D.C., April 4 and 5: 76–105. American Bar Association.

White, Richard. 2011. *Railroaded: The Transcontinentals and the Making of Modern America*. New York: Norton.

Whitman, James Q. 2007. "Consumerism versus Producerism: A Study in Comparative Law." *Yale Law Journal* 117, no. 3: 340–406.

Wiedemann, Andreas. 2021. *Indebted Societies: Credit and Welfare in Rich Democracies.* New York: Cambridge University Press.

Wilcox, Claire. 1971. *Public Policies toward Business.* 4th ed. R. D. Irwin.

Willingham, Caius Z., and Olugbenga Ajilore. 2019. *The Modern Company Town.* Washington, DC: Center for American Progress.

Wilmers, Nathan. 2018. "Wage Stagnation and Buyer Power: How Buyer-Supplier Relations Affect US Workers' Wages, 1978 to 2014." *American Sociological Review* 83, no. 2: 213–42.

Wilson, John, Anthony Webster, and Rachael Vorgerg-Rugh. 2013. "The Co-operative Movement in Britain: From Crisis to 'Renaissance,' 1950–2010." *Enterprise and Society* 14, no. 2: 271–302.

Wiltshire, Justin C. 2023. "Walmart Supercenters and Monopsony Power: How a Large, Low-Wage Employer Impacts Local Labor Markets." Job market paper, University of California, Berkeley, December 28.

Winant, Gabriel. 2020. "No Going Back: The Power and Limits of the Anti-Monopolist Tradition." *The Nation,* January 21. https://www.thenation.com/article/culture/goliath-monopoly-and-democracy-matt-stoller-review/.

Winerman, Marc. 2003. "The Origins of the FTC: Concentration, Cooperation, Control, and Competition." *Antitrust Law Journal* 71: 1–97.

Winstanley, Michael. 1983. *The Shopkeeper's World 1830–1914.* Manchester: Manchester University Press.

Wolfe, Allis Rosenberg. 1975. "Women, Consumerism, and the National Consumers' League in the Progressive Era, 1900–1923." *Labor History* 16, no. 3: 378–92.

Wolters, Lukas. 2022. "Essays on the Political Economy of Inequality, Wealth, and Money." PhD diss., Massachusetts Institute of Technology.

Wood, Alex J. 2016. "Flexible Scheduling, Degradation of Job Quality and Barriers to Collective Voice." *Human Relations* 69, no. 10: 1989–2010.

———. 2020. *Despotism on Demand: How Power Operates in the Flexible Workplace.* Ithaca, NY: Cornell University Press.

Wortmann, Michael. 2004. "Aldi and the German Model: Structural Change in German Grocery Retailing and the Success of Grocery Discounters." *Competition and Change* 8, no. 4 (December): 425–41.

———. 2021. "The German Variety of Grocery Retailing: A Historical Institutionalist Analysis of a Non-Core Industry." *Competition and Change* 25, no. 3–4 (July): 453–77.

Wright, Gavin. 1987. "The Economic Revolution in the American South." *Journal of Economic Perspectives* 1, no. 1 (Summer): 161–78.

Wrigley, N. 1992. "Antitrust Regulation and the Restructuring of Grocery Retailing in Britain and the USA." *Environment and Planning* 24: 727–49.

Yale Law Journal [no author]. 1959. "The Enforcement of Resale Price Maintenance." *Yale Law Journal* 69, no. 1: 168–92.

Yamey, B. S. 1952. "The Origins of Resale Price Maintenance: A Study of Three Branches of Retail Trade." *Economic Journal* 62, no. 247: 522–45.

———. 1966. "Introduction: The Main Economic Issues." In *Resale Price Maintenance,* edited by B. S. Yamey. Chicago: Aldine Publishing Company.

———. 1966. "United Kingdom," In *Resale Price Maintenance,* edited by B. S. Yamey. Chicago: Aldine Publishing Company.

Yeh, Chen, Claudia Macaluso, and Brad Hershbein. 2022. "Monopsony in the US Labor Market." *American Economic Review* 112, no. 7: 2099–2138.

Young, Nancy Beck. 1996. "Change and Continuity in the Politics of Running for Congress: Wright Patman and the Campaigns of 1928, 1938, 1962 and 1972." *East Texas Historical Journal* 34 (Fall): 52–64.

Zackin, Emily. 2013. *Looking for Rights in All the Wrong Places.* Princeton, NJ: Princeton University Press.

Zipser, Alfred R. 1951. "Macy's Cuts Prices 6% on 'Fixed' Items." *New York Times*, May 29.

Zulker, William Allen. 1993. *John Wanamaker: King of Merchants.* Wayne, PA: Eaglecrest Press.

Zundl, Elaine, Daniel Schneider, Kristen Harknett, and Evelyn Bellew. 2022. *Still Unstable: The Persistence of Schedule Uncertainty During the Pandemic.* Shift Project research brief. https://shift.hks.harvard.edu/still-unstable.

Princeton Studies in American Politics
Historical, International, and Comparative Perspectives
Paul Frymer, Suzanne Mettler, and Eric Schickler,
Series Editors
Ira Katznelson, Martin Shefter, and Theda Skocpol,
Founding Series Editors

A NOTE ON THE TYPE

This book has been composed in Adobe Text and Gotham. Adobe Text, designed by Robert Slimbach for Adobe, bridges the gap between fifteenth- and sixteenth-century calligraphic and eighteenth-century Modern styles. Gotham, inspired by New York street signs, was designed by Tobias Frere-Jones for Hoefler & Co.